BERTRAND RUSSELL
Critical Assessments

Russell in 1907

BERTRAND RUSSELL
Critical Assessments

Edited by A. D. Irvine

VOLUME II: LOGIC AND MATHEMATICS

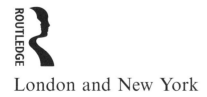

London and New York

First published 1999
by Routledge
11 New Fetter Lane, London EC4P 4EE

Simultaneously published in the USA and Canada
by Routledge
29 West 35th Street, New York, NY 10001

Typeset in Times by J&L Composition Ltd, Filey, North Yorkshire

Printed and bound in Great Britain by T.J. International Ltd,
Padstow, Cornwall

British Library Cataloguing in Publication Data

A catalogue record for this book is available from the British Library

Library of Congress Cataloguing in Publication Data

A catalogue record for this book has been requested

ISBN 0–415–13054–9 (boxed set)
ISBN 0–415–13055–7 (Vol. I)
ISBN 0–415–13056–5 (Vol. II)
ISBN 0–415–13057–3 (Vol. III)
ISBN 0–415–13058–1 (Vol. IV)

Contents

Acknowledgements

The publishers have made every effort to contact authors/copyright holders of works reprinted in *Bertrand Russell: Critical Assessments*. This has not been possible in every case, however, and we would welcome correspondence from those individuals/companies we have been unable to trace.

Cambridge University Press for the use of a photograph of page 83 of A. N. Whitehead and B. Russell, *Principia Mathematica*, vol. 2, Cambridge: Cambridge University Press, 1912. Reprinted with permission of Cambridge University Press.

University of California Press for its kind permission to reprint Gottlob Frege, 'The Russell Paradox' (1903), © 1964 The Regents of the University of California. Reprinted from Gottlob Frege, *The Basic Laws of Arithmetic*, translated by Montgomery Furth, Berkeley: University of California Press, 1964, 127–130. Used with permission.

The American Mathematical Society for its kind permission to reprint Edwin Bidwell Wilson, 'The Foundations of Mathematics', © 1904, The American Mathematical Society. Reprinted from *Bulletin of the American Mathematical Society*, 11, 74–93.

The American Mathematical Society for its kind permission to reprint James Byrnie Shaw, 'What is Mathematics?', © 1912, The American Mathematical Society. Reprinted from *Bulletin of the American Mathematical Society*, 18, 386–411.

Cambridge University Press for the use of C. E. Van Horn, 'An Axiom of Symbolic Logic', © 1916, Cambridge University Press. Reprinted from

Proceedings of the Cambridge Philosophical Society, 19, 22–31. Reprinted with the permission of Cambridge University Press.

The Mathematical Association for its kind permission to reprint F. P. Ramsey, 'Mathematical Logic', © 1926, The Mathematical Association. Reprinted from *Mathematical Gazette*, 13, 185–194.

Paul Weiss, 'The Theory of Types', © 1928, *Mind*. Reprinted from *Mind*, 37, 338–348. Used with permission.

W. V. Quine for his kind permission to reprint W. V. Quine, 'On the Theory of Types', © 1938, Association for Symbolic Logic. Reprinted from *Journal of Symbolic Logic*, 3, 125–139.

Association for Symbolic Logic for the use of W. V. Quine, 'On the Theory of Types', © 1938, Association for Symbolic Logic. Reprinted from *Journal of Symbolic Logic*, 3, 125–139. All rights reserved. This reproduction is by special permission for this publication only.

The estate of Alonzo Church for its kind permission to reprint Alonzo Church, 'Comparison of Russell's Resolution of the Semantical Antinomies with That of Tarski', © 1976, Association for Symbolic Logic. Reprinted from *Journal of Symbolic Logic*, 41, 747–760.

Association for Symbolic Logic for the use of Alonzo Church, 'Comparison of Russell's Resolution of the Semantical Antinomies with That of Tarski', © 1976, Association for Symbolic Logic. Reprinted from *Journal of Symbolic Logic*, 41, 747–760. All rights reserved. This reproduction is by special permission for this publication only.

Open Court Publishing Company for the use of Kurt Gödel, 'Russell's Mathematical Logic', in Paul Arthur Schlipp (ed.), *The Philosophy of Bertrand Russell*, 3rd edition, New York: Tudor, 1951, 123–153, © 1944, Library of Living Philosophers Inc. Reprinted from *The Philosophy of Bertrand Russell* by permission of Open Court Publishing Company, La Salle, Illinois.

Hanna Carnap Thost for the use of Rudolf Carnap, 'The Logicist Foundation of Mathematics', © 1964, Prentice Hall Inc.; © 1983 Cambridge University Press; © 1993 Hanna Carnap Thost. Translated by Gerald Massey and Erna Putnam and reprinted from Paul Benacerraf and Hilary Putnam (eds), *Philosophy of Mathematics*, 2nd ed., Cambridge: Cambridge University Press, 1983, 41–52. All rights reserved under Panamerica and International copyright conventions. Reprinted by permission of Mrs Thost.

Gerald Massey and Erna Putnam for their kind permission to reprint Rudolf Carnap, 'The Logicist Foundations of Mathematics', © 1964. Translated by Gerald Massey and Erna Putnam and reprinted from Paul Benacerraf and Hilary Putnam (eds), *Philosophy of Mathematics*, 2nd ed., Cambridge: Cambridge University Press, 1983, 41–52.

Blackwell Publishers for the use of Ludwig Wittgenstein, '*Remarks on the Foundations of Mathematics* II, §§1–14', © 1956, Blackwell Publishers. Reprinted from *Remarks on the Foundations of Mathematics*, Oxford: Blackwell, 65e–72e. Used with permission from Blackwell Publishers and the Wittgenstein Trustees.

Blackwell Publishers for the use of Geoffrey Hellman 'How to Gödel a Frege–Russell: Gödel's Incompleteness Theorems and Logicism' © 1981, Blackwell Publishers. Reprinted from *Noûs*, vol. 15, 451–468.

Kluwer Academic Publishers for its kind permission to reprint A. D. Irvine, 'Epistemic Logicism and Russell's Regressive Method', © 1989, Kluwer Academic Publishers. Reprinted from *Philosophical Studies*, 55, 303–327. Used with permission from Kluwer Academic Publishers and A. D. Irvine.

Blackwell Publishers for the use of Peter W. Hylton, 'Logic in Russell's Logicism', © 1990, Blackwell Publishers. Reprinted from David Bell and Neil Cooper (eds), *The Analytic Tradition*, vol. 1, Oxford: Blackwell, 137–172.

The University of Minnesota Press for the use of Warren D. Goldfarb, 'Russell's Reasons for Ramification', © 1989, Regents of the University of Minnesota. Reprinted from C. Wade Savage and C. Anthony Anderson (eds), *Rereading Russell: Essays on Bertrand Russell's Metaphysics and Epistemology*, Minneapolis: University of Minnesota Press, 24–40. Used with permission.

Bernard Linsky for his kind permission to reprint Bernard Linsky, 'Was the Axiom of Reducibility a Principle of Logic?', © 1990, Bernard Linsky. Reprinted from *Russell*, n.s. 10, 125–140.

George Boolos, 'The Advantages of Honest Toil over Theft', © 1994. Reprinted from Alexander George (ed.), *Mathematics and Mind*, Oxford: Oxford University Press, 27–44.

Leonard Linsky for his kind permission to reprint Leonard Linsky, 'Russell's "No Classes" Theory of Classes', © 1987, Massachusetts

Institute of Technology. Reprinted from *On Being and Saying*, edited by Judith Jarvis Thomson, Cambridge, Massachusetts: MIT Press, 21–39. Used with permission.

The MIT Press for the use of Leonard Linsky, 'Russell's "No Classes" Theory of Classes', © 1987, Massachusetts Institute of Technology. Reprinted from *On Being and Saying*, edited by Judith Jarvis Thomson, Massachusetts: MIT Press, 21–39. Used with permission.

Gregory Landini for his kind permission to reprint Gregory Landini, 'New Evidence Concerning Russell's Substitutional Theory of Classes', © 1989, Gregory Landini. Reprinted from *Russell*, n.s. 9, 26–42.

Holder–Pichler–Tempsky for their kind permission to reprint Francisco Rodríguez-Consuegra, 'Russell, Gödel and Logicism', © 1993, Holder–Pichler–Tempsky. Reprinted from Johannes Czermak (ed.), *Philosophy of Mathematics*, Vienna: Holder–Pichler–Tempsky, 223–242.

Stanford University Press for the use of Alonzo Church, 'Mathematics and Logic'. Reprinted from *Logic, Methodology and Philosophy of Science*, edited by Ernest Nagel, Patrick Suppes and Alfred Tarski, with permission of the publishers, Stanford University Press, © 1962, The Board of Trustees of the Leland Stanford Junior University, 181–186.

∗110·643. $\vdash . 1 +_c 1 = 2$

Dem.

$$\vdash . *110·632 . *101·21·28 . \supset$$
$$\vdash . 1 +_c 1 = \hat{\xi}\{(\exists y) \cdot y \in \xi . \xi - \iota'y \in 1\}$$
$$[*54·3] \quad = 2 . \supset \vdash . \text{Prop}$$

The above proposition is occasionally useful. It is used at least three times, in ∗113·66 and ∗120·123·472.

∗110·7·71 are required for proving ∗110·72, and ∗110·72 is used in ∗117·3, which is a fundamental proposition in the theory of greater and less.

∗110·7. $\vdash : \beta \subset \alpha . \supset . (\exists \mu) . \mu \in \text{NC} . \text{Nc}'\alpha = \text{Nc}'\beta +_c \mu$

Dem.

$$\vdash . *24·411·21. \supset \vdash : \text{Hp}. \supset . \alpha = \beta \cup (\alpha - \beta). \beta \cap (\alpha - \beta) = \Lambda .$$
$$[*110·32] \qquad \supset . \text{Nc}'\alpha = \text{Nc}'\beta +_c \text{Nc}'(\alpha - \beta) : \supset \vdash . \text{Prop}$$

∗110·71. $\vdash ; (\exists \mu) . \text{Nc}'\alpha = \text{Nc}'\beta +_c \mu . \supset . (\exists \delta) . \delta \text{ sm } \beta . \delta \subset \alpha$

Dem.

$$\vdash . *100·3 . *110·4 . \supset$$
$$\vdash : \text{Nc}'\alpha = \text{Nc}'\beta +_c \mu . \supset . \mu \in \text{NC} - \iota'\Lambda \qquad\qquad (1)$$
$$\vdash . *110·3 . \supset \vdash : \text{Nc}'\alpha = \text{Nc}'\beta +_c \text{Nc}'\gamma . \equiv . \text{Nc}'\alpha = \text{Nc}'(\beta + \gamma).$$
$$[*100·3·31] \qquad \supset . \alpha \text{ sm } (\beta + \gamma).$$
$$[*73·1] \qquad \supset . (\exists R) . R \in 1 \to 1.D'R = \alpha \Cup 'R = \downarrow \Lambda_\gamma \text{ "}\iota\text{"}\beta \cup \Lambda_\beta \downarrow \text{ "}\iota\text{"}\gamma.$$
$$[*37·15] \qquad \supset . (\exists R) . R \in 1 \to 1. \downarrow \Lambda_\gamma \text{ "}\iota\text{" } \beta \subset \Cup 'R . R \text{" } \downarrow \Lambda_\gamma \text{ "}\iota\text{" } \beta \subset \alpha.$$
$$[*110·12 . *73·22] \supset . (\exists \delta) . \delta \subset \alpha . \delta \text{ sm } \beta \qquad\qquad (2)$$
$$\vdash . (1) . (2) . \supset \vdash . \text{Prop}$$

The above proof depends upon the fact that "Nc' α" and "Nc' $\beta +_c \mu$" are typically ambiguous, and therefore, when they are asserted to be equal, this must hold in *any* type, and therefore, in particular, in that type for which we have $\alpha \in \text{Nc}'\alpha$, *i.e.* for $N_0c'\alpha$. This is why the use of ∗100·3 is legitimate.

∗110·72. $\vdash : (\exists \delta) . \delta \text{ sm } \beta . \delta \subset \alpha . \equiv . (\exists \mu) . \mu \in \text{NC} . \text{Nc}'\alpha = \text{Nc}'\beta +_c \mu$

Dem.

$$\vdash . *100·321 . *110·7 . \supset$$
$$\vdash : . \delta \text{ sm } \beta . \delta \subset \alpha . \supset : \text{Nc}'\delta = \text{Nc}'\beta : (\exists \mu) . \mu \in \text{NC} . \text{Nc}'\alpha = \text{Nc}'\delta +_c \mu :$$
$$[*13·12] \qquad \supset : (\exists \mu) . \mu \in \text{NC} . \text{Nc}'\alpha = \text{Nc}'\beta +_c \mu \qquad\qquad (1)$$
$$\vdash . (1) . *110·71 . \supset \vdash . \text{Prop}$$

Introduction

> Hardly anything more unwelcome can befall a scientific writer than that one of the foundations of his edifice be shaken after the work is finished.
> I have been placed in this position by a letter of Mr Bertrand Russell just as the printing of this volume was nearing completion.
>
> Gottlob Frege (1903)

These are the opening words of Gottlob Frege's Appendix to *The Basic Laws of Arithmetic*, written after receiving news from Russell that the logic of *The Basic Laws* was inconsistent. The discovery meant that Frege's hope of using his logic to derive all of arithmetic was a futile one.

Russell had made his discovery in 1901, while working on his *Principles of Mathematics* (1903). Today his insight is usually recounted in the form of a paradox arising in connection with the set of all sets which are not members of themselves. Such a set, if it exists, will be a member of itself if and only if it is not a member of itself. The question therefore arises: Is there a principled way of showing that this purported set does not exist, while at the same time leaving the rest of set theory intact?

Russell's own response came with the introduction of his theory of types in 1903. It was clear to Russell that some restrictions needed to be placed upon the original comprehension (or abstraction) axiom of naive set theory, the axiom which formalized the intuition that any coherent condition may be used to determine a set (or class). Russell's basic idea was that reference to sets such as the set of all sets which are not members of themselves could be avoided by arranging all sentences into a hierarchy (beginning with sentences about individuals at the lowest level, sentences about sets of individuals at the next lowest level, sentences about sets of sets of individuals at the next lowest level, etc.). Using the so-called "vicious circle principle" adopted by the mathematician Henri Poincaré, and his own so-called "no class" theory of classes, Russell was able to explain why the unrestricted comprehension axiom fails: propositional functions, such as "x is a set", may not be applied to themselves since self-application would involve a vicious circle. Thus, on Russell's view, all objects for which a given condition (or predicate) holds must be at the same level or of the same "type". The theory of types itself admitted of two versions, the "simple theory" and the "ramified theory". Although first introduced in 1903, the theory finds its mature expression in Russell's 1908 article "Mathematical Logic as Based on the Theory of Types" and in the monumental work he co-authored with Alfred North Whitehead, *Principia Mathematica* (1910, 1912, 1913). The theory later came under attack for being both too weak and too strong. Some saw it as being too weak since it failed to resolve all of the known paradoxes. Others saw it as being too strong since it disallowed many mathematical definitions which, although consistent, violated the vicious circle principle. Russell's response was to introduce the axiom of reducibility, an axiom which lessened the vicious circle principle's scope of application, but which many claimed was too *ad hoc* to be justified philosophically.

Of equal significance was Russell's defence of logicism, the theory that mathematics was in some important sense reducible to logic. First defended in his *Principles of Mathematics*, and later in greater detail in *Principia Mathematica*, Russell's logicism consisted of two main theses. The first is that all mathematical truths can be translated into logical truths or, in other words, that the vocabulary of mathematics constitutes a proper subset of that of logic. The second is that all mathematical proofs can be recast as logical proofs or, in other words, that the theorems of mathematics constitute a proper subset of those of logic.

Like Frege, Russell's basic idea in defending logicism was that numbers may be identified with classes of classes and that number-theoretic statements may be explained in terms of quantifiers and identity. Thus the number 1 would be identified with the class of all unit classes, the number 2 with the class of all two-membered classes, and so on. Statements such as "There are two men" would be recast as statements such as "There is a man, x, and there is a man, y, and x is not identical to y". It followed that number-theoretic operations could be explained in terms of set-theoretic operations such as intersection, union, and difference. In *Principia Mathematica*, Whitehead and Russell were able to provide detailed derivations of major theorems in set theory, finite and transfinite arithmetic, and elementary measure theory. A fourth volume on geometry was planned but never completed.

This volume begins with Frege's own response to Russell's paradox as it appeared in his Appendix to *The Basic Laws*. Reviews by Wilson and Shaw follow, giving an indication of how Russell's work in the philosophy of mathematics was originally received. Van Horn's article is representative of the first wave of more detailed logical work which followed the appearance of *Principia* and the "new logic". Ramsey, Weiss, Quine and Church then all discuss, in various detail and in various contexts, Russell's theory of types. This is followed by chapters on logicism written by three other contemporaries of Russell: Gödel, Carnap and Wittgenstein. More recent work is represented by Hellman, Irvine, Hylton, Goldfarb, Boolos, the two Linskys, Landini and Rodríguez-Consuegra. The volume ends with a second paper by Church summarizing his view of Russell's overall contribution.

The Russell Paradox

Gottlob Frege

Hardly anything more unwelcome can befall a scientific writer than that one of the foundations of his edifice be shaken after the work is finished.

I have been placed in this position by a letter of Mr Bertrand Russell just as the printing of this [second] volume [*of The Basic Laws of Arithmetic*] was nearing completion. It is a matter of my Basic Law (V). I have never concealed from myself its lack of the self-evidence which the others possess, and which must properly be demanded of a law of logic, and in fact I pointed out this weakness in the Introduction to the first volume [. . .]. I should glady have relinquished this foundation if I had known of any substitute for it. And even now I do not see how arithmetic can be scientifically founded, how numbers can be conceived as logical objects and brought under study, unless we are allowed – at least conditionally – the transition from a concept to its extension. Is it always permissible to speak of the extension of a concept, of a class? And if not, how do we recognize the exceptional cases? Can we always infer from the extension of one concept's coinciding with that of a second, that every object which falls under the first concept also falls under the second? These are the questions raised by Mr Russell's communication.

Solatium miseris, socios habuisse malorum. I too have this solace, if solace it is; for everyone who in his proofs has made use of extensions of concepts, classes, sets,[1] is in the same position. It is not just a matter of my particular method of laying the foundations, but of whether a logical foundation for arithmetic is possible at all.

But let us come to the point. Mr Russell has discovered a contradiction, which may now be set out.

No one will want to assert of the class of men that it is a man. Here we have a class that does not belong to itself. That is, I say that something belongs to a class if it falls under the concept whose extension that class is. Now let us fix our attention upon the concept *class that does not belong to itself.* The extension of this concept (if we may speak of its extension) is accordingly the class of classes that do not belong to themselves. For short we shall call it the class *C*. Now let us ask whether this class *C* belongs to itself. First let us suppose that it does. If something belongs to a class, then it falls under the concept whose extension the class is; accordingly if our class *C* belongs to itself then it is a class that does not belong to itself. Thus our first supposition leads to a self-contradiction. Second, let us suppose that our class *C* does not belong to itself; then it falls under the concept whose extension it itself is, and thus does not belong to itself: here again, a contradiction.

What should be our attitude to this? Are we to suppose that the law of excluded middle does not hold for classes? Or are we to suppose that there are cases in which to an unexceptionable concept no class corresponds as its extension? In the first case we should find ourselves obliged to deny that classes are objects in the full sense; for if classes were proper objects the law of excluded middle would have to hold for them. On the other hand there is nothing 'unsaturated', nothing 'predicative', about classes that would characterize them as functions, concepts, or relations. What we are accustomed to regard as a name of a class, e.g., 'the class of prime numbers', has rather the nature of a proper name; it cannot occur predicatively, but it can occur as grammatical subject of a singular proposition, e.g., 'the class of prime numbers comprises infinitely many objects'. If we wanted to abrogate the law of excluded middle for the case of classes, we might then think of regarding classes – and in fact courses-of-values generally – as improper objects. These then would not be permitted to occur as arguments of all first-level functions. But there would also be functions that could take as arguments both proper and improper objects; certainly the relation of identity would be of this kind. We might try to escape this by assuming a special sort of identity for improper objects, but that is completely ruled out; identity is a relation given to us in so specific a form that it is inconceivable that various kinds of it should occur. But now there would result a great multiplicity of first-level functions, namely (1) those which could take only proper objects as arguments, (2) those which could take both proper and improper objects as arguments, and (3) those which could take only improper objects as arguments. There would also result another division on the basis of the values of functions, according to which we should have to distinguish (1) functions whose values were proper objects exclusively, (2) those which had both proper and improper objects as values, and (3) those whose values were improper objects exclusively. Both of these divisions of first-level functions would hold simultaneously, so that we should obtain nine types. To these again there would correspond nine types of courses-of-values, of improper objects, among which we should have to draw logical distinctions. Classes of proper objects would have to be distinguished from classes of classes of proper objects, extensions of relations between proper objects would have to be distinguished from classes of proper objects and from classes of extensions of relations between proper objects, and so on. Thus we should obtain an incalculable multiplicity of types; and in general objects belonging to different ones of these types could not occur as arguments of the same functions. But it seems extraordinarily difficult to set up comprehensive legislation that would decide in general which objects were permissible arguments for which functions. Moreover, the justifiability of the improper objects may be doubted.

If these difficulties frighten us off from regarding classes (and hence numbers) as improper objects, and if we are nonetheless unwilling to recognize them as proper objects, namely as admissible arguments for every first-level function, then there is indeed no alternative but to regard class-names as pseudo proper names, which would thus in fact have no denotation. They would in this case have to be regarded as parts of signs that had denotation only as wholes.[2] Now of course it may be thought advantageous for some purpose to fashion different signs that are identical in some part, without thereby making them into complex signs. The simplicity of a sign certainly requires only that such parts as one can distinguish within it not have a denotation of their own. In this case, then, even what we are accustomed to regard as a sign for a number would not really be a sign at all, but a syncategorematic part of a sign. To define the sign '2' would be impossible; instead we should have to define many signs containing '2' as a syncategorematic constituent, but not construable as logical compounds of '2' and some other part. It would then be illicit to replace such a syncategorematic part by a letter, for so far as the content was concerned there would be no complexity. With this, the generality of arithmetical propositions would be lost. Again, it would be incomprehensible how on this basis we could speak of a Number of classes or a Number of numbers.

I think that this is sufficient to render this route impassable as well. Thus there is no alternative at all but to recognize the extensions of concepts, or classes, as objects in the full and proper sense of the word, while conceding that our interpretation hitherto of the words 'extension of a concept' is in need of justification . . .

Notes

1 Herr R. Dedekind's 'systems' also come under this head.
2 Cf. Vol. I [Frege, *The Basic Laws of Arithmetic*], §29, pp. 84f.

2

The Foundations of Mathematics[1]

Edwin Bidwell Wilson

1 The Problem

Pure mathematics has always been conceived in the minds of its votaries and by the world at large to be a science which makes up for whatever it lacks in human interest, and in the stimulus of close contact with the infinite variety of nature, by the sureness, the absolute accuracy, of its methods and results. Yet what has been accepted as sure and accurate in one generation has frequently required fundamental revision in the next. Euclid and his pupils could doubtless have complained of the lack of rigor and logical precision in his predecessors just as forcibly as some modern pupils of Weierstrass berate their scientific ancestors and companions. Euler, finding confusion in the theory of the infinite and infinitesimal, proceeded to explain away the difficulties, that others might be free from the prevailing errors. We cannot accept his reasoning today. At the beginning of the last century the state of infinite series was lamentable and Cauchy's memoir on the subject is said to have impressed itself on Laplace to such an extent that he postponed publishing his *Mécanique Céleste* until he became so hopeless of righting things that he gave up trying to do it. The righting has been accomplished in the present generation by Poincaré. Yet we very much doubt whether Laplace, before hearing of Cauchy's treatment, would have for a moment granted any possible inaccuracy in his own methods. Somewhat later Dirichlet treated the problem of determining a harmonic function from its boundary values and so careful a mathematician as H. Weber extended the method to the discussion of the equation $\Delta V + \lambda V = 0$ without any apparent qualms as to error. Nevertheless, nowadays, the theoretical importance and the practical use of the principles of Dirichlet and Thomson are completely obscured for many by the too great emphasis laid upon the errors in the original demonstration of the principles.

We notice that the advance toward our present rigor has been made step by step by great men who, however, were no greater – one might almost say no more careful – than their fellows in working in apparent unconsciousness of the impending trouble and perhaps even incredulous at first as to its reality. When will this revision stop? And whereunto will it finally lead? This is the problem of the ultimate foundation of mathematics. In attempting an answer one can learn only hesitancy from the past. The delicacy of the question is such that even the greatest mathematicians and philosophers of today have made what seem to be substantial slips of judgment and have shown on occasions an astounding ignorance of the essence of the problem which they were discussing. At times this has been due to the inevitable failings of individual intuition in dealing with matters that are still unsettled; but all too frequently it has been the result of a wholly unpardonable disregard of the work already accomplished by others. Even when guarding as much as may be against this latter sin, those who approach the depths of the subject upon which Russell has so courageously entered may well expect to hear the warning: "Procul, o procul este profani!"

2 The Solution

Says Russell: Pure mathematics is the class of all propositions of the form "p implies q," where p and q are propositions containing one or more variables, the same in the two propositions, and neither p nor q contains any constants except logical constants. And logical constants are all notions definable in terms of the following: Implication, the relation of a term to a class of which it is a member, the notion of *such that*, the notion of relation, and such further notions as may be involved in the general notion of propositions of the above form. In addition to these, mathematics *uses* a notion which is not a constituent of the propositions which it considers, namely the notion of truth.

This is probably the first attempt to give a complete definition of mathematics solely in terms of the laws of thought and the other necessary paraphernalia of the thinking mind. Some there are who, under the influence of arithmetic tendencies, might be tempted to give a decidedly more superficial definition in terms of integers. Some might regard a complete definition as impossible. The fact that a definition such as the above may be given – and it is the purpose of Russell's *Principles of Mathematics* to demonstrate that the definition is not illusory nor too small nor too large – is attributable to two things: first, the more careful discrimination of what *pure* mathematics is; second, the extraordinary development of logic since Boole removed it from the trammels of medieval scholasticism.

He to whom the present highly developed state of the foundations of mathematics is chiefly due is Peano – one whose work unfortunately is very little known and still less appreciated in this country. True, Leibniz had long since done much and of recent years has been ably expounded by L. Couturat;[2] true it is, too, that Boole had freed us from Aristotelianism and that C. S. Peirce[3] and Schroeder had carried the technique of logic much farther; but they had never accomplished that intimate formal relation between logic and all mathematics which was the necessary precursor to a yet more intimate philosophic relation and which has been brought about by Peano aided by a large school of pupils and fellow-workers. The advance has been made largely by introducing into symbolic logic such a simplification of notation as to relieve it of its unwieldiness and to allow its development into a powerful instrument without which one can hardly hope to get the best results in the treacherous though treasure-laden fields of the foundations of mathematics. Poincaré, to be sure, in his review of Hilbert's *Foundations of Geometry*[4] spurns this *pasigraphy*, characterizing it as disastrous in teaching, hurtful to mental development, and deadening for investigators, nipping their originality in the bud. However much we may agree in the first statements (see §7, page 91), we had best be cautious in accepting such sweeping statements as the last, even from so great an authority – especially in view of the fact that, equipped with this pasigraphy, the Italian investigators, Peano and his pupil Pieri,[5] with some rights of priority, had given a more fundamental *logical*[6] treatment of the subject on which Poincaré was writing than is to be found in the work he was praising so highly. In the fields of arithmetic and algebra, too, Burali-Forti and Padoa, adherents of Peano, had reached a point far beyond the widest view of the chief of the German school that deals with the same subjects.[7] Furthermore, on this one point Poincaré may not be regarded as an authority; for his own work[8] in the field should be characterized as subjective rather than objective, speculative and suggestive rather than purely logical.[9] Anyone who is acquainted with the articles presented to the Philosophical Congress at Paris in 1900 by Peano, Burali-Forti, Padoa, and Pieri, cannot be convinced that these authors had become deadened, and the artificiality of their system is by no means so certain as it might be. Since then, our author, Russell, has simplified and improved the older work of C. S. Peirce on the theory of relations, adapting it to the system of Peano, and has produced a coherent treatment of the great problems underlying mathematics. In view of accomplished facts one inclines more readily to the praise given by Whitehead: "I believe the invention of the Peano and Russell symbolism forms an epoch in mathematical reasoning."[10]

3 The Reason

It is not hard to detect the reason why mathematics has thus pushed its foundations back until they have come to rest solely in logic. In the first place mathematical or other reasoning presupposes a mind capable of rational, that is, non-self-contradictory ratiocinative processes. Now it always has been comfortably assumed that we can carry out such processes if only we are careful enough, that there is no need of formulating the laws of thought before beginning to reason, or even that a formulation and analysis of those laws is impossible.[11] Where then do the errors creep in? An examination of some typical cases shows that it is generally through lack of a sufficiently careful definition of the terms. This failure properly to define has led to interminable discussions which from the start could only lead either to nothing or to wrong results. In mathematics it is the absence of precise definition which brings in the erroneous statements concerning differentiation, continuity, and infinity, with a host of others. The perception of this difficulty was the origin of the principle of arithmetization and of epsilon proofs. In the end, however, after one has really mastered the principles of modern analysis he seldom needs the actual presence of epsilons to establish a theorem. Nevertheless it is a satisfaction to have this formal method to fall back on whenever challenged by one's own hesitancy or by that of others. In like manner, who has not at times during some long complicated or indirect logical demonstration felt the least bit uncertain; who would not be glad to have at his hand some formal method such as Peano's, based upon certain rudimentary propositions and concepts?

In truth it is a matter of more consequence than is sometimes thought, to have clearly in mind those processes which are definitely to be admitted as logical. The one process which stands out most definite in our consciousness is the syllogism. If a piece of reasoning can be put in the form of major premise, minor premise, conclusion, we are tolerably sure of its truth. But numerous proofs cannot be so constructed and it is one of the most frequent errors committed by the intuitive logicians to say that reasoning consists in a sequence of syllogisms. Perhaps the greatest advance made by Boole was the clear recognition of the necessity of asyllogistic reasoning.

The question then becomes of fundamental importance: What is at the bottom of our logic? When the matter is looked into, it appears that we constantly use *propositions*, passing from certain propositions as hypothesis to certain others as conclusion. The laws of implication which govern the relation between hypothesis and conclusion constitute the logical theory or calculus of propositions. Casting about for other principles we come upon *classes* or sets of objects represented in ordinary speech by common nouns. The development of the interrelations of classes produces the logical calculus of classes. This calculus has a remarkable analogy with the calculus of propositions, but the relation is not quite dual. In the third place we perceive that *relations* are of the utmost importance. Every transformation, every function is a relation. In common language the verb does but express a relation between the subject and object. Thus there appears the necessity for a calculus of relations.[12] The complete logical calculus, as now used, is a combination of these three types. The whole number of laws of thought or logical premises which seem to be required for establishing the calculus in all the generality necessary for mathematics is small. In addition to these premises there are a certain number of elementary ideas or terms such as implication, and the notions of proposition, class and relation, which must be assumed as known. It is the discussion of these questions which are of a philosophical rather than mathematical nature, that fills the first Part of Russell's *Principles*.

We may grant, then, that logic is *necessary* to mathematics. It is affirmed to be *sufficient*. This in reality is the remarkable content of the definition given by the author. So immune are we from logical error that the necessity of logic might never force us to a critical examination of its principles; but the affirmation of its sufficiency fully justifies and even renders imperative such an examination. Russell's entire volume is devoted to establishing this sufficiency. And although the subject is very new and many difficulties philosophical and mathematical are still outstanding, there can be little doubt that to an unexpectedly large extent the author is successful in his attempt and that in these *Principles* he has given a permanent set to the future philosophy of the questions which he handles.

4 Some Notions

Owing to the widespread diversity of usage in the meaning of such fundamental notions as postulates, axioms, undefined symbols, definitions, consistency, independence (of postulates), irreducibility (of undefined symbols), completeness (of systems of postulates and undefined symbols), we think it best to enter upon some slight exposition[13] of these matters instead of taking up the critical discussion of some of the more abstruse problems which are treated by the author and which could scarcely be appreciated before such exposition.

Axiom is a word which has so long been used in so many vague ways that its use in pure mathematics had probably best be abandoned. The familiar definition: An axiom is a self-evident truth, means, if it means anything, that the proposition which we call an axiom has been approved of by us in the light of our experience and intuition. In this sense pure mathematics has no axioms: for mathematics is a formal subject over which formal and not material implication reigns.[14] The proper word to use for those statements which we posit would seem to be postulate. What self-evident truths can there be concerning objects which are not dependent on any definite interpretation but are merely marks to be operated upon in accordance with the rules of formal logic? Postulates, however, may be laid down at will so long as they are not contradictory. It is the postulates which give the objects their intellectual though not physical existence. Indeed before we can apply to the physical world any of the systems of logical geometry, for instance, we have the one great axiom: This system fits nature sufficiently for our purposes. To postulate such a statement would avail us naught. We must carefully consider the totality of our experience and decide whether the statement seems to represent a truth.

Definition is a term which has long been used by philosophers to stand for a process of analysis and exemplification which brings before the mind a real consciousness of the object defined. This sort of definition has to be used in dictionaries. In mathematics, however, no such vague process is permissible. Mathematical definition is simply the attributing of a name to some object whose existence has been established or momentarily postulated. It is the process of replacing a set of statements by a single name and is resorted to solely for convenience. In any science whose development has been perfected, definitions may be entirely done away with by those who are willing to sacrifice brevity. There can be little doubt that a large number of definitions might better be thus put out of the way.[15]

Although all definitions are thus merely nominal, there are three distinct aspects[16] of definition which are worth considering in detail in connection with the theory of integers. These may be characterized as (1) the particular definition, (2) the definition by postulates, (3) the definition by abstraction. They may be illustrated as follows: Suppose (1) that it is possible to find a logical class K of which the elements are, let us say, classes or propositions. Suppose further that by means of logical processes alone we may define operations on the elements like addition and multiplication of integers. Grant that there exists in the class K an element analogous to zero (in case K is a class of classes this would be the null-class; in case K were a class of propositions it would be absurd). In fact suppose that we could set up a class K and a set of operations in K which might have the properties of integers as we use them. We then might say from a formal point of view that the class K was the class of integers, that the elements of K were the integers themselves, and that the operations we had set up were the ordinary operations of arithmetic. This would be a satisfactory though very particular definition of the integers and would have the advantage that unless there were a contradiction inherent in our logic there could be no contradiction in our system of integers. Or (2) we may assume a certain set of elementary terms, known as undefined symbols, such as number, zero, and successor. These we could connect, as Peano and Padoa have done, by a system of postulates, and thus we should have a definition of number through postulates. In order to prove the non-contradictoriness of our postulates and indefinables, that is, the existence of our elements, we should have to set up some system which afforded one interpretation of the indefinables and of the postulates. As this must be done by going back to the laws of thought we finally get very near to where we started in the other sort of definition. The definition remains, however, slightly more general: for the integers thus defined are not merely one set of elements but any set which satisfies the postulates. Or (3) we may use the principle of abstraction on which Russell places a great deal of emphasis. We may say that two classes of objects, no matter what objects they be, have the same number when there exists a one-to-one relation between their elements.[17] Thus number becomes the common property of all similar classes, and is their only common property. The class of numbers becomes the class of all similar classes. Owing to Russell's development of the theory of relations this definition becomes also merely nominal and as it seems to be the most fundamental and philosophic it may be accepted as the best thus far given.

Although the use of postulates other than the premises of logic, and the use of undefined symbols other than those of logic seem needless and to be avoided in pure mathematics, the usage is so common that we may go on to say a few words concerning consistency, independence, irreducibility, and completeness – especially as these ideas are somewhat usable in the foundations of logic. To show the consistency of the system of postulates and undefined symbols it is evidently futile to attempt to develop the consequences of the postulates until no contradiction is reached (this method of stating the thing is sufficient to show wherein lies the futility): for the most that can be accomplished in this way is to see that up to a certain point no contradiction has been reached. The method of proof consists merely in finding some system of entities known to exist and affording a possible interpretation of the undefined symbols and postulates. To make the proof really fundamental for the system of integers it seems necessary to go quite out of the field of mathematics into the domain of logic.[18] The method of showing the independence is merely to set up for each postulate one existent system of elements in which there are possible interpretations of our undefined symbols and which satisfies all the other postulates but not the particular one in question. This shows the independence of that one. If one of the undefined symbols used in the statement of the postulates can be given a nominal definition in terms of the others the system of indefinables is redundant. It was Padoa[19] who first made effective use of this idea. To show the irreducibility of the indefinables relative to the system of postulates it is necessary to set up a system of elements which satisfies all the postulates, which affords an interpretation of the undefined symbols, and which continues to satisfy these conditions when one of the undefined symbols is suitably altered: this must be done for each. The problem is quite similar to that of the independence of the postulates and is not difficult to solve in case the number of undefined symbols is small. All this difficulty is avoided in dealing with the different branches of mathematics when Russell's point of view – no new indefinables, no new postulates – is taken.

Huntington[20] seems to have been the first to bring to effective use the idea of completeness. The problem is to show that if there are two sets M and M' of objects each[21] of which satisfies the postulates and affords interpretations of the indefinables, then the two sets of objects may be brought into one-to-one correspondence in such a way as to preserve the interpretation of the symbols. With the statement of this last idea we have arrived at the limit of present ideas concerning the interrelations of the notions at the base of mathematics as defined by postulates.

5 Numbers

The analysis of number, cardinal or ordinal, finite or infinite, integral, rational, or real, with carefully drawn distinctions between the many allied ideas such as counting, quantity, magnitude, and distance, forms the content of Parts II–V, pages 111–370, of the *Principles*. To do anything like justice to this masterpiece of analysis in a field so strewn with difficulties would be impossible within the space at our command. The summaries given by the author at the close of each Part afford a clear review of the ideas which have been discussed and the points which have been won. Leaving out of account the advances which are made toward the precision of the terms which lie at the bottom of logic we can at best merely indicate some of the results which are of greatest interest to mathematicians.

It is shown that cardinal and ordinal integral numbers are inherently different, that finite cardinals and ordinals may be obtained in terms the one of the other but that this principle cannot be applied to the infinite. With the guidance of the principle of abstraction cardinal integer has been defined as a class of similar classes. This definition has the immediate advantage of giving finite and infinite cardinals at the same time. The finite may then be distinguished from the infinite by the fact that in the former the whole cannot be similar to its part, whereas in the latter it can. Another point which Russell establishes with the aid of Whitehead[22] is that by the use of logical addition the numerical addition of a finite or infinite number of finite or infinite cardinals may be and indeed (if we invoke the principle of abstraction) should be defined in such a manner that the order in which the numbers are added plays no part. This is a great victory for common sense and must appeal to everyone as a vindication of the school-child in his inherent notion that he has the same number of marbles whether he has five in one pocket and three in another or three in two pockets and two in a third, no matter which of his pockets these be. The principle of commutation and association of the terms in addition is entirely done away with, except in so far as mechanical difficulties prevent us from writing simultaneously a number of terms and the signs of addition connecting them. We may point to the fact that the work applies equally well to finite and infinite sums as an indication of its extreme generality and as evidence that at last we have a principle of addition distinctly above the plane of counting on one's fingers. In like manner the definition of multiplication is such as to be free from the laws of commutation and association of the factors and to apply equally to finite or infinite products of finite or infinite cardinals. Again a vindication of the school-child who rightly cannot see why it should make any difference whether he puts down four rows of three marks or three rows of four.

The discussion of the meaning of quantity and magnitude in Part III and its connection with number we will not pause to consider, but we pass directly to the theory of order as developed in Part IV. The treatment of this subject is greatly simplified by the theory of relations. Order is shown to be an asymmetric transitive relation, an essential property of serial relations. It is clearly pointed out and it is important to notice that when a set of objects is given the relation is not necessarily included; whereas when the relation is given the field in which it operates must also be given. If recourse is had to the principle of abstraction the ordinal integer appears as "the common property of classes of serial relations which generate ordinally similar series." As the cardinals are classes of similar classes, so the ordinals are classes of like relations. The principle of induction is intimately associated with the system of ordinals rather than with the system of cardinals although for finite numbers the distinction is not so great as for infinites. We may say that the finite ordinal is that which can be reached by induction from 1. It appears that those who generate their system of numbers by a relation of succession or by counting – that is, by successive acts of attention – must in reality be coming at something which resembles ordinals much more nearly than cardinals. The difference between the theory of infinite cardinals and infinite ordinals brings to light the important fact that in mathematics we have two kinds of infinite: the cardinal, which has the property of being similar to a part of itself, and the ordinal, which cannot be reached by induction from 1.[23] The discussion naturally brings up the old question of extensive and intensive definition. The definition of an object is said to be extensive when the object is given by the enumeration of its parts; it is said to be intensive when the object is characterized by its properties. In the treatment of these questions and of transfinite cardinals and ordinals there is much which is instructive for the mathematician and the philosopher. The author points out with his customary frank desire to state no more than the truth that there still remain difficulties to solve. Thanks to his lucid and modest presentation there is no reason why he should not find adherents who will take up the work and attempt the solution in a spirit of hearty cooperation.

There is a school of creationists who, when they find that certain infinite processes lead to no rational limit nor yet to a number which becomes infinite, postulate the existence of a limit and thus obtain the irrational numbers. The author does not consider an *ipse dixit* like this to be a sufficiently good theorem of existence. He therefore considers infinite sets of rationals and by means of them he forms a set of things which he calls real numbers. A real number is neither a rational nor an irrational; it is a certain infinite set of rationals. The real numbers thus defined are shown to satisfy the notion of a continuum. According to the method followed, the continuum appears as an idea wholly ordinal in nature. With the aids thus prepared the author is able to give a very satisfactory account of the philosophy of the infinite and of the continuous. His treatment of the paradoxes of Zeno shows that the arguments of the ancient philosopher are by no means so far from right as might be imagined and that the contradictions are more apparent than real.

6 Geometry and Mechanics

A short study of the properties of multiple series leads to a point from which it may be seen that: Geometry is the study of series of two or more dimensions.[24] In this manner the necessity of new postulates and new indefinables is avoided. The procedure is evidently reasonable. Mathematical geometry has long since been divested of all spatial relations between its elements. The above definition is but the culmination of the ideas of manifolds introduced by Grassmann and Riemann. As those who define geometry by postulates are forced to show the existence of their elements by having recourse to systems of numbers the question is quite pertinent: Why not begin with a purely nominal definition like the above and avoid the trouble of proofs of existence, of independence, and of irreducibility?

At this juncture it is interesting to compare the attitude taken in the *Principles* with that taken in the older *Foundations of Geometry*. It should be remembered that the author originally started with the study of the philosophy of dynamics and hence necessarily of geometry. To render the examination really searching the foundations of geometry had to be investigated. But, once started, the end was not so easily to be reached. Probing into the mysteries of infinity and continuity led to arithmetic in its wider sense. Trying to render precise the meaning of important words such as element, set, operation, conclusion, proof, etc., could but conduct to the study of logic, and the desire to be rid so far as possible from the contaminations of the personal element brought up at last at formal logic. And then the entire field had to be traversed in the forward direction with the necessity of constant acquisition of original results at every step! Surely the present work is a monument to patience, perseverance, and thoroughness.

In the essay on the foundations of geometry the author had not yet reached the logical stage – scarcely the arithmetic stage. He was content, as some still are, to analyse the ideas in the rough, to use a large number of indefinables, to state broad indefinite axioms instead of brief incisive postulates – in a word, to forgo all the modern technique. The result was an extremely suggestive essay – one which still can be read with profit and by rights ought to be read, if only for the sake of contrast, in connection with the newer work. Today we have mathematical geometry, then we had physical. If one wishes to read an excellent account of space from the physico-metaphysical point of view he has but to turn to the Russell of a few years since; if he would know the extreme point of modern mathematico-logical geometry he has merely to take up the Russell of today.

In Part VII the analysis proceeds to mechanics. Here space is merely a certain three- (or *n*-) dimensional series; time, a simple series. There is a relation which connects part of space (the material points) with all time, that is, $a, b, c = R(a_0, b_0, c_0, t)$, where a, b, c are the coordinates of the material points. This relation R is so chosen as to allow for the impossibility of generating or destroying matter. The relation is also chosen so that if the relation between matter and time is known at two instants it is known at every instant. In this way is stated the causality in the universe. This seems very far off from the real world. It must delight the hearts of philosophers who believe in a pure idealism. It is found that arithmetic may be handled adequately with no help save from logic. This does not surprise us. Then geometry is put in the same category. Modern mathematicians have so accustomed us to look on merely the logical side of the subject that we are not troubled. Finally comes dynamics. Why not thermodynamics, electrodynamics, biodynamics, anything we please? There is no reason why not. There is in reality no place to stop, save when we have become tired of pure logic, if once we include geometry. As a matter of fact all our concepts whether of space, or matter, or electricity, or life, are but idealizations more or less well-defined, and, if we insist on subjecting the world to purely logical explanation, they all belong in the same class.

Upon this matter we may best quote Russell who, amid all his refinements, keeps a clear idea of their proper place in the system of all knowledge. He says: The laws of motion, like the axiom of parallels in regard to space, may be viewed either as parts of a definition of a class of possible material universes, or as empirically verified assertions concerning the actual material universe. But in no way can they be taken as *a priori* truths necessarily applicable to any possible material world. The *a priori* truths involved in dynamics are only those of logic; as a system of deductive reasoning, dynamics requires nothing further, while as a science of what exists, it requires experiment and observation. Those who have admitted a similar conclusion in geometry are not likely to question it here; but it is important to establish separately every instance of the principle that knowledge as to what exists is never derivable from general philosophical considerations, but is always and wholly empirical.[25]

7 Some Conclusions

There is one conclusion in logic which suggests itself almost inevitably at this point. For there are a considerable number of systems of logic current at present. Different authors have treated the subject differently – each choosing the system of indefinables and laws of thought which seemed best to him at the time. Now it is by no means true that these various systems of logic have been proved coextensive or even not mutually contradictory. If it should appear that they cannot be brought into harmonious relation one with another there will be some instructive, if bewildering, conclusions to draw. And as we have such complex entities as infinity and continua with which to deal it might not be regarded as surprising if some points were found to stand out permanently, so that logicians will permanently disagree. In fact at present there seems to be a grave logical difficulty in our logical system as developed by Russell. This trouble had been felt by Frege and a solution had been proposed by him; but it does not seem entirely satisfactory.[26] In view of the outstanding difficulties and the possible divergence of systems of logic held by equally good authorities, we come to the conclusion that it is dangerous to accept the naïve point of view of those who claim that a certain piece of reasoning depends on the operation of logic alone but who fail to state what those operations are and to use all the means possible to avoid the intrusion of extraneous ideas. They may not fall into error, but they are merely following in the footsteps of those who "knew" what infinity and continuity were.

From the pedagogic point of view we may also draw some conclusions. It is hardly necessary to trouble the student with the commutative and associative laws in multiplication of integers or with elaborate deductions of a number system before he is readily able to appreciate the needlessness of the former and the relation which the latter bears to the theory of finite and infinite cardinals and ordinals, the ideas of compactness and continuity, and the two kinds of infinity. A clear-cut physical conception that numbers possess order and may be associated with the points on a line is a workable idea which in practice is both necessary and sufficient for ordinary rigorous analysis. An inadequate vague idea regarded as a useful working hypothesis seems, on the whole, productive of more good and less harm than an inadequate definite idea regarded as final. In geometry and mechanics the physical attitude may be taken. Axioms, things deemed worthy of credence on the basis of experience, should take the place of postulates. This does not prevent, in fact it encourages, the statement of a large number of axioms without troubling too much as to their independence. At the same time these statements should include the essential idea of order and the useful idea of continuity and other ideas which are usually passed over.[27] In short we should use and train intuition to the utmost in connection with some logic; for pure logic alone is, as Poincaré states (§2), harmful to the earlier development of the mind.

From the mathematical standpoint we have learned that many of the objects which have been thought of as individual must be regarded as classes. We cannot define Euclidean space, but we can define the class of all Euclidean spaces.[28] The principle of abstraction, here involved, seems to arise from the necessity of taking the terms in a logical equation to represent the common attribute of all the objects which may in some way satisfy the equation. As during the progress of the discussion, we have introduced no new indefinables, no new postulates, no processes other than those of logic, there is no possibility of our arriving at contradictions except through the failure of our logical system to be logical; and behind this we cannot go. It remains merely to show the existence of the classes with which we have dealt; otherwise our work would be null. To quote freely from our author: The existence of zero is derived from the fact that the null-class is a member of zero; the existence of 1, from the fact that zero is a unit-class (the null-class being its only member). By an evident induction we get all finite numbers. From the class of finite cardinals follows first the existence of the smallest of the infinite cardinals, and second, by considering them in the order of magnitude, the existence of ordinals and the smallest of the infinite ordinals. We may go on to obtain the rationals, compact enumerable series, continuous series. From the last we may see the existence of complex numbers, of the class of Euclidean spaces, of projective spaces, of hyperbolic spaces, and of spaces with various metrical properties. Finally we may prove the existence of the class of dynamical worlds. Throughout this process no entities are employed but such as are definable in terms of the fundamental logical constants. Thus the chain of definitions and existence-theorems is complete, and the purely logical nature of mathematics is established throughout.

This is as far as we are conducted. But we are promised a second volume – may it be soon forthcoming – written with the collaboration of Whitehead. Herein will be contained actual chains of deduction leading from the premises of logic through arithmetic to geometry. Herein will also be found various original developments in which the notations of Peano and Russell have been found useful. For those who wish sooner to get at the Peano–Russell point of view in the matter, we append a bibliography, which while very incomplete may still be found useful in tracing the development of the ideas:

(1) *Arithmetices principia nova methodo exposita*, Turin, Bocca Frères, 1889.

(2) *I principii di geometria logicamente esposti*, Turin, 1889.

These two works by Peano are the starting point of the whole movement. They were written in the days when a careful explanation and translation of the symbolic method was in vogue and form a good starting point for study. The *Formulaire de Mathématiques*, edited by Peano, is rather hard to begin on. The *Rivista di Matematica*, now the *Revue de Mathématiques*, also edited by Peano, furnishes much easy and instructive reading matter. *Logica matematica* by Burali-Forti in the series of Manuali Hoepli may serve as a textbook. Omitting important memoirs by Burali-Forti on arithmetic and by Pieri on geometry which we have quoted in the notes, we cite again:

(3) *Bibliothèque du congrès international de philosophie*, volume 3 (1901).

The articles by Peano, Burali-Forti, Padoa, and Pieri show the point at which the Italian school had arrived in 1900. It is since that time that most of Russell's technical work has appeared. For the present state of the science, we would note a memoir by Whitehead:

(4) "On cardinal numbers," *American Journal of Mathematics*, volume 24 (1902), pages 367–394; and a paper by Burali-Forti, "Sulla teoria generale delle grandezze e dei numeri," *Atti della R. Accademia delle Scienze di Torino*, volume 39 (January, 1904).

Notes

1 A review of Volume I of *The Principles of Mathematics* by Bertrand Russell, Cambridge, Cambridge University Press, 1903, and *Essai sur les Fondaments de la Géométrie* par Bertrand Russell, traduction par A. Cadenat, revue et annotée par l'auteur et par L. Couturat, Paris, Gauthier-Villars, 1901. We may also refer our readers to the review by L. Couturat, *Bulletin des Sciences Mathématiques*, vol. 28, pp. 129–147 (1904). So large is the work of Russell that Couturat's review and our own supplement rather than overlap one another.

2 *La Logique de Leibniz*, Paris, 1901.

3 The fundamental importance of the logic of relations (see *infra*) was emphasized by C. S. Peirce in 1880–1884: but it is only [now] beginning to have its full effect [twenty years later].

4 Translated in *Bulletin of the American Mathematical Society*, vol. 10, p. 5 (Oct., 1903).

5 "I principii della geometrica di posizione," *Memorie della R. Accademia delle Scienze di Torino*, vol. 48, pp. 1–62. And, "Della geometria elementare come sistema ipotetico-deduttivo; Monografia del punto e moto," *ibid.*, vol. 49, pp. 173–222.

6 While we appreciate and admire as much as anyone can the beauties of Hilbert's famous *Grundlagen der Geometrie*, we fail to see how the historical facts can justify what Poincaré says (*loc. cit.*, p. 23): "He has made the philosophy of mathematics take a long step in advance, comparable to those which were due

to Lobachevsky, to Riemann, to Helmholtz, and to Lie." Poincaré makes the point that Hilbert regards his geometric elements as *mere things* and on this seems to rest a large part of the praise (*loc. cit.*, bottom p. 21 and top p. 22). If this be so, it ought to be mentioned as a matter of history that Peano, in 1889, in his *Principii di Geometria* took precisely this stand, p. 24. In 1891–2, Vailati, *Rivista*, vol. 1, p. 127, vol. 2, p. 71, again formulated the principle in words. By 1897 the Italian school had gone as far beyond this point of view as to make it a *postulate* that points are classes – thus showing a twofold advance, once in recognizing the presence of a postulate, again in using the word class so as to bring the reasoning into form dependent upon precise logical processes alone. It has also been said that the idea of the independence of the axioms was due to Hilbert. As a matter of fact in 1894, Peano, "Sui fondamenti della geometria," *Rivista*, vol. 4, pp. 51 *et seq.*, states the problem and, by actually setting up simple systems of elements, proves the independence of certain axioms from certain others. So that by 1899 the idea and method were both five years old at least. Again, in 1889, Peano laid it down as a principle that there should be as few undefined symbols as possible, and he used but few. In 1897–9 Pieri used but two for projective geometry and but two for metric geometry, whereas Hilbert was using a considerable number, seven or eight. (The idea of compatibility seems to have been first stated clearly by Hilbert.) There still remains in the *Grundlagen der Geometrie* matter enough for the amplest praise. The Archimedean axiom, the theorems of Pascal and Desargues, the analysis of segments and areas, and a host of things are treated either for the first time or in a new way, and with consummate skill. We should say that it was in the technique rather than in the philosophy of geometry that Hilbert created an epoch.

7   Compare the papers below referred to in the Bibliothèque du Congrès International with No. 2 of Hilbert's Mathematical Problems, *Bulletin of the American Mathematical Society*, vol. 8, p. 447. We may refer also to Padoa, *L'Enseignement Mathématique*, vol. 5, p. 85. See also §4 of the present review. For our readers, who may be working on the problem No. 2, we may note – what we unfortunately failed to note at the time of translating – namely, that a solution along the lines proposed by Hilbert seems logically impossible. A solution has long since been proposed in the article here referred to. There are those, however, who hold that Padoa has gone so far as to overshoot the mark. Hilbert has again taken up the matter much more searchingly than in 1900. It is to be regretted that his paper which was presented at Heidelberg, August, 1904, is not at hand for comparison.

8   *La science et l'hypothèse*, Paris, 1903; and numerous scattered essays.

9   That Poincaré seems frequently to have in mind the physical rather than the mathematical, the psychological rather than the logical point of view can be seen in several places in his review. On p. 8 he asserts that we know the axioms are non-contradictory "since geometry exists." And on p. 22 he seems to complain that the logical standpoint interests the author to the utter disregard of the psychological. It should be remembered that the first chief aim of the modern researches on the foundations of geometry is to be entirely rid of the psychological element – and this for the very reason that secondly we may decide just what that psychological element must be. This latter problem belongs rather to the philosopher and psychologist than to the mathematician.

10   *American Journal of Mathematics*, vol. 24, p. 367 (October, 1902).

11   Duhamel, *Des méthodes dans les sciences*, Paris, 1875, vol. 1, p. 17.

12   Peano and his immediate followers overlook the importance of this subject – so busy are they with other important questions. It is one of the lasting services of

Russell, following very closely on the work done twenty years earlier by C. S. Peirce, to have recognized the necessity of this addition to Peano's system and to have supplied the deficiency. See his articles in the *Revue de Mathématiques*, vol. 7, nos. 2 and following (1901–1902).

13 See also E. V. Huntington on "Sets of independent postulates for the algebra of logic," *Transactions*, vol. 5, p. 288 (July, 1904).

14 In regard to logic on which mathematics rests, we should incline to use the word axiom (if indeed we do not prefer to hold to premise) and not postulate. For here we are dealing with the actual (mental) world and not with a system of marks. The basis of rationality must go deeper than a mere set of marks and postulates. It is the foundation of everything and must be more *real* than anything else.

15 Peano: *Bibliothèque du Congrès International de Philosophie à Paris, 1900*, vol. 3 (1901).

16 Compare Burali-Forti; *Bibliothèque* etc. "Sur les différentes définitions du nombre réel." We say *aspect* on account of a change in view which has been established since 1900. Also "Le classe finite", *Atti della Accademia reale di Scienze di Torino*, vol. 32, p. 34 (1896); and more recently "Sulla teoria generale della grandezze e dei numeri," *ibid.*, vol. 39 (Jan., 1904).

17 Russell shows, *Principles*, p. 113, that this idea is not dependent on the general concept number, nor even on the concept unity. Two classes which can be placed in one-to-one correspondence are called *similar*.

18 See references given in note 6. The consistency is far more important than the independence, irreducibility, or completeness: for these are merely a matter of elegance, whereas that determines whether or not all our reasoning upon the system in question is void.

19 *Bibliothèque* etc. "Essai d'une théorie algébrique des nombres entiers, précédé d'une introduction logique à une théorie déductive quelconque." This remarkable essay should be read by everyone. We may note that Padoa uses 'transformateurs' but introduces no theory of relations. In this respect Russell has introduced improvements.

20 *Transactions*, vol. 3, pp. 264–282 (1902). See also Veblen, *Transactions*, vol. 5, p. 346 (1904).

21 Serious mistakes, resulting in definitions of no essential content, have been made by forgetting that the relations which connect the elements must be in correspondence, in addition to any correspondence between the elements. See also note 24.

22 *American Journal of Mathematics*, vol. 24 (1902).

23 This would seem to render invalid the contention of Poincaré in his *La science et l'hypothèse* to the effect that the principle of induction is the essence of the infinite. We have seen that it is the essence of the finite. The difficulty seems to be that Poincaré has in mind the definition of the infinite as a growing variable. If this be so, the apparent contradiction resolves itself into a mere difference of definitions.

24 As the serial relation is emphasized rather than its domain (see discussion of order given above) the author avoids a definition which is null and which makes dimensions impossible. Compare discussion of completeness in §4 and note 18. For a fuller discussion of this important point we may refer to "The so-called foundations of geometry," by Edwin Bidwell Wilson in the *Archiv der Mathematik und Physik*, vol. 6, pp. 104–122 (1903). Toward the end of the discussion a change, which may cause some confusion, is made to the point of view of

physical geometry. The first part, however, deals solely with purely mathematical geometry.

25 It would be interesting to discuss how far this attitude is really in accord or out of accord with the apparently very different view of Poincaré (*La science et l'hypothèse*) that the question whether the parallel axiom is true or not true is devoid of sense owing to the fact that it is merely a *convenient* method of correlating experience and a *convention* can have neither truth nor falsity.

26 In a long appendix, Russell gives a detailed exposition of the important work of Frege, which culminated in the *Grundgesetze der Arithmetik*, and he discusses this troublesome contradiction again from a different standpoint. It is this contradiction which Hilbert had in mind in his Heidelberg address referred to under §2. He, therefore, attempts to recast the principles of logic and of arithmetic in such a manner as to render them sufficient for mathematical reasoning. We certainly hope that he has succeeded in doing so to the satisfaction of both mathematicians and philosophers.

27 Compare, for example, the series of articles by the reviewer on Spherical Geometry, *American Mathematical Monthly*, commencing January, 1904.

28 This apparently considerably lowers the importance of the idea of *completeness* discussed in §4. For it appears as if the one-to-one correspondence between the different Euclidean spaces were really of minor significance. This is but another instance of the fact that the elements themselves are unimportant – that it is the abstraction from them which is most fundamental. However, we believe that the idea of completeness is a new step, a step onward and toward a fuller description of the systems dealt with.

3

What is Mathematics?[1]

James Byrnie Shaw

The game of chess has always fascinated mathematicians, and there is reason to suppose that the possession of great powers of playing that game is in many features very much like the possession of great mathematical ability. There are the different pieces to learn, the pawns, the knights, the bishops, the castles, and the queen and king. The board possesses certain possible combinations of squares, as in rows, diagonals, etc. The pieces are subject to certain rules by which their motions are governed, and there are other rules governing the players. A treatise on chess contains all these. Further however it also contains openings which have been found to be advantageous to one or the other of the players and usually contains also various endings of games for the tyro to analyse, in order that he may see how to acquire skill in foreseeing the situations that may arise in any game. One has only to increase the number of pieces, to enlarge the field of the board, and to produce new rules which are to govern either the pieces or the player, to have a pretty good idea of what mathematics consists.

In mathematics the game is much more complicated. The pieces we handle are the members of ranges of a more or less elaborate character. These members may be numbers, functions, lines, operations, any set of things we can define.[2] The moves on the board are groups of operations that may be performed upon these ranges and their members. We also must take into account a feature which is present in the game of chess in one move only – that of castling. In mathematics we may handle whole combinations of elements and operations upon them, as if they were single things. That is, we must take into account complexes of operations and ranges.

With these elements we do different things, according to our taste and ability. First of all there are the developments of *structure*. These include the construction of magic squares, and other questions of tactic, arrangements and combinatory analysis, factoring, decomposition of fractions, congruences, residues, and theory of form, through the structure of groups, up to finite fields, multiple algebra, calculus of operations, symbolic logic and general algebra. Then there are developments of the *invariants* that occur in different structures. We study algebraic and arithmetic forms, group characters, projective geometry, differential forms, topology, geometry in general, and operational invariants. (We mention necessarily only a few sample cases of the problems referred to.) There is also the study of correspondences of various types, the whole field of analysis or study of *functions*. In this are such things as the functions of a real variable, trigonometric series, algebraic functions, general analysis, geometrical transformations, automorphic functions, calculus of variations, functions of a complex variable, vector fields, differential geometry, and rational mechanics. Further, and most difficult, are the studies in *inversion*. It is here that the expansions of the mathematical game take place. In this line of investigation we find algebraic corpora, ideals, modular systems, differential equations, integral equations, functional equations, and inverses of all kinds. Any theory of mathematics that would be complete is forced to account for all these different studies. To consider, for example, that one has laid the foundations of mathematics when he has produced the irrational number, is to confuse the theory of real variables with mathematics. Important as the problems of the continuum may be, the continuum is not the basis or foundation of structure. A knowledge of the different grades of ensembles does not enable one to ascertain whether a group is compound or not, or whether a number is prime or not. It does not determine the list of invariants of the decic, nor does it develop the differential parameters of a differential form of the fifth degree. The continuum has little to do with the properties of automorphic functions as functions. Cardinal and ordinal ranges do not play a prominent part in modular systems, nor in algebraic ideals, nor in functional equations. Neither likewise does a set of postulates for geometry, or some type of geometry, assist in determining how many associative algebras there are, built on twenty-four units. Indeed the postulates for associative algebras in general do not do this. So it becomes evident that when one wishes to discuss the principles of mathematics he must state what it is he refers to. If the analysis above (which was only indicated in a broad way) is correct, he may discuss the *ranges* with which mathematics has to deal, or he may discuss *operations* in general, or the principles may be those at the base of *multiple algebra*. He may mean the principles of mathematical composition and *form*, or the principles of the *invariance* in the transformations of forms, or the principles of *functionality* and correspondence in general, or the principles upon which may be founded the theory of *inversions*. For example, Russell's *Principles of Mathematics* was unable to handle the problem of the introduction of the imaginary into mathematics, and endeavored to crowd the whole theory of hypercomplex numbers into the theory of dimensionality. Peano's *Formulaire* did better, for the imaginary is defined at least by one of its examples. But the imaginary and the quaternion, and all other associative hypercomplex numbers, not to speak of those not associative, receive scant recognition in either case. A Principia Mathematica should cover the field, or it ceases to justify its title.[3]

Further we must not confuse mathematics and mathematical reasoning. It is true we infer in mathematics. But we also infer in physics, and history, and in daily life. Mathematics has no copyright on the process. To define mathematics as the science that draws necessary conclusions,[4] or as the class of all formal implications,[5] does not define at all. Other branches of human learning draw necessary conclusions, and formal implication is not unknown to them. Mathematics also uses the constructive imagination, the generalizing power, the intuition, and other mental processes. To define mathematics as "the study of ideal constructions (often applicable to real objects) and the discovery thereby of relations between the parts of these constructions, before unknown," is better.[6] This definition brings out the *ideal*, the *construction*, and the *discovery*, three features which are essential to mathematical development. For example, an abstract group is ideal. Functions of the roots of an equation are ideal constructions. The discovery lies in seeing that the properties of the one will explain the relations involved in the other. Again, algebraic numbers are ideal. We construct with them domains of rationality, and arrive at the Galois theory in the relations.

However, attention should be drawn to the fact that among the ideal elements with which we deal are many we invent or create entirely new. Examples are easily found. Quaternions were the result of Hamilton's attempt to extend the number field. The non-Euclidean geometries were the attempt to create a new geometry. If any one fact stands out prominently in mathematical investigation it is this fact of the creation of new realms of investigation. Whether these ever are applied to real objects is a matter of less importance mathematically. It is a simple affair to invent even a new logic and mode of inference. Thus, let us imagine that the contradictive process were of period three, in place of two. That is, to the proposition p there is a first contradictory p', whose first contradictory is p'', the contradictory of the last being again p. What becomes of the conventional logic now? Yet by symbolism we can develop this kind of logic as well as any. This process we may call the mathematicizing of logic. Indeed the volume before us really does something of this kind for logic, as the doctrine of types is close to the example above, and the result is labeled mathematical logic.

The outcome is interesting to mathematicians for several reasons. First of all it is a very general or abstract branch of mathematics. Secondly this book whose first volume is under consideration takes the place of a second volume of the *Principles*, in which the attempt was made to reduce all mathematics to symbolic logic, or as it is now called logistic. It is expected to demonstrate formally from these notions the derivation of the properties of cardinal and ordinal integers, irrationals, series, and eventually geometry and dynamics. We desire to examine the book from a purely mathematical point of view as to the success of the attempt.

There is an Introduction of three chapters. In some cases the fuller development farther on must be read in order to see exactly what the explanations of the Introduction mean. The first chapter gives a preliminary explanation of the notations used. These symbols are able to be themselves the elements of the entire development, and are thus very fundamental. A complete table is given here for the convenience of readers.

Symbol	Meaning	Symbol	Meaning
⊢	it is true that . .	∸	negative of relation ()
*	chapter	⊂·	relation () contained in . .
~	contradictory of . .	|	relative product of . .
v	. . or . .	R^{ι}	the referent as to relation () of . .
.	. . and . .	$R^{\iota\iota}$	referents of class α
⊃	. . implies that . .	$\breve{R}$	converse relation of R
$⊃_x$	. . implies that . . for x, formal implication	∃!	there is a case of relation
		Λ	null-relation
=	. . is identical with . .	V̇	universal relation
$=Df$	nominal definition	⌐	relation with domain limited to a class
≡	. . is equivalent to . .		
$≡_x$	. . is equivalent to . . for x, formal equivalence	⌐	relation with converse domain limited to a class
P_Δ	P-selections	⌐	relation with field limited to a class
1 → 1	one–one correspondence		
1 → Cls	one–many correspondence	↓	couplet relation, vid.
Cls	name for classes	∩	common subclass
Rel	name for relations	∪	common superclass
Cnv	converse	−	negative of class . .
Ex	existent	⊂	contained in . . .
Cls^2	class of classes	V	universal class
D$^\iota$	domain of relation . .	Λ	null class
⊲	converse domain of . .	∃!	there is a member of . .
C$^\iota$	field of . .	E!	the member of . . exists
→,	sg, referents of . .	1	the class of unit classes
←,	gs, relata of . .	1(α)	the class of unit classes of type α
$x♀$	operator of x on ()		
$♀y$	operator of () into y	φ, ψ, χ, θ	functional signs
$α♀y$	values of $x♀y$ for x over range α	↑	the . . .
R1	subrelation	ε	is a member of the class determined by . .
R1	ex existent subrelation		
$φa$	proposition about a	ι	class of one member, unit class.
$φx$	proposition about a variable	$ι^\iota α$	the only member of α
$φ\hat{x}$	propositional function		Greek capitals constants

Symbol	Meaning	Symbol	Meaning
$\varphi!\hat{x}$	predicative function		Small Greek letters usually classes
$(x) \cdot \varphi x$	proposition is true for all individuals x		Capital italics variable relations
		p, q, r	propositions
$(\exists x) \cdot \varphi x$	proposition is true for some individuals x	f, g	functions
		$t'x$	type in which x is contained
$(\imath x)\varphi x$	the x with property φ	$t_0'\alpha$	type in which α is contained
$\hat{x}(\varphi x)$	class defined by φ	$p'\kappa$	product of classes
Type	range of x such that φx is significant.	$s'\kappa$	sum of classes
		Cl	subclass
$\cap$	relation () and relation ()	Cl ex	existent subclass
$\cup$	relation () or relation ()	'	of

These symbols may be viewed in two different ways. They may be looked upon as furnishing a system of shorthand, or pasigraphy and stenography combined, intelligible to the initiated, and not only abbreviating the writing, but furnishing a mode of expression in which the usual color, shading of meaning, and associations or words are missing. This in itself would justify their use. Or we may look upon them as being symbols for the abstract elements of reasoning which have been found by the analysis, and for which no appropriate name exists. The latter formal view would not be taken by those who dislike to think that mathematics is the theory of certain combinations of symbols. But it seems to us that if we take the formal point of view, we are doing no more than when we define a rational fraction as a couple of numbers, subject to certain rules, and are able then to identify integers with those couples whose second number is 1. The foundations of arithmetic become solid. So too here if we consider that these symbols themselves, as representative of certain well-defined terms, are under consideration, we shall find a gain in clearness. In fact obscurity arises easily if we try to interpret some of the statements of the book in other ways.

We will undertake to give some notion of the ground covered in this first volume. All we can do of course in our limits of space is to discuss some of the prominent features of the book. The first thing we must consider is the meaning attached to certain words that are not used in the usual sense. The one we encouter at the beginning is the term *implication*. To this we need to devote a careful study, for it is the real basis of the further development.

Implication

The startling statement is made early that "Newton was a man" and "The sun is hot" are equivalent propositions. From the definition of implication we see also that "Newton was not a man" implies that "The sun is hot," and "The sun is cold" implies "Newton was a man," or $2 + 2 = 4$, or "John

Smith killed Pocahontas." This is a very different thing from what most of us would naturally call equivalence or implication. Implication, as used here, is a relation between two elementary propositions, or statements about particular individuals. We might raise the question as to whether there are any such propositions after all. But accepting for the time the assertion that they exist, implication is merely the statement that either the first proposition is false or else the second one is true. Now in the highly special sense in which we find terms used throughout the book, we feel instinctively that there is a certain artificial quality about every definition given or term used. Thus while we find the terms *true*, *false*, and *not true*, used, as well as *truth-value*, we find no real explanation given of the meaning of these words. Indeed we find later that there is a varying truth dependent upon the order of the statement. We must conclude then that the text throughout is concerned with a certain quality of the propositions considered, and not with the propositions themselves. When the authors talk about p and q they do not mean to discuss the significance of p and q but only a certain quality of p or of q. If the argument is about "Newton was a man," any other true proposition would do as well, for example, $2 + 2 = 4$. The assertions are not about the content of the propositions in either case but about the quality attached to either called its "truth-value." All propositions with the same truth-value are equivalent. They may in any implication be substituted, one for another. This explains how it is that "Newton was a man" and "The sun is hot" are equivalent. It also shows that the first implies the second, for either the first, irrespective of its significance, has the truth-value falsehood, or else the second has the truth-value truth. It is explained later (page 120) that we may throughout substitute the number 1 for any proposition with the truth-value truth, and the number 0 for any proposition with the truth-value falsehood, and reduce all formulas to the arithmetic of 0 and 1. The notion of truth-value is due to Frege,[7] although something similar is to be found in Boole.[8]

With regard to this view, we might suggest that whether the symbols p and q are to be regarded as equivalent or not depends upon the relationship they possess to other things in the universe, as well as upon their own significance. It would seem better to have used a different term to designate what the authors have in mind. A specific symbolism will make the matter clear. Let us agree to mark every proposition either with ° or with '. This property of being tagged we will call T, thus

T (Newton was a man) is ',   T (The sun is cold) is °.

We may then state that what is mean by implication is one of the alternatives

T(p) is ° and T(q) is °, or T(p) is ° and T(q) is ', or T(p) is ' and T(q) is '.

It is to be observed that T(q) is tagged ' if T(p) is ', otherwise it may be either. The one case excluded is evidently: tag of p is ' and tag of q is °. We may admit that this is a simple thing, but (while it may be an idiosyncrasy on our part) it does not seem to be elementary. The notion of two tags, and of the property of being tagged, are clearly involved, and unless we make the tagging a purely haphazard affair, there is also involved the problem of determining *which tag must be placed on a given symbol.* The basal assumption (not mentioned) of the entire book seems to be, that we are in a position to say with regard to any proposition p about some specific thing whether it is true or not. Often it is the truth that we are endeavoring to discover. In fact, we have here the first example of the assertion that some parts of the book become more clear if we treat the results as purely symbolic, the whole being a calculus of symbols. If we know how to tag q there is no use in mentioning p. If p happens to be false, or if p happens to be true, we still confront the fact that we must decide that we have to choose between exactly the alternatives stated above. Hence for practical inference, this kind of implication seems to be worthless, and we therefore think another name would be desirable. The definition of implication, or rather the meaning given the implication sign, by Peano,[9] seems to be more fundamental, and elementary. It reads thus:

$$p \supset q$$

de p on déduit q; si p, alors q; la p a pour conséquence la q; la q est une conséquence de la p; la p est une condition suffisante de la q; la q est une condition nécessaire de la p.

We deal here directly with the propositions p and q and not with any functions of qualities they may possess. From the formal point of view, however, we have obtained a two-valued function of the indefinite set of marks, p, q, r, etc., that is, T( ) is ' or °.

The propositional form that has a variable argument is generally expressed by φx, and we come next to the implications corresponding, that is, to *formal implication.* According to the *Principles of Mathematics,* the formal implication is the main thing in mathematics. It means that in φx we substitute for x any symbol (later it is restricted to a given type). The propositions resulting will each have a tag, as ' or °, that is, as true or false.[10] The same is done with ψx, where ψ is a form into which we put the variable x in order to arrive at a proposition. Each of these propositions is tagged. Then φx implies (formally) ψx if in each case the tag on φx is ° or else the tag on ψx is ', the same x occurring in each of the two. In other words, we must be able to assign for any given x the proper tag for φx and for ψx, and if we make out a three-column table in which the first column is marked x, the second φx, the third ψx, and then enter the values of x as arguments, and the tags as values in the proper columns, we will necessarily have in the second column both ° and ′, and in the third column also both ° and ′, but with ′ in the second will always come ′ in the third. We might also state it thus: ψx must be true at least whenever φx is true. It is explained that we do not need to know or to produce every x about which the proposition may be stated. The φ and ψ are taken intensively. This is the first case we note in which there seems to be a lack of agreement between the theory and the practice. The definition calls for a comparison of the tags on two sets of expressions, which from their character would usually be infinite in number. As the direct comparison is impossible, the practical application goes back to a problem in intension, a term the authors endeavor to the utmost to shut out of the book. Again, if φx happens to be false for x in every case, we nevertheless have ψx implied. This may be true, that from false propositions anything may be concluded, but it does not advance mathematics very much. It would seem therefore that the attempt to found the whole system on the principle of truth-values (which we have called tags) is not so very successful, and that it would be better to make the undefined implication the base of the system. Indeed the authors apparently fall into this habit unconsciously. Thus we find as one of the assertions of the book

$$*2.04 \vdash \quad : . \, p \, . \, \supset \, . \, q \supset r : \supset : q \, . \, \supset \, . \, p \supset r,$$

which they interpret: if r follows from q provided p is true, then r follows from p provided q is true. This reversal of conditions in the theory of functions would wreak havoc only too frequently. Of course the reading should be: consider {the tag on p is ° or else the tag on the statement [either the tag on q is ° or that on r is ′] is ′}, then if we mark all that has just been stated in {   } with ′, we must mark also with ′ all that follows, namely {the tag on q is ° or else the tag on the statement [either the tag on p is ° or else the tag on r is ′] is ′}. This is quite different from the Peano reading given just above.

   We have dwelt upon the idea of implication as set forth here because this idea seems to be used more as a test of the accuracy of the results obtained than as a working notion. It is held in reserve as a court of last appeal. If one starts in directly with Section A and not with the Introduction, he does not encounter the notion of truth-value until *4.01 on page 120. If implication is taken as the fundamental notion and left undefined, we can define all the other symbols in terms of it and contradiction. This was done in the *Principles*, although the method used seems unnecessarily cumbrous. However, truth-value does not appear in the symbolism, and we have practically gained the following fundamental symbols:

φa, φb, etc., definite propositions about constant subjects a, b, etc.
φx, ψx, etc., definite propositional functions but variable arguments.
$\supset$, a relation between propositions, called implication.

Propositional Functions

The propositional function is very important. It not only includes the usual predicate but may be any kind of a form with a blank place left for the entry of the argument. It is a symbol for the process that enables one to pass from a given argument term to another, the value term. The notation is as follows:

φa, a has the property φ, or of a we may say φ. This sentence is the value of φ for a.

φx, the propositional function applied to a variable argument. This is a symbol for any *one* of the values of the function, including statements which are not true as well as true statements.

$\varphi\hat{x}$, the function itself, as function. The $\hat{x}$ appears merely to assure the reader that the function really is a function of something or other. If the authors could have brought themselves to accept the Frege[11] notion and symbol $\varphi()$, the apparent argument could have been omitted.

$(x)\cdot\varphi x$, the entire list of values of φx are represented by this sign. In a large majority of them the truth-value would be ° of course. Also the x is restricted to the range called the type of φ. The expression reads "φx is every case where x belongs to the type of φ."

$(\exists x)\cdot\varphi x$, there are values of x which give φx the truth-value'.

The symbol $\hat{x}(\varphi x)$ seems to have two meanings, both at war with each other. In the early part of the book it is defined to mean the class (aggregate, ensemble) which consists of those arguments that make φx true. In other words, to be the set of individuals in the class determined by, or defined by, the function φ. Later it is defined with a symbol $\psi!\hat{x}$ which is purely a function symbol, and does not represent individuals at all. This symbol practically defines the class property. The latter meaning seems to be the one which the authors expect to use, and may be interpreted to be the class as class, and not as individuals, but considered as a *denoting* symbol. This use of the symbol to represent the predicative function that would define the class collectively seems to be necessary in the system to enable us to use classes as arguments of functions. It is explained that we do not arrive at real classes thus, but only incomplete symbols. For example it is something like this. If we desire to say "The governors of states all wore silk hats," we must recast the statement to read "Certain persons were silk-hatted governors of states." This use of the class symbol $\hat{x}(\varphi x)$ and the function symbol $\varphi\hat{x}$ is close to that of the phrase "governor of state," in two different senses, one meaning defining the qualifications necessary to be the governor of each of the states, the other defining the actual governors, so that they could be identified among other men. Both are functions. On this basis there are *no classes*, although the word "class" appears everywhere in the book. However, the claim is made that we have something just as good as a class, and in fact (page 84) "in mathematical reasoning, we can dismiss the whole apparatus of functions and think only of classes as 'quasi-things,' capable of immediate representation by a single name." An example would be the imaginary points of a curve.

However that may be as a matter of interpretation, we at least have arrived at two more symbols, from a mathematical point of view: the proposition as function, and the definition of solutions of a proposition. We have, in brief, isolated the function sign φ, and we can speak of "x such that φx." It would seem now that the fundamental thing after one has exhibited his set of elements with which he proposes to work, would be to consider functions of one variable, then synthetic processes by which these may be built up into useful structures. The importance of the propositional function is sufficiently insisted upon, but the uselessness of a mere set of isolated individuals is not dwelt upon. Nor is the character of synthetic processes in general examined at all. Of this we shall have something further to say.

Extensions

Considerable stress is laid on the assertion that mathematics is primarily concerned with extensions, despite the fact that classes have become mere ghosts of themselves. An example would be any geometric theorem from Euclid. As "Let triangle *ABC* be isosceles, then triangle *ABC* has equal base angles." We are apparently discussing the single triangle *ABC*, but in reality we expect what we say to hold good for any triangle and thus for every triangle. We have the formal implication, which holds between the two sets of elementary propositions, one for each and every triangle. The ground of the reasoning seems to be an ambiguous case, and we seem to reason from any one to all. But is it so? If in a complex mental structure one chooses to pay attention only to certain features of the structure, and discuss them, ignoring the other accompanying features, are the statements about the whole complex structure, or about the portion abstracted? In proving the theorem cited above, does the color of the crayon used in drawing the triangle also enter the argument? Does the size of each individual angle and side also enter, or only certain relations they have? In finding the limit of the expression $2 - (\frac{1}{2})^n$ do the particular values that n may take enter the argument at all? If one must answer no in these cases, that is to say, if one can abstract at all and reason about his abstraction, then we see no force in the constant appeal to extension. Is not the propositional function of the nature of an invariant rather? We say: *this* triangle has two equal sides, so *that* triangle, so also *yonder* triangle. In all the propositions of this sort that we choose to write down, we find the invariant phrase: two equal sides. It does not appear to be essentially different from any other invariant. If we were to conceive a transformation that could convert *this* into *that*, and *this* into *yonder*, the invariant of the transformation would in this case be: two equal sides, that is, isoscelism. Now the real question is, whether we can discuss invariants apart from the other circumstances in the concrete cases in which they are invariant. We certainly do this in mathematics. Indeed, is not this present book an attempt to discover what are the logical invariants in mathematics? In mathematics we are dealing with abstract elements all the time. The world of mathematics is an ideal, that is, an abstract world. We either abstract it from what we find in experience, or we create it *de novo*. For example, no such thing as *two* exists outside a mathematical mind, any more than the rainbow exists as color out there in the sky. We build our own structures and determine their relations, and no abstraction can be said to be more abstract than any other. In Socrates is mortal, Aristotle is mortal, Charlemagne is mortal, Socrates, Aristotle, and Charlemagne are abstract. No one would call them real men. They are as abstract as mortal, and as abstract as all men. Socrates is a word which represents the persistence of certain qualities of something day after day, and is thus in itself an invariant and therefore an abstraction. In one sense the whole of mathematics is the study of invariants.

If this analysis is correct, then when we say that the property φ implies the property ψ we do not need an extension to which to refer it. It is immaterial whether the extension is there or not. We can study the property as well in one case, as in a million, or an infinity of cases, if only we can isolate it itself. That is what we do in geometry, and in fact all through mathematical thinking. From this point of view (which may coincide with that which the authors denominate the philosophical, and with regard to which they admit the contention) mathematics is more concerned with intensions than extensions. These remarks apply to the extensional functions of functions. Indeed the paragraph in the middle of page 77 says:

> the functions of functions with which mathematics is specially concerned are extensional and . . . intensional functions of functions only occur where non-mathematical ideas are introduced, such as what somebody believes or affirms, or the emotions aroused by some fact.

It is difficult to see in this any more than the assertion that mathematics is not concerned with non-mathematical ideas, which no one would pretend to deny, unless it be some philosophers who thought that the *Principles of Mathematics* did not discuss mathematical ideas.

But there is a further point that we must notice. It is that the definition of function and class does not really produce the members of the extension at all. If we speak of the points of intersection of $x^2 + y^2 = 25$ and $x^2 + y^2 = 36$

what points are given as the extension of this proposition? If we speak of the roots of the equation

$$x^6 + 2x^5 - 13x^4 + x^3 - 7x^2 + 11x + 17 = 0,$$

where is the process in all the development of symbolic logic that will determine them for us? If we ask for the hypercomplex numbers that have the characteristic equation

$$\xi^4 - 4\xi\eta^2 + 5\eta^3 = 2$$

who in all the mathematical world will send us the list? Or lists, we should say, for this one equation will determine more than one certain set of such hypercomplex numbers. Quaternions satisfy the equation

$$q^2 - 2Sq\cdot q + T^2q = 0,$$

but so do other hypercomplex numbers. Take the most definite function we can find, and what does it give? Not a class in extension, but certain properties that are found in some example we may produce, yet which may exist in an infinite number of other examples we have never thought of. Mathematics is full of discoveries of just such expansions of the extension of the notions that we have been using. It is a great advance, as Poincaré says, to find that we can bring two things – that is, two extensions – under one name. As a simple case again, the notion of prime number is surely a definite thing, yet who knows how to ascertain whether 67989379012301 is a prime or not? The notion of simple group is definite, are there then simple groups of odd order, other than cyclic groups? When von Staudt called involutions on a line complex numbers, were they cases under the definition or not?

There is, as everyone knows, a vast difference between finding the value of a function for a given argument and finding the arguments that will satisfy a given function. In fact to meet the latter requirement mathematics has had to invent whole new extensions. Symbolic logic does not give us any assistance in this work of development nor any new methods. Its problem is only to criticize the character of the inferences involved in the process of development. It furnishes neither the major nor the minor premise but simply passes upon the validity of the transition from both to the conclusion. And all it furnishes in the propositional function is a sort of common invariant for many sets of classes. The classes may not exist in some sense, and may exist in others, just like the imaginary roots of an equation. But the propositional function does not point out the particular cases of members of the class it defines any more than it solves an algebraic equation. This is quite different from the explicit mathematical function,[12] like sin x or

$$\int_0^a \frac{\sin xdx}{x} \ ,$$

but analogous to the implicit function, like

$$\int \sqrt{y - x} \, dx, \text{ where } x^3y - xy^2 + y^5 = 4.$$

Types

Chapter II of the Introduction develops the part "of the *Principia* which differs most from the *Principles*, the Doctrine of types." By this doctrine the authors hope they have resolved the paradoxes of the *Principles* as well as others that have been stated in discussions provoked by the original ones or by the theory of ensembles of Cantor.

The net result of the discussion seems to be that the predicate of a sentence is of the nature of a matrix or function symbol, and cannot serve as a subject for a sentence which has it also as predicate. Thus we might consider the statement "Triangle *ABC* is scalene." The functionality involved here, scalenity, cannot be put as the subject of this sentence. Scalenity is scalene, would be an absurdity. In this form at least, we might all admit that there is a sort of hierarchy of functions, if not of types. Of course one may talk of scalenity, but scalenity does not belong to the range that is itself scalene.

The *type* of a function is the class of objects that make it significant. That is to say in substituting values for x in φx some of them will give true propositions, some will give false propositions, some will give statements that are neither true nor false. That ensemble which produces with φ a proposition, true or false, is the type. The outcome is a little curious, as it leads to a reincarnated ghost of the buried *class*. The last paragraph of page 173 is interesting reading in connection with what has gone before. The difficulty seems to be of the same type as that which certain mathematicians find in recognizing any symbolic operator as an existent entity of the same character as the things it operates upon. Strictly speaking, of course there is a difference between ⁵⁄₁ and 5, at least till we come to see that the invariant properties we spoke of above are the same in the one case as in the other, and we identify the two. In just this same way we elevate ensembles in general into the region of functions, and then we can draw a distinction between φ as function or φ as argument.

Whether we agree or disagree with the philosophy underlying the argument, we have gained one point more in our symbolism; that is, that we may make a function sign out of any symbol, simple or complex, and we may use any symbol as an argument for the proper function sign. In other words we may construct more and more complicated forms, and we may substitute for any single symbol or set of symbols, complex symbols. Incidentally we have a relativity theorem in mathematics in the doctrine of types. For no type is the bottom of all types. Types are only relative. An individual in today's discussion may be a function in tomorrow's. But do we resolve a contradiction by calling it absurd?

And it is difficult to see how the doctrine of types can be reconciled with many mathematical developments. Thus if we define the function φ by the differential equation $d\varphi x/dx = \varphi x$, we seem to have a case in opposition to the doctrine. For to define the derivative we must know an infinite set of values of the function φ, which is itself defined by means of the derivative. Apparently then we define a function in terms of the function itself. Another case more to the point possibly is the integral equation, and the integro-differential equation.

Relations and Descriptions

The third chapter of the Introduction is devoted to descriptions, classes, and relations, under the title Incomplete Symbols. It is said that these can be defined only in their use. They are analogous to the symbols $\int$, ∇, $\sin^{-1}$, etc. However, it is pointed out that

> the incomplete symbols are obedient to the same formal rules of identity as symbols which directly represent objects, so long as we consider the equivalence of the resulting variables (or constant) values of the propositional functions and not their identity. This consideration of the *identity* of propositions never enters into our formal reasoning.

Under the limitations to the use of these symbols we find that, while x is always identical with x, yet the round square is not identical with the round square, for the reason there is no round square. This surely resembles the argument: Nothing is better than heaven, a shilling is better than nothing, therefore a shilling is better than heaven.

The descriptive symbol is $(\imath x)\varphi x$. It is used in precisely the same way as, and in fact differs little from, the symbol for a class. That is to say, it is a function sign, denoting the single object in the class. For example, the author of *Waverley*. This phrase does not point out the individual Scott, yet it identifies him. The legal John Doe does the same thing for a criminal who refuses to give his real name. These are, in the sense defined, function signs.

The relation is also a function, the function however having two arguments. There are many features common to these three incomplete symbols. The logic of relatives has also many developments that are not found in the others.

With regard to the three chapters of the Introduction, we desire to remark that they are in general somewhat difficult to apprehend as they now stand, for two reasons. First the distinctions drawn seem in many cases to be confused. It is sometimes difficult to ascertain whether the authors are using words in an everyday sense, in a philosophical sense, or in a purely technical sense. It is not always clear whether a symbol is under discussion, or the meaning of the symbol, or the use of the symbol. The introduction of many more good examples might have remedied this defect in style. In the second place, the statements do not seem to be thoroughly consistent. For example, it is not easy to decide what the authors mean by extensional. In the early part it seems to mean, as ordinarily in logic, the totality of individuals constituting an ensemble or collection. Later it seems to mean anything intellectual as distinguished from the emotional and the volitional. Then on page 196:

> Propositions in which a function φ occurs may depend, for their truth-value, upon the particular function φ, or they may depend only upon the *extension* of φ. In the former case, we will call the proposition concerned an *intensional* function of φ; in the latter case an *extensional* function of φ.

Also the apparent dread the authors exhibit towards the word *concept* seems to make the explanations often involved. The root of the whole difficulty seems to lie in an unconscious, or at least unstated, philosophical theory that a general notion is only symbolic and has no real existence of its own, but is existent only as it is manifested in some supposed concrete form. This notion seems to be the source of many of the peculiar interpretations forced upon the symbols. We may in most cases interpret them otherwise, as we have tried to point out; and as a calculus of logic, the system given here is very complete. We consider next the constructive features of the work.

Elements

Substantially all that is meant by a *proposition* is to be found in the formal character of the two symbols p and $\sim p$. The latter is called the contradictory of p. It is of such a nature that the function $\sim$ is involutory, that is, $\sim\sim p$ is the same as p. If we understand then that we have a set of symbols p, q, r, or φa, φb, φc, and the like, with the duplicate set of their contradictories, we have the elements of the subject as analysed in this book. The descriptive symbol is substantially the same as we find exemplified mathematically in the symbol $^{+}\sqrt{2}$, which in the present notation would be $(\imath x)$ $(0 < x, x^2 = 2)$. That is to say, we introduce into arithmetic the indefinite symbol x with the agreement that we will insert it in our number series, and that for x^2 we will always write 2. This is, in a more general case, like the Kronecker modular theory. It is along the line of the algebraicizing of mathematics, as opposed to the arithmetizing of mathematics. It is immaterial from this point of view whether the thing x exists or not. If in any sense it does exist then we may use a single symbol for it rather than the long form $(\imath x)(\varphi x)$. Practically the idea of class is of the same kind. A mathematical example is the definition of a class of algebraic numbers by an equation, as $x^4 + 5x^3 - 2x^2 + 3x - 13 = 0$. The idea of a symbolic class ought not to disturb a geometer, for he is used to imaginary points, circular points at infinity, and the like. We talk of these ideal things as if they existed, being careful that our phrases have meaning when we find the entities do exist in any sense. The same notion occurs again in the relative. A mathematical example is the equation of a curve. Thus $x^2 + y^2 = 25$ furnishes a relation, which finds as its proper representative the *curve* itself, while the pairs of arguments x, y furnish the points on the curve. The curve is a correlating agency for bringing together these pairs of arguments. Whenever there are entities which may be considered to be represented by these symbols, then we use single letters for them and treat them in the old-fashioned manner of handling classes. This view of mathematics, and of propositions in general, we would prefer to call *functional*, rather than extensional, or intensional. It is surely mathematical, whether it is logical or not, and makes mathematics the fundamental basis of all reasoning, even more than the specialized interpretation called symbolic logic. On the philosophical side it seems to emphasize the statement that all reasoning in the last analysis is not about things but about relations between things, for every function expresses a relation between its argument and its value, and every relation may be referred to an ideal thing at least.

Combinations

We must consider next the combinations that are actually built up out of these elements. The general development is given in Part I, which extends from page 89 to page 342, and is called Mathematical Logic. We desire to consider it apart from any meaning of a specific character that might be attached to the symbols. There is a single combination introduced, represented thus: $p \lor q$. Any two symbols may be joined in this manner. It is commutative, that is $p \lor q$ is the same as $q \lor p$. Special symbols are used for the combinations $\sim p \lor q$, which is written $p \supset q$, and the combination $\sim(\sim p \lor \sim q)$, which is written $p \cdot q$, the first being called implication, the latter logical product, while the basal combination is called disjunction. Any two of these symbols may be omitted. Indeed for ease of manipulation, it seems that to express everything in terms of the symbol · would be best. Thus for p v q we write $\sim(\sim p \cdot \sim q)$, and for $\sim p$ v q we write $\sim(p \cdot \sim q)$. We agree further to certain permissible reductions or expansions. Thus, for example, we may write for p,

$$p \cdot p, \quad \text{or} \quad p \text{ v } pq, \quad \text{or} \quad p \cdot q \text{ v } p \cdot \sim q, \quad \text{or} \quad p \text{ v } (p \cdot \sim p) \cdot q,$$

whatever q may be. In fact if we consider that in any product p and $\sim p$ are incompatible and such product may be dropped after the sign v, we arrive at one of the simple methods of handling this calculus. We agree further that if we have any expression φx, where x is variable, we may write the symbol $(\exists x)\varphi x$, and likewise if we have φx and φy (*9.1 and *9.11). Further we agree that in φx we may substitute for x any symbol a of the same type as x, and also that x may run over a given range of proper type (*9.14 and *9.13). Also we agree that in any expression φa, where a is a constant, we may consider φ by itself as a function, and vice versa (*9.15). We may now take any combination of symbols and build more complicated ones with the use of the v or the ·. We add, however, to the symbolism an expression for the range, thus: (x), meaning all values of x, and $(\exists x)$ meaning those values which are solutions. The name "formal implication" is given to the combination

$$(x)\varphi x \supset \psi x \quad \text{or} \quad \varphi x \supset_x \psi x.$$

In using functions of two variables we introduce the abbreviations called relations. To indicate that x is a solution of φx we abbreviate thus: $x \in \varphi!x$.

The formulas resulting from these few elements are very numerous, and no attempt will be made to go into them. It is from the results of these combinations however that the authors expect to produce other combinations which will have all the properties of numbers, series, etc.

It is obvious that, out of all the processes the mind goes through, others might have been selected as the fundamental ones. Whether a commutative combination is in the end more useful than one that is not commutative may be a question. We often must use a non-commutative product in mathematics, as "if p is *first* true, and then q is true, it follows r is true." The whole consideration of mathematical form[13] might from certain points of view be considered to be a prerequisite to the study of any kind of combination. In Whitehead's *Universal Algebra* this is partly in evidence.

We need to note further that the few modes of combination used here are really supplemented later by a free use of relational symbols, P, Q, R, $\in$, P_Δ, in fact by so many that when we remember the few combinations used here we wonder why these in particular should have been chosen to be represented by arbitrary signs. Indeed the number of arbitrary symbols which have to be memorized is so great in the book that one is willing to conclude that a more significant system could have been worked out. But taken as it is, there remains still the mathematical problem. Stated in brief it is this: given two operations by which from elements or marks new elements or marks are produced, namely, let us say, given that from p, q we construct

$$s = \varphi p, \ t = \psi(p, q), \text{ and } u = \theta(p, q)$$

with the conditions or identities that

$$\varphi s = \varphi \varphi p = p, \ \varphi \psi(p, q) = \theta(\varphi p, \varphi q) \text{ or } \varphi \theta(p, q) = \psi(\varphi p, \varphi q),$$
$$\psi(p, q) = \psi(q, p), \ \theta(p, q) = \theta(q, p).$$

We now have the properties of these combinations as combinations to consider. This problem is one of general algebra, universal algebra, or multiple algebra, according to the title preferred, and has at its base the very fundamental question as to what a combination is logically, psychologically, and otherwise; and what the operator φ, or θ, or ψ may be, what it does to the operand, what operators are derivable from it and how; further, what the results of the operation, say s, t, u above, is; how one may pass from the operand to the result, and reversely. These are elements that seem to be overlooked in the development as given in the book. Before one uses a calculus, in other words, he should investigate the laws of his calculus.

In the course of such investigation, it turns out that structural laws are very numerous. We may investigate laws that have been assigned purely arbitrarily, as for example those that actually have been so assigned in the study of multiple algebra. The reduction of all these divers arbitrary types of structure to a few simple forms is not possible, and the introduction of extra relational symbols merely furnishes a symbolism, but does not account for the forms nor does it show that they are deducible from the primitive forms laid down in this book as the basis of all reasoning. And if what is meant is that mathematical form consists of relations, then nothing is done beyond furnishing a mere name to a class of entities. Let us put it otherwise: to single out a few combinations as worthy of special signs, and to represent all others as relations, using letters, does not substantiate the claim that all terms have been defined in terms of the few combinations. The expressions for relations $\hat{x}\hat{y}\varphi(x, y)$ are combinations and the original $p \vee q$, $p \cdot q$, and $p \supset q$ can be so expressed; for each is not different from $\varphi(a, b)$ for a properly chosen φ, hence are cases of $\varphi(x, y)$, therefore define relations. To say that ultimately all logic is reducible to propositional functions, would then be the proper outcome. And logic becomes thus a branch of general algebra.

Prolegomena to Cardinal Arithmetic

This constitutes Part II of the present book. Part III treating of Cardinal Arithmetic, Part IV of Ordinal Arithmetic, Part V of Series, are mentioned for the following volumes. The subjects treated in Part II are of high importance not only for cardinal arithmetic but for the ensemble theory. The divisions are Section A, Unit classes and couples; Section B, Sub-classes, Sub-relations, Relative types; Section C, One–many, One–one, Many–one relations; Section D, Selections; Section E, Inductive relations.

We find 1 defined here by the symbol

$$1 = \hat{\alpha} \, [(\exists x) \cdot \alpha = \iota'x] \text{ Df.}$$

In words, 1 is the class of all unit classes, or since we have abolished classes *per se*, we will paraphrase this to read: 1 is a function satisfied by nothing but those functions which are true each in one case only. Or again, one is a property possessed by functions, namely, uniqueness of argument. For example, we speak of the author of *Waverley*, the President of the United States, the sin 30°, all these enable us to put the word *the* in evidence, and the *the-ness* in their character is that common property called 1. Whether this is a logical definition of the everyday 1 or not, what is accomplished is the construction of a symbol out of those already existing which defines the property of uniqueness. We agree to use 1 in place of the longer form $\hat{\alpha}[(\exists x) \cdot \alpha = \iota'x]$. Likewise 0 is defined to be the function satisfied only by those functions which are never true. For example, ( ) is not identical with itself, ( ) is true when its contradictory is true, and such like. These are in no case true, and the property of their impossibility is the number represented by 0. The cardinal 2 is defined similarly as a function satisfied only by functions which define couples. If the couple defined were an ordered couple, then we define 2_r, the ordinal 2. For example, 2 is a property possessed by quadratic equations, when we confine our attention to the solutions they have. From the purely symbolic point of view we use 0 and 2 to abbreviate the forms

$$0 = \iota'\Lambda \quad 2 = \hat{\alpha}[(\exists x, y) \cdot x \neq y \cdot \alpha = \iota'x \, \mathrm{v} \, \iota'y] \quad \text{Df.}$$

Mathematically we have thus found that if the words one, none, two are used, we must have in mind the *uniqueness* of certain classes, the *impossibility* of certain classes, or the *dyad character* of certain classes. We may accept or reject this view of what the symbols mean, but practically we have placed 0, 1, 2, in the list of symbols which form the range of classes of classes. They belong to the second order symbols. The symbolic point of view is nearly the same as saying that we start with objects, these are entities of any order m. Then we make a set of tags to enable us to distinguish the objects without being concerned with their other qualities. These tags are $m + 1$ order symbols (classes). We then make a set of symbols to enable us to talk about the tags. This set of symbols is the set of cardinal numbers, and is of the $m + 2$ order in the process of symbolizing or abstracting.

We begin now to reach arithmetic. As one example of what it looks like, we will quote the theorem which is to prove later that $1 + 1 = 2$. It runs thus

$$*54.43 \vdash : . \; \alpha, \beta \in 1 . \supset : \alpha \cap \beta = \Lambda . \equiv . \; \alpha \cup \beta \epsilon 2.$$

That is in English, if α and β are unit-classes with no common members, then their smallest superclass is a couplet.

In Section A we find also the ordinal 2_r, which does not differ from the class of alio-vids of C. S. Peirce; and also the ordinal $\dot{2}$, which does not differ from the class of vids. An ordinal 1 might be defined by $\dot{2} - 2_r$, which is the common subclass of vids and vids that are not alio-vids, that is the class of idem-vids. The connection with the cardinal 2 is in the fact that an alio-vid – that is, an asymmetric relation – must have two distinct terms. The relation here, being a vid, is between one object of thought and one other object of thought. Of course we are not far from the theory of quadrate algebras and matrices in general after we have arrived at this result.[14]

We pass over the next three sections, although they are of high importance, to Section E, which treats of generalized mathematical induction. The notion of *hereditary* class is defined, μ is a hereditary class with respect to the relation R if successors of μ's are μ's. For example if μ is the peerage, μ is hereditary with respect to the relation of father to eldest son. If μ is numbers greater than 100, μ is hereditary with respect to the relation of v to $v + 1$. Mathematical induction is evidently included in this class of relations, and by means of it we pass from any finite integral case to any greater integral case, but finite. No such proof holds for any infinity. Thus we may say the binomial theorem is proved in this manner for *any* finite integral exponent, but not for *all* finite integral exponents. Indeed the word *all* here has no sense. We are led to consider powers of relations and the analysis of the field of a relation. This belongs to the general theory of operations.

The whole of the second Part really is mathematical logic of a little more specialized character than Part I, and this first volume could have properly been called a treatise on the mathematics of logic.

Summary

In summary, the object that we have had in mind was to show that this first volume of the *Principia* is in reality an application of mathematical methods of definition and synthetic combination to the relationships between the abstract things that logic chooses to discuss. By means of a symbolism, which awkward as it is, is sufficiently comprehensive, a study is made of functions: as related to terms in propositions, and as shown in the particular forms of descriptions, classes, and relations. In one sense the highly ideal character of mathematical objects is made more evident. In another sense the real mathematical object, though already ideal, is sublimated still further into a logical object. The book is a culmination of the critical investigation of mathematical foundations of recent years, and will no doubt advance the systematization and mutual readjustment of mathematical treatments. It will assist in discovering tacit hypotheses, and in putting into formal shape the demonstration of many facts that have been brought to light by the intuition. If it eventually helps in any substantial manner to unify different theories and show their common features it will do enough.[15]

But while we may admit that it has perhaps placed the fundamental principles of the theory of ranges in a more definite form, and has done something for the theory of relations, we insist that the other great theories of mathematics are barely touched upon if, indeed, at all. These, we pointed out, were the theory of structure and form, the theory of invariance, the theory of functions as functions, the theory of inversions. That these can receive a general treatment we do not doubt, inasmuch as some of them are receiving such development. In logistic then we find only a very definite *branch* of mathematics, and in this volume we have the most complete treatment of logistic that exists. The question that many have asked naturally "How far does it assist in building up synthetic systems of mathematics" is easily answered. It reaches arithmetic only after one volume of 666 pages. We would not expect the complete treatise then to furnish much that would be of a synthetic nature. Indeed that would be as unreasonable as to expect to build Eiffel towers and Eads bridges from a study of postulates and axioms for the foundation of geometry. While design rests upon these things in a sense, design antedates them just as language antedates grammar. It is not fair to the book or its aim to assert that it does nothing synthetic. Its problem is philosophical and analytical. It does enough if it shows us what are the characteristic features of reasoning and generalizes the types of reasoning. In this respect it is scientific as well as philosophical. It examines the rules of the great mathematical game. But it does not play the game nor undertake to teach its strategy.

Notes

1 *Principia Mathematica* by Alfred North Whitehead and Bertrand Russell Volume I, Cambridge, 1910.
2 Cf. E. H. Moore, "Introduction to a form of General Analysis," New Haven Math. Colloquium, 1910, p. 2.
3 Cf. Poincaré, *Rev. Mét. et Morale*, vol. 13 (1905), pp. 815–835; vol. 14 (1906), pp. 17–34, 294–317, 866–868. Hilbert, Verh. III. Int. Math. Kongr. Heidelberg (1904), pp. 174–185. Russell, *Rev. Mét. et Morale*, vol. 14 (1906), pp. 627–650. Bôcher, *Bull. of Am. Math. Soc.*, vol. 11 (1904), pp. 115–135.
4 B. Peirce, *Amer. Jour. Math.*, vol. 4 (1881), p. 97.
5 B. Russell, *Principles of Mathematics*, p. 3.
6 *Century Dictionary* (C. S. Peirce).
7 Russell, "The theory of implication," *Amer. Jour. Math.*, vol. 28 (1906), p. 160.
8 *Laws of Thought*, 1854, p. 70.
9 *Formulaire*, 4 éd., page 4; 5 éd., p. 3.
10 If absurd, they are not propositions.
11 See *Principles*, p. 505.
12 Russell, *Revue Mét. et Morale*, vol. 13 (1905), pp. 906–917.
13 Cf. Kempe, *Trans. R. Soc. London*, vol. 177 (1886), pp. 1–70; *Nature*, vol. 43 (1890), 156–162; *Proc. Lond. Math. Soc.*, vol. 26 (1894), 5–15.
14 C. S. Peirce, *Amer. Jour. Math.*, vol. 4 (1881), p. 221.
15 M. Winter, *Revue Mét. et Morale*, vol. 15 (1907), pp. 186–216. E. Borel, ibid., pp. 273–383. H. Poincaré, ibid., vol. 17 (1909), pp. 451–482, 620–653. H. Dufumier, *Bull. des Sciences Math.*, vol. 35 (1911), pp. 213–221.

4

An Axiom in Symbolic Logic

C. E. Van Horn

Philosophy's task is a search for the primal and fundamental elements of the world. Its face is turned in the opposite direction to that of science and mathematics. Philosophy hands back to them its results, and they as best they can construct systematic bodies of doctrine that purport to show us what the world may be on the one hand (science) and what the world might be on the other (mathematics). As philosophy advances in the pursuit of its task it is continually vacating old ground to science and mathematics. The history of this change of boundary can be traced in the changes in the nomenclature of human knowledge: Natural Philosophy has become Physics; Mental Philosophy has become Psychology; Moral Philosophy is becoming the inductive science of Ethics. Thus (paradoxically speaking) philosophy's advance is to be marked by the retreat of her boundaries.

It is interesting to watch this retreat in a field occupied by philosophy from its very beginning, and until recently supposed to be its permanent possession. I refer to the field of the foundations of mathematics. Here large areas once occupied by philosophy by sovereign right of long control are slowly passing into the possession of pure mathematics; and by the way both are gainers by the transfer.[1]

To facilitate the mathematical treatment of these new areas a new instrument of investigation had to be invented, namely, Mathematical, or Symbolic, Logic. This new logic, which is infinitely more powerful than the traditional logic, and which embraces all that is really self-consistent in the old logic, makes possible a precise and easy handling of all the highly abstract and complex ideas occurring in the new fields. For example, both philosophy and the old logic found themselves involved in many a tangle on questions concerning classes and relations because neither possessed the requisite instruments of analysis. Again, philosophy had wandered into a veritable labyrinth of difficulties concerning infinity, quantity, continuity, and so on. Here too the secret of the trouble lay in the inadequacy of the instruments of analysis afforded by the traditional logic.

Now however the matter is all changed. Philosophy, equipped with the latest instruments of mathematical logic, is able to deal successfully with the problems of these fields. In fact so fully have these ideas been analysed that at last philosophy as such has relinquished these fields to pure mathematics. Even more, the whole field of deduction has now become the foundation-branch of mathematics and has developed into a precise Calculus of Propositions. Out of it grow by easy stages the Calculus of Classes and the Calculus of Relations, and these in turn grow by equally easy stages into all the manifold branches of pure mathematics as more commonly known. It is in these and similar ways that philosophy and pure mathematics are both gainers by the transfer of the fields recently acquired by mathematics from philosophy.

It is now easy to understand why the axioms of mathematical logic (and so of all pure mathematics) lie in the borderland between philosophy and mathematics, and are thus the concern of the philosopher equally with the mathematician. To depart entirely from our figures and adopt others, the rootage of mathematics is in philosophy. It is here too that we meet the innovations of mathematical logic that appear so fantastic to the philosopher trained only in the old logic. Its definitions and treatment of some of the common terms of language seem so at variance with what the traditional logician is familiar with that he often views the new logic as the victim of some delusion. It appears however from the nature of the case itself that many of those peculiarities, which from the viewpoint of traditional logic would be described as abnormal, do not deserve to be so described; that in fact it is in the theories of the traditional logician and philosopher that the abnormalities really occur.[2]

In order to indicate what seems to me a possible simplification of the axiomatic basis of mathematical logic I wish to introduce in a new form an idea advocated by Sheffer. Its importance lies in the fact that in terms of it Sheffer was able to define the four fundamental operations of logic, namely, Negation, Disjunction, Implication, and Conjunction or Joint Assertion. It is a familiar fact that Kronecker found the use of certain auxiliary quantities (let us call them 'parameters') of great value in his algebraic investigations, the chief value lying in the fact that their disappearance led to desired relations among numbers essential to his investigations. It is a precisely similar use of Sheffer's idea that I desire to make in the field of the philosophy of logic. In terms of it I define, after him, the four fundamental operations of logic. Then, unlike him, I work by means of an *axiom* to *eliminate* that idea from the formulae, and in so doing to arrive at the desired properties and relations of the four fundamental operations. The chief excellence of my method seems to reside in the fact that proceeding as indicated above I have been able to prove *as propositions of mathematical logic* some of the axioms hitherto laid down at the basis of this logic.

In its most satisfactory form the axiomatic basis of mathematical logic has been stated by Bertrand Russell in the first volume of the *Principia Mathematica*.[3] In *1 of Vol. I, pp. 98–101, of the *Principia* will be found the primitive propositions required for the theory of deduction as applied to elementary propositions. I confine myself to these purposely, for it is here that I have succeeded, I believe, in simplifying the axiomatic basis of mathematical logic.

Let p and q be any two elementary propositions. The four fundamental operations give us (1) $\sim p$ (not-p), (2) $p \vee q$ (either p or q), (3) $p \supset q$ (p implies q), and (4) $p \cdot q$ (both p and q). After Sheffer, I define these four results in terms of a single undefinable operation. I will call this undefinable operation *Deltation*. The result of performing this operation upon two elementary propositions p and q is symbolized, after Sheffer, '$p \Delta q$' (read 'p *deltas* q'). The four fundamental operations of logic can be expressed as logical functions of this parameter thus:

Negation:	$\sim p . = . p \Delta p$	Df.
Disjunction:	$p \vee q . = . \sim p \Delta \sim q$	Df.
Implication:	$p \supset q . = . p \Delta \sim q$	Df.
Conjunction:	$p \cdot q . = . \sim (p \Delta q)$	Df.

These definitions of the four fundamental operations of logic as functions of the one undefined parameter, Deltation, are made relevant to our discussion by means of the following axiom.

Axiom. *If p and q are of the same truth-value, then '$p \Delta \theta$' is of the opposite truth-value; but if p and q are of opposite truth-values, then '$p \Delta q$' is true.*

For convenience of reference it might be well for me to state at this point Russell's primitive propositions concerning elementary propositions as he enunciates them in *1 of the first volume of the *Principia*.

*1.1 Anything implied by a true elementary proposition is true. Pp.[4]

*1.11 When ϕx can be asserted, where x is a real variable, and '$\phi x \supset \psi x$' can be asserted, where x is a real variable, then ψx can be asserted, where x is a real variable. Pp.

*1.2 $\vdash : p \vee p . \supset . p$ Pp.

*1.3 $\vdash : q . \supset . p \vee q$ Pp.

*1.4 $\vdash : p \vee q . \supset . q \vee p$ Pp.

*1.5 $\vdash : p \vee (q \vee r) . \supset . q \vee (p \vee r)$ Pp.

*1.6 $\vdash : . q \supset r . \supset : p \vee q . \supset . p \vee r$ Pp.

*1.7 If p is an elementary proposition, $\sim p$ is an elementary proposition. Pp.

*1.71 If p and q are elementary propositions 'p v q' is an elementary proposition.   Pp.

*1.72 If ϕp and ψp are elementary propositional functions which take elementary propositions as arguments, 'ϕp v ψp' is an elementary propositional function.   Pp.

These are all the primitive propositions that are needed for the development of the theory of deduction, as applied to elementary propositions, according to Russell's method of treatment.

It is my purpose to show that by means of my axiom Russell's primitive propositions *1.2 to *1.71 can be demonstrated. I do this by starting at the very beginning and developing the immediate consequences of three of the axioms which I lay down as the basis of the theory of deduction as applied to elementary propositions. The resulting deductive development at length reaches a point where it includes among its theorems Mr Russell's seven primitive propositions and two others that can take the place of his definitions of Implication and Conjunction. Altogether I prove seventeen theorems. Some of these theorems occur as propositions in the first volume of the *Principia*. Although many more theorems can be proved as simply as the ones given, to economize space I shall stop at the point where my development of Mathematical Logic includes the nine theorems mentioned above.

I will now state the three axioms used in this paper. The first is *1.1 given above, the last is my axiom as already enunciated.

Axiom 1. *Anything implied by a true elementary proposition is true.*

Axiom 2. *If p and q are elementary propositions, then '$p \Delta q$' is an elementary proposition.*

Axiom 3. *If p and q are of the same truth-value, then '$p \Delta q$' is of the opposite truth-value; but if p and q are of opposite truth-values, then '$p \Delta q$' is true.*

Theorem 1

If p is an elementary position, $\sim p$ is an elementary proposition.

Dem.
Axiom 2 gives us '$p \Delta p$' elementary when p is elementary; '$p \Delta p$' is $\sim p$, by Definition of Negation. Hence the theorem.

This is a proof of Mr Russell's primitive proposition *1.7 given above.

Theorem 2

If p and q are elementary propositions, 'p v q' is an elementary proposition.

Dem.
By Theorem 1, if p and q are elementary so are $\sim p$ and $\sim q$. Therefore, by Axiom 2, '$\sim p \, \Delta \sim q$' is elementary; but this, by Definition of Disjunction, is '$p \lor q$'. Hence the theorem.

This is Mr Russell's primitive proposition *1.71 quoted above.

Theorem 3

The propositions p and $\sim p$ are of opposite truth-values.

Dem.
Two possibilities can occur:
    $1°$: p true. By Axiom 3, '$p \, \Delta \, p$' is false; but this by Definition of Negation is $\sim p$; hence in this case p and $\sim p$ are opposite in truth-value.
    $2°$: p false. By Axiom 3, '$p \, \Delta \, p$' is true; but this by Definition of Negation is $\sim p$; hence in this case also p and $\sim p$ are opposite in truth-value. Hence the theorem.

This theorem states in precise form the information usually given in textbooks on logic in more or less vague statements that are called 'definitions' of negation.

Theorem 4

$\vdash . p \supset p.$

Dem.
[Th.3]	$\vdash . p$ and $\sim p$ of opposite truth-values	(1)
[(1). Ax. 3]	$\vdash . p \, \Delta \sim p$	(2)
[(2). Def. of Implication]	$\vdash .$ theorem.	

This is proposition *2.08[5] of the *Principia*.

Theorem 5

If p is false, '$p \, \Delta \, q$' is always true.

Dem.
Two possibilities can occur: either q true, or q false. In either case '$p \, \Delta \, q$' is true by Ax. 3.

Theorem 6

If q is false, 'p Δ q' is always true.
Proof similar to that of preceding theorem.

Theorem 7

The propositions 'p Δ q' and 'q Δ p' have the same truth-value.

Dem.
If p and q are of the same truth-value then, by Ax. 3, 'p Δ q' and 'q Δ p' are both of the opposite truth-value. If p and q are of opposite truth-values then, by Ax. 3, 'p Δ q' and 'q Δ p' are both true. Hence the theorem.

Theorem 8

The proposition

$$\sim p \, \Delta \sim (\sim q \, \Delta \sim r)$$

is true if any one or more of the propositions p, q, r are true; but if all of these propositions are false then the proposition

$$\sim p \, \Delta \sim (\sim q \, \Delta \sim r)$$

is false.

Dem.
Eight possibilities can occur:
  1° : p, q, r all true. Then (Th. 3) $\sim p$, $\sim q$, $\sim r$ are all false. Hence (Ax. 3) '$\sim q \, \Delta \sim r$' is true. Hence (Th. 3) $\sim (\sim q \, \Delta \sim r)$ is false. Hence (Ax. 3) the proposition $\sim p \, \Delta \sim (\sim q \, \Delta \sim r)$' is true in this case.
  2° : p and q true, but r false. By Th. 3, $\sim p$ and $\sim q$ are false, while $\sim r$ is true. Hence (Ax. 3) '$\sim q \, \Delta \sim r$' is true. Hence (Th. 3) $\sim (\sim q \, \Delta \sim r)$ is false. Hence (Ax. 3) the proposition is true in this case. In a similar manner in the following cases:

  3° : p true, q false, r true;
  4° : p false, q, r true;
  5° : p true, q, r false;
  6° : p false, q true, r false;
  7° : p, q false, r true;

we have '$\sim p \, \Delta \sim (\sim q \, \Delta \sim r)$' true.

But in 8° : p, q, r false, we have $\sim p, \sim q, \sim r$ all true, by Th. 3. Hence (Ax. 3) '$\sim q \wedge \sim r$' is false, making $\sim (\sim q \wedge \sim r)$ true (Th. 3). Hence (Ax. 3) in this case the proposition is false.

Hence the theorem.

Theorem 9

The propositions

$$\text{'}\sim p \wedge \sim (\sim q \wedge \sim r)\text{'}, \text{'}\sim q \wedge \sim (\sim p \wedge \sim r),$$

always have the same truth-value.

This follows at once from Th. 8.

At this point I introduce Mr Russell's definition of Equivalence[6] as it occurs in the *Principia*.

Equivalence: $p \equiv q \, . \, = \, . \, \mathrm{p} \supset q \cdot q \supset p$ Df.

Theorem 10

$\vdash . \, p \equiv \sim (\sim p).$

Dem.

We first prove $\vdash . \, p \supset \sim (\sim p)$. Two cases arise:

1° : p true. By Theorem 3, $\sim p$ is false, $\sim (\sim p)$ is true, and $\sim [\sim (\sim p)]$ is false. Hence

[Ax. 3]	$\vdash . \, p \wedge \sim [\sim (\sim p)]$ (1)
[(1). Def. Implica.]	$\vdash . \, p \supset \sim (\sim p)$ (2)

2° : p false. By Th. 3, $\sim p$ is true, $\sim (\sim p)$ is false, and $\sim [\sim (\sim p)]$ is true.

[Ax. 3]	$\vdash . \, p \wedge \sim [\sim (\sim p)]$ (3)
[(1). Implica.]	$\vdash . \, p \supset \sim (\sim p)$ (4)
Hence in all cases we have	
	$\vdash . \, p \supset \sim (\sim p)$ (5)
We now prove	$\vdash . \, \sim (\sim p) \supset p.$
[Th. 3]	$\vdash . \, q$ and $\sim q$ of opposite truth-values (6)
[(6). Ax. 3]	$\vdash . \, \sim q \wedge q$ (7)
[(7). $\dfrac{\sim p}{q}$]	$\vdash . \, \sim (\sim p) \wedge \sim p$ (8)
[(8). Def. Implica.]	$\vdash . \, \sim (\sim p) \supset p$ (9)
[(5). (9). Def. Equiv.]	$\vdash . \,$ theorem.

This is proposition *4.13 of the *Principia*.[7] It is the Principle of Double Negation, and asserts that any proposition is logically equivalent to the denail of its negation.

Theorem 11

$\vdash: p \lor p. \supset . p.$

Dem.

[Ax. 3]	$\vdash .\sim p$ and '$\sim p \,\Delta \sim p$' of opposite truth-values	(1)
[(1). Ax. 3]	$\vdash: \sim p \,\Delta \sim p . \Delta . \sim p$	(2)
[(2). Def. Disjunc. Implica.]	$\vdash$. theorem.	

This is Mr Russell's primitive proposition *1.2 given above.

Theorem 12

$\vdash: q . \supset . p \lor q.$

Dem.

Two cases need only be treated:

1° : q true. Then (Th. 3) $\sim q$ is false. Hence (Th. 6) '$\sim p \,\Delta \sim q$' is true. Hence $\sim (\sim p \,\Delta \sim q)$ is false, by Th. 3. Hence

[Ax. 3]	$\vdash: q . \Delta . \sim (\sim p \,\Delta \sim q)$	(1)
2° : q false.		
[Th. 5. $\dfrac{q, \ \sim (\sim p \,\Delta \sim q)}{p, \qquad q}$]	$\vdash. q . \Delta . \sim (\sim p \,\Delta \sim q)$	(2)
[(1). (2). Def. Disjunc. Implica.]	$\vdash$. theorem.	

This is Mr Russell's primitive proposition *1.3 given above.

Theorem 13

$\vdash: p \lor q . \supset . q \lor p.$

Dem.

[Th. 7]	$\vdash:$ '$\sim p \,\Delta \sim q$' and '$\sim q \,\Delta \sim p$' of the same truth-value	(1)
[(1). Th. 3. Ax. 3]	$\vdash: \sim p \,\Delta \sim q . \Delta . \sim (\sim q \,\Delta \sim p)$	(2)
[(2). Def. Disjunc. Implica.]	$\vdash:$ theorem.	

This is Mr Russell's primitive proposition *1.4 given above.

Theorem 14

$\vdash : p \vee (q \vee r) . \supset . q \vee (p \vee r).$

Dem.
[Th. 9] $\vdash$: '$\sim p \, \Delta \sim (\sim q \, \Delta \sim r)$' and
'$\sim q \, \Delta \sim (\sim p \, \Delta \sim r)$' of the same truth-value   (1)
[(1). Th. 3. Ax. 3] $\vdash: \sim p \, \Delta \sim (\sim q \, \Delta \sim r)$'
$. \, \Delta . \sim [\sim q \, \Delta \sim (\sim p \, \Delta \sim r)]$ (2)
[(2). Def. Disjunc. Implica.] $\vdash$: theorem.
   This is Mr Russell's primitive proposition *1.5 given above.

Theorem 15

$\vdash : . \, q \supset r . \supset : p \vee q . \supset . p \vee r.$

Dem.
There are three cases to be discussed:
   $1°$: If p is true, or if r is true, or if both p and r are true, q being *any* elementary proposition.

[Th. 8] $\vdash : \sim l . \Delta . \sim (\sim p \, \Delta \sim r)$ (1)

[(1). $\dfrac{\sim l}{l}$. Th. 10] $\vdash : l . \Delta . \sim (\sim p \, \Delta \sim r)$ (2)

[(2). $\dfrac{\sim p \, \Delta \sim q}{l}$] $\vdash : \sim p \, \Delta \sim q . \Delta . \sim (\sim p \, \Delta \sim r)$ (3)

[(3). Th. 3. Th. 6]
$\vdash : q \, \Delta \sim r . \Delta . \sim [\sim p \, \Delta \sim q . \Delta . \sim (\sim p \, \Delta \sim r)]$ (4)
Taken together with the Definitions of Implication and Disjunction, (4) gives the theorem in this case.
   $2°$: If both p and r are false, but q true. In this case $\sim p$ and $\sim r$ are true by Th. 3. Hence (Ax. 3) '$\sim p \, \Delta \sim r$' is false. The proof in this case proceeds as follows:

[Th. 3] $\vdash : \sim (\sim p \, \Delta \sim r)$ (5)
Since q is true, $\sim q$ is false (Th. 3).
[Th. 6] $\vdash . \sim p \, \Delta \sim q$ (6)
[(5). (6). Th. 3. Ax. 3] $\vdash : \sim [\sim p \, \Delta \sim q . \Delta . \sim (\sim p \, \Delta \sim r)]$ (7)
By Ax. 3, '$q \, \Delta \sim r$' is in this case false.
[(7). Ax. 3]
$\vdash : q \, \Delta \sim r . \Delta . \sim [\sim p \, \Delta \sim q . \Delta . \sim (\sim p \, \Delta \sim r)]$ (8)
As in the previous case this result gives the theorem.
   $3°$: All three false. Hence $\sim p$ and $\sim r$ true as before. In this case '$\sim p \, \Delta \sim q$' is false by Ax. 3. The proof in this last case proceeds thus:

[Th. 3, as in 2°] $\vdash . \sim (\sim p \wedge \sim r)$ (9)
[(9). Ax. 3] $\vdash : \sim p \wedge \sim q . \wedge . \sim (\sim p \wedge \sim r)$ (10)
In this case q and $\sim r$ are of opposite truth-values.
[Ax. 3] $\vdash : q \wedge \sim r$ (11)
[(10). Th. 3. (11). Ax. 3]
$$\vdash : q \wedge \sim r . \wedge . \sim [\sim p \wedge \sim q . \wedge . \sim (\sim p \wedge \sim r)] \quad (12)$$

As in the two preceding cases, this result, together with the Definitions of Implication and Disjunction, gives the theorem.

No other cases can arise. Hence the theorem.

This is Mr Russell's primitive proposition *1.6 given above. It asserts that an alternative may be added to both premise and conclusion in any implication without impairing the truth of the implication.

This completes the list of Mr Russell's primitive propositions that I proposed for proof by means of my axiom, on the basis of the definitions given in this paper of the four fundamental operations of logic.

I now propose to prove two propositions which can take the place of his definitions of Implication[8] and Conjunction[9], or Joint Assertion.

Theorem 16

$\vdash : p \supset q . \equiv . \sim p \vee q.$

Dem.

[Th. 4 $\dfrac{p \wedge \sim q}{p}$] $\vdash : p \wedge \sim q . \supset . p \wedge \sim q$ (1)

[Th. 10] $\vdash : p \wedge \sim q . \supset . \sim (\sim p) \wedge \sim q$ (2)

[(2). Def. Implica. Disjunc.] $\vdash : p \supset q . \supset . \sim p \vee q$ (3)

[(1). Th. 10] $\vdash : \sim (\sim p) \wedge \sim q . \supset . p \wedge \sim q$ (4)

[(4). Def. Implica. Disjunc.] $\vdash : \sim p \vee q . \supset . p \supset q$ (5)

[(3). (5). Def. Equiv.] $\vdash :$ theorem.

Theorem 17

$\vdash : p \cdot q . \equiv . \sim (\sim p \vee \sim q).$

Dem.

[Th. 4 $\dfrac{\sim (p \wedge q)}{p}$] $\vdash : \sim (p \wedge q) . \supset . \sim (p \wedge q)$ (1)

[Th. 10] $\vdash : \sim (p \wedge q) . \supset . \sim [\sim (\sim p) \wedge \sim (\sim q)]$ (2)

[(2). Def. Conjunc. Disjunc.] $\vdash : p \cdot q . \supset . \sim (\sim p \vee q)$ (3)

[(1). Th. 10] $\vdash : \sim [\sim (\sim p) \wedge \sim (\sim q)] . \supset . \sim (p \wedge q)$ (4)

[(4). Def. Conjunc. Disjunc.] $\vdash : \sim (\sim p \text{ v} \sim q) . \supset . p \cdot q$ (5)
[(3). (5). Def. Equiv.] $\vdash$: theorem.

With these theorems established the development of the *Principia Mathematica* can proceed as given by its authors. All that I have done is to reduce the number of axioms needed for that development.

Notes

1 Much valuable light is thrown upon the details of this process in the writings of Bertrand Russell, especially in the preface and introductory chapters of the *Principia Mathematica*, Vol. I, 1910; and more recently in his *Scientific Method in Philosophy*, 1914.
2 Cf. Russell, *Scientific Method in Philosophy*, chap. I.
3 Whitehead and Russell, *Principia Mathematica*, Vol. I, 1910; Vol. II, 1912; Vol. III, 1913 (Cambridge University Press).
4 Russell uses the letters 'Pp' to stand for 'primitive proposition', as does Peano.
5 *Principia*, Vol. I, p. 105.
6 Ibid., p. 120, *4.01.
7 Ibid., p. 122.
8 Ibid., p. 98, *1.01.
9 Ibid., p. 116, *3.01.

5

Mathematical Logic

F. P. Ramsey

I have been asked to speak about developments in Mathematical Logic since the publication of *Principia Mathematica*, and I think it would be most interesting if, instead of describing various definite improvements of detail, I were to discuss in outline the work which has been done on entirely different lines, and claims to supersede altogether the position taken up by Whitehead and Russell as to the nature of mathematics and its logical foundations.

Let me begin by recalling what Whitehead and Russell's view is: it is that mathematics is part of formal logic, that all the ideas of pure mathematics can be defined in terms which are not distinctively mathematical but involved in complicated thought of any description, and that all the propositions of mathematics can be deduced from propositions of formal logic, such as that if p is true, then either p or q is true. This view seems to me in itself plausible, for so soon as logic has been developed beyond its old syllogistic nucleus, we shall expect to have besides the forms 'All men are mortal', 'Some men are mortal', the numerical forms 'Two men are mortal' and 'Three men are mortal', and number will have to be included in formal logic.

Frege was the first to maintain that mathematics was part of logic, and to construct a detailed theory on that basis. But he fell foul of the famous contradictions of the theory of aggregates, and it appeared that contradictory consequences could be deduced from his primitive propositions. Whitehead and Russell escaped this fate by introducing their Theory of Types, of which it is impossible here to give an adequate account. But one of its implications must be explained if later developments are to be intelligible.

Suppose we have a set of characteristics given as all characteristics of a certain sort, say A, then we can ask about anything, whether it has a characteristic of the sort A. If it has, this will be another characteristic of it, and the question arises whether this characteristic, the characteristic of having a characteristic of the kind *A*, can itself be of the kind *A*, seeing that it presupposes the totality of such characteristics. The Theory of Types held that it could not, and that we could only escape contradiction by saying that it was a characteristic of higher order, and could not be included in any statement about all characteristics of lower order. And more generally that any statement about all characteristics must be regarded as meaning all of a certain order. This seemed in itself plausible, and also the only way of avoiding certain contradictions which arose from confusing these orders of characteristics. Whitehead and Russell also hold that statements about classes or aggregates are to be regarded as really about the characteristics which define the classes (a class being always given as the class of things possessing a certain character), so that any statement about all classes will be really about all characteristics, and will be liable to the same difficulties with regard to the order of these characteristics.

Such a theory enables us easily to avoid the contradictions of the Theory of Aggregates, but it has also the unfortunate consequence of invalidating an ordinary and important type of mathematical argument, the sort of argument by which we ultimately establish the existence of the upper bound of an aggregate, or the existence of the limit of a bounded monotonic sequence. It is usual to deduce these propositions from the principle of Dedekindian section, that if the real numbers are divided completely into an upper and a lower class, there must be a dividing number which is either the least of the upper class or the greatest of the lower. This in turn is proved by regarding real numbers as sections of rationals; sections of rationals are a particular kind of classes of rationals, and hence a statement about real numbers will be a statement about a kind of classes of rationals, that is about a kind of characteristics of rationals, and the characteristics in question will have to be limited to be of a certain order.

Now suppose we have an aggregate *E* of real numbers; that will be a class of characteristics of rationals. ξ, the upper bound of *E*, is defined as a section of rationals which is the sum of the members of *E*; i.e. ξ is a section whose members are all those rationals which are members of any member of *E*, that is, all those rationals which have the characteristic of having any of the characteristics which give the members of *E*. So the upper bound ξ is a section whose defining characteristic is one of higher order than those of the members of *E*. Hence if all real numbers means all sections of rationals defined by characteristics of a certain order, the upper bound will, in general, be a section of rationals defined by a characteristic of higher order, and will not be a real number. This means that analysis as ordinarily understood is entirely grounded on a fallacious kind of argument, which when applied in other fields leads to self-contradictory results.

This unfortunate consequence of the Theory of Types Whitehead and

Russell tried to avoid by introducing the Axiom of Reducibility, which asserted that to any characteristic of higher order there was an equivalent characteristic of the lowest order – equivalent in the sense that everything that has the one has the other, so that they define the same class. The upper bound, which we saw was a class of rationals defined by a characteristic of higher order, would then also be defined by the equivalent characteristic of lower order, and would be a real number. Unfortunately the axiom is certainly not self-evident, and there is no reason whatever to suppose it true. If it were true this would only be, so to speak, a happy accident, and it would not be a logical truth like the other primitive propositions.

In the Second Edition of *Principia Mathematica*, of which the first volume was published last year, Mr Russell has shown how mathematical induction, for which the Axiom of Reducibility seemed also to be required, can be established without it, but he does not hold out any hope of similar success with the Theory of Real Numbers, for which the ingenious method used for the whole numbers is not available. The matter is thus left in a profoundly unsatisfactory condition.

This was pointed out by Weyl, who published in 1918 a little book called *Das Kontinuum*, in which he rejected the Axiom of Reducibility and accepted the consequence that ordinary analysis was wrong. He showed, however, that various theorems, such as Cauchy's General Principle of Convergence, could still be proved.

Since then Weyl has changed his view and become a follower of Brouwer, the leader of what is called the intuitionist school, whose chief doctrine is the denial of the Law of Excluded Middle, that every proposition is either true or false.[1] This is denied apparently because it is thought impossible to know such a thing *a priori*, and equally impossible to know it by experience, because if we do not know either that it is true or that it is false we cannot verify that it is either true or false. Brouwer would refuse to agree that either it was raining or it was not raining, unless he had looked to see. Although it is certainly difficult to give a philosophical explanation of our knowledge of the laws of logic, I cannot persuade myself that I do not know for certain that the Law of Excluded Middle is true; of course, it cannot be proved, although Aristotle gave the following ingenious argument in its favour. If a proposition is neither true nor false, let us call it doubtful; but then if the Law of Excluded Middle be false, it need not be either doubtful or not doubtful, so we shall have not merely three possibilities but four, that it is true, that it is false, that it is doubtful, and that it is neither true, false, nor doubtful. And so on *ad infinitum*.

But if it be answered 'Why not?', there is clearly nothing more to be said, and I do not see how any common basis can be found from which to discuss the matter. The cases in which Brouwer thinks the Law of Excluded Middle false are ones in which, as I should say, we could not tell whether the proposition was true or false; for instance, is $2^{\sqrt 2}$ rational or irrational? We cannot tell, but Brouwer would say it was neither. We cannot find integers m, n so that $m/n = 2^{\sqrt 2}$; therefore it is not rational: and we cannot show that it is impossible to find such integers; therefore it is not irrational. I cannot see that the matter is not settled by saying that it is either rational or irrational, but we can't tell which. The denial of the Law of Excluded Middle renders illegitimate the argument called a dilemma, in which something is shown to follow from one hypothesis and also from the contradictory of that hypothesis, and it is concluded that it is true unconditionally. Thus Brouwer is unable to justify much of ordinary mathematics, and his conclusions are even more sceptical than those of Weyl's first theory.

Weyl's second theory is very like Brouwer's, but he seems to deny the Law of Excluded Middle for different reasons, and in a less general way. He does not appear to deny that any proposition is either true or false, but denies the derived law that either every number has a given property, or at least one number does not have it. He explains his denial first of all for real numbers in the following way. A real number is given by a sequence of integers, for instance as an infinite decimal; this sequence we can conceive as generated either by a law or by successive acts of choice. If now we say there is a real number or sequence having a certain property, this can only mean that we have found a law giving one; but if we say all sequences have a property, we mean that to have the property is part of the essence of a sequence, and therefore belongs to sequences arising not only by laws but from free acts of choice. Hence it is not true that either all sequences have the property or there is a sequence not having it. For the meaning of sequence is different in the two clauses. But I do not see why it should not be possible to use the word consistently. However this may be, nothing similar can be urged about the whole numbers which are not defined by sequences, and so another more fundamental reason is put forward for denying the Law of Excluded Middle. This is that general and existential propositions are not really propositions at all. If I say '2 is a prime number', that is a genuine judgment asserting a fact; but if I say 'There is a prime number' or 'All numbers are prime', I am not expressing a judgment at all. If, Weyl says, knowledge is a treasure, the existential proposition is a paper attesting the existence of a treasure but not saying where it is. We can only say 'There is a prime number' when we have previously said 'This is a prime number' and forgotten or chosen to disregard which particular number it was. Hence it is never legitimate to say 'There is a so-and-so' unless we are in possession of a construction for actually finding one. In consequence, mathematics has to be very considerably altered; for instance, it is impossible to have a function of a real variable with more than a finite number of discontinuities. The foundation on which this rests, namely the view that existential and general propositions are not genuine judgments, I shall come back to later.

But first I must say something of the system of Hilbert and his followers, which is designed to put an end to such scepticism once and for all. This is to be done by regarding higher mathematics as the manipulation of meaningless symbols according to fixed rules. We start with certain rows of symbols called axioms: from these we can derive others by substituting certain symbols called constants for others called variables, and by proceeding from the pair of formulae p, if p then q, to the formula q.

Mathematics proper is thus regarded as a sort of game, played with meaningless marks on paper rather like noughts and crosses; but besides this there will be another subject called metamathematics, which is not meaningless, but consists of real assertions about mathematics, telling us that this or that formula can or cannot be obtained from the axioms according to the rules of deduction. The most important theorem of metamathematics is that it is not possible to deduce a contradiction from the axioms, where by a contradiction is meant a formula with a certain kind of shape, which can be taken to be $0 \neq 0$. This I understand Hilbert has proved, and has so removed the possibility of contradictions and scepticism based on them.

Now, whatever else a mathematician is doing, he is certainly making marks on paper, and so this point of view consists of nothing but the truth; but it is hard to suppose it the whole truth. There must be some reason for the choice of axioms, and some reason why the particular mark $0 \neq 0$ is regarded with such abhorrence. This last point can, however, be explained by the fact that the axioms would allow anything whatever to be deducted from $0 \neq 0$, so that if $0 \neq 0$ could be proved, anything whatever could be proved, which would end the game for ever, which would be very boring for posterity. Again, it may be asked whether it is really possible to prove that the axioms do not lead to contradiction, since nothing can be proved unless some principles are taken for granted and assumed not to lead to contradiction. This objection is admitted, but it is contended that the principles used in the metamathematical proof that the axioms of mathematics do not lead to contradiction, are so obviously true that not even the sceptics can doubt them. For they all relate not to abstract or infinitely complex things, but to marks on paper, and though anyone may doubt whether a subclass of a certain sort of infinite series must have a first term, no one can doubt that if = occurs on a page, there is a place on the page where it occurs for the first time.

But, granting all this, it must still be asked what use or merit there is in this game the mathematician plays, if it is really a game and not a form of knowledge; and the only answer which is given is that some of the mathematician's formulae have or can be given meaning, and that if these can be proved in the symbolic system their meanings will be true. For Hilbert shares Weyl's opinion that general and existential propositions are meaningless, so that the only parts of mathematics which mean anything are particular assertions about finite integers, such as '47 is a prime' and conjunctions and disjunctions of a finite number of such assertions like 'There is a prime between 50 and 100', which can be regarded as meaning 'Either 51 is a prime or 52 is a prime, etc., up to, or 99 is a prime.' But as all such propositions of simple arithmetic can be easily proved without using higher mathematics at all, this use for it cannot be of great importance. And it seems that although Hilbert's work provides a new and powerful method, which he has successfully applied to the Continuum problem, as a philosophy of mathematics it can hardly be regarded as adequate.

We see then that these authorities, great as are the differences between them, are agreed that mathematical analysis as ordinarily taught cannot be regarded as a body of truth, but is either false or at best a meaningless game with marks on paper; and this means, I think, that mathematicians in this country should give some attention to their opinions, and try to find some way of meeting the situation.

Let us then consider what sort of a defence can be made for classical mathematics, and Russell's philosophy of it.

We must begin with what appears to be the crucial question, the meaning of general and existential propositions, about which Hilbert and Weyl take substantially the same view. Weyl says that an existential proposition is not a judgment, but an abstract of a judgment, and that a general proposition is a sort of cheque which can be cashed for a real judgment when an instance of it occurs.

Hilbert, less metaphorically, says that they are ideal propositions, and fulfil the same function in logic as ideal elements in various branches of mathematics. He explains their origin in this sort of way; a genuine finite proposition such as 'There is a prime between 50 and 100', we write 'There is a prime which is greater than 50 and less than 100', which appears to contain a part, '51 is a prime, or 52 is a prime, etc., *ad inf.*', and so be an infinite logical sum, which, like an infinite algebraic sum, is first of all meaningless, and can only be given a secondary meaning subject to certain conditions of convergence. But the introduction of these meaningless forms so simplifies the rules of inference that it is convenient to retain them, regarding them as ideals, for which a consistency theorem must be proved.

In this view of the matter there seem to me to be several difficulties. First it is hard to see what use these ideals can be supposed to be; for mathematics proper appears to be reduced to elementary arithmetic, not even algebra being admitted, for the essence of algebra is to make general assertions. Now any statement of elementary arithmetic can be easily tested or proved without using higher mathematics, which if it be supposed to exist solely for the sake of simple arithmetic seems entirely pointless. Secondly, it is hard to see how the notion of an ideal can fail to presuppose the possibility of general knowledge. For the justification of ideals lies in the fact that *all* propositions not containing ideals which can be proved by means of them are true. And so Hilbert's metamathematics, which is agreed to be genuine truth, is bound to consist of general propositions about all possible mathematical proofs, which, though each proof is a finite construct, may well be infinite in number. And if, as Weyl says, an existential proposition is a paper attesting the existence of a treasure of knowledge but not saying where it is, I cannot see how we explain the utility of such a paper, except by presupposing its recipient capable of the existential knowledge that there is a treasure somewhere.

Moreover, even if Hilbert's account could be accepted so long as we confine our attention to mathematics, I do not see how it could be made plausible with regard to knowledge in general. Thus, if I tell you 'I keep a dog', you appear to obtain knowledge of a fact; trivial, but still knowledge. But 'I keep a dog' must be put into logical symbolism as 'There is something which is a dog and kept by me'; so that the knowledge is knowledge of an existential proposition, covering the possibly infinite range of 'things'. Now it might possibly be maintained that my knowledge that I keep a dog arose in the sort of way Hilbert describes by my splitting off incorrectly what appears to be part of a finite proposition, such as 'Rolf is a dog and kept by me', but your knowledge cannot possibly be explained in this way, because the existential proposition expresses all you ever have known, and probably all you ever will know about the matter.

Lastly, even the apparently individual facts of simple arithmetic seem to me to be really general. For what are these numbers, that they are about? According to Hilbert marks on paper constructed out of the marks 1 and +. But this account seems to me inadequate, because if I said 'I have two dogs', that would also tell you something; you would understand the word 'two', and the whole sentence could be rendered something like 'There are x and y, which are my dogs and are not identical with one another.' This statement appears to involve the idea of existence, and not to be about marks on paper; so that I do not see that it can be seriously held that a cardinal number which answers the question 'How many?' is merely a mark on paper. If then we take one of these individual arithmetical facts, such as $2 + 2 = 4$, this seems to me to mean 'If the p's are two in number, and the q's also, and nothing is both a p and a q, then the number of things which are either p's or q's is four.' For this is the meaning in which we must take $2 + 2 = 4$ in order to use it, as we do, to infer from I have two dogs and two cats to I have four pets. This apparently individual fact, $2 + 2 = 4$, then contains several elements of generality and existentiality, firstly because the p's and q's are absolutely general characteristics, and secondly because the parts of the proposition, such as 'if the p's are two in number', involve as we have seen the idea of existence.

It is possible that the whole assertion that general and existential propositions cannot express genuine judgments or knowledge is purely verbal; that it is merely being decided to emphasize the difference between individual and general propositions by refusing to use the words judgment and knowledge in connection with the latter. This, however, would be a pity, for all our natural associations to the words judgment and knowledge fit general and existential propositions as well as they do individual ones; for in either case we can feel greater or lesser degrees of conviction about the matter, and in either case we can be in some sense right or wrong. And the suggestion which is implied, that general and existential knowledge exists simply for the sake of individual knowledge, seems to me entirely false. In theorizing what we principally admire is generality, and in ordinary life it may be quite sufficient to know the existential proposition that there is a bull somewhere in a certain field, and there may be no further advantage in knowing that it is this bull and here in the field, instead of merely a bull somewhere.

How then are we to explain general and existential propositions? I do not think we can do better than accept the view which has been put forward by Wittgenstein as a consequence of his theory of propositions in general. He explains them by reference to what may be called atomic propositions, which assert the simplest possible sort of fact, and could be expressed without using even implicitly any logical terms such as or, if, all, some. 'There is red' is perhaps an instance of an atomic proposition. Suppose now we have, say, n atomic propositions; with regard to their truth or falsity, there are 2^n mutually exclusive ultimate possibilities. Let us call these the truth-possibilities of the n atomic propositions; then we can take any sub-set of these truth-possibilities and assert that it is a possibility out of this sub-set which is, in fact, realized. We can choose this sub-set of possibilities in which we assert the truth to lie in 2^{2^n} ways; and these will be all the propositions we can build up out of these n atomic propositions. Thus to take a simple instance, 'If p, then q' expresses agreement with the three possibilities, that both p and q are true, that p is false and q true, and that p is false and q false, and denies the remaining possibility that p is true and q false.

We can easily see that from this point of view there is a redundancy in all ordinary logical notations, because we can write in many different ways what is essentially the same proposition, expressing agreement and disagreement with the same sets of possibilities.

Mr Wittgenstein holds that all propositions express agreement and disagreement with truth-possibilities of atomic propositions, or, as we say, are truth-functions of atomic propositions; although often the atomic propositions in question are not enumerated, but determined as all values of a certain propositional function. Thus the propositional function 'x is red' determines a collection of propositions which are its values, and we can assert that all or at least one of these values are true by saying 'For all x, x

is red' and 'There is an x such that x is red' respectively. That is to say, if we could enumerate the values of x as a, b . . . z, 'For all x, x is red' would be equivalent to the proposition 'a is red and b is red and . . . and z is red'. It is clear, of course, that the state of mind of a man using the one expression differs in several respects from that of a man using the other, but what might be called the logical meaning of the statement, the fact which is asserted to be, is the same in the two cases.

It is impossible to discuss now all the arguments which might be used against this view, but something must be said about the argument of Hilbert, that if the variable has an infinite number of values, if, that is to say, there are an infinite number of things in the world of the logical type in question, we have here an infinite logical sum or product which, like an infinite algebraic sum or product, is initially meaningless and can only be given a meaning in an indirect way. This seems to me to rest on a false analogy; the logical sum of a set of propositions is the proposition that one of the set at least is true, and it doesn't appear to matter whether the set is finite or infinite. It is not like an algebraic sum to which finitude is essential, since this is extended step by step from the sum of two terms. To say that anything possibly involving an infinity of any kind must be meaningless is to declare in advance that any real theory of aggregates is impossible.

Apart from providing a simple account of existential and general propositions, Wittgenstein's theory settles another question of the first importance by explaining precisely the peculiar nature of logical propositions. When Mr Russell first said that mathematics could be reduced to logic, his view of logic was that it consisted of all true absolutely general propositions, propositions, that is, which contained no material (as opposed to logical) constants. Later he abandoned this view, because it was clear that some further characteristic besides generality was required. For it would be possible to describe the whole world without mentioning any particular thing, and clearly something may by chance be true of anything whatever without having the character of necessity which belongs to the truths of logic.

If, then, we are to understand what logic, and so on Mr Russell's view mathematics is, we must try to define this further characteristic which may be vaguely called necessity, or from another point of view tautology. For instance, 'p is either true or false' may be regarded either as necessary truth or as a mere tautology. This problem is incidentally solved by Wittgenstein's theory of propositions. Propositions, we said, expressed agreement and disagreement with the truth-possibilities of atomic propositions. Given n atomic propositions, there are 2^n truth-possibilities, and we can agree with any set of these and disagree with the remainder. There will then be two extreme cases, one in which we agree with all the possibilities, and disagree with none, the other in which we agree with none and disagree with all. The former is called a tautology, the latter a contradiction.

The simplest tautology is '*p* or not *p*': such a statement adds nothing to our knowledge, and does not really assert a fact at all; it is, as it were, not a real proposition, but a degenerate case. And it will be found that all propositions of logic are in this sense tautologies; and this is their distinguishing characteristic. All the primitive propositions in *Principia Mathematica* are tautologies except the Axiom of Reducibility, and the rules of deduction are such that from tautologies only tautologies can be deduced, so that were it not for the one blemish, the whole structure would consist of tautologies. We thus are brought back to the old difficulty, but it is possible to hope that this too can be removed by some modification of the Theory of Types which may result from Wittgenstein's analysis.

A Theory of Types must enable us to avoid the contradictions; Whitehead and Russell's theory consisted of two distinct parts, united only by being both deduced from the rather vague 'Vicious-Circle Principle'. The first part distinguished propositional functions according to their arguments, i.e. classes according to their members; the second part created the need for the Axiom of Reducibility by requiring further distinctions between orders of functions with the same type of arguments.

We can easily divide the contradictions according to which part of the theory is required for their solution, and when we have done this we find that these two sets of contradictions are distinguished in another way also. The ones solved by the first part of the theory are all purely logical; they involve no ideas but those of class, relation and number, could be stated in logical symbolism, and occur in the actual development of mathematics when it is pursued in the right direction. Such are the contradictions of the greatest ordinal, and that of the class of classes which are not members of themselves. With regard to these Mr Russell's solution seems inevitable.

On the other hand, the second set of contradictions are none of them purely logical or mathematical, but all involve some psychological term, such as meaning, defining, naming or asserting. They occur not in mathematics, but in thinking about mathematics; so that it is possible that they arise not from faulty logic or mathematics, but from ambiguity in the psychological or epistemological notions of meaning and asserting. Indeed, it seems that this must be the case, because examination soon convinces one that the psychological term is in every case essential to the contradiction, which could not be constructed without introducing the relation of words to their meaning or some equivalent.

If now we try to apply to the question Wittgenstein's theory of generality, we can, I think, fairly easily construct a solution along these lines. To explain this adequately would require a paper to itself, but it may be possible to give some idea of it in a few words. On Wittgenstein's theory a general proposition is equivalent to a conjunction of its instances, so that the kind of fact asserted by a general proposition is not essentially different from that asserted by a conjunction of atomic propositions. But the symbol for a general proposition means its meaning in a different way from that in which the symbol for an elementary proposition means it, because the latter contains names for all the things it is about, whereas the general proposition's symbol contains only a variable standing for all its values at once. So that though the two kinds of symbol could mean the same thing, the senses of meaning in which they mean it must be different. Hence the orders of propositions will be characteristics not of what is meant, which is alone relevant in mathematics, but of the symbols used to mean it.

First-order propositions will be rather like spoken words; the same word can be both spoken and written, and the same proposition can theoretically be expressed in different orders. Applying this *mutatis mutandis* to propositional functions, we find that the typical distinctions between functions with the same arguments apply not to what is meant, but to the relation of meaning between symbol and object signified. Hence they can be neglected in mathematics, and the solution of the contradictions can be preserved in a slightly modified form, because the contradictions here relevant all have to do with the relation of meaning.

In this way I think it is possible to escape the difficulty of the Axiom of Reducibility, and remove various other more philosophical objections, which have been made by Wittgenstein, thus rehabilitating the general account of the Foundations of Mathematics given by Whitehead and Russell. But there still remains an important point in which the resulting theory must be regarded as unsatisfactory, and that is in connection with the Axiom of Infinity.

According to the authors of *Principia Mathematica* there is no way of proving that there are an infinite number of things in any logical type; and if there are not an infinite number in any type, the whole theory of infinite aggregates, sequences, differential calculus and analysis in general breaks down. According to their theory of number, if there were only ten individuals, in the sense of number appropriate to individuals all numbers greater than ten would be identical with the null-class and so with one another. Of course there would be 2^{10} classes of individuals, and so the next type of numbers would be all right up to 2^{10}, and so by taking a high enough type any finite number can be reached.

But it will be impossible in this way to reach $\aleph_0$. There are various natural suggestions for getting out of this difficulty, but they all seem to lead to reconstituting the contradiction of the greatest ordinal.

It would appear then impossible to put forward analysis except as a consequence of the Axiom of Infinity; nor do I see that this would in general be objectionable, because there would be little point in proving propositions about infinite series unless such things existed. And on the other hand the mathematics of a world with a given finite number of members is of little theoretical interest, as all its problems can be solved by a mechanical procedure.

But a difficulty seems to me to arise in connection with elementary propositions in the theory of numbers which can only be proved by transcendental methods, such as Dirichlet's evaluation of the class number of quadratic forms. Let us consider such a result of the form 'Every number has the property p', proved by transcendental methods only for the case of an infinite world; besides this, if we knew the world only contained, say, 1,000,000 things, we could prove it by testing the numbers up to 1,000,000. But suppose the world is finite and yet we do not know any upper limit to its size, then we are without any method of proving it at all.

It might be thought that we could escape this conclusion by saying that although no infinite aggregate may exist, the notion of an infinite aggregate is not self-contradictory, and therefore permissible in mathematics. But I think this suggestion is no use, for three reasons: firstly, it appears as a result of some rather difficult, but I think conclusive, reasoning by Wittgenstein that, if we accept his theory of general and existential propositions (and it was only so that we could get rid of the Axiom of Reducibility), it will follow that if no infinite aggregate existed the notion of such an aggregate would be self-contradictory; secondly, however that may be, it is generally accepted that the only way of demonstrating that postulates are compatible is by an existence theorem showing that there actually is and not merely might be a system of the kind postulated; thirdly, even if it were granted that the notion of an infinite aggregate were not self-contradictory, we should have to make large alterations in our system of logic in order to validate proofs depending on constructions in terms of things which might exist but don't. The system of *Principia* would be quite inadequate.

What then can be done? We can try to alter the proofs of such propositions, and it might therefore be interesting to try to develop a new mathematics without the Axiom of Infinity; the methods to be adopted might resemble those of Brouwer and Weyl. These authorities, however, seem to me to be sceptical about the wrong things in rejecting not the Axiom of Infinity, but the clearly tautologous Law of Excluded Middle. But I do not feel at all confident that anything could be achieved on these lines which would replace the transcendental arguments at present employed.

Another possibility is that Hilbert's general method should be adopted, and that we should use his proof that no contradiction can be deduced from the axioms of mathematics including an equivalent of the Axiom of Infinity. We can then argue thus: whether a given number has or has not the property p can always be found out by calculation. This will give us a formal proof of the result for this particular number, which cannot contradict the general result proved from the Axiom of Infinity which must therefore be valid.

But this argument will still be incomplete, for it will only apply to numbers which can be symbolized in our system. And if we are denying the Axiom of Infinity, there will be an upper limit to the number of marks which can be made on paper, since space and time will be finite, both in extension and divisibility, so that some numbers will be too large to be written down, and to them the proof will not apply. And these numbers being finite will be existent in a sufficiently high type, and Hilbert's theory will not help us to prove that they have the property p.

Another serious difficulty about the Axiom of Infinity is that, if it is false, it is difficult to see how mathematical analysis can be used in physics, which seems to require its mathematics to be true and not merely to follow from a possibly false hypothesis. But to discuss this adequately would take us too far.

As to how to carry the matter further. I have no suggestion to make; all I hope is to have made it clear that the subject is very difficult, and that the leading authorities are very sceptical as to whether pure mathematics as ordinarily taught can be logically justified, for Brouwer and Weyl say that it cannot, and Hilbert proposes only to justify it as a game with meaningless marks on paper. On the other hand, although my attempted reconstruction of the view of Whitehead and Russell overcomes, I think, many of the difficulties, it is impossible to regard it as altogether satisfactory.

Note

1 For instance, as the White Knight said: 'Everybody that hears me sing it – either it brings the *tears* into their eyes, or else – '. 'Or else what?' said Alice, for the Knight had made a sudden pause. 'Or else it doesn't, you know.'

6

The Theory of Types[1]

Paul Weiss

It would seem from the interpretation that Whitehead and Russell put on the theory of types, that it is impossible or meaningless to state propositions which have an unrestricted possible range of values, or which, in any sense, are arguments to themselves. Thus on the acceptance of the principle that statements about all propositions are meaningless,[2] it would be illegitimate to say, "all propositions are respresentable by symbols," "all propositions involve judgment," "all propositions are elementary or not elementary," and if no statement could be made about all the members of a set,[3] it would be impossible to say, "all meanings are limited by a context," "all ideas are psychologically conditioned," "all significant assertions have grammatical structures," etc., all of which are intended to apply to themselves as well. The theory seems also to make ineffective a familiar form of refutation. General propositions are frequently denied because their enunciation or acknowledgment depends on the tacit supposition of the truth of a contradictory or contrary proposition. Such refutations assume that the general proposition should be capable of being an argument of the same type and to the same function as its own arguments, so that according to Whitehead and Russell, they fallaciously refute "by an argument which involves a vicious circle fallacy."[4]

That these limitations on the scope of assertions or on the validity of refutations are rarely heeded is apparent even from a cursory examination of philosophical writings since 1910. Thus Russell, apropos to Bergson's attempt to state a formula for the comic says,[5] "it would seem to be impossible to find any such formula as M. Bergson seeks. Every formula treats what is living as if it were mechanical, and is therefore by his own rules a fitting object of laughter." The characterisation of all formulæ, even though it refers to a totality, seems to Mr Russell to be of the same type as the formulæ characterised.

If the theory were without any embarrassments of its own, and were indispensable for the resolution of the so-called paradoxes[6] (which no one seems to believe), there would be nothing to do but to acknowledge the impossibility of cosmic formulations, as well as the inadequacy of philosophic criticisms, and to pass charitably over such remarks as Russell's as mere accidents in a busy life. However, the statement of the theory itself involves the following difficulties in connection with (1) its scope, (2) its applicability to propositions made about it, and (3) its description.

1. It is either about all propositions or it is not.

A. If it were about all propositions it would violate the theory of types and be meaningless or self-contradictory.

B. If it were not about all propositions, it would not be universally applicable. To state it, its limitations of application would have to be specified. One cannot say that there is a different theory of types for each order of the hierarchy, for the proposition about the hierarchies introduces the difficulty over again.

2. Propositions about the theory of types (such as the present ones, as well as those in the *Principia*) are subject to the theory of types, or they are not.

A. If they were, the theory would include within its own scope propositions of a higher order, and thus be an argument to what is an argument to it.[7]

B. If they were not, there would be an unlimited number of propositions, not subject to the theory, that could be made directly or indirectly about it. Among these propositions there might be some which refer to a totality and involve functions which have arguments presupposing the function.

3. The statement of the theory of types is either a proposition or a propositional function, neither or both.

A. If it were a proposition, it would be either elementary, first order, general, etc., have a definite place in a hierarchy and refer only to those propositions which are of a lower order. If it were held to be a proposition of the last order, then the number of orders would have a last term, and there could not be meaningful propositions made about the theory. The *Principia* should not be able to say, on that basis, just what the purpose, character and application of the theory is.

B. Similarly, if it were a propositional function, it would have a definite place in a hierarchy, being derived from a proposition by generalisation. It could not refer to all propositions or propositional functions, but only to those of a lower order.

C. If it were neither it could not be true or false, nor refer to anything that was true or false. It could not apply to propositions, for only propositions or propositional functions, in a logic, refer to propositions.

D. If both at once, it would be necessarily self-reflexive.

a. If as function it had itself as value, it would refer to itself. But the theory of types denies that a function can have itself as value.

b. If as function it had something else as value, it would conform to the theory, which insists that functions have something else as values. The theory then applies to itself and is self-reflexive, and thus does not apply to itself. As, by hypothesis, it is a value of some other function, there must be propositions of a higher order and wider range than the theory of types.

It is no wonder that the perpetrators of the theory have not been altogether happy about it! What is sound in it – and there is much that is – is best discovered by forgetting their statements altogether, and by endeavouring to analyse the problems it was designed to answer, without recourse to their machinery. The result will be an acknowledgment of a theory of types having a limited application, and a formulation of a principle which will permit certain kinds of unrestricted general propositions.

To do this we shall deal in detail with two apparent paranoumena dealt with in the *Principia*, where the difficulty is largely *methodological*. We shall then treat of Weyl's "heterological–autological" problem, where the difficulty is due to a confusion in *meanings*. Those problems which cannot be dealt with under either heading will be those which need a theory of types for their resolution.

1. *Epimenides.* The proposition "All Cretans are liars" must be false if it applies to Epimenides as well, for it cannot be true, and only as false has it meaning. If it were true, it would involve its own falsity. When taken as false, no contradiction, or even paradox, is involved, for the truth would then be "*some* Cretans tell the truth." The truth could not be "all Cretans tell the truth" for Epimenides must be a liar for that to be true and by that token it must be false. Epimenides himself would be one of the lying Cretans, and one of the lies that the Cretans were wont to make would be "all Cretans are liars." Thus if Epimenides meant to include all his own remarks within the scope of the assertion, he would contradict himself or state a falsehood. If it be denied that a contradictory assertion can have meaning, he must be saying something false if he is saying anything significant. Had he meant to refer to all other Cretans there is, of course, no difficulty, for he then invokes a kind of theory of types by which he makes a remark not intended to apply to himself. All difficulty disappears when it is recognised that the formal implication, "all Cretanic statements are lies" can as a particular statement be taken as one of the values of the terms of this implication. Letting $Ep \, ! \, p$ represent "Epimenides once asserted p"; ϕ represent "Cretanic" and p represent a statement or proposition, then for "all Cretanic statements are false (or lies)," we have:

1. $\phi p \, . \supset_p . \sim p.$

And as Epimenides is a Cretan, for any assertion he makes we have:

2. $Ep \mathbin{!} p . \supset_p . \phi p.$

As #1 is an argument to the above – it being Epimenides' present remark –
we get:

3. $Ep \mathbin{!} \{\phi p . \supset_p . \sim p\} . \supset . \phi \{\phi p . \supset_p . \sim p\}$

#1, as a Cretanic statement, is an argument to #1 as a formal implication
or principle about Cretanic statements, so that:

3A. $\phi \{\phi p . \supset_p \sim p\} . \supset . \sim \{\phi p . \supset_p . \sim p\}$

#3 and #3A by the syllogism yield:

3B. $Ep \mathbin{!} \{\phi p . \supset_p . \sim p\} . \supset . \sim \{\phi p . \supset_p . \sim p\}$

so that in this instance Epimenides lied.

It is important to note that #1 states a formal implication, and that #3,
#3A and #3B employ #1 as a particular assertion or specific argument to
their functions. #3A is an instance of the implication expressed by #1, and
is this instance because of the particular argument it does have. It states the
fact that "'all Cretanic statements are false' is a Cretanic Statement,"
implies that "'all Cretanic statements are false' is false." Substitution of
another argument would give a different instance; though of course of the
same implication. The implication contained in its argument does not have
instances. "'Some Cretanic statements are false' is a Cretanic statement" or
"'This Cretanic statement is false' is a Cretanic statement" are not
instances of "'All Cretanic statements are false' is a Cretanic statement,"
but of "P is a Cretanic statement." These three propositions have different
subjects; they are different values of the same propositional function. That
these subjects have relations to one another is of no moment. "My wife
loves me" and "my mother-in-law is old (or loves me)" are two distinct and
logically independent propositions, even though there is a relationship
between the two subjects.

It is because any considered general proposition is at once an individual
fact, and a formal implication or principle, with many possible arguments,
that it is capable of being taken as an argument to itself. All propositions
about words, logic, truth, meaning, ideas, etc., take arguments which fall in
these same categories, and in so far as such a general proposition is stated
in words, determined by logic, etc., it should, as such a fact, be an argument to itself as a formal implication. The principle must be false if this
cannot be done, for it is sufficient, in order to overthrow a proposition of

this kind, to produce one argument for which it does not hold. One may limit the principle by asserting that it holds for "all but . . .", in which case it is a *restricted* general proposition. Nominalism, association of ideas, scepticism, the theory of universal tautology, the denial of logic are defended in propositions which cannot take themselves as arguments, and which as facts are arguments to contradictory principles. Their contradictory principles therefore hold sometimes at least, so that these doctrines must be false if they are put forward without restriction, and cannot be universally true, if, in Bradley's words, they "appear."

2. "I am lying" – if it be taken in isolation from all fact – is a meaningless statement. There must be some objective truth that is distorted, and unless it is provided the assertion has no significance. This proposition means either, "I am lying about X"; "I always lie," or "I have always lied." The first can be either true or false without giving rise to any problem, except where "all my assertions" is made an argument to X, in which case it is equivalent to either the second or third formulation. "I always lie" involves the same situation as with Epimenides, and the proposition is false. The supposition of its truth would involve a contradiction; the supposition of its falsity means simply that I sometimes lie and sometimes tell the truth. If what is meant is that "I have always lied" that does not involve a contradiction, for what is intended is a restricted proposition, applying to *all but* the present one. It can be true because it does not apply to all propositions; if it were false, then sometimes I lied and sometimes I did not. In short, there is nothing like a self-reflective universal liar, which is an interesting moral conclusion to derive from a logical analysis. Similarly, there cannot be a thorough scepticism held by the sceptic to be valid.

Prof. Whitehead (to whom I am also indebted for the notation) has pointed out to me that wherever a conjunction of propositions results in a *reductio ad absurdum*, there is no way of determining on logical grounds alone which of the antecedents fails, or is false (though one at least must be). Thus in the case of Epimenides we have:

$$4. \underset{\text{(A)}}{\{\phi p . \supset_p . \sim p\}} . \underset{\text{(B)}}{\{Ep \: ! \: p . \supset_p . \phi p\}}$$
$$. \underset{\text{(C)}}{Ep \: ! \: \{\phi p . \supset_p . \sim p\}} . \supset . \underset{\text{(D)}}{\sim \{\phi p . \supset_p . \sim p\}}$$

It is because B and C are in that case assumed to hold, that we can say that A must fail. If the truths of all these antecedents were undetermined, we should have merely the general rule: a *reductio ad absurdum* has as a necessary condition the conjunction of one or more false propositions. Transposition,

$$4'. \ \{\phi p . \supset_p . \sim p\} . \supset . \sim \{\phi p . \supset_p . \sim p\}$$
$$\text{(D)} \qquad\qquad\qquad \text{(A)}$$
$$. \lor . \sim \{Ep \ ! \ p . \supset_p . \ \phi p\}. \lor . \sim Ep \ ! \ \{\phi p . \supset_p . \sim p\}$$
$$\text{(B)} \qquad\qquad\qquad\qquad \text{(C)}$$

makes it apparent that to deny the conclusion of a *reductio ad absurdum* is to imply that at least one of the antecedents is false.

In connection with the *reductio ad absurdum* involved in the assertions, "I always lie" and "I always doubt," #4B reduces to the tautologies: "If I assert p, p is my assertion," and "If I doubt, the doubt is mine." In these cases, the only alternatives left are the denial of the fact of the assertion (#4C), or the truth of the principle itself (#4A).

3. Weyl's heterological–autological contradiction[8] is the result of a material fallacy of amphiboly in connection with the employment of adjectives. The simplest form of such a fallacy is due to a failure to distinguish between an adjective as substantive and an adjective as attribute. Thus if we treat both the subject and attribute in "large is small" and "small is large" as attributes united by a copula expressing identity (instead of reading it as "large is a small word," "small is a large word") we could say "whatever is small is large, and whatever is large is small." No one, I believe, since the Megarics, has been troubled by this particular confusion.

The present problem is the result of a confusion, not between substantive and adjective, but between an adjective which expresses a property, and an adjective which expresses a relation between this property and the substantive. All words can be described in terms of a property – they are long, short, beautiful, melodious, etc., words. They can be classified in accordance with these properties, giving us the class of long words, short words, etc. They can also be classified as either "autological" or "heterological," depending on whether or not the same word is at once substantive and property-adjective; the terms "autological" and "heterological" expressing relationships between the substantive and adjective.

The autological class is made up of words, each of which expresses a property which it possesses; though all of them have unique properties. If "short" be short, and if "melodious" be melodious, they would both be members of the autological class; though in addition, "short" would be a member of the class of short words, and "melodious" would be a member of the class of melodious words.

The heterological class is made up of words, each of which expresses a property which it does not possess. If "long" be short, and if "fat" be thin, they would both be members of the heterological class; although here also "long" would be a member of the class of short words, and "fat" would be a member of the class of thin words. Though when classified according to the relationship of the adjective to the substantive, "short" would be an autological word and "long" a heterological word, they would both be members of that class which was defined in terms of the properties of words – being in this case, members of the class of short words.

Now if heterologicality were a property that a word could have, and if the word "heterological" had that property, it would be a member of the autological class, for it would then possess a property that it expressed. But it would also be a member of a class of words which had the *property* of heterologicality. This class is determined by taking the properties of words, and if it be called "heterological," must be distinguished from that class which was determined not by properties, but by the relationship between properties and substantives.

If there were a property like autologicality and if "heterological" had that property,[9] it would be a member of the heterological class, for it would express a property which it did not possess. But it would also be a member of the class of words which possessed autologicality and could be thus classified.

Thus if "heterological" had the property of autologicality, it would be in the heterological class owing to the *relation* which held between the property and substantive (or between a property it possessed and the property it expressed); but it would be in the class of autological words, owing to a *property* it possessed. If it had the property of heterologicality, it would be in the autological class on the basis of the *relation*, and in the class of heterological words on the basis of *property* classification. There is no difficulty in considering something as a member of two distinct classes, owing to the employment of different methods of classification. There is no contradiction in saying: "'heterological' expresses the property heterologicality, possesses the property autologicality, and the relation between these properties is heterological, in that it expresses and possesses the property heterologicality and the relation between them is autological." Similarly, Richard's contradiction, Berry's contradiction, and that involving the least indefinable ordinal, are resolvable by recognising that "nameable" and "indefinable" are used in two sharply distinguishable senses. They do not require a hierarchy, but a discrimination in the methods of description.

When a distinction is made between a class and its membership (the distinction between a number of numbers and a number is a particular case of this), and between a relation of objects and a relation of relations, the requirements for the solution of the other mathematical problems are provided. A class is other than its members, and a relation, like all universals, transcends any given instance or totality of instances. As they have characters of their own, universals can be described in terms of other universals, which in turn transcend them. Arguments are of a different "type" than functions, just so far as they have different logical characteristics, i.e. are different kinds of logical facts. The class which is an argument to a function about classes has, as argument, a different logical import than the function, and its arguments have a different import from it. This is true of all functions, restricted and unrestricted alike, for it means simply that they are discriminable from their arguments. They can, despite this difference, have characteristics in common with their arguments, and are to that extent unrestricted. Thus in the case of "the class of those classes which are identical with themselves," the class of classes can be taken simply as a class, without logical embarrassment. Yet a class of classes differs from a class, and must therefore be capable of a different characterisation, and thus also be an argument to a function of a different type. With some classes, it may not be possible to consider them as arguments to their own functions, without uncovering a contradiction. In such cases (e.g. the class of those classes which are not members of themselves, and the relations which are connected by their contradictories), it is the difference between the function and the argument that is of moment. That *some* cannot take themselves as arguments does not indicate that all classes or functions are restricted in scope, but simply that classes and functions are *non-restricted*. Some classes and functions are restricted and some are not. To say that all are because some are is an obvious fallacy.

Whenever, as individual, a general proposition is in the class of those objects of which it treats, but cannot be considered as an argument to itself, it is either false or restricted in scope. If the second, its range of arguments must be specified. Accordingly, we can state as a *necessary* condition for the truth of a general proposition, whose scope is unspecified, that when it has a character, which is one of the characters about which it speaks, it *must* be an argument to itself. Thus if Bergson adequately described the comic, his formula should be an object of laughter, and if the theory of types is universal in application, it should be capable of being subject to itself. Conformity to this condition indicates that the unrestricted proposition is *possibly* true; not that it is necessarily true. To demonstrate that such a proposition was necessarily true, it would be essential to show that the supposition of its falsity assumes its truth. That there is danger in applying this rule can be seen from the consideration of some such proposition as: "Everything is made up of language elements." Its denial will be made up of language elements, and would seem to demonstrate that the proposition was necessarily true. Supposition of the falsity of a proposition, however, means verbal denial only in so far as the proposition applies to the realm of language. If it applies to everything, supposition of its falsity involves the positing of the objects of assertions; not the assertions. A necessary unrestricted proposition about everything can be supported only by a demonstration that the supposition of an argument for which it does not hold is self-contradictory. If the proposition has to do with grammar, meaning, logic, judgment, etc., the conditions for a necessarily true and unrestricted proposition would be: 1. the assertion of it is an argument to it; 2. any possible denial is an argument to it. That "any possible denial" rather than "any given denial" is required, is apparent from the consideration of the following propositions: "All sentences are made up of eight words," "No sentence is made up of eight words." Each of these contains eight words. It is because of the fact that we can formulate propositions such as, "It is false that every proposition must be made up of eight words," that the condition is seen not to have been met.

An unrestricted proposition applies to every member of the category, and has some aspect of itself as value. It is in some sense then a determinate in the category which it determines. If the proposition refers to some other category than the one to which it as fact, or some aspect of it as fact, belongs, it is restricted. Thus "all men are mortal" is neither man nor mortal, and as condition does not determine itself as fact. Any proposition referring to that statement would be a different type, and would deal with its truth, falsity, constituents, historical place, logical structure, etc. Though the unrestricted propositions have no limitations, the category to which they refer may have. Epimenides' remark, for example, referred only to Cretans. As his assertion was a determinate in the category, and as his statement of the supposed conditions imposed on the members of that category was not a possible argument to the general proposition, the general proposition was seen to be false or restricted. Had he said, "All Cretans tell the truth," he would have stated an unrestricted proposition which was possibly true. It could not be said to be necessarily true unless Cretan and lie, against the evidence of history, were actually contradictories.

Accordingly, we shall say: *All true unrestricted propositions are arguments to themselves; or by transposition, those propositions which are not arguments to themselves are either restricted or false.* As this proposition can take itself as argument it is possibly true. Unless no proposition is possible which does not conform to it, it cannot be said to be necessarily true. I have not been able to demonstrate this and therefore accept it as a definition or "methodological principle of validation." The theory of types, in its most general form, may be stated as: *A proposition or function of order n, which cannot be an argument to itself, is, as fact, an argument of a proposition or function of order n + 1.*

In accordance with the scheme of the criticism of the theory of types, we can describe our principle as (1) applying to all propositions, including (2) those which refer to it. It (3) is a formal implication with itself as one of its arguments. The theory of types, on the other hand, (1) does not apply to all propositions, but only to those which are restricted, (2) *may* apply to those propositions which refer to it, and (3) is a formal implication which cannot take itself as argument.

The theory of types cannot be an unrestricted proposition about all restricted propositions. As an unrestricted proposition it must take itself as argument; but its arguments are only those propositions which are *not* arguments to themselves. It cannot therefore be unrestricted without being restricted. Nor can it be a restricted proposition about all restricted propositions for it would then be one of the restricted propositions, and would have to take itself as argument – in which case it would be unrestricted. Hence it cannot be restricted without being unrestricted. Three possible solutions may be advanced. The first is that the theory of types is restricted and does not apply to *all* restricted propositions, but only to *some* of them. It is not an argument to itself but to some other proposition about restricted propositions. This in turn will have to be restricted and refer only to some propositions, and so on, giving us theories of types of various orders. The proposition made about the totality of these orders would be of a still higher order and would in turn presuppose a higher order *ad infinitum*. The theory of types thus depends on theories of types of theories of types without end. This seems probable on the ground that the theory is based on the recognition that no proposition can be made about all restricted propositions, so that it must by that very fact admit that it cannot apply to all of them. Instead, therefore, of the theory of types applying to all propositions, and determining them in various orders, it does not even apply to all of a given class of them. This interpretation would not affect unrestricted propositions, and would merely show that the determination of restricted propositions is subject to determinations without end.

The second possibility is suggested by the consideration of a proposition such as: "all truths are but partially true." If that were absolutely true, it would contradict itself, and if it were not, could only apply to some truths. Considered as referring to the necessary limitations which any finite statement must have, it would take itself as argument in so far as it was finite, thus indicating that it was absolutely true about finite propositions, and yet not absolutely true as regards all truths. By pointing out the limitations of a finite statement it indicates that there is an absolute truth in terms of which it is relatively true. On this interpretation, any condition which imposes universal limitations is unlimited in terms of what it limits, but limited in turn by some other condition. One might hold, therefore, that the theory would be unrestricted as regards restricted propositions, and restricted as regards all propositions, and would point to a higher principle which limits it.

The third possibility is to allow for "intensive" propositions which are neither restricted nor unrestricted, being incapable of any arguments. The theory of types could be viewed as such an intensive proposition, and, what we have called its arguments, would merely "conform" to it. This interpretation means the downfall of a completely extensional logic, and a determination of an extensional logic as subordinate to an intensional one.

There are difficulties in each of these interpretations. We shall not now choose among them. In any of these cases, however, a restricted proposition which refers to some other than the restricted aspect of the theory would be subject to the theory and the principle we have laid down about unrestricted propositions could still hold. Those restricted propositions which refer to the restricted character of the theory would not be an argument to it on the first, would be an argument to it on the second, and would neither be nor not be an argument to it on the third solution.

To briefly summarise: The theory of types must be limited in application. Not all the problems it was designed to answer require it; another principle of greater logical import is desirable; while for the resolution of the problems in which it is itself involved, very drastic remedies are necessary. No matter how the theory fares, the possibility of the methodological principle and the possibility of other solutions for the so-called paradoxes, indicate that it is at least not as significant an instrument as it was originally thought to be.

Notes

1 Chap. II, *Principia Mathematica*.
2 Ibid., p. 37 (2nd edn).
3 Ibid.
4 Ibid., p. 38.
5 "Prof. Guide to Laughter," *Cambridge Review*, Vol. 32, 1912, and Jourdain's *Philosophy of Mr. B*tr*nd R*ss*ll*, pp. 86–7.
6 Paradoxes, though contrary to common opinion, may be and frequently are true. Paranoumena, violating principles of logic or reason, if they are not meaningless, are false, and it is only they which are capable of logical analysis and resolution. What the *Principia* attempts to do is to solve apparent paranoumena by a paradox.
7 *Principia Mathematica*, p. 39.
8 Briefly stated it is: all words which express a property they possess are autological; all words which express a property they do not possess are heterological. If "heterological" is heterological it expresses a property it possesses and is thus autological; if it is autological, it expresses a property it does not possess and is therefore heterological. *Das Kontinuum*, p. 2.
9 "Heterological," in fact, has the properties of being long, polysyllabic, etc., and it is questionable whether there are properties like autologicality and heterologicality possessed by words. If there be no such properties, "heterological" is a member of the class of long words, polysyllabic words, etc. In addition it would be one of the terms related by the heterological relation, which fact would not make it have the *property* of heterologicality.

7

On the Theory of Types[1]

W. V. Quine

In this paper the theory of logical types will be examined, and certain departures from it will be suggested. Though the purpose of the paper is not primarily expository, an approach has been possible which presupposes no familiarity with special literature. Matters at variance with such an approach have been confined to appendices and notes.

In the early pages the logical paradoxes will be considered – an infinite series of them, of which Russell's paradox is the first. Then Russell's simple theory of types will be formulated, in adaptation to a minimal set of logical primitives: inclusion and abstraction. Two aspects of the theory will be distinguished: an *ontological doctrine* and a *formal restriction*. It will be found that by repudiating the former we can avoid certain unnatural effects of the type theory – notably the reduplication of logical constants from type to type, and the apparent dependence of finite arithmetic upon an axiom of infinity. But the formal restriction itself has unnatural effects, which survive, even in an aggravated form, after the type ontology has been dropped. A liberalization of the formal restriction will be proposed which removes the more irksome of these anomalies.

1 Basic Formal Concepts

Use will be made of the following logical notions and notations:

Membership: "$(x \epsilon y)$" means that x is a member of the class y. (In this and the ensuing notations, parentheses will be suppressed when there is no risk of ambiguity.)

Inclusion: "$(x \subset y)$" means that the class x is included in the class y; i.e., that every member of x is a member of y.

Identity: "$(x = y)$" means that x and y are the same object.

Conditional, Biconditional, Conjunction, Denial: "(. . . ⊃ _ _ _)", "(. . . ≡ _ _ _)", "(. . . · _ _ _)", and "~ . . ." mean respectively "If . . . then _ _ _", ". . . if and only if _ _ _", ". . . and _ _ _", and "It is not the case that . . .", where the blanks are filled by any statements.

Abstraction: "$\hat{x}$ . . ." denotes the class whose members are just the objects x satisfying the condition ". . .". (The blank is filled by any statement, ordinarily one containing "x".)

Universal quantification: "(x) . . ." means that the condition ". . ." is satisfied by all values of "x".

Universal class: V is the class to which everything belongs.

Null class: Λ is the class to which nothing belongs.

Unit class: ιx is the class whose sole member is x.

It is well known that these notions are sufficient for mathematical logic and indeed for mathematics generally. The further mathematical and logical notions are constructible from this basis by definition. The above list is in fact much longer than necessary, for various notions of the list are definable in terms of the remainder. Thus "V", "Λ", and "xεy" are definable as abbreviations respectively of "$\hat{x}(x = x)$", "$\hat{x}$~$(x = x)$", and "ι$x \subset y$"; and "ιx" is definable in turn as an abbreviation of "$\hat{y}(y = x)$". Further definitions are possible, until finally the twelve items of the list are reduced to just two; *inclusion* and *abstraction*.[2] Every mathematical or logical term (noun) or formula (statement) thus becomes a definitional abbreviation of a term or formula which is built up from variables merely by alternating the devices of inclusion and abstraction in the following fashion: Variables, which are our simplest *terms*, are joined by the inclusion notation to make a *formula*; from this formula a new *term* is made by abstraction; i.e., by prefixing a variable bearing a circumflex accent; two such terms, in turn, or one such term and one variable, are then joined by the inclusion notation to make a new *formula*; and so on.

"Term" and "formula", in this sense, are more rigorously describable with help of a rudimentary metamathematical symbolism. Let us use Greek letters (other than "ι", "ε") to *denote* any unspecified *expressions*. Then let us write "ζIη" to denote the *inclusion compound* of ζ and η. That is, "ζIη" denotes the expression formed by putting ζ and η, whatever they may be, in the respective blanks of "($\subset$)". E.g., where ζ is "$\hat{x}(x \subset x)$" and η is "y", ζIη is "$(\hat{x}(x \subset x) \subset y)$". Finally, let us write "ζ_α" to denote the *abstract* of ζ with respect to α. That is, "ζ_α" denotes the expression formed by applying a circumflex accent to the expression α, whatever it may be, and prefixing this to the expression ζ. E.g., where α is "x" and ζ is "$(x \subset y)$", ζ_α is $\hat{x}$ $(x \subset y)$". These notations involving Greek letters do not form part of the notation of logic, but aid us merely in talking about the notation of logic.

Now the *terms* are describable recursively thus:

(I) *Variables* (letters "x", "y", . . .) *are* terms, *and if* ζ *and* η *are terms and* α *is a variable then* $(\zeta I \eta)_\alpha$ *is a* term.

"Term" is of course to be construed in the narrowest way conformable to (I). In other words, the terms constitute the smallest class which embraces all variables and all expressions $(\zeta I \eta)_\alpha$ such that ζ and η are in the class and α is a variable.

Finally, the *formulae* are directly describable thus:

(II) Formulae *are the expressions* $\zeta I \eta$ *such that* ζ *and* η *are terms.*

2 The Paradoxes

It is clear from the explanation of abstraction that any statement of the form

$$\text{``}(z \in \hat{x} \ldots x \ldots) \equiv \ldots z \ldots\text{''} \tag{1}$$

should be true, where ". . . x . . ." is any statement about x and " . . . z . . ." is the result of substituting "z" for "x" therein. But it is equally clear that any statement of the form

$$\text{``}\underline{\hspace{2cm}} \equiv \sim \underline{\hspace{2cm}}\text{''} \tag{2}$$

is a self-contradiction and must be rejected as false. Next let "K" be short for "$\hat{x}\sim(x\in x)$". Now

$$\text{``}(K\in K) \equiv \sim (K\in K)\text{''} \tag{3}$$

is of the form (2), and should hence be false; yet it is the same as

$$\text{``}(K\in \hat{x}\sim(x\in x)) \equiv \sim(K\in K)\text{''},$$

which is of the form (1) and should hence be true.

This difficulty, known as *Russell's paradox*, arises in precisely similar fashion when we confine ourselves to the primitive notation of inclusion and abstraction. For, the signs "$\equiv$", "$\sim$", and "$\in$" used in the above account are merely abbreviations of our primitive notation, according to the series of definitions alluded to in section 1. The paradox then shows that our simple grammatical rule, whereby inclusion and abstraction are applied alternately to produce terms and formulae, is too liberal; it enables us to get a freak combination such as (3), or rather the formula whereof (3) is a definitional abbreviation. This formula is a freak in that it illustrates a form which should be false in all cases, according to the meanings of our signs, and at the same time illustrates another form which should be true in all cases.

Our already very rudimentary equipment for generating terms and formulae must therefore be further restricted, so as to exclude such freak results. By way of such an added restriction, however, we cannot content ourselves with the direct stipulation that a formula is to be discarded as meaningless if, like (3), it is an instance simultaneously of a valid and a contradictory form. The fault of this stipulation is the lack of any finite test for the general case. We are trying to purify our language of idioms which might deceive us into contradicting ourselves; hence a restriction is of no avail which remains inapplicable until we have discovered ourselves in contradiction. Rather, we must isolate some immediately observable or at least finitely testable feature which (3) and similar freak cases have in common; then we may discard as meaningless all formulae exhibiting that feature.

Examination of (3) suggests that we could avoid Russell's paradox by rejecting as meaningless all formulae of *self-membership* – all formulae of the form "$x \epsilon x$". More accurately, since "ϵ" is not one of our primitive signs, the proposal would be to reject as meaningless all formulae of the kind which the definitions would *abbreviate* in the form "$x \epsilon x$"; rejecting also, of course, all formulae having any such meaningless formulae as parts.

This would indeed dispose of (3), but it is easily seen that other paradoxes analogous to Russell's would still arise in spite of the suggested restriction. Namely, let K' be $\hat{x}(y) \sim (x\epsilon y \cdot y\epsilon x)$; i.e., let "K'" be used as an abbreviation of the *term* (built up of inclusion and abstraction) which the series of definitions would abbreviate as "$\hat{x}(y) \sim (x\epsilon y \cdot y\epsilon x)$". The principle (1) tell us us, then, that

$$\text{``}(z\epsilon K') \equiv (y) \sim (z\epsilon y \cdot y\epsilon z)\text{''}$$

should be true, and hence also, in particular,

$$\text{``}(\iota K'\ \epsilon K') \equiv (y) \sim (\iota K'\epsilon y \cdot y\epsilon\iota K')\text{''}. \tag{4}$$

But familiar logical principles transform the right side of (4) successively into

$$\text{``}(y)\,((y\epsilon\iota K') \supset \sim (\iota K'\epsilon y))\text{''}, \tag{5}$$

$$\text{``}(y)\,((y = K') \supset \sim (\iota K'\epsilon y))\text{''}, \tag{6}$$

$$\text{``}\sim (\iota K'\epsilon K')\text{''}. \tag{7}$$

We thus have the contradiction

$$\text{"}(\iota K'\epsilon K') \equiv\, \sim (\iota K'\epsilon K')\text{"}. \tag{8}$$

Yet no self-membership was involved here: no expression of the form "$x\epsilon x$", either explicitly or implicitly through definitional abbreviations.

Russell's paradox and this one are merely the first two of a series. In the general case, we take $K^{(n)}$ as

$$\hat{x}(y_1)(y_2)\ldots(y_n) \sim (x\epsilon y_1 \cdot y_1\epsilon y_2 \cdot y_2\epsilon y_3 \cdot \ldots y_n\epsilon x);$$

then, analogously to (4), we have

$$\text{"}(\iota^n K^{(n)}\epsilon K^{(n)}) \equiv (y_1)(y_2)\ldots(y_n) \sim (\iota^n K^{(n)}\, \epsilon y_1 \cdot y_1\epsilon y_2 \cdot \ldots y_n\, \epsilon\iota^n K^{(n)})\text{"} \tag{9}$$

where "ι^n" represents n occurrences of "ι". We next transform the right side of (9) into

$$\text{"}(y_1)(y_2)\ldots(y_n)((y_n\epsilon\iota^n K^{(n)})\supset((y_{n-1}\epsilon y_n)\supset\ldots((y_1\epsilon y_2)\supset\sim(\iota^n K^{(n)}\epsilon y_1))\ldots))\text{"},$$

and finally we reduce this to "$\sim (\iota\ ^n K^{(n)}\, \epsilon K^{(n)})$" by n steps each of which is analogous to the step from (5) to (7).

It might appear that all the paradoxes would drop out if we strengthened our restriction to exclude all formulae which contain an *epsilon cycle*; i.e., all formulae which contain parts having the forms "$x\epsilon y_1$", "$y_1\epsilon y_2$", . . . and "$y_n\epsilon x$" (or the primitive expansions of these). Actually even this restriction is too mild, for there are formulae which contain no epsilon cycles but are logically equivalent to others which do. A simple example is

$$\text{"}(y)((x = y) \supset (x\epsilon y))\text{"} \tag{10}$$

(or its expansion into primitives); this contains no epsilon cycle, but it is logically equivalent to "$x\epsilon x$" and hence leads to an equivalent of Russell's paradox.

3 The Theory of Types

A set of restrictions which does presumably avoid all paradoxes is provided by Russell's *theory of types*.[3] We must distinguish between the *metaphysical* or *ontological* aspect of this theory and the *metalogical* or *formal* aspect. In its ontological aspect the theory stipulates that if an individual is a member of a class x, then x must be composed exclusively of individuals; if an individual is a member of a member of a class x, then x must be composed exclusively of classes composed exclusively of individuals; and so on. Individuals are said to be of *type* 0, and classes of objects of type n are said to be of *type n* + 1; and in these terms the theory of types amounts, in its ontological aspect, to demanding that all the members of a class be alike with respect to type.

The metalogical or formal aspect of the type theory is commonly set forth in terms which are not altogether formal, but involve reference also to the type ontology. Thus expressed, the formal aspect of the theory consists essentially of this stipulation: it is to be regarded as *meaningless*, rather than merely false, to indicate the relation of membership as holding between objects which are not of consecutive ascending types; likewise meaningless, rather than false, to indicate inclusion or identity as holding between objects which are not of the same type. Thus "$x\epsilon y$", "$x \subset z$", "$x = z$", and all contexts thereof, become meaningless unless the values of "x", "y", and "z" are thought of as restricted to the respective types n, $n + 1$, and n (for some n).

The formal side of the type theory is studied most easily in application to our primitive notation of inclusion and abstraction, since the modes of notational combination to be scrutinized for meaningfulness are here reduced to a minimum. Thus applied, the stipulation is merely that "$\subset$" be used only between terms which designate things of the same type.

This is not yet formal enough, because inspection of a term (variable or abstract) suggests no one appropriate type. A natural course, therefore, would be to modify our notation to the extent of attaching numerical indices to variables, thus indicating what type of objects each variable is to admit as values.[4] Then, since a class is of next higher type than its members, an abstract would denote a term of next higher type than the type indicated for its circumflexed variable. The formal aspect of the theory of types would thus reduce to this explicitly formal stipulation: The sign "$\subset$" must occur only between terms with equal index numbers – the index number of an abstract being understood as the index number of the circumflexed variable plus one.

Russell's practice, however, which is more usual and more convenient, is to dispense with such indices; to leave the variables "typically ambiguous," in the sense of allowing them to denote objects of *any* types conformable to the context.[5] Applied to our primitive notation, this procedure of "typical ambiguity" consists in recognizing as meaningful any term or formula such that indices *could* be attached to all variables conformably with the described requirement on "$\subset$".

Thus, as applied to our primitive notation, the formal aspect of the theory of types comes to consist of the following stipulation:

(III) *a term or formula ζ is to be retained as meaningful only if all terms occurring in ζ can be assigned numbers in such a way that* (a) *"$\subset$" connects only terms having like assignments, and* (b) *whatever number is assigned to an abstract θ_α, the next lower number is assigned to the variable α.*

But this formulation is still not quite accurate. It proceeds on the understanding that all recurrences of a letter are recurrences of the same variable, and hence subject to the same numerical assignment. But actually such uniformity of assignment is in certain cases unnecessary. In "$\hat{x}(x \subset y) \subset x$" or "$\hat{x}(x \subset y) \subset \hat{x}(x \subset z)$", obviously the first two occurrences of "x" have nothing to do with subsequent ones; the circumflexed variable of abstraction is relevant only to the abstract to which it belongs, and any recurrence of the same letter outside that abstract is merely an alphabetical coincidence. In the examples cited, the first two occurrences of "x" could be rewritten as "w" without any change in meaning. In general, the circumflexed prefix of an abstract θ_α affects only those occurrences of α which are *free* in θ: i.e., which are in θ but are not in any abstract η_α within θ.[6]

In a refined formulation of (III), then, we would speak of assigning numbers to individual *term occurrences* rather than to terms. Instead of (b), we would say merely that, whatever number is assigned to an *occurrence* of an abstract θ_α, the next lower number is assigned to each *free occurrence* of α in that occurrence of θ. This compels like assignments to all free occurrences of α in the occurrence of θ, but imposes no uniformity on assignments to other occurrences of α. Finally, we need an added condition to deal with occurrences of α which lie outside all abstracts θ_α; i.e., occurrences of α which are free in the original term or formula ζ. These free occurrences must of course still have like assignments among themselves. We thus arrive at this formulation of the formal aspect of type theory:

(IV) *A term or formula ζ is to be retained as meaningful only if all term occurrences in ζ can be assigned numbers in such a way that*

(a) *"$\subset$" connects only term occurrences having like assignments;*

(b) *whatever number is assigned to an occurrence of an abstract θ_α, the next lower number is assigned to each free occurrence of α in that occurrence of θ;*

(c) *any two free occurrences in ζ of the same variable have like assignments.*

It is generally believed that the restrictions imposed by the formal aspect of the theory of types are sufficient to rescue logic and mathematics from the paradoxes. If the particular formulae (3)–(10) which led to the paradoxes of section 2 were written out in full primitive notation, it could easily be seen that they are all rejected as meaningless by (IV). The same is true of the terms "K", "K'", etc.

4 Abandonment of the Type Ontology

One especially unnatural and awkward effect of the type theory is the infinite reduplication of each logically definable class. There is no longer one universal class V to which everything belongs, for the theory of types demands that the members of a class be alike in type. We must thus content ourselves with a separate universal class for each type. The same reduplication affects all other classes definable in logical terms; even the numbers 0, 1, etc. lose their uniqueness, giving way to a duplicate for every type.

This reduplication is particularly strange in the case of the null class. One feels that classes should differ only with respect to their members, and this is obviously not true of the various null classes. A unique null class indeed still seems permissible, vacuously, if we think only of the requirement that members be alike in type. However, other requirements of type theory would be violated. For example, we want the null class to be included in each class; hence, inasmuch as it is regarded as meaningless to relate classes of unlike types by inclusion, we need a new null class to be included in each class of new type.

The constants "V", "Λ", "0", "1", etc. are thus "typically ambiguous," just as is the case with variables. Indeed, since our terms are built up of variables by means solely of inclusion and abstraction, *all* our terms are typically ambiguous; and the constants under consideration are merely definitional abbreviations of certain of these terms.

Another effect of the type theory appears in connection with a theorem of arithmetic, namely the theorem to the effect that $n \neq n + 1$ for finite n. The proof of this theorem depends on producing a class of at least n members; and this is accomplished as follows. We start with V and Λ, determined as of any one type. Then there are four classes having none, one, or both of V and Λ as members. Then there are 16 classes having none, one, two, three, or all of these four classes as members. After a finite number of steps of this kind we reach a level providing at least n classes. These, together, compose a class of at least n members as was required.

But observe that this process carries us higher and higher in the hierarchy of types. Consequently the proof establishes only that $n \neq n + 1$ when the numbers are construed as of sufficiently high types. Within lower types the theorem may still fail.

A remedy suggested by Whitehead and Russell is an axiom, valid for each type, to the effect that there is an infinite class.[7] Some such axiom is in any case presumably needed for the theory of infinite numbers; but that it should be needed for proving finite inequalities is an anomalous effect merely of the theory of types.

But this is part of a broader problem, raised by the device of typical ambiguity. This device operates in such a way that Whitehead and Russell *could* have proved their theorem of inequality after all, in its full generality, without adding any axiom of infinity. That is, if they considered merely their logical formalism they could present in symbolic form precisely the proof outlined above. In some of the intermediate steps of the proof it would be contextually apparent, despite the typical ambiguity of the symbols, that the classes dealt with were of progressively higher types; but these contextual evidences would have dropped out by the time one reached the conclusion "$n \neq n + 1$".

Such a proof, though admitted by the apparent formalism of *Principia Mathematica* and related systems, seems to involve an abuse of typical ambiguity: a theorem is unconditionally asserted which, judged merely on its internal structure, admits determinations of type not covered by the proof. Hence Whitehead and Russell did not choose this easy way; indeed, to avoid being deceived into this fallacious sort of argument they even brought in a heuristic notation of suffixes for keeping track of the range of types covered by a proof.[8] No such precautions were explicit in the initial formalism of their system, and indeed it would be a matter of some complexity to incorporate them explicitly. Obviously the abuse of typical ambiguity would be much more convenient. Further, despite its apparent lack of cogency, this practice seems never to yield any intrinsically undesirable theorems.

The awkward situations thus far considered actually depend, not on the formal aspect of type theory, but only on the ontological aspect. Let us then try abandoning the ontological aspect altogether, retaining only the formal restrictions: for if the theory of types is adequate at all as a safeguard against contradictions, it must be adequate in its formal aspect alone.

The whole notion of type is now dropped. Some classes may now contain both individuals and classes as members, and some classes may even be members of themselves. Typical ambiguity of variables disappears; each variable may henceforward be thought of simply as having the unrestricted universe as its range. Typical ambiguity of constants similarly disappears; the sign "V" now denotes just the unique universal class, to which absolutely everything belongs; the sign "Λ" a unique null class; the sign "0" a unique number 0; and so on.

Such expressions as "VϵV", "$\sim(\Lambda\epsilon\Lambda)$", etc., can now be taken literally; the universal class *is* indeed a member of itself, the null class not. These expressions were also countenanced under the standard theory of types; but one took care to explain that in "VϵV" the typical ambiguity of the sign "V" was to be resolved differently in the two occurrences. For the first occurrence the type was to be lower by one than for the second. A similar remark would be applied to "$\sim(\Lambda\epsilon\Lambda)$", "$\Lambda\epsilon$V", "$\Lambda\epsilon0$", "$\sim(0\epsilon0)$", etc. But in discarding the type ontology we slough off this complication; we abandon typical ambiguity, restore the uniqueness of the logically definable classes, and cease to be offended in general by self-membership and other so-called confusions of type.

The effect is observable not only in the case of variables and constants, but also in the case of functions. For example the *negate* $\bar{x}$, defined as $\hat{y}\sim(y\epsilon x)$, is construed under the theory of types as comprising as members not *all* the non-members of x, but just those non-members of x which are of appropriate type for membership in x. Abandoning the type ontology, however, we restore $\bar{x}$ to its common-sense status: the class of absolutely everything except the members of x.

Abandonment of the type ontology disposes also of such difficulties as the one about numerical inequalities. In effect, we now adopt without question the practice described above as abuse of typical ambiguity; but the procedure no longer turns upon typical ambiguity, nor involves any special assumption. Construction of *any* class of n or more members now provides a proof that *the* number n is distinct from *the* number $n + 1$.

All this freedom is gained without altering the restriction (IV) on meaningful terms and formulae. We merely divorce this restriction from any connotations of type. The type ontology was at best only a graphic representation or metaphysical rationalization of the formal restrictions; and though some such rationalization may well be desired, it seems clear in particular that the type ontology afforded less help than hindrance.

5 Relaxation of the Formal Restriction

Removed from its background of types and viewed as an ultimate restriction, (IV) itself remains arbitrary and unnatural. We shall see that the unnatural features can in large part be eliminated by moderating (IV) in a certain way; but let us consider first what some of the unnatural features are.

Note that the meaninglessness of a given *term* is not, in general, difficult to conceive – quite apart from any theory of types. An abstract purports to denote a class whose members are all and only the objects x satisfying a given formula; but, for certain formulae, there may *be* no such corresponding class – every class may either miss some of those objects or else contain some others in addition. Russell's paradox shows, e.g., by *reductio ad absurdum*, that there can be no class corresponding to the formula "$\sim(x \epsilon x)$".

Moreover, if we concede the meaninglessness of a given term we are of course ready to concede also the meaninglessness of any formula containing that term. There remains, however, the case of a meaningless formula containing only meaningful terms. Every formula, in primitive notation, is an inclusion compound; so the case now under consideration is the case of two meaningful terms, say abstracts, joined by "$\subset$" to make a meaningless formula. The whole is a *meaningless* statement of inclusion concerning two *genuine* classes. Having abandoned the type ontology, we can no longer excuse ourselves with the thought that the two classes are of different types; and hence it is hard to admit that it means nothing to say that the one is included in the other.

Another somewhat unnatural effect of (IV) is that many terms and formulae such as "$x \epsilon y$" (or its primitive expansion) are retained as meaningful while certain substitution instances thereof, such as "$x \epsilon x$", are rejected as meaningless. And there is a still more unnatural effect, which is the reverse: many formulae such as "$x \epsilon x$" are rejected as meaningless, while substitution instances thereof, such as "$V \epsilon V$", are retained as meaningful. Intuitively it would seem, e.g., that "$x \epsilon x$" can be meaningless only through meaninglessness in general of self-membership; and that "$V \epsilon V$" should then be meaningless by the same token. We no longer have the excuse originally provided by the theory of types, namely that because of typical ambiguity "$V \epsilon V$" is really not a case of self-membership.

These anomalies of substitution were illustrated just now with definitionally abbreviated formulae "$x \epsilon y$", "$x \epsilon x$", "$V \epsilon V$". But simple examples in primitive notation are also easily found, e.g.

$$\text{``}\hat{x}(x \subset z) \subset w\text{''}, \qquad \text{``}\hat{x}(x \subset z) \subset z\text{''}, \qquad \text{``}\hat{x}(x \subset \hat{y}(y \subset y)) \subset \hat{y}(y \subset y)\text{''}.$$

Another anomaly is the fact that a conjunction, conditional, or other truth function composed of meaningful formulae may itself be meaningless; e.g., "$x = y$" and "$x \epsilon y$" are meaningful but "$x = y \cdot x \epsilon y$" is meaningless. From an intuitive standpoint it is hard to concede that two formulae can be meaningful separately, understood separately, and yet meaningless in conjunction. Nor can we appeal any longer to "confusion of type" as an excuse.

Now all those anomalies can be swept away by one simple change in the restriction (IV). We merely omit (c), obtaining the following:

(V)[9] *A term or formula ζ is to be retained as meaningful only if all term occurrences in ζ can be assigned numbers in such a way that*

    (a) *"$\subset$" connects only term occurrences having like assignments, and*

    (b) *whatever number is assigned to an occurrence of an abstract θ_α, the next lower number is assigned to each free occurrence of α in that occurrence of θ.*

The difference between (IV) and (V) is illustrated by "$\hat{x}(x \subset y) \subset y$". This formula becomes meaningful; for, (a) and (b) are fulfilled by assigning 0 to "x", 0 to the first occurrence of "y", 1 to "$\hat{x}(x \subset y)$", and 1 to the second occurrence of "y". On the other hand such assignment of 0 and 1 to the occurrences of "y" would have violated (c) of (IV). Other expressions which (IV) renders meaningful include the formulae "$x \epsilon x$", "$\sim(x \epsilon x)$", and "$x = y \cdot x \epsilon y$" (or their primitive expansions); also the formula (10) of section 2; also the terms "$\hat{x}(x = y \cdot x \epsilon y)$" and "$\hat{x} \sim (x = y \cdot x \epsilon y)$"; not, however, "$\hat{x}(x \epsilon x)$", nor any of the series "K", "K'", "K''", . . . of section 2. In general, it is easily seen that the terms and formulae which are meaningful under (V) comprise just those which would be meaningful also according to (IV) if all free occurrences of variables were replaced by distinct letters.

Though (V) is a much milder restriction than (IV), no threat of paradox has appeared; and a scheme as liberal as (V), published earlier,[10] has already had expert scrutiny.[11] There is indeed no proof that paradoxes are excluded, but then neither is there such a proof for the original theory of types.[12]

6 Disappearance of the Anomalies

Under (V) it ceases to be true that a formula can be meaningless and yet contain only meaningful terms. For, consider a formula $\zeta I \eta$ such that ζ and η are meaningful terms according to (V). Then numbers can be assigned to all term occurrences in ζ conformably with (a) and (b); and similarly for η. Let S_1 be such a system of assignments for ζ, and let m be the number which it assigns to the occurrence of ζ itself; and let S_2 and n be similarly related to η. If S_2 is changed by adding $m - n$ to each of the assigned numbers, the result S_3 will still satisfy (a) and (b); this is apparent from the purely relative nature of (a) and (b). Now S_1 and S_3 constitute together a system of assignments S_4 for $\zeta I \eta$ as a whole. Each occurrence of "$\subset$", within ζ or η connects term occurrences having like assignments under S_4, since S_1 and S_3 fulfill (a); and the remaining occurrence of "$\subset$" in $\zeta I \eta$ also connects term occurrences having like assignments under S_4, for it connects ζ and η, both of which are assigned m. Thus S_4 satisfies (a). Furthermore, S_4 satisfies (b); for, S_1 and S_3 both satisfy (b), and there is no abstract θ_α in $\zeta I \eta$ which is not in ζ or η. Hence $\zeta I \eta$ is a formula according to (V).

Thus every inclusion compound of meaningful terms is now meaningful. Terms are the essential locus of meaninglessness; a formula can be meaningless only derivatively, though containing a meaningless term.

Equivalently, indeed, we might omit the reference to formulae in (V), omit also the original description (II) of formulae, and then simply describe a meaningful formula once and for all as an expression $\zeta I \eta$ such that ζ and η are meaningful terms.

Another anomaly which disappears is the possibility of a meaningless truth function of meaningful formulae. By examining the definitions whereby denial, conjunction, the conditional, etc. are introduced in terms of inclusion and abstraction, it could easily be seen that all truth functions of meaningful formulae are meaningful according to (V).

Finally, the anomalies of substitution also disappear. It becomes true that every substitution instance of a meaningful term or formula is meaningful, and that every term or formula having a meaningful substitution instance is meaningful. Preparatory to establishing this, we need an explicit formulation of *logical substitution*: *A term or formula ζ' is said to result from* substituting *a term η for a variable β in a term of formula ζ if ζ' is formed by putting η for all free occurrences of β in ζ, and no free occurrence of β in ζ stands within a term θ_α such that α has a free occurrence in η.*[13] Now what is to be proved is that, if η is a meaningful term according to

(V), and ζ and ζ' are as just now described, then ζ is meaningful if and only if ζ' is.

Suppose first that ζ is meaningful, and hence admits of a system S_1 of assignments conforming to (a) and (b). Likewise η admits of such a system S_2. Let $m_i, \ldots m_k$ be the numbers assigned by S_1 to the respective free occurrences of β in ζ, and let n be the number assigned by S_2 to the occurrence of η in itself. Now let S_3 be the following system of assignments to all term occurrences in ζ': throughout that occurrence of η which supplants the ith free occurrence of β in ζ, we make assignments as in S_2 but with $m_i - n$ added to each assignment; and to all other term occurrences in ζ' we make assignments just as in S_1. Since $n + (m_i - n) = m_i$, we see that S_3 assigns the same numbers to the substitute occurrences of η, in ζ', which S_1 assigned to the corresponding occurrences of β in ζ. Outside such occurrences of η, further, S_3 simply duplicates S_1. Then, since S_1 conforms to (a), it follows that S_3 also conforms to (a) in so far at least as concerns any occurrence of "$\subset$" outside the substitute occurrences of η.

Now consider an occurrence of an abstract θ_α in ζ'. Even if this occurrence of θ contains some of the substitute occurrences of η, we know from the definition of substitution that the free occurrences of α in θ will fall outside such occurrences of η. Hence, in all cases at least except where the occurrence of θ_α is wholly inside one of the substitute occurrences of η, S_3 will agree with S_1 in its assignments to the free occurrences of α in θ. Then, since S_1 conforms to (b), we see that S_3 conforms to (b) in so far at least as concerns occurrences of θ_α not within the substitute occurrences of η.

But S_3 also conforms to (a) and (b) in so far as concerns any occurrence of "$\subset$" or θ_α within the ith substitute occurrence of η; for, S_2 conformed to (a) and (b), and addition of a constant $m_i - n$ to each assignment does not affect this property. Hence S_3 conforms completely to (a) and (b). Hence ζ' is meaningful according to (V).

It remains to prove, conversely, that ζ is meaningful if ζ' is. If ζ' is meaningful, it has a system S_1 of assignments conforming to (a) and (b). Now let S_2 be the following set of assignments to all term occurrences in ζ: the free occurrences of β in ζ receive the same assignments which the corresponding occurrences of η received under S_1, and all other term occurrences receive the same assignments as in S_1. Now it is immediately apparent that S_2, like S_1, conforms to (a). Next consider any occurrence of an abstract θ_α in ζ. No occurrence of α in that occurrence of θ is simultaneously a free occurrence of β in ζ, by the definition of freedom (Section 3). Hence all occurrences of α in the occurrence of θ are assigned numbers by S_2 in accordance with S_1. Then, since S_1 conforms to (b), so does S_2. Therefore ζ is meaningful according to (V).

Appendix A. Elimination of the Retroactive Feature

As formulated, the theory of types performs a peculiar function of expurgation: a totality of terms and formulae is first specified as in (I)–(II), and afterward certain of these are weeded out by (IV). The case is similar under (V).

Both theories can be freed of this retroactive feature. The recursive description of term given in (I) can be supplanted by a narrower one which provides, from the very beginning, just those terms which would be left standing by (IV). The same is possible with regard to (V).

These formulations are more complicated than the formulations presented earlier, and they appear to be less convenient technically. It may be worth while, however, to record them. Proof of their equivalence with the previous formulations will not be undertaken.

The recursive description of *term* which would supplant (I) and (IV) is the following. It is at the same time a recursive description of an auxiliary notion of *rank*.

(VI) (a) *A variable is a* term *and has* rank 0 *with respect to itself.*

(b) *If α is a variable, ζ and η are terms, and for each variable γ there is at most one number r such that ζ or η has rank r with respect to γ, then $(\zeta I \eta)_\alpha$ is a* term; *and if ζ or η has rank m with respect to α, and ζ or η has rank n with respect to a variable β distinct from α, then $(\zeta I \eta)_\alpha$ has rank $n - m + 1$ with respect to β.*

Now the *formulae* are describable thus:

(VII) Formulae *are the expressions ζ such that ζ_α is a term if α is a variable.*

Granted that (VI) yields as terms just those terms in the sense (I) which are meaningful according to (IV), it is then obvious also that (VII) will yield as formulae just those formulae in the sense (I)–(II) which are meaningful according to (IV).

For a recursive definition of *term* supplanting (I) and (V), we change (VI) to just this extent: instead of "for each variable . . . with respect to γ," we put "there is at most one number m such that ζ or η has rank m with respect to α." The *formulae* are then describable as in (VII), or, equivalently and more simply, as in (II).

Appendix B. Two Deductive Systems

The question of the consistency of (V) has no precise meaning until a deductive system is specified. Such a system will now be presented, comprising just two postulates and four rules of inference. The postulates, expressed with help of the abbreviations "ϵ" and "$\supset$" (as defined in Quine [11]), are these:

$$(x \subset y) \supset ((y \subset z) \supset (x \subset z))$$
$$(\hat{w}(w\epsilon y \supset w\epsilon z) \subset \hat{w}(w\epsilon x \supset w\epsilon y)) \supset (x \subset y)$$

In stating the rules of inference, I shall write "ζ repl η" to mean that when ζ is put for an occurrence of η in any theorem the result is a theorem. I shall write "$\zeta E\eta$" to denote the expression formed by putting ζ and η in the respective blanks of "(ϵ)" and expanding the result into primitives according to the definitions in [11]. "Term" and "formula" are to be understood in the sense of (I)–(II); and "meaningful" is to be understood in the sense of (V). The four rules, then, are these:

(1) *If ζ and η_α are meaningful terms and η is a theorem, $\zeta I\eta_\alpha$ is a theorem.*
(2) *If ζ and $\zeta_\alpha I\eta_\beta$ are theorems, so is η.*
(3) *If ζ results from substituting the term η for the variable α in the formula θ, then ζ repl $\eta E\theta_\alpha$.*
(4) *If ζ is a term containing no free occurrence of the variable α, then $(\alpha E\zeta)_\alpha$ repl ζ.*

Rules (1)–(3) are essentially R3–5 of [11]. Rule (4) allows, indirectly, alphabetical change of a variable of abstraction; no such rule was included in [11], because the above two postulates were rendered in [11] as rules R1′–2′ with unspecified variables.

The above rules are so framed that no formula can become a theorem if meaningless according to (V). It seems likely, however, that even this degree of restriction is unnecessary. Presumably the stipulation of the meaningfulness of η_α can be dropped from (1) without contradiction. The thus liberalized system will yield theorems violating (V); hence the word "meaningful," in connection with (V), should be abandoned in favor of a more neutral word. Let us adopt rather the word "stratified" to denote conformity to (V). (This word now acquires a broader sense, of course, than in Quine [9].) The system then assumes this form:

Postulates as before.

Rules: (1′) *If ζ is a stratified term, α is a variable, and η is a theorem, then $\zeta I\eta_\alpha$ is a theorem.*

(2)–(4) as before.

By giving (1) the relaxed form (1′), we let down the bars to unstratified terms η_α such that η is a theorem; such terms, e.g., as "$\hat{x}(x\epsilon x \supset x\epsilon x)$" (or its primitive expansion). In effect, thus, we recognize such terms as meaningful. Stratification (conformity to (V)) becomes merely a sufficient condition for meaningfulness, not a necessary one. The question of a necessary condition for meaningfulness is abandoned.

This course is strongly recommended by intuitive considerations. The meaninglessness of an unstratified term η_α is conveniently thought of in general as non-existence of the class which η_α purports to describe; yet if η is a theorem, the term η_α (e.g. "$\hat{x}(x\epsilon x \supset x\epsilon x)$") would still seem to describe a genuine enough class, namely V. More generally, on similar grounds, we should like to allow for the meaningfulness of an unstratified term η_α whenever there is a meaningful term ζ_α such that ζ and η are equivalent. The system under consideration permits all this.

Technically, also, the system under consideration is more convenient than the system involving (1). Much less attention to (V) is required in the course of deductions. This is especially striking in the case of inference by substitution for free variables – a form of inference not listed among the above rules, but capable of justification on the basis of rules (1) (or (1')) and (3).[14] Under the version (1)–(4) we must, in effect, inspect not just the substituted term but the whole resulting formula for conformity to (V); under the version (1')–(4), on the other hand, we need inspect only the substituted term.

Notes

1 The main ideas of this paper were presented in an address before the mathematical fraternity Pi Mu Epsilon and the New York University Philosophical Society at their annual joint meeting in New York February 24, 1938.

2 See Quine [11], pp. 145–147. (Bracketed numerals refer to listings at the end of the paper.) In what follows, use will be made of the fact that definitional reduction to inclusion and abstraction is possible; but familiarity with the actual definitions will not be presupposed, nor indeed any acquaintance with [11].

3 What is relevant here is Russell's simple theory of class types. His theory took on a more complex form when applied to relations; and underlying his classical types and relational types there was his still more elaborate theory of types of so-called propositional functions. (See Whitehead and Russell [16], Vol. I, pp. 37–65). But later work has made it apparent that both of these more complicated parts of the theory are superfluous. The complication regarding relations is eliminated through the reduction of relations to classes by Wiener [17] and Kuratowski [6]. (See also Gödel [5], p. 176; Tarski [15], pp. 363–364; Quine [10], pp. 123–124.) The superfluousness of the other complication, at the level of "propositional functions", was first suggested by Chwistek [3]. (See also Ramsey [12], pp. 20–29; Church [2], p. 169; Quine [8].)

4 Such a notation has been used in some works, e.g. Tarski [14], pp. 97–103. To facilitate comparison with Tarski [14], it was used also in Quine [11].

5 To some extent, in the notation of Whitehead and Russell [16], type differences are reflected by styles of variables; but this is an inessential mnemonic device. See Quine [7], pp. 30–31.

6 Note that the variable "x" in a context of quantification "(x) . . ." turns out to be a variable of abstraction, having the context "$\hat{x}$ . . .", when the definitions of Quine [11] are applied.

7 See Whitehead and Russell [16], Vol. II, pp. 203.

8 See Whitehead and Russell [16], Vol. I, pp. 415–417; Vol. II, pp. vii–xxxi, 5–12, 285–290.

9 If one prefers the kind of notation which attaches indices to the variables (see section 3), he will find that the moderated theory embodied in (V) is easily adapted also to that procedure. The indices would be viewed as belonging, not to

the general notation of variables, but to the notation of abstraction; only variables of abstraction would bear them. A variable α would bear an index at its initial circumflexed occurrence in θ_α, and the same index at all of its free occurrences in the formula θ; but no index outside such contexts. As previously, we would define the index number of an abstract as one plus the index number of its circumflexed variable; and we would forbid use of "$\subset$" between terms with unequal index numbers. But unindexed variables would remain unaffected by the restriction.

10 Quine [9], pp. 79–80. The primitives in [9] are different, and abstraction is not among them. But [9] is related to the present scheme in this way: if an abstract "$\hat{x}$ . . ." (lacking "y") is meaningful under (V), then we can prove in [9] that $(\exists y)$ $(x)\,((x\epsilon y) \equiv \ldots)$; i.e., that there *is* a class such as "$\hat{x}$ . . ." purports to express. This is seen as follows. Suppose "$\hat{x}$ - - -" formed from "$\hat{x}$ . . ." by replacing all free occurrences of variables by new and distinct letters. As observed above, then, "$\hat{x}$ - - -" and hence also "- - -" will be meaningful under (IV). But the formulae meaningful under (IV) are just those which are "stratified" in the sense of [9] – due allowance being made for the difference in primitive notation. Hence R3′ of [9] yields "$(\exists y)\,(x)\,((x\epsilon y) \equiv$ - - -$)$". From this, by substitution on the free variables (a form of inference allowed by the rules of [9]), we derive "$(\exists y)\,(x)\,((x\epsilon y) \equiv \ldots)$".

Note, incidentally, these four corrections of [9]. (i) Of the two explanations of stratification on page 78, only the first is relevant; the second was included because it was erroneously supposed equivalent. Cf. Bernays [1]. (ii) The dated postscript at the end of [9] leads nowhere. Cf. Quine [10], note 4; or, indeed, section 2 above. (iii) R1 should end with "ω" instead of "ψ". (iv) R4 should end with "χ" instead of ψ".

11 See Rosser [13]; also Bernays [1], Curry [4].

12 See Appendix B.

13 Cf. Tarski [14], p. 103, or Quine [11], p. 146.

14 Cf. Quine [11], p. 152 (M27).

References

[1] Paul Bernays. Review of [9]. *Journal of Symbolic Logic*, vol. 2 (1937), pp. 86–87.

[2] Alonzo Church. Review of Chwistek. *Journal of Symbolic Logic*, vol. 2 (1937), pp. 168–170.

[3] Leon Chwistek. "Antynomje logiki formalnej." *Przeglad filozoficzny*, vol. 24 (1921), pp. 164–171.

[4] H. B. Curry. Review of [9]. *Zentralblatt für Mathematik*, vol. 16 (1937), p. 193.

[5] Kurt Gödel. "Ueber formal unentscheidbare Sätze der Principia Mathematica und verwandter Systeme I." *Monatshefte für Mathematik und Physik*, vol. 38 (1931), pp. 173–198.

[6] Casimir Kuratowski. *Sur la notion de l'ordre dans la théorie des ensembles. Fundamenta mathematicae*, vol. 2 (1920), pp. 161–171.

[7] W. V. Quine. *A system of logistic.* Cambridge, Mass., 1934.

[8] —— "On the axiom of reducibility." *Mind*, vol. 45 NS (1936), pp. 498–500.

[9] —— "New foundations for mathematical logic." *The American mathematical monthly*, vol. 44 (1937), pp. 70–80.

[10] —— "On Cantor's theorem." *Journal of Symbolic Logic*, vol. 2 (1937), pp. 120–124.

[11] —— "Logic based on inclusion and abstraction." *Journal of Symbolic Logic*, Vol. 2 (1937), pp. 145–152.

[12] F. P. Ramsey. *The foundations of mathematics and other logical essays.* New York and London, 1931.

[13] J. B. Rosser. "On the consistency of Quine's 'New foundations for mathematical logic.'" Abstract in the *Bulletin of the American Mathematical Society*, vol. 44 (1938), p. 43.

[14] Alfred Tarski. "Einige Betrachtungen über die Begriffe der ω-Widerspruchsfreiheit und der ω-Vollständigkeit." *Monatshefte für Mathematik und Physik*, vol. 40 (1933), pp. 97–112.

[15] —— "Der Wahrheitsbegriff in den formalisierten Sprachen." *Studia philosophica*, vol. 1 (1935), pp. 261–405.

[16] A. N. Whitehead and Bertrand Russell. *Principia Mathematica* (2nd edition). Cambridge, England, 1925–27.

[17] Norbert Wiener. "A simplification of the logic of relations." *Proceedings of the Cambridge Philosophical Society*, vol. 17 (1912–14), pp. 387–390.

8

Comparison of Russell's Resolution of the Semantical Antinomies with That of Tarski

Alonzo Church*

1 Ramified Theory of Types

In this paper we treat the ramified type theory of Russell [6], afterwards adopted by Whitehead and Russell in *Principia Mathematica* [12], so that we may compare Russell's resolution of the semantical antinomies by ramified type theory with the now widely accepted resolution of them by the method of Tarski in [7], [8], [9].

To avoid impredicativity the essential restriction is that quantification over any domain (type) must not be allowed to add new members to the domain, as it is held that adding new members changes the meaning of quantification over the domain in such a way that a vicious circle results. As Whitehead and Russell point out, there is no one particular form of the doctrine of types that is indispensable to accomplishing this restriction, and they have themselves offered two different versions of the ramified hierarchy in the first edition of *Principia* (see Preface, p. vii).[1] The version in §§58–59 of the writer's [1], which will be followed in this paper, is still slightly different.[2]

To distinguish Russellian types or types in the sense of the ramified hierarchy from types in the sense of the simple theory of types,[3] let us call the former *r-types*.

There is an r-type i to which the individual variables belong. If β_1, β_2, . . ., β_m are given r-types, $m \geq 0$, there is an r-type $(\beta_1, \beta_2, \ldots, \beta_m)/n$ to which there belong m-ary functional variables of level n, $n \geq 1$. The r-type $(\alpha_1, \alpha_2, \ldots, \alpha_m)/k$ is said to be *directly lower* than the r-type $(\beta_1, \beta_2, \ldots, \beta_m)/n$ if $\alpha_1 = \beta_1, \alpha_2 = \beta_2, \ldots, \alpha_m = \beta_m, k < n$.

The intention is that the levels shall be cumulative in the sense that the range of a variable of given r-type shall include the range of every variable of directly lower r-type.

The *order* of a variable is defined recursively as follows. The order of an individual variable is 0. The order of a variable of r-type $(\beta_1, \beta_2, \ldots, \beta_m)/n$ is $N + n$, where N is the greatest of the orders that correspond to the types $\beta_1, \beta_2, \ldots, \beta_m$ (and $N = 0$ if $m = 0$). This is Russell's notion of order as modified by the cumulative feature which was just described.

The notations for r-types are abbreviated by writing the numeral m to stand for $(i, i, \ldots, i)$, m being the number of i's between the parentheses. For example ( )$/n$ is abbreviated as $0/n$, $(i, i, i)/n$ is abbreviated as $3/n$, and $((i)/2, ( )/2)/1$ is abbreviated as $(1/2, 0/2)/1$.

There must be a separate alphabet of variables for each r-type, the r-type being indicated by a superscript on the letter. In writing well-formed formulas (wffs) we may often omit these r-type-superscripts as an abbreviation, if it is clear from the context what the superscript should be or if explained in words accompanying the formula. Or we may write the superscript on only the first occurrence of a particular letter, understanding the superscript to be the same on all later occurrences of the same letter – not only in a particular formula but even throughout a particular passage such as a proof.

We take the range of a variable of r-type $0/n$ as propositions of level n, counting propositions as 0-ary propositional functions.[4] And the range of a variable of r-type $(\beta_1, \beta_2, \ldots, \beta_m)/n$ where $m > 0$, is to consist of m-ary propositional functions which are of level n and for which the appropriate arguments are of r-types $\beta_1, \beta_2, \ldots, \beta_m$ respectively.

The formation rules provide that a propositional variable (i.e., a variable of one of the r-types $0/n$) shall constitute a wff when standing alone. Also a formula $\mathbf{f}(\mathbf{x}_1, \mathbf{x}_2, \ldots, \mathbf{x}_m)$ is well-formed (wf) if and only if $\mathbf{f}$ is a variable (or a primitive constant) of some r-type $(\beta_1, \beta_2, \ldots, \beta_m)/n$, where $m > 0$, and $\mathbf{x}_1$ is a variable (or a primitive constant) whose r-type is β_1 or directly lower than β_1, and $\mathbf{x}_2$ is a variable (or a primitive constant) whose r-type is β_2 or directly lower than β_2, and $\ldots$, and $\mathbf{x}_m$ is a variable (or a primitive constant) whose r-type is β_m or directly lower than β_m.

Besides an infinite alphabet of variables in each r-type and the notation for application of a function to its arguments (already used in the preceding paragraph), the primitive symbols comprise an unspecified list of primitive constants,[5] each of definite r-type, and the usual notations for negation, disjunction, and the universal quantifier.[6] The remaining formation rules, not already stated, provide that $\sim \mathbf{P}$, $[\mathbf{P} \vee \mathbf{Q}]$, and $(\mathbf{a})\mathbf{P}$ are wf whenever $\mathbf{P}$ and $\mathbf{Q}$ are wf and $\mathbf{a}$ is a variable.

In abbreviating wffs we follow the conventions of [1], as adapted to the present context.[7] The signs of material implication, conjunction,[8] and material equivalence are of course introduced by the definitions *1.01, *3.01, *4.01 of [12]. And as explained in note 6, *10.01 is used as definition of the existential quantifier.

We do not follow the rules of inference and axioms of either [6] or [12], as these are in some respects insufficient and also involve some oddities[9] (as they would now seem). But rather we suppose that a system of rules and axioms for propositional calculus and laws of quantifiers is adopted from some standard source. And to these we adjoin the two following comprehension axiom schemata: [10]

$$(\exists \mathbf{p}) \, . \, \mathbf{p} \equiv \mathbf{P},$$

where $\mathbf{p}$ is a propositional variable of r-type $0/n$, the bound (in Russell's terminology, "apparent") variables of $\mathbf{P}$ are all of order less than n, and the free (in Russell's terminology, "real") variables of $\mathbf{P}$ and the constants of $\mathbf{P}$ are all of order not greater than n;

$$(\exists \mathbf{f}) \, . \, \mathbf{f}(\mathbf{x}_1, \mathbf{x}_2, \ldots, \mathbf{x}_m) \equiv_{x_1 x_2 \, \ldots \, x_m} \mathbf{P}$$

where $\mathbf{f}$ is a functional variable of r-type $(\beta_1, \beta_2, \ldots, \beta_m)/n$, and $\mathbf{x}_1, \mathbf{x}_2, \ldots,$ $\mathbf{x}_m$ are distinct variables of r-types $\beta_1, \beta_2, \ldots, \beta_m$, and the bound variables of $\mathbf{P}$ are all of order less than the order of $\mathbf{f}$, and the free variables of $\mathbf{P}$ (among which of course some or all of $\mathbf{x}_1, \mathbf{x}_2, \ldots, \mathbf{x}_m$ may be included) and the constants occurring in $\mathbf{P}$ are all of order not greater than the order of $\mathbf{f}$.

From the comprehension axiom schemata there follow rules of substitution for propositional and functional variables[11] which are like *510 in [1], as generalized to higher types, but have the two following restrictions: (i) the wff $\mathbf{P}$ which is substituted for $\mathbf{p}$ or the wff $\mathbf{P}$ which is substituted for $\mathbf{f}(\mathbf{x}_1, \mathbf{x}_2, \ldots, \mathbf{x}_m)$ must obey the same conditions that are attached to the comprehension axiom schemata; (ii) all occurrences of the variable $\mathbf{p}$ or $\mathbf{f}$ in the wff $\mathbf{A}$ into which the substitution is made must be at extensional places.[12]

Using this reconstruction of the logic of *Principia Mathematica* (with ramified type theory), as just outlined, we shall present proofs in the manner of [1] – making use in particular of the deduction theorem. The following abbreviations will be used to refer to certain primitive and derived rules of inference, as indicated:

mod. pon.: The rule of *modus ponens*, from $\mathbf{P} \supset \mathbf{Q}$ and $\mathbf{P}$ to infer $\mathbf{Q}$.

P: Laws of propositional calculus.

ded. thm.: The deduction theorem.

univ. inst.: The rule of universal instantiation, from $(\mathbf{a})\mathbf{P}$ to infer the result of substituting $\mathbf{b}$ for all free occurrences of $\mathbf{a}$ throughout $\mathbf{P}$, if $\mathbf{a}$ is a variable, if $\mathbf{b}$ is a variable or a constant and is either of the same r-type as $\mathbf{a}$ or of r-type directly lower than that of $\mathbf{a}$, and (in case $\mathbf{b}$ is a variable) if there is no capture of $\mathbf{b}$ that results by the substitution described.

ex. gen.: The rule of existential generalization, from $\mathbf{Q}$ to infer $(\exists \mathbf{a})\mathbf{P}$, where $\mathbf{Q}$ is the result of substituting $\mathbf{b}$ for all free occurrences of $\mathbf{a}$ throughout **P**, and where **a**, **b**, and **P** obey the same conditions which were just stated in connection with the rule of universal instantiation.

ex. inst.: The rule of existential instantiation,[13] if $\mathbf{P}_1, \mathbf{P}_2, \ldots, \mathbf{P}_m, \mathbf{Q} \vdash \mathbf{S}$ and if the variable **a** is free in none of the wffs except **Q**, then $\mathbf{P}_1, \mathbf{P}_2, \ldots,$ $\mathbf{P}_m (\exists \mathbf{a}) \mathbf{Q} \vdash \mathbf{S}$; also if $\mathbf{P}_1, \mathbf{P}_2, \ldots, \mathbf{P}_m, \mathbf{Q}, \mathbf{R} \vdash \mathbf{S}$ and if the variable **a** is free in none of the wffs except **Q** and **R**, then $\mathbf{P}_1, \mathbf{P}_2, \ldots, \mathbf{P}_m ((\exists \mathbf{a}) . \mathbf{QR} \vdash \mathbf{S}$.

2 Grelling's Antinomy

As an example of one of the semantical antinomies we select Grelling's[14] as being perhaps the simplest to reproduce in a formalized language, although it is not one of the antinomies ("contradictions") that are discussed in [6] and [12]. Applied to one of the familiar natural languages, such as English or German, Grelling's antinomy is concerned with *adjectives* and with *properties* which the adjectives express.[15] In the formalized language which we are here treating it is propositional forms with one free variable that most nearly take the place of adjectives. But the semantics appropriate to such a *propositional form* is rather that it has a *value* for each value of its free variable, and we shall follow this in reproducing Grelling's antinomy.

We assume that symbols and formulas are to be counted among the individuals. This choice is convenient for our purpose and is allowable on the ground that any well-defined domain may be taken as the individuals. It is believed that a different choice will make no important difference in what follows.[16]

It will be sufficient to deal with the case of propositional forms having just one free variable and to assume that this is an individual variable, although there are evident generalizations of the antinomy which concern the case of propositional forms having more than one free variable or free variables of higher r-type or both. Therefore we introduce the infinite list of primitive constants $\text{val}^2, \text{val}^3, \text{val}^4, \ldots,$ with the intention that val^{n+1} $(a^i, v^i, F^{1/n})$ shall mean that a^i is an individual variable and v^i is a wff (propositional form) having no other free variable than a^i and for every value x^i of the variable a^i the value of v^i is $F^{1/n}(x^i)$.[17]

As no reason to the contrary appears, we take the constants val^{n+1} to be of level 1 (i.e., in Russell's terminology, predicative). The r-type of val^{n+1} is therefore $(i, i, 1/n)/1$, and it may indeed be convenient to regard the notation val^{n+1} as an abbreviation for $\text{val}^{(i, i, 1/n)/1}$. The order of val^{n+1} is $n + 1$.

Based on the intended meaning the following postulates involving the constants val^{n+1} suggest themselves as evident.

First there is the principle of univocacy, which may be taken in the strong form:

$$\text{val}^{m + 1}(a, v, F^{1/m}) \supset_{avf} . \text{val}^{n + 1}(a, v, G^{1/n}) \supset_G . F = G. \tag{1}$$

Since $[F = G]$ is defined as $(H) \cdot H(F) \supset H(G)$, where the type of H is $(1/k)/1$ (with k chosen as the greater of m and n), we may infer from (1):

$$\text{val}^{m + 1}(a, v, F^{1/m}) \supset_{avF} . \text{val}^{n + 1}(a, v, G^{1/n}) \supset_G . F(x) \equiv_x G(x). \tag{2}$$

We shall need only the weak, or extensional principle of univocacy (2). Then there is the following postulate schema, which (without extending the formalized language) can be stated only in the extensional form shown, and whose truth (for each **P**) may be seen informally by taking v to be the propositional form **P** and a to be the individual variable 'x':

$$(\exists a) (\exists v) (\exists F^{1/n}) . \text{val}^{n + 1}(a, v, F) . F(x) \equiv_x \mathbf{P}, \tag{3}$$

where **P** is a wff in which there is no free variable other than 'x', in which all the bound variables are of order less than n, and in which all the constants are of order not greater than n. And finally there are the following postulates which express the cumulative character of the constants $\text{val}^{n + 1}$ that was implicit in our informal explanation of the meaning:

$$\text{val}^{n + 1}(a, v, F^{1/n}) \supset \text{val}^m (a, v, F^{1/n}), \text{ where } m > n + 1. \tag{4}$$

Corresponding to the word "heterological" that appears in the verbal statement of Grelling's antinomy, we make the definition: [18]

$$\text{het}^{n + 1}(v) \rightarrow (\exists a) (\exists F^{1/n}) . \text{val}^{n + 1}(a, v, F) . \sim F(v).$$

Then we prove the following theorems:

$$\text{het} n^{+ 1}(v) \supset \text{het}^{m + 1}(v), \text{ if } m \geqq n. \tag{5}$$

Proof. Suppose that $m \geqq n$.
By (4) and P, $\text{val}^{n + 1}(a, v, F^{1/n}) \vdash \text{val}^{m + 1}(a, v, F)$.
Hence by P, $\text{val}^{n + 1}(a, v, F) . \sim F(v) \vdash \text{val}^{m + 1}(a, v, F) . \sim F(v)$.
Hence by ex. gen.,[19] $\text{val}^{n + 1}(a, v, F) . \sim F(v) \vdash \text{het}^{m + 1}(v)$.
Hence by ex. inst., $\text{het}^{n + 1}(v) \vdash \text{het}^{m + 1}(v)$.
Hence (5) follows by ded. thm.

$$[\text{val}^{m + 2}(a, v, G^{1/m + 1}) . G(x) \equiv_x \text{het}^{m+1}(x)] \supset \sim \text{het}^{n + 1}(v), \text{ if } m \geqq n. \tag{6}$$

Proof. Suppose that $m \geqq n$.
By (2), univ. inst., and mod. pon., $\text{val}^{m + 2}(a, v, G^{1/m + 1})$,

$$\text{val}^{n + 1}(a, v, F^{1/n}) \vdash F(x) \equiv_x G(x).$$

Hence, by univ. inst. and **P**, $\text{val}^{m + 2}(a, v, G)$,

$$\text{val}^{n + 1}(a, v, F), \sim F(v) \vdash \sim G(v).$$

Hence by ex. inst., $\text{val}^{m + 2}(a, v, G)$, $\text{het}^{n + 1}(v) \vdash \sim G(v)$.
Hence by ded. thm., $\text{val}^{m + 1}(a, v, G) \vdash \text{het}^{n + 1}(v) \supset \sim G(v)$.
Hence by univ. inst. and **P**, $\text{val}^{m + 2}(a, v, G)$,

$$G(x) \equiv_x \text{het}^{m + 1}(x) \vdash \text{het}^{n + 1}(v) \supset \sim \text{het}^{m + 1}(v).$$

Hence by (5) and **P**, $\text{val}^{m + 2}(a, v, G)$,

$$G(x) \equiv_x \text{het}^{m + 1}(x) \vdash \sim \text{het}^{n + 1}(v).$$

Hence (6) follows by **P** and ded. thm.

$$[\text{val}^{m + 2}(a, v, G^{1/m + 1}) \, . \, G(x) \equiv_x \text{het}^{m + 1}(x)] \supset \text{het}^{n + 1}(v), \text{ if } m < n. \quad (7)$$

Proof. Suppose that $m < n$.
By **P** and ex. gen., $\text{val}^{m + 2}(a, v, G^{1/m + 1}), \sim G(v) \vdash \text{het}^{m + 2}(v)$.
Hence by univ. inst. and **P**, $\text{val}^{m + 2}(a, v, G)$,

$$G(x) \equiv_x \text{het}^{m + 1}(x), \sim \text{het}^{m + 1}(v) \vdash \text{het}^{m + 2}(v).$$

Hence by (5) (used twice) and **P**, $\text{val}^{m + 2}(a, v, G)$,

$$G(x) \equiv_x \text{het}^{m + 1}(x), \sim \text{het}^{n + 1}(v) \vdash \text{het}^{n + 1}(v).$$

Hence by ded. thm. and **P**, $\text{val}^{m + 2}(a, v, G)$,

$$G(x) \equiv_x \text{het}^{m + 1}(x) \vdash \text{het}^{n + 1}(v).$$

Hence (7) follows by **P** and ded. thm.
Also as an instance of (3) we have:

$$(\exists a) \, (\exists v) \, (\exists \, G^{1/m + 1}) \, . \, \text{val}^{m + 2}(a, v, G) \, . \, G(x) \equiv_x \text{het}^{m + 1} (x). \quad (8)$$

If we reduce to simple type theory by dropping all level indicators, the infinitely many constants $\text{val}^{n + 1}$ coalesce into a single constant, val, whose type (in the sense of simple type theory) is $(i, i, (i))$. The informal explanation of the meaning of $\text{val}^{n + 1}$ then becomes an explanation of the meaning of val, and the postulates (1), (3) still seem to be evident from this intended meaning; moreover (2) is still a consequence of (1), and (4) becomes tautologous. The proofs of theorems (5)–(8) still hold, after dropping the level indicators, and the last three theorems then constitute a contradiction. This is Grelling's antinomy, as it arises in simple type theory.

The resolution of the antinomy by ramified type theory consists not merely in the fact that, after restoration of the level indicators, theorems (6)–(8) are no longer a contradiction, but also in that the question "Is the propositional form $\text{het}^{m+1}(x)$ autological or heterological?" can now be answered: namely it is (by (6)) autological at all levels $\leq m + 1$, and it is (by (7)) heterological at all levels $> m + 1$.

3 The Language L

Now let L be the language of ramified type theory (as here formulated) with addition of all of the constants

$$\text{val}^{(i,\ i,\ \ldots,\ i(\beta_1,\beta_2,\ \ldots,\ \beta_m)/n)/1}$$

and appropriate postulates involving them. Here m is any non-negative integer, $\beta_1, \beta_2, \ldots, \beta_m$ are any m r-types, n is any level ≥ 1, and in the superscript

$$(i,\ i,\ \ldots,\ i,\ (\beta_1,\ \beta_2,\ \ldots,\ \beta_m)/n)/1$$

that indicates the r-type of the constant there are to be exactly $m + 1$ i's preceding the r-type-symbol

$$(\beta_1,\ \beta_2,\ \ldots,\ \beta_m)/n.$$

The constants val^{n+1} that were introduced above are special cases, corresponding to $m = 1$, $\beta_1 = i$. Generally, the wff

$$\text{val}^{(i,\ i,\ \ldots,\ i,(\beta_1,\beta_2,\ \ldots,\ \beta_m)/n)/1}(a_1, a_2, \ldots, a_m, v, F^{(\beta_1,\ \beta_2,\ \ldots,\ \beta_m)/n})$$

shall mean that $a_1, a_2, \ldots, a_m$ are distinct variables of types $\beta_1, \beta_2, \ldots, \beta_m$ respectively, and v is a wff having no other free variables than $a_1, a_2, \ldots, a_m$, and for every system of values

$$x_1^{\beta_1}, x_2^{\beta_2}, \ldots, x_m^{\beta_m}$$

of the variables $a_1, a_2, \ldots, a_m$ the value of v is

$$F^{(\beta_1,\ \beta_2,\ \ldots,\ \beta_m)/n}(x_1^{\beta_1}, x_2^{\beta_2}, \ldots, x_m^{\beta_m}).$$

(Compare note 17.)

We put down only the postulates that are generalizations of (1), (3), (4) above.[20] As an abbreviation in stating these we take the r-type of F to be always

$$(\beta_1, \beta_2, \ldots, \beta_m)/n;$$

and the r-type of G is to be

$$(\beta_1, \beta_2, \ldots, \beta_m)/k;$$

and the r-type of val is to be, at each occurrence, the lowest that is compatible with its arguments, unless the contrary is said. The postulates are:

$$\text{val}(a_1, a_2, \ldots, a_m, v, F) \supset_{a_1 a_2 \ldots a_m v F} \text{val}(a_1, a_2, \ldots, a_m, v, G) \supset_G . F = G, \quad (9)$$

$$(\exists a_1)(\exists a_2) \ldots (\exists a_m)(\exists v)(\exists F) . \text{val}(a_1, a_2, \ldots, a_m, v, F) .$$
$$F(x_1, x_2, \ldots, x_m) \equiv_{x_1 x_2 \ldots x_m} \mathbf{P}, \quad (10)$$

where $\mathbf{P}$ is a wff in which there are no free variables other than 'x_1', 'x_2', ..., 'x_m' and in which all the bound variables are of order less than the order of 'F' and all the constants of order not greater than the order of 'F'.

$$\text{val} (a_1, a_2, \ldots, a_m, v, F) \supset \text{val} (a_1, a_2, \ldots, a_m, v, F), \quad (11)$$

where the constant, val, on the right is of the lowest r-type that is compatible with the arguments it has, while that on the left is of any other r-type that is compatible with these arguments.

For $n = 1, 2, 3, \ldots$, let L_n be the sublanguage of L obtained by deleting all variables and constants of order greater than n, and allowing the variables of order n to occur only as free variables.

Then L_1 is a functional calculus of first order[21] in the presently standard sense, i.e., only individual variables occur as bound variables. None of the semantical constants, val, are in L_1, as the lowest order of these is 2. And the propositional and functional variables in L_1 are of first order, having superscripts of the form $m/1$ ($m = 0, 1, 2, \ldots$).

In L_2 there are propositional and functional variables with superscripts $m/2$, where $m \geq 0$; and also propositional and functional variables with superscripts $(\beta_1, \beta_2, \ldots, \beta_m)/1$, $m \geq 0$, where each of $\beta_1, \beta_2, \ldots, \beta_m$ is either i or of the form $k/1$, $k \geq 0$. But only individual variables and propositional and functional variables of first order are used as bound variables. And the semantical constants, val, which are present in L_2 are those having the r-types $(i, i, \ldots, i, m/1)/1$, $m = 0, 1, 2, \ldots$, and thus are precisely those needed for the semantical metatheory of L_1.

We may therefore regard L_2 as a semantical meta-language of L_1. However, L_2 is stronger than L_1 not only in having the semantical predicates (semantical functional constants) that are needed for the semantics of L_1 but also in having additional free variables beyond those of L_1, namely the variables of second order, and in admitting as bound variables certain variables which appear only as free variables in L_1, namely the variables of first order.

And so we may continue through the hierarchy of languages L_1, L_2, L_3, $\ldots$, the situation being always that L_{n+1} is a semantical meta-language of L_n, containing the semantical predicates that are applicable to L_n, and containing also L_n itself plus additional r-types of free variables and additional r-types of bound variables that are not present in L_n. Moreover it is quite indifferent whether we speak of a single language L and a hierarchy of orders of variables and predicates within it or whether we speak of an infinite hierarchy of languages L_1, L_2, L_3, $\ldots$, as it is evident that the distinction is merely terminological.

4 Comparison with Tarski

It is Tarski's solution of the problem of the semantical antinomies that the semantical predicates for a particular language must be contained, not in the language itself, but always in a meta-language. Indeed the semantical predicates val are intensional, whereas Tarski at the date of [7] and [8] is concerned only with the extensional semantical notions of truth and satisfaction and perhaps would have denied corresponding intensional notions. But it is intensional semantical predicates that are primarily appropriate to the language L (or to L_1, L_2, etc.). The essential point of the resolution of the semantical antinomies by Tarski is unrelated to a distinction of intension and extension, and is simply that the semantical predicates (and propositional forms) appropriate to a language must be put into a meta-language of it.

In the light of this it seems justified to say that Russell's resolution of the semantical antinomies is not a different one than Tarski's but is a special case of it.

This conclusion may be supported by supplying in L (or in L_2, L_3, etc.) the following definitions to express the extensional semantical notions, that v is a true sentence of L_n,

$$\mathrm{tr}^{n+1}(v) \to (\exists p^{0/n}) \,.\, \mathrm{val}^{(i,0/n)/1}(v, p) \,.\, p,$$

and that v is a propositional form of L_{N+n} and is satisfied by the values x_1, $x_2, \ldots, x_m$ of the variables $a_1, a_2, \ldots, a_m$,

$$\text{sat}^{N+n+1}(a_1, a_2, \ldots, a_m, x_1, x_2, \ldots, x_m, v) \to (\exists F) . \text{val}(a_1, a_2, \ldots, a_m, v, F).$$
$$F(x_1, x_2, \ldots, x_m)$$

where in the latter definition, F is of r-type $(\beta_1, \beta_2, \ldots, \beta_m)/n$ and order $N + n$, and val is of r-type $(i, i, \ldots, i, (\beta_1, \beta_2, \ldots, \beta_m)/n)/1$, and $x_1, x_2, \ldots, x_m$ are of r-types $\beta_1, \beta_2, \ldots, \beta_m$ respectively (where $m \geqq 1$, $n \geqq 1$).

As the propositional form $\text{tr}^{n+1}(v)$ contains a bound variable of order n, a constant of order $n + 1$, and as its only free variable, the individual variable 'v', it follows that $\text{tr}^{n+1}(v)$ belongs to the language L_{n+1} but not to L_n. Similarly the propositional form $\text{sat}^{N+n+1}(a_1, a_2, \ldots, a_m, x_1, x_2, \ldots, x_m, v)$ belongs to the language L_{N+n+1} but not to L_{N+n}. And this is just what Tarski's resolution of the semantical antinomies requires.

It should be remarked that if we *begin* with extensional semantics, we may then naturally take as primitive a predicate or infinite list of predicates, tr, which require an individual variable as argument, and an infinite list of predicates, sat, which require $2m + 1$ arguments of r-types $i, i, \ldots, i$, $\beta_1, \beta_2, \ldots, \beta_m, i$. In this case the levels of the primitive predicates, tr and sat, must be assigned *ad hoc* to avoid antinomy, and the ramified theory of types may seem to play only a secondary role.

However, such priority of extensional semantics is just not appropriate to the language L – and does not accord with the way in which the resolution of the "contradictions" is informally explained in [6] and [12].[22] Moreover, as we have just seen, we are able by taking the intensional predicates val as primitive to supply definitions of $\text{tr}^{n+1}(v)$ and sat^{N+n+1} $(a_1, a_2, \ldots, a_m, x_1, x_2, \ldots, x_m, v)$. But the reverse does not hold: if the predicates tr and sat of various r-types are primitive, we are unable from them to define val $(a_1, a_2, \ldots, a_m, v, F)$ suitably, but only an extensional analogue which we may call valext $(a_1, a_2, \ldots, a_m, v, F)$. For example, if

$$\text{valext}^{n+1}(a, v, F^{1/n}) \to F(x) \equiv_x \text{sat}^{(i, i, i)/n+1}(a, x, v),$$

we have for $\text{valext}^{n+1}(a, v, F)$, unlike $\text{val}^{n+1}(a, v, F)$, that if it is satisfied by given values of the variables a, v, F, then it is satisfied also by the same values of a and v and any coextensive (or formally equivalent) value of F.

By taking the intensional semantics as prior, and proceeding from it to the extensional semantical notions, ramified type theory resolves the semantical antinomies in a straightforward way, without *ad hoc* additional assumptions, and it is seen only after the event that the resolution is a subcase of Tarski's.

5 Axioms of Reducibility

To secure adequacy for classical mathematics it is necessary to adjoin to the language L an axiom of infinity, axioms of choice in some form, and the axioms of reducibility.[23]

As our concern is with the resolution of the semantical antinomies by ramified type theory, it is only the axioms of reducibility that need concern us here. They are:

$$(F^{(\beta_1, \beta_2, \ldots, \beta_m)/n)}) (\exists G^{(\beta_1, \beta_2, \ldots, \beta_m)/1}) . F(x_1, x_2, \ldots, x_m) \equiv_{x_1 x_2 \ldots x_m}$$
$$G(x_1, x_2, \ldots, x_m),$$

where $m = 1, 2, 3, \ldots,$[24] and the variables $x_1, x_2, \ldots, x_m$ are of r-types $\beta_1,$ $\beta_2, \ldots, \beta_m$ respectively.

The effect of the axioms is that the range of the functional variables is already extensionally complete at level 1, in the sense that it contains a propositional function that is extensionally (or in the terminology of [12], "formally") equivalent to any propositional function which enters as a value of the functional variables at any higher level; and that it is only in intension that we are to think of additional values of the functional variables as arising at each new level. Thus the rejection of impredicative definition is annulled in extensional but not in intensional matters.[25] And this much is enough for classical mathematics, especially mathematical analysis.

The danger may be feared that the axiom of reducibility will restore the semantical antinomies which it was intended to avoid by means of the ramified type hierarchy. But this does not appear to be realized, at least not in any obvious way.

Let us take the case of Grelling's antinomy as an illustration. By using the appropriate one of the axioms of reducibility, we may indeed prove:

$$(\exists H^{1/1}) . H(v) \equiv_v (\exists a) (\exists F^{1/n}) . \mathrm{val}^{n+1}(a, v, F) . \sim F(v). \tag{12}$$

Then if we take as hypothesis

$$H^{1/1}(v) \equiv_v (\exists a) (\exists F^{1/n}) . \mathrm{val}^{n+1}(a, v, F) . \sim F(v), \tag{13}$$

we may repeat the proofs of (6) and (7) in modified form, treating them as proofs from the hypothesis (13). In this way we get, as proved from the hypothesis (13), both

$$[\mathrm{val}^2 (a, v, G^{1/1}) . G(x) \equiv_x H(x)] \supset \sim H(v)$$

and

$$[\mathrm{val}^2\ (a,\ v,\ G^{1/1})\ .\ G(x) \equiv_x H(x)] \supset H(v).$$

No contradiction results, as it does not appear that a similar analogue of (8) can be obtained. But from the two last formulas we get by propositional calculus

$$G(x) \equiv_x H(x) \supset\ \sim \mathrm{val}^2\ (a,\ v,\ G),$$

still as proved from the hypothesis (13); then deduction theorem and a substitution for the functional variable H enable us to prove the theorem:

$$G^{1/1}\ (x) \equiv_x \mathrm{het}^{n\,+\,1}\ (x) \supset_{avG}\ \sim \mathrm{val}^2\ (a,\ v,\ G). \tag{14}$$

Also by alphabetic changes of bound variable in (12):

$$(\exists G^{1/1})\ .\ G(x) \equiv_x \mathrm{het}^{n\,+\,1}\ (x). \tag{15}$$

This is an empiric justification of the axioms of reducibility, based on the failure of the direct attempt to restore Grelling's antinomy by means of them, and on the fact that the resulting situation as expressed by (14) and (15) not only is intelligible but even is to be expected in the light of Tarski's theorem about truth.[26] If the axioms of reducibility are included in the hierarchy of languages L_1, L_2, L_3, . . ., each at its appropriate place, it therefore seems that the resulting hierarchy of languages will still conform to Tarski's resolution of the semantical antinomies.[27] But this again is only an empiric justification because the actual conformity to Tarski's plan of resolution of the antinomies depends on the unprovability of certain theorems,[28] which must here remain a conjecture.

The principal significance of theorems (14) and (15) is that there must be, among the values of the variables in L_1 of r-type 1/1, propositional functions such that no coextensive function is expressible by a propositional form in L_1, but only in some language arbitrarily far along in the hierarchy L_1, L_2, L_3, ...

Notes

* This research has been supported by the National Science Foundation, grant no. GP-43517.
1 Russell's earlier version of the ramified type hierarchy is in [6] and in the Introduction to the first edition of [12]. The later version is in *12 and in (Russell's) Introduction to the Second Edition of [12].
2 Differences among the three versions of ramified type theory are unimportant for the purpose of resolving the antinomies. The version which is here adopted from [1] is close to Russell's earlier version. But by using "levels" in addition to, and

partly in place of, Russell's "orders" and by allowing levels and orders to be cumulative in a sense in which Russell's orders are not, it facilitates comparison both with the simple theory of types and with the hierarchy of languages and meta-languages that enters into Tarski's resolution of the semantical antinomies.

3 It is types in the sense of the simple theory that are called simply *types* in [1]. See footnote 578 on page 349.

The writer takes the opportunity to make a correction to his "Russellian simple type theory" (*Proceedings and addresses of the American Philosophical Association*, vol. 47, pp. 21–33), the need for which was called to his attention by John M. Vickers. In line 21 on p. 26, after the words "may be empty" it is necessary to add "and the domains $\mathfrak{T}$ and $\mathfrak{F}$ must be disjoint." Instead of this it would be possible to correct by changing the words "and otherwise the value of **(a)P** is in $\mathfrak{F}$" in line 15 on p. 27 to "and the value of **(a)P** is in $\mathfrak{F}$ if the value of **P** is in $\mathfrak{F}$ for some value of **a**." This alternative correction may not be without interest on its own account. But it was not the original intention of the paper. Moreover, it is not historically accurate; i.e., it is not anything which might be supposed to have been intended by Russell, even implicitly, or even at a time when he still maintained the notion of proposition.

4 Thus we take propositions as values of the propositional variables, on the ground that this is what is clearly demanded by the background and purpose of Russell's logic, and in spite of what seems to be an explicit denial by Whitehead and Russell in [12], pp. 43–44.

In fact Whitehead and Russell make the claim: "that what we call a 'proposition' (in the sense in which this is distinguished from the phrase expressing it) is not a single entity at all. That is to say, the phrase which expresses a proposition is what we call an 'incomplete' symbol . . ." They seem to be aware that this fragmenting of propositions requires a similar fragmenting of propositional functions. But the contextual definition or definitions that are implicitly promised by the "incomplete symbol" characterization are never fully supplied, and it is in particular not clear how they would explain away the use of bound propositional and functional variables. If some things that are said by Russell in IV and V of his Introduction to the second edition may be taken as an indication of what is intended, it is probable that the contextual definitions would not stand scrutiny.

Many passages in [6] and [12] may be understood as saying or as having the consequence that the values of the propositional variables are sentences. But a coherent semantics of Russell's formalized language can hardly be provided on this basis (notice in particular that, since sentences are also substituted for propositional variables, it would be necessary to take sentences as names of sentences). And since the passages in question seem to involve confusions of use and mention or kindred confusions that may be merely careless, it is not certain that they are to be regarded as precise statements of a semantics.

5 It is intended that additions to the list of primitive constants may be made from time to time, so that Russell's formalized language is an open language rather than a language of fixed vocabulary.

6 This means that we use the definition *10.01 of the existential quantifier rather than to take it as primitive.

The Frege–Russell assertion sign, ⊢, should properly be listed as one of the primitives. But we here follow [1] in taking the mere writing of a wff on a separate line or lines as a sign of assertion (unless the context shows otherwise), and in introducing the sign ⊢ in a different (syntactical) sense.

Historically, it must be confessed, this change of notation is unfortunate. For Frege is right that an asserted sentence has a different meaning from a sentence occurring e.g. as antecedent or consequent of an implication. And the assertion *of* a wff (sentence or propositional form) is of course not the same as the assertion *about* the wff that it is a theorem, or that it is a demonstrable consequence of certain listed wffs.

7 The use of dots as brackets follows a simplified form of the Peano–Russell conventions that is explained in [1]. Briefly a bold dot stands for an omitted pair of brackets with the scope extending from the point at which the dot appears, forward, either to the end of the innermost explicitly written pair of brackets, [ ], within which the dot appears or to the end of the formula if there is no such explicitly written pair of brackets; and if square brackets are omitted without replacement by a dot, the restoration of the brackets is to follow the convention of association to the left and the convention about categories, as these are explained on pp. 74–79, 171.

We also allow that any wf part of a wff may first be enclosed in square brackets (if not already so enclosed) and then these square brackets may be eliminated by replacing the first of the pair by a bold dot in accordance with the same conventions about scope of the omitted brackets that are used in other cases of replacement of brackets by dots. This may often increase the perspicuity of the abbreviated formula when dots are used for brackets.

The foregoing statement of the conventions about the use of dots as brackets is sufficient for our present purpose, and indeed is sufficient in most contexts in which very complicated formulas are not used. For cases of the kind represented by the displayed formulas on p. 80 of [1], the convention which is there intended requires some restatement for accuracy (as was pointed out by Philip Tartaglia in 1963); perhaps the shortest way of putting the required amendment is to provide that the convention about higher and lower categories that is introduced on page 79 shall be used only when none of the connectives (with which the affected bracket-pairs belong) is written with a bold dot after it.

8 The conjunction of **P** and **Q** is to be written simply as [**PQ**], or when the brackets are omitted, as **PQ**. If in the expression of a conjunction a bold dot appears between **P** and **Q**, this dot represents an omitted pair of brackets in accordance with the conventions explained in note 7 – not excluding, however, the case described in the second paragraph of note 7, in which the dot, by representing a fictitious pair of brackets, serves only the purpose of perspicuity.

9 Some of the oddities arise from the fact that Russell does not use a different alphabet of variables for each r-type but in effect has only one alphabet, thus leaving the r-types (or rather the relative r-types) to be determined from the wff itself in which the variables appear. And this seems to be due in turn to Russell's intention (see §II of [6]) that, in an asserted wff, although each bound variable must be restricted to a particular r-type as its range, the free variables may have a wider range.

10 Readers not previously familiar with ramified type theory should notice that the significance of the notion of order, which we have not yet explained, first becomes clear in the restrictions that are attached to these schemata.

11 The proof is similar to that in Henkin [5].

12 That is, places at which substitutivity of material equivalence holds.

13 For want of a better we adopt this name from "natural inference" logic, notwithstanding its inappropriateness in the present context.

14 This first appears in [4], where it is credited to Grelling.

15 An adjective is called autological if it has the property which it expresses, and otherwise it is called heterological. For example, if the language is English, the adjectives "polysyllabic" and "unequivocal" are autological, while the adjectives

"long" and "unusual" are heterological. Then is the adjective "heterological" autological or heterological?

16 Not even a choice that puts primitive symbols and formulas into different types, or different r-types.

17 In this sentence, those who wish to be very accurate about use-mention distinctions may enclose the constants, 'val^1', 'val^2', 'val^3' and the wff 'val^n (a^i, v^i, $F^{1/n}$)' in Frege's single quotation marks to show that they are mentioned rather than used. But observe that nothing else in the sentence is to be enclosed in single quotation marks. There should be no confusion over the point that, since individual variables are included among the individuals, the individual variable 'a^i' may have an individual variable as value (which latter individual variable is then spoken of as "the variable a^i"). [*Added in proof*: The writer has just noticed that the use of quotation marks that is suggested in the first sentence of this note is itself inaccurate; but the note may nevertheless serve its purpose of clearing up a possible misunderstanding of what is said in the text.]

18 For strict accuracy the letters v and a should be in bold type – i.e., syntactical variables, as in [1]. If we here follow the common informal practice of using object-language variables, it is to avoid obtruding use-mention distinctions where they are not in fact important for understanding of what is being said.

19 We here follow the strong form of the rule of existential generalization as this is stated above, taking **b** to be $F^{1/n}$ and **a** to be $F^{1/m}$.

20 Additional postulates relating the semantical propositional functions, val, to the syntax of L can be expressed only after adding still further primitives enabling us to express the syntax of L. There are indeed some additional things holding that can be expressed without introducing new primitives, for example:

$$\text{val}\,(a,\, v,\, F) \supset .\ \text{val}\,(b,\, v,\, F) \supset .\ a = b \lor (x)F(x) \lor (x) \sim F(x),$$

$$\text{val}\,(a,\, b,\, v,\, F) \supset .\ \text{val}\,(b,\, a,\, v,\, G) \supset .\ F(x, y) \equiv_{xy} G(y, x),$$

$$a = b \supset\ \sim \text{val}\,(a,\, b,\, v,\, F).$$

But our present purpose does not make it necessary to explore the question of additional postulates which may therefore be wanted.

21 The terminology, functional calculus of first order, second order, etc., is appropriate primarily to simple type theory and represents a different meaning of the word "order" from that which is needed in connection with ramified type theory. The hierarchy of languages L_1, L_2, L_3, . . . is in fact quite different from the hierarchy of functional calculi of first, second, third, . . . orders. And except in such phrases as "functional calculus of second order" we shall always use the word "order" in the sense (essentially Russell's) which was defined at the beginning of this paper. (Footnote 578 of [1] overlooks that the notion of "level," though useful, cannot wholly supersede Russell's notion of "order" in treating ramified type theory.)

22 For example, in his explanation regarding the Epimenides antinomy in §I of [6] or p. 62 of [12], when Russell says that the notion of "all propositions" is illegitimate and that a statement about all propositions of some order must be itself of higher order, we may take a "statement" or a "proposition" (the two words seem to be synonymous) to be "in the sense in which this is distinguished from the phrase expressing it," or we may take it to be a declarative sentence *considered together with* its meaning. But for a sentence, either as a finite sequence of sounds (or of printed or written characters) or as a class or class

concept of such, organized by a particular syntax but not yet associated with a meaning, there is in the nature of the case nothing illegitimate in the totality of all sentences. And in setting up the language L we have in fact taken the symbols, sentences, and propositional forms of L as being, all of them, members of a single r-type.

23 We treat the system of the first edition of [12], with ramified type theory and axioms of reducibility. The modification which is suggested in Russell's Introduction to the second edition (and is based on ideas of Wittgenstein), to replace the axioms of reducibility by axioms of extensionality, one in each type, is unsatisfactory – because the resulting system is not adequate for classical mathematics (as Russell admits, see pp. xiv, xxix, xliv–xlv, and compare Weyl [10]), and because if Russell's attempt is successful, in Appendix C of the second edition of [12], to be rid of intensional contexts, he thereby abandons some of his own important contributions to logic. As regards this last, we have already seen how a strictly extensional approach prejudices the resolution of the semantical antinomies by ramified type theory; and Russell's theory of descriptions loses its point as a solution of the puzzle about King George IV and the author of *Waverley* if there are no intensional contexts.

24 Only the cases $m = 1, 2$ are used in [6] and [12], but the case of greater m is referred to briefly.

25 That the restoration of impredicative definition is confined to extensional contexts might be defended on the ground that there are antinomies which are about intensional matters but are not semantical in character. For example, Bouleus believes that he is sometimes mistaken, but (with the possible exception of some that are logically implied by this one together with his true beliefs) all his other beliefs are in fact true. Is it then true that Bouleus is sometimes mistaken?

This is implicitly a correction of the first paragraph of §59 of [1], as it is only by confining attention to extensional logic that it can be said that ramified type theory with axioms of reducibility has no interest as an intermediate position between pure ramified type theory and simple type theory.

26 In fact consider the case that the superscript $n + 1$ in (14) and (15) is 2, and let (14′) and (15′) be the sentences obtained from (14) and (15) respectively by replacing 'het$^2(x)$' by 'tr$^2(x)$'. Suppose further that the languages L_1 and L_2 are consistent and that 'tr$^2(x)$', as a propositional form of L_2, is satisfied by those and only those values of 'x' which are true sentences of L_1. Then (15′) must hold if the range of the singulary functional variables of L_1 is to be extensionally complete; and (14′) can be taken as an expression of Tarski's theorem.

And that what holds of truth – i.e., expressibility only in a meta-language – must be expected to hold also of other semantical notions, including heterologicality, is already implicit in the description of Tarski's resolution of the semantical antinomies as we gave it above.

27 Weyl's use [10] of Grelling's antinomy to support what is in effect ramified type theory without axioms of reducibility is therefore not in itself compelling. That is, it is not demonstrated that a system which allows impredicative definition must therefore be inconsistent. But if one agrees with Weyl [10], [11] that impredicative definition is intrinsically unsound, a *circulus vitiosus* whether or not it leads to antinomy, then indeed ramified type theory without axioms of reducibility is what results; and while first-order arithmetic can be obtained by adjoining either Peano's postulates for the natural numbers (under some appropriate choice of r-types for the variables and constants occurring in them) or an

axiom of infinity strong enough to yield this, it will still be impossible to obtain more than a weakened form of the classical theory of real numbers.

28 For example sat$^2(a, x, v)$, defined as $(\exists F^{1/1})$. val$^2(a, v, F)$. $F(x)$, is supposed to express the semantical satisfaction relation only as it applies to L_1; if theorems could be proved by which it could be regarded as expressing this relation also for L_2, the Tarski plan for avoiding antinomy would be violated. Something may depend on whether postulates (4) and (11) are assumed only in the weak form which was given to them above or whether they are strengthened by putting $\equiv$ in place of $\supset$. It is conjectured that L remains consistent after adjoining both the axioms of reducibility and the strong form of postulates (4) and (11). But this conjecture, if correct, deserves support by a relative consistency proof, relative perhaps to the consistency of the simple theory of types or of standard axiomatic set theory.

References

[1] Alonzo Church, *Introduction to mathematical logic*, Volume 1, Princeton, 1956.

[2] Irving M. Copi, *The theory of logical types*, London, 1971.

[3] Abraham A. Fraenkel and Yehoshua Bar-Hillel, *Foundations of set theory*, Amsterdam, 1958; second edition 1973, by Fraenkel, Bar-Hillel, and Azriel Levy with collaboration of Dirk van Dalen.

[4] Kurt Grelling and Leonard Nelson, "Bemerkungen zu den Paradoxieen von Russell und Burali-Forti," *Abhandlungen der Fries'schen Schule*, n.s. vol. 2 (1907–08), pp. 301–324.

[5] Leon Henkin, "Banishing the rule of substitution for functional variables," *Journal of Symbolic Logic*, vol. 18 (1953), pp. 201–208.

[6] Bertrand Russell, "Mathematical logic as based on the theory of types," *American Journal of Mathematics*, vol. 30 (1908), pp. 222–262.

[7] Alfred Tarski, "Pojęcie prawdy w językach nauk dedukcyjnych," *Travaux de la Société des Sciences et des Lettres de Varsovie, Classe III*, no. 34, Warsaw, 1933.

[8] —— "Der Wahrheitsbegriff in den formalisierten Sprachen" (German translation of [7] with added Nachwort), *Studia Philosophica*, vol. 1 (1936), pp. 261–405.

[9] —— "The concept of truth in formalized languages" (English translation of [8]), *Logic, Semantics, Metamathematics, Papers from 1923 to 1938, by Alfred Tarski*, London, 1956, pp. 152–278.

[10] Hermann Weyl, "Das Kontinuum," *Kritische Untersuchungen über die Grundlagen der Analysis*, Leipzig, 1918.

[11] —— "Der circulus vitiosus in der heutigen Begründung der Analysis," *Jahresbericht der Deutschen Mathematiker-Vereinigung*, vol. 28 (1919), pp. 85–92.

[12] A. N. Whitehead and Bertrand Russell, *Principia Mathematica* (three volumes), Cambridge, 1910–1913; second edition, Cambridge, 1925–1927.

9

Russell's Mathematical Logic

Kurt Gödel*

Mathematical logic, which is nothing else but a precise and complete formulation of formal logic, has two quite different aspects. On the one hand, it is a section of Mathematics treating of classes, relations, combinations of symbols, etc., instead of numbers, functions, geometric figures, etc. On the other hand, it is a science prior to all others, which contains the ideas and principles underlying all sciences. It was in this second sense that Mathematical Logic was first conceived by Leibniz in his *Characteristica universalis*, of which it would have formed a central part. But it was almost two centuries after his death before his idea of a logical calculus really sufficient for the kind of reasoning occurring in the exact sciences was put into effect (in some form at least, if not the one Leibniz had in mind) by Frege and Peano.[1] Frege was chiefly interested in the analysis of thought and used his calculus in the first place for deriving arithmetic from pure logic. Peano, on the other hand, was more interested in its applications within mathematics and created an elegant and flexible symbolism, which permits expressing even the most complicated mathematical theorems in a perfectly precise and often very concise manner by single formulas.

It was in this line of thought of Frege and Peano that Russell's work set in. Frege, in consequence of his painstaking analysis of the proofs, had not gotten beyond the most elementary properties of the series of integers, while Peano had accomplished a big collection of mathematical theorems expressed in the new symbolism, but without proofs. It was only in *Principia Mathematica* that full use was made of the new method for actually deriving large parts of mathematics from a very few logical concepts and axioms. In addition, the young science was enriched by a new instrument, the abstract theory of relations. The calculus of relations had been developed before by Peirce and Schröder, but only with certain restrictions and in too close analogy with the algebra of numbers. In *Principia* not only Cantor's set theory but also ordinary arithmetic and the theory of measurement are treated from this abstract relational stand-point.

It is to be regretted that this first comprehensive and thoroughgoing presentation of a mathematical logic and the derivation of Mathematics from it is so greatly lacking in formal precision in the foundations (contained in *1–*21 of *Principia*), that it presents in this respect a considerable step backwards as compared with Frege. What is missing, above all, is a precise statement of the syntax of the formalism. Syntactical considerations are omitted even in cases where they are necessary for the cogency of the proofs, in particular in connection with the "incomplete symbols." These are introduced not by explicit definitions, but by rules describing how sentences containing them are to be translated into sentences not containing them. In order to be sure, however, that (or for what expressions) this translation is possible and uniquely determined and that (or to what extent) the rules of inference apply also to the new kind of expressions, it is necessary to have a survey of all possible expressions, and this can be furnished only by syntactical considerations. The matter is especially doubtful for the rule of substitution and of replacing defined symbols by their *definiens*. If this latter rule is applied to expressions containing other defined symbols it requires that the order of elimination of these be indifferent. This however is by no means always the case ($\varphi ! \hat{u} = \hat{u} [\varphi ! u]$, e.g., is a counter-example). In *Principia* such eliminations are always carried out by substitutions in the theorems corresponding to the definitions, so that it is chiefly the rule of substitution which would have to be proved.

I do not want, however, to go into any more details about either the formalism or the mathematical content of *Principia*,[2] but want to devote the subsequent portion of this essay to Russell's work concerning the analysis of the concepts and axioms underlying Mathematical Logic. In this field Russell has produced a great number of interesting ideas some of which are presented most clearly (or are contained only) in his earlier writings. I shall therefore frequently refer also to these earlier writings, although their content may partly disagree with Russell's present standpoint.

What strikes one as surprising in this field is Russell's pronouncedly realistic attitude, which manifests itself in many passages of his writings. "Logic is concerned with the real world just as truly as zoology, though with its more abstract and general features," he says, e.g., in his *Introduction to Mathematical Philosophy* (edition of 1920, p. 169). It is true, however, that this attitude has been gradually decreasing in the course of time[3] and also that it always was stronger in theory than in practice. When he started on a concrete problem, the objects to be analyzed (e.g., the classes or propositions) soon for the most part turned into "logical fictions." Though perhaps this need not necessarily mean (according to the sense in which Russell uses this term) that these things do not exist, but only that we have no direct perception of them.

The analogy between mathematics and a natural science is enlarged upon by Russell also in another respect (in one of his earlier writings). He compares the axioms of logic and mathematics with the laws of nature and logical evidence with sense perception, so that the axioms need not necessarily be evident in themselves, but rather their justification lies (exactly as in physics) in the fact that they make it possible for these "sense perceptions" to be deduced; which of course would not exclude that they also have a kind of intrinsic plausibility similar to that in physics. I think that (provided "evidence" is understood in a sufficiently strict sense) this view has been largely justified by subsequent developments, and it is to be expected that it will be still more so in the future. It has turned out that (under the assumption that modern mathematics is consistent) the solution of certain arithmetical problems requires the use of assumptions essentially transcending arithmetic, i.e., the domain of the kind of elementary indisputable evidence that may be most fittingly compared with sense perception. Furthermore it seems likely that for deciding certain questions of abstract set theory, and even for certain related questions of the theory of real numbers, new axioms based on some hitherto unknown idea will be necessary. Perhaps also the apparently insurmountable difficulties which some other mathematical problems have been presenting for many years are due to the fact that the necessary axioms have not yet been found. Of course, under these circumstances mathematics may lose a good deal of its "absolute certainty"; but, under the influence of the modern criticism of the foundations, this has already happened to a large extent. There is some resemblance between this conception of Russell and Hilbert's "supplementing the data of mathematical intuition" by such axioms as, e.g., the law of excluded middle which are not given by intuition according to Hilbert's view; the borderline however between data and assumptions would seem to lie in different places according to whether we follow Hilbert or Russell.

An interesting example of Russell's analysis of the fundamental logical concepts is his treatment of the definite article "the." The problem is: what do the so-called descriptive phrases (i.e., phrases as, e.g., "the author of *Waverley*" or "the king of England") denote or signify[4] and what is the meaning of sentences in which they occur? The apparently obvious answer that, e.g., "the author of *Waverley*" signifies Walter Scott, leads to unexpected difficulties. For, if we admit the further apparently obvious axiom, that the signification of a composite expression, containing constituents which have themselves a signification, depends only on the signification of these constituents (not on the manner in which this signification is expressed), then it follows that the sentence "Scott is the author of *Waverley*" signifies the same thing as "Scott is Scott"; and this again leads almost inevitably to the conclusion that all true sentences have the same signification (as well as all false ones).[5] Frege actually drew this conclusion; and he meant it in an almost metaphysical sense, reminding one somewhat of the Eleatic doctrine of the "One." "The True" – according to Frege's view – is analyzed by us in different ways in different propositions; "the True" being the name he uses for the common signification of all true propositions.[6]

Now according to Russell, what corresponds to sentences in the outer world is facts. However, he avoids the term "signify" or "denote" and uses "indicate" instead (in his earlier papers he uses "express" or "being a symbol for"), because he holds that the relation between a sentence and a fact is quite different from that of a name to the thing named. Furthermore, he uses "denote" (instead of "signify") for the relation between things and names, so that "denote" and "indicate" together would correspond to Frege's "*bedeuten*." So, according to Russell's terminology and view, true sentences "indicate" facts and, correspondingly, false ones indicate nothing.[7] Hence Frege's theory would in a sense apply to false sentences, since they all indicate the same thing, namely nothing. But different true sentences may indicate many different things. Therefore this view concerning sentences makes it necessary either to drop the above mentioned principle about the signification (i.e., in Russell's terminology the corresponding one about the denotation and indication) of composite expressions or to deny that a descriptive phrase denotes the object described. Russell did the latter[8] by taking the viewpoint that a descriptive phrase denotes nothing at all but has meaning only in context; for example, the sentence "the author of *Waverley* is Scottish," is defined to mean: "There exists exactly one entity who wrote *Waverley* and whoever wrote *Waverley* is Scottish." This means that a sentence involving the phrase "the author of *Waverley*" does not (strictly speaking) assert anything about Scott (since it contains no constituent denoting Scott), but is only a roundabout way of asserting something about the concepts occurring in the descriptive phrase. Russell adduces chiefly two arguments in favor of this view, namely (1) that a descriptive phrase may be meaningfully employed even if the object described does not exist (e.g., in the sentence: "The present king of France does not exist"). (2) That one may very well understand a sentence containing a descriptive phrase without being acquainted with the object described; whereas it seems impossible to understand a sentence without being acquainted with the objects about which something is being asserted. The fact that Russell does not consider this whole question of the interpretation of descriptions as a matter of mere linguistic conventions, but rather as a question of right and wrong, is another example of his realistic attitude, unless perhaps he was aiming at a merely psychological investigation of the actual processes of thought. As to the question in the logical sense, I cannot help feeling that the problem raised by Frege's puzzling conclusion has only been evaded by Russell's theory of descriptions and that there is something behind it which is not yet completely understood.

There seems to be one purely formal respect in which one may give preference to Russell's theory of descriptions. By defining the meaning of sentences involving descriptions in the above manner, he avoids in his logical system any axioms about the particle "the," i.e., the analyticity of the theorems about "the" is made explicit; they can be shown to follow from the explicit definition of the meaning of sentences involving "the." Frege, on the contrary, has to assume an axiom about "the," which of course is also analytic, but only in the implicit sense that it follows from the meaning of the undefined terms. Closer examination, however, shows that this advantage of Russell's theory over Frege's subsists only as long as one interprets definitions as mere typographical abbreviations, not as introducing names for objects described by the definitions, a feature which is common to Frege and Russell.

I pass now to the most important of Russell's investigations in the field of the analysis of the concepts of formal logic, namely those concerning the logical paradoxes and their solution. By analyzing the paradoxes to which Cantor's set theory had led, he freed them from all mathematical technicalities, thus bringing to light the amazing fact that our logical intuitions (i.e., intuitions concerning such notions as: truth, concept, being, class, etc.) are self-contradictory. He then investigated where and how these common-sense assumptions of logic are to be corrected and came to the conclusion that the erroneous axiom consists in assuming that for every propositional function there exists the class of objects satisfying it, or that every propositional function exists "as a separate entity";[9] by which is meant something separable from the argument (the idea being that propositional functions are abstracted from propositions which are primarily given) and also something distinct from the combination of symbols expressing the propositional function; it is then what one may call the notion or concept defined by it.[10] The existence of this concept already suffices for the paradoxes in their "intensional" form, where the concept of "not applying to itself" takes the place of Russell's paradoxical class.

Rejecting the existence of a class or concept in general, it remains to determine under what further hypotheses (concerning the propositional function) these entities do exist. Russell pointed out (*loc. cit.*, note 9) two possible directions in which one may look for such a criterion, which he called the zig-zag theory and the theory of limitation of size, respectively, and which might perhaps more significantly be called the intensional and the extensional theory. The second one would make the existence of a class or concept depend on the extension of the propositional function (requiring that it be not too big), the first one on its content or meaning (requiring a certain kind of "simplicity," the precise formulation of which would be the problem).

The most characteristic feature of the second (as opposed to the first) would consist in the non-existence of the universal class or (in the intensional interpretation) of the notion of "something" in an unrestricted sense. Axiomatic set theory as later developed by Zermelo and others can be considered as an elaboration of this idea as far as classes are concerned.[11] In particular the phrase "not too big" can be specified (as was shown by J. v. Neumann)[12] to mean: not equivalent with the universe of all things, or, to be more exact, a propositional function can be assumed to determine a class when and only when there exists no relation (in intension, i.e., a propositional function with two variables) which associates in a one-to-one manner with each object, an object satisfying the propositional function and vice versa. This criterion, however, does not appear as the basis of the theory but as a consequence of the axioms and inversely can replace two of the axioms (the axiom of replacement and that of choice).

For the second of Russell's suggestions too, i.e., for the zig-zag theory, there has recently been set up a logical system which shares some essential features with this scheme, namely Quine's system.[13] It is, moreover, not unlikely that there are other interesting possibilities along these lines.

Russell's own subsequent work concerning the solution of the paradoxes did not go in either of the two aforementioned directions pointed out by himself, but was largely based on a more radical idea, the "no-class theory," according to which classes or concepts *never* exist as real objects, and sentences containing these terms are meaningful only to such an extent as they can be interpreted as a *façon de parler*, a manner of speaking about other things (cf. p. [123]). Since in *Principia* and elsewhere, however, he formulated certain principles discovered in the course of the development of this theory as general logical principles without mentioning any longer their dependence on the no-class theory, I am going to treat of these principles first.

I mean in particular the vicious circle principle, which forbids a certain kind of "circularity" which is made responsible for the paradoxes. The fallacy in these, so it is contended, consists in the circumstance that one defines (or tacitly assumes) totalities, whose existence would entail the existence of certain new elements of the same totality, namely elements definable only in terms of the whole totality. This led to the formulation of a principle which says that "no totality can contain members definable only in terms of this totality, or members involving or presupposing this totality" (vicious circle principle). In order to make this principle applicable to the intensional paradoxes, still another principle had to be assumed, namely that "every propositional function presupposes the totality of its values" and therefore evidently also the totality of its possible arguments.[14] (Otherwise the concept of "not applying to itself" would presuppose no totality – since it involves no quantifications[15] – and the vicious circle principle would not prevent its application to itself.) A corresponding vicious circle principle for propositional functions which says that nothing defined in terms of a propositional function can be a possible argument of this function is then a consequence.[16] The logical system to which one is led on the basis of these principles is the theory of orders in the form adopted, e.g., in the first edition of *Principia*, according to which a propositional function which either contains quantifications referring to propositional functions of order n or can be meaningfully asserted of propositional functions of order n is at least of order $n + 1$, and the range of significance of a propositional function as well as the range of a quantifier must always be confined to a definite order.

In the second edition of *Principia*, however, it is stated in the Introduction (pp. XI and XII) that "in a limited sense" also functions of a higher order than the predicate itself (therefore also functions defined in terms of the predicate as, e.g., in $p'\kappa \, \varepsilon \, \kappa$) can appear as arguments of a predicate of functions; and in Appendix B such things occur constantly. This means that the vicious circle principle for propositional functions is virtually dropped. This change is connected with the new axiom that functions can occur in propositions only "through their values," i.e., extensionally, which has the consequence that any propositional function can take as an argument any function of appropriate type, whose extension is defined (no matter what order of quantifiers is used in the definition of this extension). There is no doubt that these things are quite unobjectionable even from the constructive standpoint (see p. [120]), provided that quantifiers are always restricted to definite orders. The paradoxes are avoided by the theory of simple types,[17] which in *Principia* is combined with the theory of orders (giving as a result the "ramified hierarchy") but is entirely independent of it and has nothing to do with the vicious circle principle (cf. p. [127]).

Now as to the vicious circle principle proper, as formulated on p. [118], it is first to be remarked that, corresponding to the phrases "definable only in terms of," "involving," and "presupposing," we have really three different principles, the second and third being much more plausible than the first. It is the first form which is of particular interest, because only this one makes impredicative definitions[18] impossible and thereby destroys the derivation of mathematics from logic, effected by Dedekind and Frege, and a good deal of modern mathematics itself. It is demonstrable that the formalism of classical mathematics does not satisfy the vicious circle principle in its first form, since the axioms imply the existence of real numbers definable in this formalism only by reference to all real numbers. Since classical mathematics can be built up on the basis of *Principia* (including the axiom of reducibility), it follows that even *Principia* (in the first edition) does not satisfy the vicious circle principle in the first form, if "definable" means "definable within the system" and no methods of defining outside the system (or outside other systems of classical mathematics) are known except such as involve still more comprehensive totalities than those occurring in the systems.

I would consider this rather as a proof that the vicious circle principle is false than that classical mathematics is false, and this is indeed plausible also on its own account. For, first of all one may, on good grounds, deny that reference to a totality necessarily implies reference to all single elements of it or, in other words, that "all" means the same as an infinite logical conjunction. One may, e.g., follow Langford's and Carnap's[19] suggestion to interpret "all" as meaning analyticity or necessity or demonstrability. There are difficulties in this view; but there is no doubt that in this way the circularity of impredicative definitions disappears.

Secondly, however, even if "all" means an infinite conjunction, it seems that the vicious circle principle in its first form applies only if the entities involved are constructed by ourselves. In this case there must clearly exist a definition (namely the description of the construction) which does not refer to a totality to which the object defined belongs, because the construction of a thing can certainly not be based on a totality of things to which the thing to be constructed itself belongs. If, however, it is a question of objects that exist independently of our constructions, there is nothing in the least absurd in the existence of totalities containing members, which can be described (i.e., uniquely characterized)[20] only by reference to this totality.[21] Such a state of affairs would not even contradict the second form of the vicious circle principle, since one cannot say that an object described by reference to a totality "involves" this totality, although the description itself does; nor would it contradict the third form, if "presuppose" means "presuppose for the existence" not "for the knowability."

So it seems that the vicious circle principle in its first form applies only if one takes the constructivistic (or nominalistic) standpoint[22] toward the objects of logic and mathematics, in particular toward propositions, classes and notions, e.g., if one understands by a notion a symbol together with a rule for translating sentences containing the symbol into such sentences as do not contain it, so that a separate object denoted by the symbol appears as a mere fiction.[23]

Classes and concepts may, however, also be conceived as real objects, namely classes as "pluralities of things" or as structures consisting of a plurality of things and concepts as the properties and relations of things existing independently of our definitions and constructions.

It seems to me that the assumption of such objects is quite as legitimate as the assumption of physical bodies and there is quite as much reason to believe in their existence. They are in the same sense necessary to obtain a satisfactory system of mathematics as physical bodies are necessary for a satisfactory theory of our sense perceptions and in both cases it is impossible to interpret the propositions one wants to assert about these entities as propositions about the "data," i.e., in the latter case the actually occurring sense perceptions. Russell himself concludes in the last chapter of his book on *Meaning and Truth*, though "with hesitation," that there exist "universals," but apparently he wants to confine this statement to concepts of sense perceptions, which does not help the logician. I shall use the term "concept" in the sequel exclusively in this objective sense. One formal difference between the two conceptions of notions would be that any two different definitions of the form $\alpha\,(x) = \varphi\,(x)$ can be assumed to define two different notions α in the constructivistic sense. (In particular this would be the case for the nominalistic interpretation of the term "notion" suggested above, since two such definitions give different rules of translation for propositions containing α.) For concepts, on the contrary, this is by no means the case, since the same thing may be described in different ways. It might even be that the axiom of extensionality[24] or at least something near to it holds for concepts. The difference may be illustrated by the following definition of the number two: "Two is the notion under which fall all pairs and nothing else." There is certainly more than one notion in the constructivistic sense satisfying this condition, but there might be one common "form" or "nature" of all pairs.

Since the vicious circle principle, in its first form does apply to constructed entities, impredicative definitions and the totality of all notions or classes or propositions are inadmissible in constructivistic logic. What an impredicative definition would require is to construct a notion by a combination of a set of notions to which the notion to be formed itself belongs. Hence if one tries to effect a retranslation of a sentence containing a symbol for such an impredicatively defined notion it turns out that what one obtains will again contain a symbol for the notion in question.[25] At least this is so if "all" means an infinite conjunction; but Carnap's and Langford's idea (mentioned on p. [120]) would not help in this connection, because "demonstrability," if introduced in a manner compatible with the constructivistic standpoint towards notions, would have to be split into a hierarchy of orders, which would prevent one from obtaining the desired results.[26] As Chwistek has shown,[27] it is even possible under certain assumptions admissible within constructivistic logic to derive an actual contradiction from the unrestricted admission of impredicative definitions. To be more specific, he has shown that the system of simple types becomes contradictory if one adds the "axiom of intensionality" which says (roughly speaking) that to different definitions belong different notions. This axiom, however, as has just been pointed out, can be assumed to hold for notions in the constructivistic sense.

Speaking of concepts, the aspect of the question is changed completely. Since concepts are supposed to exist objectively, there seems to be objection neither to speaking of all of them (cf. p. [124]) nor to describing some of them by reference to all (or at least all of a given type). But, one may ask, isn't this view refutable also for concepts because it leads to the "absurdity" that there will exist properties φ such that $\varphi\,(a)$ consists in a certain state of affairs involving all properties (including φ itself and properties defined in terms of φ), which would mean that the vicious circle

principle does not hold even in its second form for concepts or propositions? There is no doubt that the totality of all properties (or of all those of
a given type) does lead to situations of this kind, but I don't think they
contain any absurdity.[28] It is true that such properties φ (or such propositions φ (*a*)) will have to contain themselves as constituents of their content
(or of their meaning), and in fact in many ways, because of the properties
defined in terms of φ; but this only makes it impossible to construct their
meaning (i.e., explain it as an assertion about sense perceptions or any other
non-conceptual entities), which is no objection for one who takes the
realistic standpoint. Nor is it self-contradictory that a proper part should
be identical (not merely equal) to the whole, as is seen in the case of
structures in the abstract sense. The structure of the series of integers,
e.g., contains itself as a proper part and it is easily seen that there exist
also structures containing infinitely many different parts, each containing
the whole structure as a part. In addition there exist, even within the domain
of constructivistic logic, certain approximations to this self-reflexivity of
impredicative properties, namely propositions which contain as parts of
their meaning not themselves but their own formal demonstrability.[29]
Now formal demonstrability of a proposition (in case the axioms and rules
of inference are correct) implies this proposition and in many cases is
equivalent to it. Furthermore, there doubtlessly exist sentences referring
to a totality of sentences to which they themselves belong as, e.g., the
sentence: "Every sentence (of a given language) contains at least one
relation word."

Of course this view concerning the impredicative properties makes it
necessary to look for another solution of the paradoxes, according to
which the fallacy (i.e., the underlying erroneous axiom) does not consist
in the assumption of certain self-reflexivities of the primitive terms but in
other assumptions about these. Such a solution may be found for the
present in the simple theory of types and in the future perhaps in the
development of the ideas sketched on pp. [117f.] and [129]. Of course, all
this refers only to concepts. As to notions in the constructivistic sense there
is no doubt that the paradoxes are due to a vicious circle. It is not surprising that the paradoxes should have different solutions for different interpretations of the terms occurring.

As to classes in the sense of pluralities or totalities it would seem that
they are likewise not created but merely described by their definitions and
that therefore the vicious circle principle in the first form does not apply. I
even think there exist interpretations of the term "class" (namely as a
certain kind of structure), where it does not apply in the second form
either.[30] But for the development of all contemporary mathematics one
may even assume that it does apply in the second form, which for classes as
mere pluralities is, indeed, a very plausible assumption. One is then led to
something like Zermelo's axiom system for set theory, i.e., the sets are split

up into "levels' in such a manner that only sets of lower levels can be elements of sets of higher levels (i.e., $x \ \varepsilon \ y$ is always false if x belongs to a higher level than y). There is no reason for classes in this sense to exclude mixtures of levels in one set and transfinite levels. The place of the axiom of reducibility is now taken by the axiom of classes (Zermelo's *Aussonderungsaxiom*) which says that for each level there exists for an arbitrary propositional function $\varphi(x)$ the set of those x of this level for which $\varphi(x)$ is true, and this seems to be implied by the concept of classes as pluralities.

Russell adduces two reasons against the extensional view of classes, namely the existence of (1) the null class, which cannot very well be a collection, and (2) the unit classes, which would have to be identical with their single elements. But it seems to me that these arguments could, if anything, at most prove that the null class and the unit classes (as distinct from their only element) are fictions (introduced to simplify the calculus like the points at infinity in geometry), not that all classes are fictions.

But in Russell the paradoxes had produced a pronounced tendency to build up logic as far as possible without the assumption of the objective existence of such entities as classes and concepts. This led to the formulation of the aforementioned "no class theory," according to which classes and concepts were to be introduced as a *façon de parler*. But propositions, too, (in particular those involving quantifications)[31] were later on largely included in this scheme, which is but a logical consequence of this standpoint, since e.g., universal propositions as objectively existing entities evidently belong to the same category of idealistic objects as classes and concepts and lead to the same kind of paradoxes, if admitted without restrictions. As regards classes this program was actually carried out; i.e., the rules for translating sentences containing class names or the term "class" into such as do not contain them were stated explicitly; and the basis of the theory, i.e., the domain of sentences into which one has to translate is clear, so that classes can be dispensed with (within the system *Principia*), but only if one assumes the existence of a concept whenever one wants to construct a class. When it comes to concepts and the interpretation of sentences containing this or some synonymous term, the state of affairs is by no means as clear. First of all, some of them (the primitive predicates and relations such as "red" or "colder") must apparently be considered as real objects;[32] the rest of them (in particular according to the second edition of *Principia*, all notions of a type higher than the first and therewith all logically interesting ones) appear as something constructed (i.e., as something not belonging to the "inventory" of the world); but neither the basic domain of propositions in terms of which finally everything is to be interpreted, nor the method of interpretation is as clear as in the case of classes (see below).

This whole scheme of the no-class theory is of great interest as one of the few examples, carried out in detail, of the tendency to eliminate assumptions about the existence of objects outside the "data" and to replace them by constructions on the basis of these data.[33] The result has been in this case essentially negative; i.e., the classes and concepts introduced in this way do not have all the properties required for their use in mathematics, unless one either introduces special axioms about the data (e.g., the axiom of reducibility), which in essence already mean the existence in the data of the kind of objects to be constructed, or makes the fiction that one can form propositions of infinite (and even non-denumerable) length,[34] i.e., operate with truth-functions of infinitely many arguments, regardless of whether or not one can construct them. But what else is such an infinite truth-function but a special kind of an infinite extension (or structure) and even a more complicated one than a class, endowed in addition with a hypothetical meaning, which can be understood only by an infinite mind? All this is only a verification of the view defended above that logic and mathematics (just as physics) are built up on axioms with a real content which cannot be "explained away."

What one can obtain on the basis of the constructivistic attitude is the theory of orders (cf. p. [119]); only now (and this is the strong point of the theory) the restrictions involved do not appear as *ad hoc* hypotheses for avoiding the paradoxes, but as unavoidable consequences of the thesis that classes, concepts, and quantified propositions do not exist as real objects. It is not as if the universe of things were divided into orders and then one were prohibited to speak of all orders; but, on the contrary, it is possible to speak of all existing things; only, classes and concepts are not among them; and if they are introduced as a *façon de parler*, it turns out that this very extension of the symbolism gives rise to the possibility of introducing them in a more comprehensive way, and so on indefinitely. In order to carry out this scheme one must, however, presuppose arithmetic (or something equivalent) which only proves that not even this restricted logic can be built up on nothing.

In the first edition of *Principia*, where it was a question of actually building up logic and mathematics, the constructivistic attitude was, for the most part, abandoned, since the axiom of reducibility for types higher than the first together with the axiom of infinity makes it absolutely necessary that there exist primitive predicates of arbitrarily high types. What is left of the constructive attitude is only: (1) The introduction of classes as a *façon de parler*; (2) the definition of $\sim$, v, ., etc., as applied to propositions containing quantifiers (which incidentally proved its fecundity in a consistency proof for arithmetic); (3) the step-by-step construction of functions of orders higher than 1, which, however, is superfluous owing to the axiom of reducibility; (4) the interpretation of definitions as mere typographical abbreviations, which makes every symbol introduced by definition an incomplete symbol (not one naming an object described by the definition). But the last item is largely an illusion, because, owing to the axiom of reducibility, there always exist real objects in the form of primitive predicates, or combinations of such, corresponding to each defined symbol. Finally, Russell's theory of descriptions is also something belonging to the constructivistic order of ideas.

In the second edition of *Principia* (or to be more exact, in the introduction to it) the constructivistic attitude is resumed again. The axiom of reducibility is dropped and it is stated explicitly that all primitive predicates belong to the lowest type and that the only purpose of variables (and evidently also of constants) of higher orders and types is to make it possible to assert more complicated truth-functions of atomic propositions,[35] which is only another way of saying that the higher types and orders are solely a *façon de parler*. This statement at the same time informs us of what kind of propositions the basis of the theory is to consist, namely of truth-functions of atomic propositions.

This, however, is without difficulty only if the number of individuals and primitive predicates is finite. For the opposite case (which is chiefly of interest for the purpose of deriving mathematics) Ramsey (*loc. cit.*) took the course of considering our inability to form propositions of infinite length as a "mere accident," to be neglected by the logician. This of course solves (or rather cuts through) the difficulties; but it is to be noted that, if one disregards the difference between finite and infinite in this respect, there exists a simpler and at the same time more far reaching interpretation of set theory (and therewith of mathematics). Namely, in case of a finite number of individuals, Russell's *aperçu* that propositions about classes can be interpreted as propositions about their elements becomes literally true, since, e.g., "$x \, \varepsilon \, m$" is equivalent to "$x = a_1 \vee x = a_2 \vee \ldots \vee x = a_k$" where the a_i are the elements of m; and "there exists a class such that . . ." is equivalent to "there exist individuals $x_1, x_2, \ldots x_n$ such that . . . ",[36] provided n is the number of individuals in the world and provided we neglect for the moment the null class which would have to be taken care of by an additional clause. Of course, by an iteration of this procedure one can obtain classes of classes, etc., so that the logical system obtained would resemble the theory of simple types except for the circumstance that mixture of types would be possible. Axiomatic set theory appears, then, as an extrapolation of this scheme for the case of infinitely many individuals or an infinite iteration of the process of forming sets.

Ramsey's viewpoint is, of course, everything but constructivistic, unless one means constructions of an infinite mind. Russell, in the second edition of *Principia*, took a less metaphysical course by confining himself to such truth-functions as can actually be constructed. In this way one is again led to the theory of orders, which, however, appears now in a new light, namely as a method of constructing more and more complicated truth-functions of atomic propositions. But this procedure seems to presuppose arithmetic in some form or other (see next paragraph).

As to the question of how far mathematics can be built up on this basis (without any assumptions about the data – i.e., about the primitive predicates and individuals – except, as far as necessary, the axiom of infinity), it is clear that the theory of real numbers in its present form cannot be obtained.[37] As to the theory of integers, it is contended in the second edition of *Principia* that it can be obtained. The difficulty to be overcome is that in the definition of the integers as "those cardinals which belong to every class containing o and containing $x + 1$ if containing x," the phrase "every class" must refer to a given order. So one obtains integers of different orders, and complete induction can be applied to integers of order n only for properties of order n; whereas it frequently happens that the notion of integer itself occurs in the property to which induction is applied. This notion, however, is of order $n + 1$ for the integers of order n. Now, in Appendix B of the second edition of *Principia*, a proof is offered that the integers of any order higher than 5 are the same as those of order 5, which of course would settle all difficulties. The proof as it stands, however, is certainly not conclusive. In the proof of the main lemma *89.16, which says that every subset α (of arbitrary high order)[38] of an inductive class β of order 3 is itself an inductive class of order 3, induction is applied to a property of β involving α (namely $\alpha - \beta \neq \Lambda$, which, however, should read $\alpha - \beta \sim \varepsilon$ Induct$_2$ because (3) is evidently false). This property, however, is of an order > 3 if α is of an order > 3. So the question whether (or to what extent) the theory of integers can be obtained on the basis of the ramified hierarchy must be considered as unsolved at the present time. It is to be noted, however, that, even in case this question should have a positive answer, this would be of no value for the problem whether arithmetic follows from logic, if propositional functions of order n are defined (as in the second edition of *Principia*) to be certain finite (though arbitrarily complex) combinations (of quantifiers, propositional connectives, etc.), because then the notion of finiteness has to be presupposed, which fact is concealed only by taking such complicated notions as "propositional function of order n" in an unanalyzed form as primitive terms of the formalism and giving their definition only in ordinary language. The reply may perhaps be offered that in *Principia* the notion of a propositional function of order n is neither taken as primitive nor defined in terms of the notion of a finite combination, but rather quantifiers referring to propositional functions of order n (which is all one needs) are defined as certain infinite conjunctions and disjunctions. But then one must ask: Why doesn't one define the integers by the infinite disjunction: $x = 0 \vee x = 0 + 1 \vee x = 0 + 1 + 1 \vee \ldots$. *ad infinitum*, saving in this way all the trouble connected with the notion of inductiveness? This whole objection would not apply if one understands by a propositional function of order n one "obtainable from such truth-functions of atomic propositions as presuppose for their definition no totalities except those of the propositional functions of order < *n* and of individuals"; this notion, however, is somewhat lacking in precision.

The theory of orders proves more fruitful if considered from a purely mathematical standpoint, independently of the philosophical question whether impredicative definitions are admissible. Viewed in this manner, i.e., as a theory built up within the framework of ordinary mathematics, where impredicative definitions are admitted, there is no objection to extending it to arbitrarily high transfinite orders. Even if one rejects impredicative definitions, there would, I think, be no objection to extend it to such transfinite ordinals as can be constructed within the framework of finite orders. The theory in itself seems to demand such an extension since it leads automatically to the consideration of functions in whose definition one refers to all functions of finite orders, and these would be functions of order ω. Admitting transfinite orders, an axiom of reducibility can be proved. This, however, offers no help to the original purpose of the theory, because the ordinal α – such that every propositional function is extensionally equivalent to a function of order α – is so great that it presupposes impredicative totalities. Nevertheless, so much can be accomplished in this way, that all impredicativities are reduced to one special kind, namely the existence of certain large ordinal numbers (or, well ordered sets) and the validity of recursive reasoning for them. In particular, the existence of a well ordered set, of order type ω_1 already suffices for the theory of real numbers. In addition this transfinite theorem of reducibility permits the proof of the consistency of the Axiom of Choice, of Cantor's Continuum-Hypothesis and even of the generalized Continuum-Hypothesis (which says that there exists no cardinal number between the power of any arbitrary set and the power of the set of its subsets) with the axioms of set theory as well as of *Principia*.

I now come in somewhat more detail to the theory of simple types which appears in *Principia* as combined with the theory of orders; the former is, however (as remarked above), quite independent of the latter, since mixed types evidently do not contradict the vicious circle principle in any way. Accordingly, Russell also based the theory of simple types on entirely different reasons. The reason adduced (in addition to its "consonance with common sense") is very similar to Frege's, who, in his system, already had assumed the theory of simple types for functions, but failed to avoid the paradoxes because he operated with classes (or rather functions in extension) without any restriction. This reason is that (owing to the variable it contains) a propositional function is something ambiguous (or, as Frege says, something unsaturated, wanting supplementation) and therefore can occur in a meaningful proposition only in such a way that this ambiguity is eliminated (e.g., by substituting a constant for the variable or applying quantification to it). The consequences are that a function cannot replace an individual in a proposition, because the latter has no ambiguity to be removed, and that functions with different kinds of arguments (i.e., different ambiguities) cannot replace each other; which is the essence of the theory of simple types. Taking a more nominalistic viewpoint (such as suggested in the second edition of *Principia* and in *Meaning and Truth*) one would have to replace "proposition" by "sentence" in the foregoing considerations (with corresponding additional changes). But in both cases, this argument clearly belongs to the order of ideas of the "no class" theory, since it considers the notions (or propositional functions) as something constructed out of propositions or sentences by leaving one or several constituents of them undetermined. Propositional functions in this sense are, so to speak, "fragments" of propositions, which have no meaning in themselves, but only in so far as one can use them for forming propositions by combining several of them, which is possible only if they "fit together," i.e., if they are of appropriate types. But, it should be noted that the theory of simple types (in contradistinction to the vicious circle principle) cannot in a strict sense follow from the constructive standpoint, because one might construct notions and classes in another way, e.g., as indicated on p. [125], where mixtures of types are possible. If on the other hand one considers concepts as real objects, the theory of simple types is not very plausible, since what one would expect to be a concept (such as, e.g., "transitivity" or the number two) would seem to be something behind all its various "realizations" on the different levels and therefore does not exist according to the theory of types. Nevertheless, there seems to be some truth behind this idea of realizations of the same concept on various levels, and one might, therefore, expect the theory of simple types to prove useful or necessary at least as a stepping-stone for a more satisfactory system, a way in which it has already been used by Quine.[39] Also Russell's "typical ambiguity" is a step in this direction. Since, however, it only adds certain simplifying symbolic conventions to the theory of types, it does not *de facto* go beyond this theory.

It should be noted that the theory of types brings in a new idea for the solution of the paradoxes, especially suited to their intensional form. It consists in blaming the paradoxes not on the axiom that every propositional function defines a concept or class, but on the assumption that every concept gives a meaningful proposition, if asserted for any arbitrary object or objects as arguments. The obvious objection that every concept can be extended to all arguments, by defining another one which gives a false proposition whenever the original one was meaningless, can easily be dealt with by pointing out that the concept "meaningfully applicable" need not itself be always meaningfully applicable.

The theory of simple types (in its realistic interpretation) can be considered as a carrying through of this scheme, based, however, on the following additional assumption concerning meaningfulness: "Whenever an object *x* can replace another object *y* in one meaningful proposition, it can do so in every meaningful proposition."[40] This of course has the consequence that the objects are divided into mutually exclusive ranges of significance, each range consisting of those objects which can replace each other; and that therefore each concept is significant only for arguments belonging to one of these ranges, i.e., for an infinitely small portion of all objects. What makes the above principle particularly suspect, however, is that its very assumption makes its formulation as a meaningful proposition impossible,[41] because x and y must then be confined to definite ranges of significance which are either the same or different, and in both cases the statement does not express the principle or even part of it. Another consequence is that the fact that an object x is (or is not) of a given type also cannot be expressed by a meaningful proposition.

It is not impossible that the idea of limited ranges of significance could be carried out without the above restrictive principle. It might even turn out that it is possible to assume every concept to be significant everywhere except for certain "singular points" or "limiting points," so that the paradoxes would appear as something analogous to dividing by zero. Such a system would be most satisfactory in the following respect: our logical intuitions would then remain correct up to certain minor corrections, i.e., they could then be considered to give an essentially correct, only somewhat "blurred," picture of the real state of affairs. Unfortunately the attempts made in this direction have failed so far;[42] on the other hand, the impossibility of this scheme has not been proved either, in spite of the strong inconsistency theorems of Kleene and Rosser.[43]

In conclusion I want to say a few words about the question whether (and in which sense) the axioms of *Principia* can be considered to be analytic. As to this problem it is to be remarked that analyticity may be understood in two senses. First, it may have the purely formal sense that the terms occurring can be defined (either explicitly or by rules for eliminating them from sentences containing them) in such a way that the axioms and theorems become special cases of the law of identity and disprovable propositions become negations of this law. In this sense even the theory of integers is demonstrably non-analytic, provided that one requires of the rules of elimination that they allow one actually to carry out the elimination in a finite number of steps in each case.[44] Leaving out this condition by admitting, e.g., sentences of infinite (and non-denumerable) length as intermediate steps of the process of reduction, all axioms of *Principia* (including the axioms of choice, infinity and reducibility) could be proved to be analytic for certain interpretations (by considerations similar to those referred to on p. [125]).[45] But this observation is of doubtful value, because the whole of mathematics as applied to sentences of infinite length has to be presupposed in order to prove this analyticity, e.g., the axiom of choice can be proved to be analytic only if it is assumed to be true.

In a second sense a proposition is called analytic if it holds, "owing to the meaning of the concepts occurring in it," where this meaning may perhaps be undefinable (i.e., irreducible to anything more fundamental).[46] It would seem that all axioms of *Principia*, in the first edition (except the axiom of infinity), are in this sense analytic for certain interpretations of the primitive terms, namely if the term "predicative function" is replaced either by "class" (in the extensional sense) or (leaving out the axiom of choice) by "concept," since nothing can express better the meaning of the term "class" than the axiom of classes (cf. p. [123]) and the axiom of choice, and since, on the other hand, the meaning of the term "concept" seems to imply that every propositional function defines a concept.[47] The difficulty is only that we don't perceive the concepts of "concept" and of "class" with sufficient distinctness, as is shown by the paradoxes. In view of this situation, Russell took the course of considering both classes and concepts (except the logically uninteresting primitive predicates) as non-existent and of replacing them by constructions of our own. It cannot be denied that this procedure has led to interesting ideas and to results valuable also for one taking the opposite viewpoint. On the whole, how-ever, the outcome has been that only fragments of Mathematical Logic remain, unless the things condemned are reintroduced in the form of infinite propositions or by such axioms as the axiom of reducibility which (in case of infinitely many indivduals) is demonstrably false unless one assumes either the existence of classes or of infinitely many "*qualitates occultae.*" This seems to be an indication that one should take a more conservative course, such as would consist in trying to make the meaning of the terms "class" and "concept" clearer, and to set up a consistent theory of classes and concepts as objectively existing entities. This is the course which the actual development of Mathematical Logic has been taking and which Russell himself has been forced to enter upon in the more construc-tive parts of his work. Major among the attempts in this direction (some of which have been quoted in this essay) are the simple theory of types (which is the system of the first edition of *Principia* in an appropriate interpreta-tion) and axiomatic set theory, both of which have been successful at least to this extent, that they permit the derivation of modern mathematics and at the same time avoid all known paradoxes. Many symptoms show only too clearly, however, that the primitive concepts need further elucidation.

It seems reasonable to suspect that it is this incomplete understanding of the foundations which is responsible for the fact that Mathematical Logic has up to now remained so far behind the high expectations of Peano and others who (in accordance with Leibniz's claims) had hoped that it would facilitate theoretical mathematics to the same extent as the decimal system of numbers has facilitated numerical computations. For how can one expect to solve mathematical problems systematically by mere analysis of the concepts occurring, if our analysis so far does not even suffice to set up the axioms? But there is no need to give up hope. Leibniz, in his writings about the *Characteristica universalis*, did not speak of a utopian project; if we are to believe his words he had developed this calculus of reasoning to a large extent, but was waiting with its publication till the seed could fall on fertile ground.[48] He went even so far[49] as to estimate the time which would be necessary for his calculus to be developed by a few select scientists to such an extent "that humanity would have a new kind of an instrument in increasing the powers of reason far more than any optical instrument has ever aided the power of vision." The time he names is five years, and he claims that his method is not any more difficult to learn than the mathematics or philosophy of his time. Furthermore, he said repeatedly that, even in the rudimentary state to which he had developed the theory himself, it was responsible for all his mathematical discoveries; which, one should expect, even Poincaré would acknowledge as a sufficient proof of its fecundity.

Notes

* I wish to express my thanks to Professor Alonzo Church of Princeton University, who helped me to find the correct English expressions in a number of places.

1 Frege has doubtless the priority, since his first publication about the subject, which already contains all the essentials, appeared ten years before Peano's.

2 Cf. in this respect W. V. Quine's article in the Whitehead volume of the Library of Living Philosophers series.

3 The above quoted passage was left out in the later editions of the *Introduction*.

4 I use the term "signify" in the sequel because it corresponds to the German word "*bedeuten*" which Frege, who first treated the question under consideration, used in this connection.

5 The only further assumptions one would need in order to obtain a rigorous proof would be: (1) that "φ (*a*)" and the proposition "*a* is the object which has the property φ and is identical with *a*" mean the same thing, and (2) that every proposition "speaks about something," i.e., can be brought to the form φ (*a*). Furthermore one would have to use the fact that for any two objects *a*, *b*, there exists a true proposition of the form φ (*a*, *b*) as, e.g., $a \neq b$ or $a = a \cdot b = b$.

6 Cf. "Sinn und Bedeutung," *Zeitschrift für Philosophie und philosophische Kritik*, Vol. 100 (1892), p. 35.

7 From the indication (*Bedeutung*) of a sentence is to be distinguished what Frege called its meaning (*Sinn*) which is the conceptual correlate of the objectively existing fact (or "the True"). This one should expect to be in Russell's theory a possible fact (or rather the possibility of a fact), which would exist also in the case of a false proposition. But Russell, as he says, could never believe that such "curious shadowy" things really exist. Thirdly, there is also the psychological correlate of the fact which is called "signification" and understood to be the corresponding belief in Russell's latest book [*An Inquiry into Meaning and Truth*]. "Sentence" in contradistinction to "proposition" is used to denote the mere combination of symbols.

8 He made no explicit statement about the former; but it seems it would hold for the logical system of *Principia*, though perhaps more or less vacuously.

9 In Russell's first paper about the subject: "On Some Difficulties in the transfinite

Numbers and Order Types," *Proc. London Math. Soc.*, Second Series, Vol. 4, 1906, p. 29. If one wants to bring such paradoxes as "the liar" under this viewpoint, universal (and existential) propositions must be considered to involve the class of objects to which they refer.

10 "Propositional function" (without the clause "as a separate entity") may be understood to mean a proposition in which one or several constituents are designated as arguments. One might think that the pair consisting of the proposition and the argument could then for all purposes play the role of the "propositional function as a separate entity," but it is to be noted that this pair (as one entity) is again a set or a concept and therefore need not exist.

11 The intensional paradoxes can be dealt with, e.g., by the theory of simple types or the ramified hierarchy, which do not involve any undesirable restrictions if applied to concepts only and not to sets.

12 Cf. "Über eine Widerspruchfreiheitsfrage in der axiomatischen Mengenlehre," *Journal für reine und angewandte Mathematik*, Vol. 160, 1929, p. 227.

13 Cf. "New Foundations for Mathematical Logic," *Amer. Math. Monthly*, Vol. 44, p. 70.

14 Cf. *Principia Mathematica*, Vol. I, p. 39.

15 Quantifiers are the two symbols ($\exists x$) and (x) meaning respectively, "there exists an object x" and "for all objects x." The totality of objects x to which they refer is called their range.

16 Cf. *Principia Mathematica*, Vol. I, p. 47, section IV.

17 By the theory of simple types I mean the doctrine which says that the objects of thought (or, in another interpretation, the symbolic expressions) are divided into types, namely: individuals, properties of individuals, relations between individuals, properties of such relations, etc. (with a similar hierarchy for extensions), and that sentences of the form: "a has the property φ," "b bears the relation R to c," etc. are meaningless, if a, b, c, R, φ are not of types fitting together. Mixed types (such as classes containing individuals and classes as elements) and therefore also transfinite types (such as the class of all classes of finite types) are excluded. That the theory of simple types suffices for avoiding also the epistemological paradoxes is shown by a closer analysis of these. (Cf. F. P. Ramsey's paper, quoted in note 21, and A. Tarski, *Der Wahrheitsbegriff in den formalisierten Sprachen, Stud. phil.*, Vol. I, Lemberg, 1935, p. 399.)

18 These are definitions of an object α by reference to a totality to which α itself (and perhaps also things definable only in terms of α) belong. As, e.g., if one defines a class α as the intersection of all classes satisfying a certain condition φ and then concludes that α is a subset also of such classes u as are defined in terms of α (provided they satisfy φ).

19 See Rudolf Carnap in *Erkenntnis*, Vol. 2, p. 103, and *Logical Syntax of Language*, p. 162, and C. H. Langford, *Bulletin of the American Mathematical Society*, Vol. 33 (1927), p. 599.

20 An object a is said to be described by a propositional function $\varphi(x)$ if $\varphi(x)$ is true for $x = a$ and for no other object.

21 Cf. F. P. Ramsey, "The Foundations of Mathematics," in *Proc. London Math Soc.*, Series 2, Vol. 25 (1926), p. 338. (Reprinted in *The Foundations of Mathematics*, New York and London, 1931, p. 1.)

22 I shall use in the sequel "constructivism" as a general term comprising both these standpoints and also such tendencies as are embodied in Russell's "no class" theory.

23 One might think that this conception of notions is impossible, because the sentences into which one translates must also contain notions so that one would

get into an infinite regress. This, however, does not preclude the possibility of maintaining the above viewpoint for all the more abstract notions, such as those of the second and higher types, or in fact for all notions except the primitive terms which might be only a very few.

24 That is, that no two different properties belong to exactly the same things, which, in a sense, is a counterpart to Leibniz's *Principium identitatis indiscernibilium*, which says no two different things have exactly the same properties.

25 Cf. Carnap, *loc. cit.*, note 19 above.

26 Nevertheless the scheme is interesting because it again shows the constructibility of notions which can be meaningfully asserted of notions of arbitrarily high order.

27 See *Erkenntnis*, Vol. 3, p. 367.

28 The formal system corresponding to this view would have, instead of the axiom of reducibility, the rule of substitution for functions described, e.g., in Hilbert–Bernays, *Grundlagen der Mathematik*, vol. I (1934), p. 90, applied to variables of any type, together with certain axioms of intensionality required by the concept of property which, however, would be weaker than Chwistek's. It should be noted that this view does not necessarily imply the existence of concepts which cannot be expressed in the system, if combined with a solution of the paradoxes along the lines indicated on p. [128].

29 Cf. my paper in *Monatshefte für Mathematik und Physik*, Vol. 38 (1931), p. 173, or R. Carnap, *Logical Syntax of Language*, §35.

30 Ideas tending in this direction are contained in the following papers by D. Mirimanoff: "Les antinomies de Russell et de Buraliforte et le problème fondamental de la théorie des ensembles," *L'Enseignment mathématique*, Vol. 19 (1917), pp. 37–52, and "Remarques sur la théorie des ensembles et les antinomies Cantoriennes," *L'Enseignment mathématique*, vol. 19 (1917), pp. 209–217 and vol. 21 (1920), pp. 29–52. Cf. in particular Vol. 19, p. 212.

31 Cf. "Les paradoxes de la logique," *Rev. de Métaph. et de Morale*, Vol. 14 (1906), p. 627.

32 In Appendix C of *Principia* a way is sketched by which these also could be constructed by means of certain similarity relations between atomic propositions, so that these latter would be the only ones remaining as real objects.

33 The "data" are to be understood in a relative sense here, i.e., in our case as logic without the assumption of the existence of classes and concepts.

34 Cf. Ramsey, *loc. cit.*, note 21 above.

35 That is, propositions of the form $S(a)$, $R(a, b)$, etc., where S, R are primitive predicates and a, b individuals.

36 The x_i may, of course, as always, be partly or wholly identical with each other.

37 As to the question how far it is possible to build up the theory of real numbers, presupposing the integers, cf. Hermann Weyl, *Das Kontinuum*, reprinted, 1932.

38 That the variable α is intended to be of undetermined order is seen from the later applications of *89.17, and from the note to *89.17. The main application is in line (2) of the proof of *89.24, where the lemma under consideration is needed for α's of arbitrarily high orders.

39 *Loc. cit.*, cf. note 13 above.

40 Russell formulates a somewhat different principle with the same effect, in *Principia*, Vol. I, p. 95.

41 This objection does not apply to the symbolic interpretation of the theory of types, spoken of on p. [128], because there one does not have objects but only symbols of different types.

42 A formal system along these lines is Church's (cf. "A Set of Postulates for the

Foundation of Logic," *Annals of Mathematics*, Vol. 33 (1932), p. 346 and Vol. 34 (1933), p. 839), where, however, the underlying idea is expressed by the somewhat misleading statement that the law of excluded middle is abandoned. However, this system has been proved to be inconsistent. See note 43.

43 Cf. S. C. Kleene and J. B. Rosser, "The Inconsistency of Certain Formal Logics," *Annals of Math.*, Vol. 36 (1935), p. 630.

44 Because this would imply the existence of a decision-procedure for all arithmetical propositions. Cf. A. M. Turing, *Proc. Lond. Math. Soc.*, Vol. 42 (1936), p. 230.

45 Cf. also F. P. Ramsey, *loc. cit.*, (note 21), where, however, the axiom of infinity cannot be obtained, because it is interpreted to refer to the individuals in the world.

46 The two significations of the term *analytic* might perhaps be distinguished as tautological and analytic.

47 This view does not contradict the opinion defended above that mathematics is based on axioms with a real content, because the very existence of the concept of, e.g., "class" already constitutes such an axiom; since, if one defined, e.g., "class" and "ε" to be "the concepts satisfying the axioms," one would be unable to prove their existence. "Concept" could perhaps be defined in terms of "proposition" (cf. p. [128], although I don't think that this would be a natural procedure); but then certain axioms about propositions, justifiable only with reference to the undefined meaning of this term, will have to be assumed. It is to be noted that this view about analyticity makes it again possible that every mathematical proposition could perhaps be reduced to a special case of $a = a$, namely if the reduction is effected not in virtue of the definitions of the terms occurring, but in virtue of their meaning, which can never be completely expressed in a set of formal rules.

48 *Die philosophischen Schriften von G. W. Leibniz*, herausgegeben von C. J. Gerhardt, Vol. 7 (1890), p. 12. Cf. also G. Vacca, "La logica di Leibniz" (section VII), *Riv. di Mat.*, Vol. 8 (1902–06), p. 72, and the preface in the first volume of the first series of *Leibniz's Sämtliche Briefe und Schriften*, herausgegeben von der Preussischen Akademie der Wissenschaften (1923–).

49 Leibniz, *Philosophische Schriften* (ed. Gerhardt), Vol. 7, p. 187.

10

The Logicist Foundations of Mathematics

Rudolf Carnap*

The problem of the logical and epistemological foundations of mathematics has not yet been completely solved. This problem vitally concerns both mathematicians and philosophers, for any uncertainty in the foundations of the "most certain of all the sciences" is extremely disconcerting. Of the various attempts already made to solve the problem none can be said to have resolved every difficulty. These efforts have taken essentially three directions: *Logicism*, the chief proponent of which is Russell; *Intuitionism*, advocated by Brouwer; and Hilbert's *Formalism*.

Since I wish to draw you a rough sketch of the salient features of the logicist construction of mathematics, I think I should not only point out those areas in which the logicist program has been completely or at least partly successful but also call attention to the difficulties peculiar to this approach. One of the most important questions for the foundations of mathematics is that of the relation between mathematics and logic. *Logicism* is the thesis that mathematics is reducible to logic, hence nothing but a part of logic. Frege was the first to espouse this view (1884). In their great work, *Principia Mathematica*, the English mathematicians A. N. Whitehead and B. Russell produced a systematization of logic from which they constructed mathematics.

We will split the logicist thesis into two parts for separate discussion:

1 The *concepts* of mathematics can be derived from logical concepts through explicit definitions.
2 The *theorems* of mathematics can be derived from logical axioms through purely logical deduction.

The Derivation of Mathematical Concepts

To make precise the thesis that the concepts of mathematics are derivable from logical concepts, we must specify the logical concepts to be employed in the derivation. They are the following. In propositional calculus, which deals with the relations between unanalyzed sentences, the most important concepts are: the negation of a sentence p, "not-p" (symbolized "$\sim p$"); the disjunction of two sentences, "p or q" ("$p \vee q$"); the conjunction, "p and q" ("$p \cdot q$"); and the implication, "if p, then q" ("$p \supset q$"). The concepts of functional calculus are given in the form of functions, e.g., "$f(a)$" (read "f of a") signifies that the property f belongs to the object a. The most important concepts of functional calculus are universality and existence: "$(x)f(x)$" (read "for every x, f of x") means that the property f belongs to every object; "$(\exists x)f(x)$" (read "there is an x such that f of x") means that f belongs to at least one object. Finally there is the concept of identity: "$a = b$" means that "a" and "b" are names of the same object.

Not all these concepts need be taken as undefined or primitive, for some of them are reducible to others. For example, "$p \vee q$" can be defined as "$\sim (\sim p \cdot \sim q)$" and "$(\exists x)f(x)$" as "$\sim(x)\sim f(x)$". It is the logicist thesis, then, that the logical concepts just given suffice to define all mathematical concepts, that over and above them no specifically mathematical concepts are required for the construction of mathematics.

Already before Frege, mathematicians in their investigations of the interdependence of mathematical concepts had shown, though often without being able to provide precise definitions, that all the concepts of arithmetic are reducible to the natural numbers (i.e., the numbers 1, 2, 3, . . . which are used in ordinary counting). Accordingly, the *main problem* which remained for logicism was to derive the natural numbers from logical concepts. Although Frege had already found a solution to this problem, Russell and Whitehead reached the same results independently of him and were subsequently the first to recognize the agreement of their work with Frege's. The crux of this solution is the correct recognition of the logical status of the natural numbers; they are logical attributes which belong, not to things, but to concepts. That a certain number, say 3, is the number of a concept means that three objects fall under it. We can express the very same thing with the help of the logical concepts previously given. For example, let "$2_m (f)$" mean that at least two objects fall under the concept f. Then we can define this concept as follows (where "$=_{\mathrm{Df}}$" is the symbol for definition, read as "means by definition"):

$$2_m (f) =_{\mathrm{Df}} (\exists x)(\exists y)[\sim(x = y) \cdot f(x) \cdot f(y)]$$

or in words: there is an x and there is a y such that x is not identical with y and f belongs to x and f belongs to y. In like manner, we define 3_m, 4_m, and so on. Then we define the number two itself thus:

$$2(f) = {}_{\mathrm{Df}} 2_m(f) \cdot \sim 3_m(f)$$

or in words: at least two, but not at least three, objects fall under f. We can also define arithmetical operations quite easily. For example, we can define addition with the help of the disjunction of two mutually exclusive concepts. Furthermore, we can define the concept of natural number itself.

The derivation of the other kinds of numbers – i.e., the positive and negative numbers, the fractions, the real and the complex numbers – is accomplished, not in the usual way by adding to the domain of the natural numbers, but by the construction of a completely new domain. The natural numbers do not constitute a subset of the fractions but are merely correlated in obvious fashion with certain fractions. Thus the natural number 3 and the fraction ¾ are not identical but merely correlated with one another. Similarly we must distinguish the fraction ½ from the real number correlated with it. In this paper, we will treat only the definition of the real numbers. Unlike the derivations of the other kinds of numbers which encounter no great difficulties, the derivation of the real numbers presents problems which, it must be admitted, neither logicism, intuitionism, nor formalism has altogether overcome.

Let us assume that we have already constructed the series of fractions (ordered according to magnitude). Our task, then, is to supply definitions of the real numbers based on this series. Some of the real numbers, the rationals, correspond in obvious fashion to fractions; the rest, the irrationals, correspond as Dedekind showed (1872) to "gaps" in the series of fractions. Suppose, for example, that we divide the (positive) fractions into two classes, the class of all whose square is less than 2, and the class comprising all the rest of the fractions. This division forms a "cut" in the series of fractions which corresponds to the irrational real number $\sqrt{2}$. This cut is called a "gap" since there is no fraction correlated with it. As there is no fraction whose square is two, the first or "lower" class contains no greatest member, and the second or "upper" class contains no least member. Hence, to every real number there corresponds a cut in the series of fractions, each irrational real number being correlated with a gap.

Russell developed further Dedekind's line of thought. Since a cut is uniquely determined by its "lower" class, Russell defined a real number as the lower class of the corresponding cut in the series of fractions. For example, $\sqrt{2}$ is defined as the class (or property) of those fractions whose square is less than two, and the rational real number ⅓ is defined as the class of all fractions smaller than the fraction ⅓. On the basis of these definitions, the entire arithmetic of the real numbers can be developed. This development, however, runs up against certain difficulties connected with so-called "impredicative definition," which we will discuss shortly.

The essential point of this method of introducing the real numbers is that they are *not postulated but constructed*. The logicist does not establish the existence of structures which have the properties of the real numbers by laying down axioms or postulates; rather, through explicit definitions, he produces logical constructions that have, by virtue of these definitions, the usual properties of the real numbers. As there are no "creative definitions," definition is not creation but only name-giving to something whose existence has already been established.

In similarly constructivistic fashion, the logicist introduces the rest of the concepts of mathematics, those of analysis (e.g., convergence, limit, continuity, differential, quotient, integral, etc.) and also those of set theory (notably the concepts of the transfinite cardinal and ordinal numbers). This "constructivistic" method forms part of the very texture of logicism.

The Derivation of the Theorems of Mathematics

The second thesis of logicism is that the *theorems of mathematics* are derivable from logical axioms through logical deduction. The requisite system of logical axioms, obtained by simplifying Russell's system, contains four axioms of propositional calculus and two of functional calculus. The rules of inference are a rule of substitution and a rule of implication (the *modus ponens* of ancient logic). Hilbert and Ackermann have used these same axioms and rules of inference in their system.

Mathematical predicates are introduced by explicit definitions. Since an explicit definition is nothing but a convention to employ a new, usually much shorter, way of writing something, the *definiens* or the new way of writing it can always be eliminated. Therefore, as every sentence of mathematics can be translated into a sentence which contains only the primitive logical predicates already mentioned, this second thesis can be restated thus: Every provable mathematical sentence is translatable into a sentence which contains only primitive logical symbols and which is provable in logic.

But the derivation of the theorems of mathematics poses certain difficulties for logicism. In the first place it turns out that some theorems of arithmetic and set theory, if interpreted in the usual way, require for their proof besides the logical axioms still other special axioms known as the *axiom of infinity* and the *axiom of choice* (or multiplicative axiom). The axiom of infinity states that for every natural number there is a greater one. The axiom of choice states that for every set of disjoint non-empty sets, there is (at least) one selection-set, i.e., a set that has exactly one member in common with each of the member sets. But we are not concerned here with the content of these axioms but with their logical character. Both are existential sentences. Hence, Russell was right in hesitating to present them as logical axioms, for logic deals only with possible entities and cannot make assertions about whether something does or does not exist. Russell found a way out of this difficulty. He reasoned that since mathematics was also a purely formal science, it too could make only conditional, not categorical, statements about existence: if certain structures exist, then there also exist certain other structures whose existence follows logically from the existence of the former. For this reason he transformed a mathematical sentence, say S, the proof of which required the axiom of infinity, I, or the axiom of choice, C, into a conditional sentence; hence S is taken to assert not S, but $I \supset S$ or $C \supset S$, respectively. This conditional sentence is then derivable from the axioms of logic.

A greater difficulty, perhaps the greatest difficulty, in the construction of mathematics has to do with another axiom posited by Russell, the so-called *axiom of reducibility*, which has justly become the main bone of contention for the critics of the system of *Principia Mathematica*. We agree with the opponents of logicism that it is inadmissible to take it as an axiom. As we will discuss more fully later, the gap created by the removal of this axiom has certainly not been filled in an entirely satisfactory way. This difficulty is bound up with Russell's *theory of types* which we shall now briefly discuss.

We must distinguish between a "simple theory of types" and a "ramified theory of types." The latter was developed by Russell but later recognized by Ramsey to be an unnecessary complication of the former. If, for the sake of simplicity, we restrict our attention to one-place functions (properties) and abstract from many-place functions (relations), then type theory consists in the following classification of expressions into different "types": To type 0 belong the names of the objects ("individuals") of the domain of discourse (e.g., a, b, . . .). To type 1 belong the properties of these objects (e.g., $f(a)$, $g(a)$, . . .). To type 2 belong the properties of these properties (e.g., $F(f)$, $G(f)$, . . .); for example, the concept $2(f)$ defined above belongs to this type. To type 3 belong the properties of properties of properties, and so on. The basic rule of type theory is that every predicate belongs to a determinate type and can be meaningfully applied only to expressions of the next lower type. Accordingly, sentences of the form $f(a)$, $F(f)$, $2(f)$ are always meaningful, i.e., either true or false; on the other hand combinations like $f(g)$ and $f(F)$ are neither true nor false but meaningless. In particular, expressions like $f(f)$ or $\sim f(f)$ are meaningless, i.e., we cannot meaningfully say of a property either that it belongs to itself or that it does not. As we shall see, this last result is important for the elimination of the antinomies.

This completes our outline of the simple theory of types, which most proponents of modern logic consider legitimate and necessary. In his system, Russell introduced the ramified theory of types, which has not found much acceptance. In this theory the properties of each type are further subdivided into "orders." This division is based, not on the kind of objects to which the property belongs, but on the form of the definition which introduces it. Later we shall consider the reasons why Russell believed this further ramification necessary. Because of the introduction of the ramified theory of types, certain difficulties arose in the construction of mathematics, especially in the theory of real numbers. Many fundamental theorems not only could not be proved but could not even be expressed. To overcome this difficulty, Russell had to use brute force; i.e., he introduced the axiom of reducibility by means of which the different orders of a type could be reduced in certain respects to the lowest order of the type. The sole justification for this axiom was the fact that there seemed to be no other way out of this particular difficulty engendered by the ramified theory of types. Later Russell himself, influenced by Wittgenstein's sharp criticism, abandoned the axiom of reducibility in the second edition of *Principia Mathematica* (1925). But, as he still believed that one could not get along without the ramified theory of types, he despaired of the situation. Thus we see how important it would be, not only for logicism but for any attempt to solve the problems of the foundations of mathematics, to show that the simple theory of types is sufficient for the construction of mathematics out of logic. A young English mathematician and pupil of Russell, Ramsey (who unfortunately died this year, i.e., 1930), in 1926 made some efforts in this direction which we will discuss later.

The Problem of Impredicative Definition

To ascertain whether the simple theory of types is sufficient or must be further ramified, we must first of all examine the reasons which induced Russell to adopt this ramification in spite of its most undesirable consequences. There were two closely connected reasons: the necessity of eliminating the logical antinomies and the so-called "vicious circle" principle. We call "logical antinomies" the contradictions which first appeared in set theory (as so-called "paradoxes") but which Russell showed to be common to all logic. It can be shown that these contradictions arise in logic if the theory of types is not presupposed. The simplest antinomy is that of the concept "impredicable." By definition a property is "impredicable" if it does not belong to itself. Now is the property "impredicable" itself impredicable? If we assume that it is, then since it belongs to itself it would be, according to the definition of "impredicable," not impredicable. If we assume that it is not impredicable, then it does not belong to itself and hence, according to the definition of "impredicable," is impredicable. According to the law of excluded middle, it is either impredicable or not, but both alternatives lead to a contradiction. Another example is Grelling's antinomy of the concept "heterological." Except that it concerns predicates rather than properties, this antinomy is completely analogous to the one just described. By definition, a predicate is "heterological" if the property designated by the predicate does not belong to the predicate itself. (For example, the word "monosyllabic" is heterological, for the word itself is not monosyllabic.) Obviously both the assumption that the word "heterological" is itself heterological as well as the opposite assumption lead to a contradiction. Russell and other logicians have constructed numerous antinomies of this kind.

Ramsey has shown that there are two completely different kinds of antinomies. Those belonging to the first kind can be expressed in logical symbols and are called "logical antinomies" (in the narrower sense). The "impredicable" antinomy is of this kind. Ramsey has shown that this kind of antinomy is eliminated by the simple theory of types. The concept "impredicable," for example, cannot even be defined if the simple theory of types is presupposed, for an expression of the form, a property does not belong to itself ($\sim f(f)$), is not well formed, and meaningless according to that theory.

Antinomies of the second kind are known as "semantical" or "epistemological" antinomies. They include our previous example, "heterological," as well as the antinomy, well-known to mathematicians, of the smallest natural number which cannot be defined in German with fewer than 100 letters. Ramsey has shown that antinomies of this second kind cannot be constructed in the symbolic language of logic and therefore need not be taken into account in the construction of mathematics from logic. The fact that they appear in word languages led Russell to impose certain restrictions on logic in order to eliminate them – namely, the ramified theory of types. But perhaps their appearance is due to some defect of our ordinary word language.

Since antinomies of the first kind are already eliminated by the simple theory of types and those of the second kind do not appear in logic, Ramsey declared that the ramified theory of types and hence also the axiom of reducibility were superfluous.

Now what about Russell's second reason for ramifying the theory of types – namely, the vicious circle principle? This principle, that "no whole may contain parts which are definable only in terms of that whole," may also be called an "injunction against impredicative definition." A definition is said to be "impredicative" if it defines a concept in terms of a totality to which the concept belongs. (The concept "impredicative" has nothing to do with the aforementioned pseudo-concept "impredicable.") Russell's main reason for laying down this injunction was his belief that antinomies arise when it is violated. From a somewhat different standpoint Poincaré before, and Weyl after, Russell also rejected impredicative definition. They pointed out that an impredicatively defined concept was meaningless because of the circularity in its definition. An example will perhaps make the matter clearer:

We can define the concept "inductive number" (which corresponds to the concept of natural number including zero) as follows: A number is said to be "inductive" if it possesses all the hereditary properties of zero. A property is said to be "hereditary" if it always belongs to the number $n + 1$ whenever it belongs to the number n. In symbols,

$$\text{Ind}\ (x) = {}_{\text{Df}} (f)[(\text{Her}\ (f) \cdot f\ (0)) \supset f\ (x)]$$

To show that this definition is circular and useless, one usually argues as follows: In the *definiens* the expression "(f)" occurs, i.e., "for all properties (of numbers)." But since the property "inductive" belongs to the class of all properties, the very property to be defined already occurs in a hidden way in the *definiens* and thus is to be defined in terms of itself, an obviously inadmissible procedure. It is sometimes claimed that the meaninglessness of an impredicatively defined concept is seen most clearly if one tries to establish whether the concept holds in an individual case. For example, to ascertain whether the number three is inductive, we must, according to the definition, investigate whether every property which is hereditary and belongs to zero also belongs to three. But if we must do this for every property, we must also do it for the property "inductive" which is also a property of numbers. Therefore, in order to determine whether the number three is inductive, we must determine among other things whether the property "inductive" is hereditary, whether it belongs to zero, and finally – this is the crucial point – whether it belongs to three. But this means that it would be impossible to determine whether three is an inductive number.

Before we consider how Ramsey tried to refute this line of thought, we must get clear about how these considerations led Russell to the ramified theory of types. Russell reasoned in this way: Since it is inadmissible to define a property in terms of an expression which refers to "all properties," we must subdivide the properties (of type 1): To the "first order" belong those properties in whose definition the expression "all properties" does not occur; to the "second order" those in whose definition the expression "all properties of the first order" occurs; to the "third order" those in whose definition the expression "all properties of the second order" occurs, and so on. Since the expression "all properties" without reference to a determinate order is held to be inadmissible, there never occurs in the definition of a property a totality to which it itself belongs. The property "inductive," for example, is defined in this no longer impredicative way: A number is said to be "inductive" if it possesses all the hereditary properties of the first order which belong to zero.

But the ramified theory of types gives rise to formidable difficulties in the treatment of the real numbers. As we have already seen, a real number is defined as a class, or what comes to the same thing, as a property of fractions. For example, we saw that $\sqrt{2}$ is defined as the class or property of those fractions whose square is less than two. But since the expression "for all properties" without reference to a determinate order is inadmissible under the ramified theory of types, the expression "for all real numbers" cannot refer to all real numbers without qualification but only to the real numbers of a determinate order. To the first order belong those real numbers in whose definition an expression of the form "for all real numbers" does not occur; to the second order belong those in whose definition such an expression occurs, but this expression must be restricted to "all real numbers of the first order," and so on. Thus there can be neither an admissible definition nor an admissible sentence which refers to all real numbers without qualification.

But as a consequence of this ramification, many of the most important definitions and theorems of real number theory are lost. Once Russell had recognized that his earlier attempt to overcome it – namely, the introduction of the axiom of reducibility – was itself inadmissible, he saw no way out of this difficulty. The *most difficult problem* confronting contemporary studies in the foundations of mathematics is this: How can we develop logic if, on the one hand, we are to avoid the danger of the meaninglessness of impredicative definitions and, on the other hand, are to reconstruct satisfactorily the theory of real numbers?

Attempt at a Solution

Ramsey (1926) outlined a construction of mathematics in which he courageously tried to resolve this difficulty by declaring the forbidden impredicative definitions to be perfectly admissible. They contain, he contended, a circle but the circle is harmless, not vicious. Consider, he said, the description "the tallest man in this room." Here we describe something in terms of a totality to which it itself belongs. Still no one thinks this description inadmissible since the person described already exists and is only singled out, not created, by the description. Ramsey believed that the same considerations applied to properties. The totality of properties already exists in itself. That we men are finite beings who cannot name individually each of infinitely many properties but can describe some of them only with reference to the totality of all properties is an empirical fact that has nothing to do with logic. For these reasons Ramsey allows impredicative definition. Consequently, he can both get along with the simple theory of types and still retain all the requisite mathematical definitions, particularly those needed for the theory of the real numbers.

Although this happy result is certainly tempting, I think we should not let ourselves be seduced by it into accepting Ramsey's basic premise; v12., that the totality of properties already exists before their characterization by definition. Such a conception, I believe, is not far removed from a belief in a Platonic realm of ideas which exist in themselves, independently of *if* and *how* finite human beings are able to think them. I think we ought to hold fast to Frege's dictum that, in mathematics, only that may be taken to exist whose existence has been proved (and he meant proved in finitely many steps). I agree with the intuitionists that the finiteness of every logical–mathematical operation, proof, and definition is not required because of some accidental empirical fact about man but is required by the very nature of the subject. Because of this attitude, intuitionist mathematics has been called "anthropological mathematics." It seems to me that, by analogy, we should call Ramsey's mathematics "theological mathematics," for when he speaks of the totality of properties he elevates himself above the actually knowable and definable and in certain respects reasons from the standpoint of an infinite mind which is not bound by the wretched necessity of building every structure step by step.

We may now rephrase our crucial question thus: Can we have Ramsey's result without retaining absolutist conceptions? His result was this: Limitation to the simple theory of types and retention of the possibility of definitions for mathematical concepts, particularly in real number theory. We can reach this result if, like Ramsey, we allow impredicative definition, but can we do this without falling into his conceptual absolutism? I will try to give an affirmative answer to this question.

Let us go back to the example of the property "inductive" for which we gave an impredicative definition:

$$\text{Ind }(x) = {}_{\text{Df}} (f)[(\text{Her}(f) \cdot f(0)) \supset f(x)]$$

Let us examine once again whether the use of this definition, i.e., establishing whether the concept holds in an individual case or not, really leads to circularity and is therefore impossible. According to this definition, that the number two is inductive means:

$$(f)[(\text{Her}(f) \cdot f(0)) \supset f(2)]$$

in words: Every property f which is hereditary and belongs to zero belongs also to two. How can we verify a universal statement of this kind? If we had to examine every single property, an unbreakable circle would indeed result, for then we would run headlong against the property "inductive." Establishing whether something had it would then be impossible in principle, and the concept would therefore be meaningless. But the verification of a universal logical or mathematical sentence does not consist in running through a series of individual cases, for impredicative definitions usually refer to infinite totalities. The belief that we must run through all the individual cases rests on a confusion of "numerical" generality, which refers to objects already given, with "specific" generality.[1] We do not establish specific generality by running through individual cases but by logically deriving certain properties from certain others. In our example, that the number two is inductive means that the property "belonging to two" follows logically from the property "being hereditary and belonging to zero." In symbols, "$f(2)$" can be derived from an arbitrary f from "Her$(f) \cdot f(0)$" by logical operations. This is indeed the case. First, the derivation of "$f(0)$" from "Her$(f) \cdot f(0)$" is trivial and proves the inductiveness of the number zero. The remaining steps are based on the definition of the concept "hereditary":

$$\text{Her}(f) =_{\text{Df}} (n)[f(n) \supset f(n + 1)].$$

Using this definition, we can easily show that "$f(0 + 1)$" and hence "$f(1)$" are derivable from "Her$(f) \cdot f(0)$" and thereby prove that the number one is inductive. Using this result and our definition, we can derive "$f(1 + 1)$" and hence "$f(2)$" from 'Her$(f) \cdot f(0)$', thereby showing that the number two is inductive. We see then that the definition of inductiveness, although impredicative, does not hinder its utility. That proofs that the defined property obtains (or does not obtain) in individual cases can be given shows that the definition is meaningful. If we reject the belief that it is necessary to run through individual cases and rather make it clear to ourselves that the complete verification of a statement about an arbitrary property means nothing more than its logical (more exactly, tautological) validity for an arbitrary property, we will come to the conclusion that impredicative definitions are logistically admissible. If a property is defined impredicatively, then establishing whether or not it obtains in an individual case may, under certain circumstances, be difficult, or it may even be impossible if there is no solution to the decision problem for that logical system. But in no way does impredicativeness make such decisions impossible in principle for all cases. If the theory just sketched proves feasible, logicism will have been helped over its greatest difficulty, which consists in steering a safe course between the Scylla of the axiom of reducibility and the Charybdis of the allocation of the real numbers to different orders.

Logicism as here described has several features in common both with intuitionism and with formalism. It shares with intuitionism a constructivistic tendency with respect to definition, a tendency which Frege also emphatically endorsed. A concept may not be introduced axiomatically but must be constructed from undefined, primitive concepts step by step through explicit definitions. The admission of impredicative definitions seems at first glance to run counter to this tendency, but this is only true for constructions of the form proposed by Ramsey. Like the intuitionists, we recognize as properties only those expressions (more precisely, expressions of the form of a sentence containing one free variable) which are constructed in finitely many steps from undefined primitive properties of the appropriate domain according to determinate rules of construction. The difference between us lies in the fact that we recognize as valid not only the rules of construction which the intuitionists use (the rules of the so-called "strict functional calculus"), but in addition, permit the use of the expression "for all properties" (the operations of the so-called "extended functional calculus").

Further, logicism has a methodological affinity with formalism. Logicism proposes to construct the logical–mathematical system in such a way that, although the axioms and rules of inference are chosen with an interpretation of the primitive symbols in mind, nevertheless *inside the system* the chains of deductions and of definitions are carried through formally as in a pure calculus, i.e., without reference to the meaning of the primitive symbols.

Notes

* Translated by Erna Putnam and Gerald J. Massey.
1 Cf. F. Kaufmann, *Das Unendliche in der Mathematik und seine Ausschaltung* (Vienna, 1930).

11

Remarks on the Foundations of Mathematics, II, §§1–14

Ludwig Wittgenstein

1 "A mathematical proof must be perspicuous." Only a structure whose reproduction is an easy task is called a "proof". It must be possible to decide with certainty whether we really have the same proof twice over, or not. The proof must be a configuration whose exact reproduction can be certain. Or again: we must be sure we can exactly reproduce what is essential to the proof. It may for example be written down in two different handwritings or colours. What goes to make the reproduction of a proof is not anything like an exact reproduction of a shade of colour or a hand-writing.

It must be easy to write down *exactly* this proof again. This is where a written proof has an advantage over a drawing. The essentials of the latter have often been misunderstood. The drawing of a Euclidian proof may be inexact, in the sense that the straight lines are not straight, the segments of circles not exactly circular, etc. etc. and at the same time the drawing is still an exact proof; and from this it can be seen that this drawing does not – e.g. – demonstrate that such a construction results in a polygon with five equal sides; that what it proves is a proposition of geometry, not one about the properties of paper, compass, ruler and pencil.

[Connects with: proof a *picture* of an experiment.]

2 I want to say: if you have a proof-pattern that cannot be taken in, and by a change in notation you turn it into one that can, then you are producing a proof, where there was none before.

Now let us imagine a proof for a Russellian proposition stating an addition like "$a + b = c$", consisting of a few thousand signs. You will say: Seeing whether this proof is correct or not is a purely external difficulty, of no mathematical interest. ("One man takes in easily what someone else takes in with difficulty or not at all" etc., etc.)

The assumption is that the definitions serve merely to abbreviate the expression for the convenience of the calculator; whereas they are part of the calculation. By their aid expressions are produced which could not have been produced without it.

3   But how about the following: "While it is true that we cannot – in the ordinary sense – multiply 234 by 537 in the Russellian calculus, still there is a Russellian calculation corresponding to this multiplication." What kind of correspondence is this? It might be like this: we can carry out this multiplicaiton in the Russellian calculus too, only in a different symbolism – just as, as we should certainly say, we can carry it out in a different number system. In that case, then, we could e.g. solve the practical problems for which we use that multiplication by means of the calculation in the Russellian calculus too, only in a more roundabout way.

Now let us imagine the cardinal numbers explained as $1, 1 + 1, (1 + 1) + 1, ((1 + 1) + 1) + 1$, and so on. You say that the definitions introducing the figures of the decimal system are a mere matter of convenience; the calculation 703000×40000101 could be done in that wearisome notation too. But is that true? – "Of course it's true! I can surely write down, construct, a calculation in that notation corresponding to the calculation in the decimal notation." But how do I know that it corresponds to it? Well, because I have derived it from the other by a given method. But now if I look at it again half an hour later, may it not have altered? For one cannot command a clear view of it.

Now I ask: could we also find out the truth of the proposition $7034174 + 6594321 = 13628495$ by means of a proof carried out in the first notation? Is there such a proof of this proposition? The answer is: no.

4   But still doesn't Russell teach us *one* way of adding?

Suppose we proved by Russell's method that $(\exists \, a \ldots g) \, (\exists a \ldots l) \supset (\exists \, a \ldots s)$ is a tautology; could we reduce our result to $g + l$'s being s? Now this presupposes that I can take the three bits of the alphabet as representatives of the proof. But does Russell's proof show this? After all I could obviously also have carried out Russell's proof with groups of signs in the brackets whose sequence made no characteristic impression on me, so that it would not have been possible to represent the group of signs between brackets by its last term.

Even assuming that the Russellian proof were carried out with a notation such as $x_1x_2 \ldots x_{10}x_{11} \ldots x_{100} \ldots$ as in the decimal notation, and there were 100 members in the first pair of brackets, 300 in the second and 400 in the third, does the proof itself show that $100 + 300 = 400$? What if this proof led at one time to this result, and at another to a different one, for example $100 + 300 = 420$? What is needed in order to see that the result of the proof, if it is correctly carried out, always depends solely on the last figures of the first two pairs of brackets?

But still for small numbers Russell does teach us to add; for then we take the groups of signs in the brackets in at a glance and we can take *them* as numerals; for example "xy", "xyz", "$xyzuv$".

Thus Russell teaches us a new calculus for reaching 5 from 2 and 3; and that is true even if we say that a logical calculus is only frills tacked on to the arithmetical calculus.

The *application* of the calculation must take care of itself. And that is what is correct about "formalism".

The reduction of arithmetic to symbolic logic is supposed to show the point of application of arithmetic, as it were the attachment by means of which it is plugged in to its application. As if someone were shown, first a trumpet without the mouthpiece – and then the mouthpiece, which shows how a trumpet is used, brought into contact with the human body. But the attachment which Russell gives us is on the one hand too narrow, on the other hand too wide; too general and too special. The calculation takes care of its own application.

We extend our ideas from calculations with small numbers to ones with large numbers in the same kind of way as we imagine that, if the distance from here to the sun *could* be measured with a footrule, then we should get the very result that, as it is, we get in a quite different way. That is to say, we are inclined to take the measurement of length with a footrule as a model even for the measurement of the distance between two stars.

And one says, e.g. at school: "If we imagine rulers stretching from here to the sun . . ." and seems in this way to explain what we understand by the distance between the sun and the earth. And the use of such a picture is all right, so long as it is clear to us that we can measure the distance from us to the sun, and that we cannot measure it with footrules.

5   Suppose someone were to say: "The only real proof of 1000 + 1000 = 2000 is after all the Russellian one, which shows that the expression . . . is a tautology"? For can I not prove that a tautology results if I have 1000 members in each of the two first pairs of brackets and 2000 in the third? And if I can prove that, then I can look at it as a proof of the arithmetical proposition.

In philosophy it is always good to put a *question* instead of an answer to a question.

For an answer to the philosophical question may easily be unfair; disposing of it by means of another question is not.

Then should I put a *question* here, for example, instead of the answer that that arithmetical proposition cannot be proved by Russell's method?

6   The proof that ( )¹ ( )² ⊃ ( )³ is a tautology consists in always crossing out a term of the third pair of brackets for a term of (1) or (2). And there are many methods for such collating. Or one might even say: there are many ways of establishing the success of a 1–1 correlation. One way, for example, would be to construct a star-shaped pattern for the left-hand side of the implication and another one for the right-hand side and then to compare these in their turn by making an ornament out of the two of them.

Thus the rule could be given: "If you want to know whether the numbers A and B together actually yield C, write down an expression of the form . . . and correlate the variables in the brackets by writing down (or trying to) the proof that the expression is a tautology."

My objection to this is *not* that it is arbitrary to prescribe just this way of collating, but that it cannot be established in this way that 1000 + 1000 = 2000.

7 Imagine that you had written down a "formula" a mile long, and you showed by transformation that it was tautologous ("if *it* has not altered meanwhile", one would have to say). Now we *count* the terms in the brackets or we divide them up and make the expression into one that can be taken in, and it comes out that there are 7566 terms in the first pair of brackets, 2434 in the second, 10000 in the third. Now have I proved that 2434 + 7566 = 10000? That depends – one might say – on whether you are certain that the counting has really yielded the number of terms which stood between the brackets in the course of the proof.

Could one say: "Russell teaches us to write as many variables in the third pair of brackets as were in the first two together"? But really: he teaches us to write a variable in (3) for every variable in (1) and (2).

But do we learn from this what number is the sum of two given numbers? Perhaps it is said: "Of course, for in the third pair of brackets we have the paradigm, the prototype of the new number." But in what sense is | | | | | | | | | | | | | | | | the paradigm of a number? Consider how it can be used as such.

8 Above all, the Russellian tautology corresponding to the proposition $a + b = c$ does not show us in what notation the number c is to be written, and there is no reason why it should not be written in the form $a + b$. For Russell does not teach us the technique of, say, adding in the decimal system. But could we perhaps derive it from his technique?

Let us just ask the following question: Can one derive the technique of the decimal system from that of the system 1, 1 + 1, (1 + 1) + 1, etc.?

Could this question not also be formulated as follows: if one has one technique of calculation in the one system and one in the other, how is it shown that the two are equivalent?

9 "A proof ought to show not merely that this is how it is, but this is how it has to be."

In what circumstances does counting show this?

One would like to say: "When the figures and the thing being counted yield a memorable configuration. When this configuration is now used in place of any fresh counting." But here we seem to be talking only of *spatial* configurations: but if we know a series of words by heart and then co-ordinate two such series, one to one, saying for example: "First – Monday; second – Tuesday; third – Wednesday; etc." – can we not *prove* in this way that from Monday to Thursday is four days?

For the question is: What do we call a "memorable configuration"? What is the criterion for its being impressed on our minds? Or is the answer to that: "That we use it as a paradigm of identity!"?

10   We do not make *experiments* on a sentence or a proof in order to establish its properties.

How do we reproduce, how do we copy, a proof? – Not e.g. by taking measurements of it.

Suppose a proof were so hugely long that it could not possibly be taken in? Or let us look at a different case: Let there be a long row of strokes engraved in hard rock which is our paradigm for the number that we call 1000. We call this row the proto-thousand and if we want to know whether there are a thousand men in a square, we draw lines or stretch threads. (1–1 correlation.)

Now here the sign of the number 1000 has the identity, not of a shape, but of a physical object. We could imagine a "proto-hundred" similarly, and a proof, which we could not take in at a glance, that 10 × 100 = 1000.

The figure for 1000 in the system of 1 + 1 + 1 + 1 . . . cannot be recognized by its *shape*.

11 ||||||||||||||||||||||||||||||| |||||||||||||||||
Is this pattern a proof of 27 + 16 = 43, because one reaches "27" if one counts the strokes on the left-hand side, "16" on the right-hand side, and "43" when one counts the whole row?

Where is the queerness of calling the pattern the proof of this proposition? It lies in the kind of way this proof is to be reproduced or known again; in its not having any characteristic visual shape.

Now even if that proof has not any such visual shape, still I can copy (reproduce) it exactly – so isn't the figure a proof after all? I might e.g. have it engraved on a bit of steel and passed from hand to hand. So I should tell someone: "Here you have the proof that 27 + 16 = 43." Well, can't one say *after all* that he proves the proposition with the aid of the pattern? Yes; but the pattern is not the proof.

This, however, would surely be called a proof of 250 + 3220 = 3470: one counts on from 250 and at the same time begins counting from 1 and co-ordinates the two counts:

$$251 . . . . 1$$
$$252 . . . . 2$$
$$253 . . . . 3$$
$$\text{etc.}$$
$$3470 . . . . 3220$$

That could be called a proof in 3220 steps. It is surely a proof – and can it be called perspicuous?

12   What is the invention of the decimal system really? The invention of

a system of abbreviations – but what is the system of the abbreviations? Is it simply the system of the new signs or is it also a system of applying them for the purpose of abbreviation? And if it is the latter, then it *is* a new way of looking at the old system of signs.

Can we start from the system of $1 + 1 + 1$ . . . and learn to calculate in the decimal system through mere abbreviations of the notation?

13   Suppose that following Russell I have proved a proposition of the form $(\exists \ xyz \ . . .) \ (\exists \ uvw \ . . .) \supset (\exists \ abc \ . . .)$ – and now "I make it perspicuous" by writing signs x_1, x_2, x_3 . . . over the variables – am I to say that following Russell I have proved an arithmetical proposition in the decimal system?

But for every proof in the decimal system there is surely a corresponding one in Russell's system! How do we know there is? Let us leave intuition on one side. But it can be proved.

If a number in the decimal system is defined in terms of $1, 2, 3, . . . 9, 0$, and the signs $0, 1 . . . 9$ in terms of $1, 1 + 1, (1 + 1) + 1, . . .$ can one then use the recursive explanation of the decimal system to reach a sign of the form $1 + 1 + 1 . . .$ from any number?

Suppose someone were to say: Russellian arithmetic agrees with ordinary arithmetic up to numbers less than 10^{10}; but then it diverges from it. And now he produces a Russellian proof that $10^{10} + 1 = 10^{10}$. Now why should I not trust such a proof? How will anybody convince me that I must have miscalculated in the Russellian proof?

But then do I need a proof from another system in order to ascertain whether I have miscalculated in the first proof? Is it not enough for me to write down that proof in a way that makes it possible to take it in?

14   Is not my whole difficulty one of seeing how it is possible, without abandoning Russell's logical calculus, to reach the concept of the *set of variables* in the expression "$(\exists \ xyz \ . . .)$", where this expression cannot be taken in?

Well, but it can be made surveyable by writing: $(\exists \ x_1, x_2, x_3, \text{etc.})$. And still there is something that I do not understand: the criterion for the identity of such an expression has now surely been changed: I now see in a different way that the set of signs in two such expressions is the same.

What I am tempted to say is: Russell's proof can indeed be continued step by step, but at the end one does not rightly know what one has proved – at least not by the old criteria. By making it possible to command a clear view of the Russellian proof, I prove something about this proof.

I want to say: one need not acknowledge the Russellian technique of calculation at all – and can prove by means of a different technique of calculation that there *must* be a Russellian proof of the proposition. But in that case, of course, the proposition is no longer based upon the Russellian proof.

Or again: its being possible to imagine a Russellian proof for every proved proposition of the form $m + n = l$ does not show that the proposition is based on this proof. For it is conceivable that the Russellian proof of one proposition should not be distinguishable from the Russellian proof of another and should be called different only because they are the translations of two recognizably different proofs.

Or again: something stops being a proof when it stops being a paradigm, for example Russell's logical calculus; and on the other hand any other calculus which serves as a paradigm is acceptable.

12

How to Gödel a Frege–Russell

Gödel's Incompleteness Theorems and Logicism*

Geoffrey Hellman

Any viable philosophy of mathematics must square with incontrovertible metamathematical results. Thus, as is well known, any version of formalism committed to identifying mathematical truth with provability in some formal system is to be rejected in light of Gödel's first incompleteness theorem, according to which any consistent formal system capable of representing the primitive recursive number-theoretic functions has an undecidable sentence. In fact, Gödel showed how, given any such system, one could construct such a sentence which, on the standard interpretation of its symbols, makes a definite claim about natural numbers. Thus, either such a Gödel sentence or its negation must be an arithmetical truth, but neither is provable in the system for which it was constructed. Any formalist philosophy which respects "arithmetical truth" runs afoul of the first incompleteness theorem.[1]

The impact of Gödel's incompleteness theorems on *logicism*, however, is not so straightforwardly assessed. While there are independent grounds for regarding logicism (as conceived by Frege and Russell) as a lost cause, it remains instructive to examine the force of Gödel's theorems in this quarter. In fact, a negative result (i.e. incompatibility of logicism with a metatheorem) could be quite powerful, especially if it does not depend on a particularly restrictive way of drawing the controversial line between logic and non-logic. The purpose of this note is to present precisely this kind of argument: so long as logic is taken to be formalizable (i.e. logically valid formulas form a recursively enumerable set), a natural thesis of epistemological logicism is, modulo quite elementary assumptions, incompatible with Gödel's *second* incompleteness theorem.[2] However, for this argument, it needs to be assumed that the logicist system is to be finitely axiomatized. Extending the argument to the infinite case turns out to depend on a crucial step whose justification is by no means trivial. Thus, the situation is seen to be in sharp contrast to the intuitive expectation that Gödel's first incompleteness theorem rules out logicism (on the grounds that we know or can know the undecidable Gödel sentences). As it turns out, however, the weakened extension we are able to establish for an infinitely axiomatizable system has an interesting epistemic analogue: even though a (non-finitely-axiomatizable) logicist system may exist, it must, on pain of contradiction, remain unknowable of any particular system that it meets the logicist's demands.

We focus on epistemological logicism of the sort recently considered by Mark Steiner ([12]), leaving aside what might be called "ontological logicism," the thesis that all mathematics can be understood to be about a realm of "logical entities" (classes or propositional functions?). In his book, Steiner lists several claims of epistemological logicism, intended to spell out the vague initial claim that "mathematical knowledge is reducible to logical knowledge" ([12]: 25–26). It is really only the first of these claims that we need consider. It runs:

(1) There is some formal system of logic such that mathematics can be effectively generated from it. ([12]: 25)

At first blush, this looks suspiciously like formalism, and, indeed, if "mathematics" were construed as "all mathematical truths" or even as "all arithmetic truths," we would have a formalist thesis directly ruled out by Gödel's first theorem. The thesis should not, however, be read in such a way because the epistemological logicist need not seek to identify mathematical truth with formal derivability. Rather, what logicism seeks to identify with formal derivability is knowable mathematical truth. It is consistent with logicism that there be mathematical truths we can't know. In fact, as will emerge in a moment, it is precisely this shift that protects this version of logicism from the kind of application of Gödel's first theorem that spoils formalism.[3]

Without worrying about demarcating logic, we may, with Steiner, take logicism to be committed to the existence of a formal system that, in some sense to be specified, embraces mathematical knowledge. In light of what has been said so far, the following thesis should serve as a minimal component of epistemological logicism:

EL: There is a formal system K such that
    (i) for any knowable mathematical claim, P, there is a sentence S in the language of K such that S represents P and S is a theorem of K; and
    (ii) Any theorem S of K represents some knowable mathematical claim.

This is vague on two major counts. First, there is the matter of representation. This is evidently what upset Wittgenstein, since, typically, formulas of a strict logistic system are recognizable as representatives only with difficulty if at all. Here we will simply assume that, given abbreviational devices and patience, the well-formed formulas of a formal system could be said to represent sentences of mathematical discourse so that a proof of a well-formed formula would count as establishing a corresponding claim that might be made in, say, mathematical English. The second point of vagueness, of course, concerns "knowable." Roughly, what is intended is "knowable by an intelligent human mathematician, abstracting from limitations of computing time and space, storage limitations, and other aspects of endurance." Equally roughly, a mathematical claim counts as knowable if idealized mathematicians would come to know the claim were they (perhaps collectively) to search long enough and widely enough. It will turn out that the only further dissipation of this fog that will be needed for the main argument is the following principle of "constancy of mathematical truth":

> CMT: The same mathematical truths hold in all the "worlds" that are relevant to determining whether a mathematical claim is "knowable."

This is, of course, uncontroversial to anyone who views mathematical claims as necessarily true or necessarily false, but it should be acceptable to others as well (if there really are others!).

At this point, it is worth considering a tempting argument that the thesis EL is ruled out by Gödel's first incompleteness theorem. The argument is simply that the undecidable sentence that Gödel shows us how to construct for a given system K – a sentence A which says, in effect, "I am unprovable in K" – is unprovable in K but at the same time represents a knowable mathematical truth. This latter claim would be supported by appealing to our understanding of what A says together with our understanding of Gödel's argument that A is undecidable, hence unprovable. As it stands, of course, this argument is fallacious, since the Gödel proof of A's undecidability is not unconditional but depends on the hypothesis that the system K in question is consistent. (For simplicity, we are throughout working with Rosser's extension of Gödel's theorems, which replaces Gödel's stronger hypothesis of ω-consistency with that of consistency.) What we can come to know by following Gödel's proof (of the first incompleteness theorem) is this:

> (*) If K is consistent, the Gödel sentence A for K is true, i.e., there is no proof in K whose last line is A.

This we can know and do know. Is *it* a counterexample to EL; that is, is it represented by no theorem of K? No, in fact, (*) can be formalized and proved in K (if K comes within the purview of the first incompleteness theorem); it is precisely this observation that leads to the second incompleteness theorem. (The consequent of (*) is represented by A itself; using a provability predicate, one can represent the antecedent; if it were provable, by *modus ponens* A would be also, contrary to the first theorem.) As it stands, (*) does not outrun theoremhood in K and poses no threat to logicism.

Can we strengthen our knowledge claims to reach A itself? If so, we would have a direct conflict with EL. However, it is clear that in order to know (or come to know) A itself, it is necessary and sufficient that we know (or come to know) that K is consistent. (Clearly, it suffices, since we do know Gödel's first theorem; and it is necessary, in that knowing anything to be unprovable suffices for knowing consistency.)[4] Well, do we know that K is consistent? That certainly depends on what system K is taken to be. If, for instance, it is taken as Zermelo–Fraenkel set theory, it is highly debatable that we know any such thing. If the system is quite weak, say first-order Peano arithmetic, then it might be argued that we know this system to be consistent if we know anything about the infinite at all. The debate over this is interesting, but it need not detain us because we do know that this system is too weak for classical analysis, which, we assume, logicism must incorporate. That is, even if we can claim knowledge of the Gödel sentence for Peano arithmetic, this cannot be the relevant system purported to exist by EL. However, we can be confident that, in a system strong enough for classical analysis, the existence of a model of Peano arithmetic would be demonstrable, so that, once again, our knowledge of the Gödel sentence for the weaker system would not outstrip the logicist's provability. The relevant question would then be whether we can know a new Gödel sentence for a stronger system, adequate to logicist purposes. Again this would depend on whether we can know that this system is consistent.

Generalizing a bit, this suggests that logicism may be safe from Gödel's first incompleteness theorem and even the second, as well. If we do not and cannot know the consistency of a putative logicist system, then we are probably no better off with regard to mathematical knowledge than *it* is (assuming it is otherwise powerful enough). And, if we can know of a system that it is consistent, then, for the benefit of logicism, we should regard the system as too weak to be the relevant one for logicism, and we should step up to a stronger system. One might picture the search for the logicist framework as a climb beginning with arithmetic at the ground level and proceeding to higher and higher levels in a hierarchy of types (possibly into the transfinite). With each step, we gain a wider view of mathematical truth while, at the same time, our foothold becomes less and less sure as knowledge of consistency of the system we're occupying recedes further and further from our grasp. A limit of this process would be the logicist pinnacle, a system strong enough to embrace all the mathematical truths we can know, yet at the same time too strong to admit of any consistency argument that we would find rationally conclusive. Is there such a limit?

A simple, if somewhat curious, argument shows that such a limit cannot exist. We break the argument down into two cases corresponding, respectively, to the requirement that the logicist system asserted to exist in EL be finitely axiomatized, and that it be merely recursively axiomatized. As will emerge, the latter case involves an additional assumption that the more constructively minded may question. If we read "mathematical claim" in the EL thesis as "true mathematical claim," both arguments will depend on an inference from knowability to truth, which we may state in the form of

Lemma 1: If P is a mathematical statement that is knowable (in the sense above), then P expresses a mathematical truth.

Reason: Obvious from the constancy of mathematical truth (CMT, in the sense above) and the generally accepted implication from actual knowledge (in a world) to truth (in that world).[5]

In addition we will need two more lemmas. The first is rather trivial: for any sentence in the language of any EL system, if it is knowable, then that it is true is also knowable. Here we assume no more than that it is possible to name the sentences in a standard way and that the Tarski T-sentences of the form

$$p \text{ iff True}_{L(K)} (P),$$

where P designates p, constitute invariant knowledge in the sense that coming to know one side does not upset knowledge of the *iff* connection. Note that we require only that such knowledge be statable in some meta-language for L(K); there is no need to claim that it is translatable into the putative EL system itself. Thus, using "$\Diamond Kn$" for "is knowable"[6] we have

Lemma 2: For any system K meeting EL and any sentence X in the language of K, L(K):

$$\Diamond \ Kn(X) \rightarrow \Diamond \ Kn \ (\ulcorner \text{True}_{L(K)} (X) \urcorner).^{7}$$

The final lemma we require expresses a similar connection between truth and consistency. Roughly, if it is knowable that a sentence is true, it is also knowable that it is consistent in the sense of implying no contradiction. Of course, if this were interpreted to mean consistent in the overall EL system itself, we would not have any such connection without begging the very question at hand (whether the consistency of such a system is knowable). However, this can be gotten around in the following way. We assume, without any essential loss of generality, that any EL system can be represented in some functional calculus F^n in the sense of Church ([3]) or even in $F^\omega = \cup_i F^i$, $i = 1, 2, 3, \ldots$ Of course, such a representation presupposes *only that the deductive machinery of an EL system* correspond to a functional calculus; in addition any number of predicate and function constants and axioms governing these may be added.[8] They may be called "extra-logical" postulates, but only to mark the syntactic distinction between them and the axioms of F^n (F^ω), without implying anything at issue concerning logicism. Let us call the F^n-(F^ω-) axioms and rules of inference occurring in a representation of any (putative) EL system K the "underlying logic of K," abbreviated "UL(K)". Now the following is invariant knowledge: For any EL system K and sentence X in L(K):

$True_{L(K)}(X) \to A \& \sim A$ is not provable from X in UL(K), i.e., $X \nvdash_{UL(K)} A \& \sim A$.

This is invariant knowledge in the sense that coming to know the antecedent for any particular K and X does not upset knowledge of the if–then connection, so that the consequent also becomes known. Moreover, the reason why this is knowledge at all is because we know how to construct soundness proofs for any F^n (see [3]: 310), and for F^ω as well (by the compactness of $\vdash$). We summarize this in

Lemma 3: For any system K meeting EL and any sentence X in the language of K, L(K):

$$\Diamond \ Kn \ (\ulcorner True_{L(K)}(X) \urcorner) \to \Diamond \ Kn(X \nvdash_{UL(K)} A \& \sim A).$$

Now, the pieces are in place and we can proceed to

Metametatheorem I. There is no formal system that is finitely axiomatizable and that meets the conditions of the epistemological logicist thesis.

Proof: Suppose the contrary. Let K^* be a system meting EL and let C be the conjunction of axioms of K^* (exclusive of any axioms in $UL(K^*)$). (This exclusion allows $UL(K^*)$ to be F^ω.) Then we have:

1	$\vdash_{K^*} C$	Df. of "$\vdash$" and the rule of conjunction.
2	$\Diamond \ Kn \ (C)$	EL hypothesis.
3	$\Diamond \ Kn \ (\ulcorner True_{L(K^*)}(C) \urcorner)$	Lemma 2.
4	$\Diamond \ Kn \ (C \nvdash_{UL(K)^*} A \& \sim A)$	Lemma 3.
5	$\Diamond \ Kn \ (\nvdash_{K^*} A \& \sim A)$	Df. of proof from premises and hypothesis that C is a conjunction of axioms of $K^* - UL(K^*)$.

6 "$\not\vdash_{K*} A \mathbin{\&} \sim A$" is a mathe-   5, Lemma 1, and fact that this
matical truth   sentence is expressible in the
    language of arithmetic.

7 "$\not\vdash_{K*} A \mathbin{\&} \sim A$" asserts the consistency of K* and, as a statement of
number theory, has a translate in L(K*), abbreviated "Con(K*)".

8 $\vdash_{K*}$ Con (K*)   5, 6, 7, EL hypothesis.

Line 8, however, contradicts Gödel's second incompleteness theorem. Therefore, the hypothesis is wrong and the proof is complete.[9]

Although the condition of finite axiomatizability is a real restriction (at least for systems formulated in F^ω), note that some very powerful systems of set theory are finitely axiomatizable (such as NGB). (See, e.g., [4].) Also, note that the logicist system may be of arbitrary finite order. (In well-known cases, such as number theory, finite-axiomatizability is achieved by moving from a first to a second order formulation.) Nevertheless, it is interesting to consider what happens when we relax the finite-axiomatizability requirement to recursive axiomatizability. In that case, surprisingly perhaps, matters are not so straightforward.

Let K be a system meeting the requirements of EL and containing infinitely many axioms in the recursive set $\Gamma = \{A_1, A_2, \ldots \}$. Let $\{B_i\}$ be the sequence of finite conjunctions of the first i members of Γ. By the hypothesis that K satisfies EL, we have

(i) $\forall i \; \Diamond \; Kn \ulcorner B_i \text{ is true} \urcorner$

i.e. for each finite conjunction of axioms, it is possible to know it. Now, if we could move from (i) to

(ii) $\Diamond \; Kn \ulcorner \forall i \; B_i \text{ is true} \urcorner$,

we could reason exactly as in the finite case: truth of all the B_i suffices for consistency of Γ, a known connection: knowability of the antecedent yields knowability of the consequent, whence incompatability of EL and Gödel's second theorem. However, passing from (i) to (ii) is certainly not generally valid. Each of the infinite set of sentences may be knowable singly without there being any possible situation in which it is known that all are true. Moving quantifiers across intensional operators is a notorious business, and here we have two of them.

We can imagine a world in which a mathematical community survives indefinitely, forever amassing mathematical truths without loss. Countenancing such a world could allow us to move the universal quantifier of (i) across the possibility-sign (assuming we regard our knowledge operator as applying to the community at large). Still, there is the epistemic barrier. Crossing it amounts to passing from the "potential" to the "actual" infinite. In some world, it is known of each of infinitely many statements that it is true. But can we say that there or elsewhere it is known *that they are all true*? Such knowledge would encompass an infinite totality. Thus, passing from (i) to (ii) depends in general on the conditions under which it is possible to know quantified statements ranging over infinite sets, a central question of mathematical epistemology.

Normally, within mathematics proper, one justifies such statements by a proof, frequently employing mathematical induction. Thereby we can know not only of each natural number, say, that it is uniquely factorable into primes, but that all are. Justifying induction itself was, of course, one of the main goals of logicism and was perceived, by some, such as Poincaré, as an insuperable obstacle to logicism. That, however, is not the issue here. For, even if one accepted mathematical inductions as primitive, one simply has no way of knowing, independently of the particular system K, whether an inductive argument could be constructed leading to the universal sentence of (ii).

My aim here is not to try to justify the move from (i) to (ii) in general, since that seems to me to be impossible at this level of generality. Rather it is to urge that it is a genuine problem on whose resolution the application of the Gödel theorems to logicism depends. Thus, it is worth stressing that, even if we are willing, as we were above, to relativize our knowledge operator to a whole, eternal, mathematical community, we cannot by any means automatically pass from ⌜$\forall i\ \mathrm{Kn}\ \ulcorner B_i$ is true⌝ to ⌜$\mathrm{Kn}\ \ulcorner \forall i\ B_i$ is true.⌝ Even if we do not require that every bit of community knowledge be localized in some individual knower (or other), we must make sense of a community's knowing an "extremal clause" to the effect "and these are all the sentences in question (i.e., finite conjunctions from Γ)" before we can attribute knowledge of the universal claim.[10]

Thus, at this abstract level, we do not have a categorical extension of metametatheorem I to the infinite case, but rather a conditional one:

Metametatheorem II: No recursively axiomatizable formal system for which the (material) conditional "if (i) then (ii)" holds can meet the conditions of the epistemological logicist thesis (EL).[11]

It is to be emphasized that the awkward phrasing making reference to the material conditional is intentional. Many systems – perhaps all that would be acceptable to logicism on other grounds – may be ruled out by the argument proving this theorem, without there being any claim whatever of an "implication" in any sense of (ii) by (i).[12]

Thus, the impact of Gödel's theorems on epistemological logicism is by no means trivially negative, once we relax the restriction of finite axiomatizability. Everything turns on some formally subtle but highly significant quantifier manipulations, the ultimate status of which we are in no position to decide.

However, there is an interesting *epistemic analogue* of metametatheorem II which should not be overlooked. Although there is a window left open through which the EL thesis can pass, *it can never be known of any recursively axiomatizable system* (to which the Gödel theorems apply) *that it passes through*! For, suppose there were such a system, K, of which it could be known (in the relevant sense) that it satisfied the conditions of EL. Then the following would be knowable:

Every theorem of K represents a knowable mathematical claim.

But then (because the connection between knowability and truth is invariant knowledge) it would also be knowable that every theorem of K represents a mathematical truth, whence follows the knowability that K is consistent. Thus, K would have to contain a theorem asserting its own consistency, contradicting Gödel's second theorem after all. In short, the escape route left open for EL exists only in principle: there may possibly be in fact a system satisfying EL, containing infinitely many axioms such that it is not knowable that all of them are true, and it may conceivably even be knowable that this is the case; but it literally could not be known *of* any individual system that it is such a system. In this epistemic sense, codifying the limits of mathematical knowledge must transcend those limits.

Finally, it should be remarked that some may wish to extend the term "logic" to systems that are not even recursively axiomatized. Whether a logicist thesis appropriate to such a relaxed conception is tenable depends on just how non-constructive one is willing to be. For a wide class of "non-constructive logics," such as those obtained by taking limits of sequences of recursive axiom sets along paths in the constructive ordinals, analogues of Gödel's incompleteness theorems hold.[13] For such systems, we would expect what has been said above regarding recursively axiomatized systems and EL to carry over. Saving epistemological logicism from Gödel, then, would seem to require giving up any natural way of grounding logic, even indirectly, on constructive methods. Whether such "logic" would be better named "theologic" I will not attempt to decide.

Appendix

In quite a different context, Paul Benacerraf (in [1]) has formulated an argument concerning the "provability of consistency" that bears some resemblance to the main argument we have used above (in the proof of the first metametatheorem). It will be instructive to draw some comparisons. As we shall see, an examination of Benacerraf's argument suggests that we overlooked a simple way of by-passing the restriction we thought we needed in the infinite case (to systems satisfying the move from (i) to (ii)). Investigating this may also shed light on the status of Benacerraf's argument, which has provoked a good deal of discussion.

That argument was intended to represent "what underlies the vague one" of J. R. Lucas (in [9]) to the effect that Gödel's incompleteness theorems rule out "mechanism," the view that human minds are essentially complex computing mechanisms. Crudely put, Lucas wanted to claim he could not be a Turing machine (properly modelled as one?) because he could "prove" his own consistency, something no Turing machine can do, by an application of Gödel's second incompleteness theorem. This is not the place to enter into the substantive debate over "mechanism."[14] Rather, I want to focus on the early stages of Benacerraf's reconstruction of Lucas. The upshot of that argument was not that mechanism is false, but that

> if I am a Turing machine, not only can I not ascertain which one, but neither can I ascertain of any instantiation of the machine that I happen to be that it is an instantiation of that machine. ([1]: 29)

Some have, according to Benacerraf, seen in this the conclusion that "psychology is impossible," whereas Benacerraf himself, in an appendix to the same paper that contained the reconstruction of Lucas, presented another argument to the effect that the principles underlying the first argument lead to contradiction.[15] In any case, the status of the first argument has remained unclear. How does it get off the ground? Here are the first four steps as they originally appeared:

1 Let S = {x: I can prove x}

S represents my deductive output. It may be viewed as consisting of sentences under an interpretation. The sense of 'prove' involved is not one which limits S to the output of a machine, but it *does* involve the assumption of correctness which we saw Lucas making and without which his arguments don't go through. It must be a sense of 'prove' which Lucas can use.

2 Let S* = {x: S ⊢ x}

S* is the closure of S under the rules of first order logic with identity . . .

3 S* is consistent.

Since every member of S is true – I can't prove what is false – and first order logic preserves truth, every member of S* is true. S* is therefore highly consistent.

4 "Con(S*)" ∈ S

Since 1–3 above constitutes a proof that S* is consistent, and since I produced that proof, it follows that I can prove that S* is consistent. Therefore, by the definition of S, "Con(S*)" ∈ S. ([1]: 23–24)

This kind of reasoning is used once more to obtain in S* the statement that every recursively enumerable subset of S* is consistent. Then a tripartite assumption (step 9) – roughly, that some recursively enumerable set is known to extend arithmetic, is known not to outstrip S*, and in fact is not outstripped by S* – is seen to lead to contradiction. Each part of step 9 gets used in the derivation, and there is room for debate over which to reject. Crucially, step 4, which concerns us, is used as well.

The analogy between the above four steps and the argument for our first theorem should be clear. A sense of 'can prove' is adopted which guarantees truth, corresponding to our assumption that 'can be known' guarantees truth. Next the obvious connection between truth and consistency is invoked to arrive at some special status for the statement that the system in question is consistent. In my own argument, the status is "knowability," hence provability in any system meeting the conditions of the epistemological logicist thesis (EL). For Benacerraf, the special status is "provability," whence it is claimed the statement of consistency belongs to the (theorems of the) system asserted to be consistent (S*). Notice, however, that Benacerraf encounters no problem about "proving" consistency for non-finitely axiomatizable systems. This is because the truth of every member of S* is simply assumed at the outset. But, did we not in effect make the same assumption in starting off our argument with the supposition that some system satisfying EL exists? Such a system has only knowable theorems, and, by hypothesis, these are all true. This suggests that perhaps we "created a problem" where none existed, namely the problem of extending the argument to the infinite case (the move from (i) to (ii)). Specifically, couldn't we have followed Benacerraf's chain of reasoning as follows:

"Suppose there is a system K meeting EL, with finite sets of axioms B_i as before. By hypothesis

(1)′ $\forall i \; \Diamond \; Kn \ulcorner B_i$ is true$\urcorner$.

But then each of the B_i is true, since knowability implies truth, i.e.

(2)′ $\forall i \ulcorner B_i$ is true$\urcorner$

Therefore, the system K is consistent,

(3)′ $Con(K)$.

But now we have

(4)′   '$Con(K)$' (a representative thereof) is a theorem of K, *contra* Gödel, because (1)′–(3)′ above constitutes a proof that K is consistent, and since I produced that proof, it follows that it can be known that K is consistent. Therefore, by EL, 'Con(K)' must be represented by a theorem of K'"?

Can this be right? Does the fact that (3)′ follows from (1)′ – or, more precisely, the fact that I exhibit this – establish that the conclusion, line (3)′, is knowable? Surely this is achieving epistemic competence a bit too easily. In fact, nothing of the sort follows. We derived (3)′ correctly all right; but for a derivation to establish knowledge (or knowability), the premises must occupy the status of knowledge (or knowability). But, of course, no such status exists for (1)′ or (2)′; (1)′ is rather a hypothesis, with a dummy label for a system K, in a *reductio* argument. The knowledge we establish in moving from (1)′ to (3)′ is not (3)′ or (4)′ but

(5)′ ($\forall$K) (K satisfies EL $\supset$ Con (K)).

We certainly cannot yet conclude

(6)′ ($\forall$K) (K satisfies EL $\supset$ $\Diamond$ Kn Con (K)),

since *the knowability of "Con(K)"* has nowhere been derived. In sum, we were right not to reason in this manner, and the problem in extending the argument to the infinite case is genuine.

If Benacerraf's mode of reasoning would have been fallacious for us, is it still all right for Benacerraf? Of course, one can point out that, in the dialectical enterprise of showing charity to one's opponent (in this case, Lucas), faulty inferences are a good investment so long as no self-serving capital is made on them. But, as indicated above, Benacerraf's argument has taken on a life of its own.

Looking back at steps 1–4, we see that the first two are just definitions, and that 3 certainly follows: any set of truths is indeed consistent. The problem comes with step 4 where it is said that 1–3 constitute a "proof" that S* is consistent. What does this mean? At first it is said that S consists in "deductive output," but immediately thereafter it is stipulated that to be provable in the relevant sense is sufficient for truth. If this were all there were to it, I suppose step 4 would be unobjectionable; 3 was obtained as "deductive output," and, by hypothesis, it is true. But the whole purpose of Lucas is to argue that humans' mathematical knowledge distinguishes them from any machine. "Proof" in the relevant sense must serve to *establish the conclusion* as true, not merely *have* a true conclusion. Viewed in this light, what does the argument 1–3 establish? Simply that some (ill-defined) set of (established?) truths is consistent. Surely as an argument that anyone's real (even rationally reconstructed) deductive output (logically closed) is consistent, it is entirely question-begging, since, as already noted, the truth of each sentence of the "output" is *stipulated*. (Whether all such sentences can be true, or are simultaneously satisfiable, is precisely what is at issue.) Until we have a more definite characterization of the initial set S (intended to reflect human mathematical competence), we really don't yet know what we're talking about. But of this we may be sure: if the characterization builds in truth, a "proof" of consistency is an epistemically useless triviality; whereas, if the characterization does not build in truth, then (as Benacerraf suggests) we simply haven't been presented with an argument.

There is one conceivable counter to this. It might be alleged (in defense of Benacerraf's first four steps) that an ingredient of human creativity is entering at step 3, where the baby-logical link between truth and consistency is employed. Thus, the argument might be said to transcend the algorithmic character of mechanical reasoning at just this point, and that would be enough for the purposes at hand (exploring the limits of "mechanism"). This objection is wrong, however, on the relevant facts, since there is no reason why a machine cannot derive the consistency of a set of sentences given to be true by stipulation![16]

Does this mean a machine can prove "its own" consistency? Not if the quoted expression is taken to mean its total output as standardly specified, and we understand by "prove", "formally prove in the system itself (without adding new axioms)". If, however, we are talking not about standard specification of total output and are allowing proofs to be in an extended system, then machines and we can easily provide such consistency proofs. But of course Gödel's theorems have nothing to say about this latter sort of "proof."[17]

Notes

* In 1975, David Kaplan published a paper in the *Journal of Philosophy* entitled, "How to Russell a Frege–Church." By requiring of each successor title that it share at least two names with its predecessor, perhaps the unfortunate sequence can soon be terminated.

1 A finitistic formalism, of the kind sometimes associated with Hilbert, is not thus ruled out, since unbounded quantified formulas are not viewed as having truth-values. In any case, it is Gödel's second incompleteness theorem that upsets Hilbert's *program*. For a good discussion, see [10].

2 The second theorem asserts that any sufficiently strong formal system meeting the conditions of the first theorem (including consistency) cannot have as a theorem any standard formalization of the claim that the system is consistent.

N.B. Throughout, whenever we speak of formal consistency proofs it is to be assumed that standard consistency predicates (or sentences) are at issue. This restriction is necessary due to results of Feferman to the effect that Gödel's second theorem does not apply to certain systems (capable of proving the consistency of their finite subsystems) provided a kind of "pathological" proof predicate is employed in the statement of consistency. (Also, if the system is weak in certain ways, it may prove its consistency stated in terms that appear non-pathological (Cf. [7]). I am indebted to Mic Detlefsen for calling this to my attention.) Although in particular cases, what counts as "pathological" may be clear, there remains (to my knowledge) the problem of justifying a precise, general criterion. See [5]. For an informal presentation and helpful discussion, see [10].

3 It is not being claimed that Frege or Russell (or Carnap) ever explicitly formulated such a epistemological thesis. Rather, such a thesis may be seen as an interesting one in its own right, designed to take into account the most obvious limitations on formalization deriving from Gödel's theorems, while remaining within the spirit of the logicist program in so far as it sought to provide the grounds of mathematical knowledge (Cf. [12], Ch. 1).

4 In a different sense, the necessity is not so obvious: need the knowledge of consistency figure in coming to know the undecidable sentence? Divine revelation aside, it's hard to see how we could establish unprovability of A apart from a proof such as Gödel's, or a model-theoretic argument; in either case, consistency must be assumed. Our knowledge of the status of A depends on our knowledge of the consistency of K.

5 There is a sense of "knowable" that seems automatically to entail truth. On this reading, of course, this lemma is just excess baggage.

6 We employ the modal operator "$\diamond$" for "it is possible that" in order to exhibit logical complexity that will emerge below when we consider non-finitely axiomatizable systems, without intending any commitment to "metaphysical possibility," which, in the present context, it seems unnecessary to consider.

7 It must be emphasized that nowhere in the ensuing argument need it be assumed that "True$_{L(K)}$(C)" is knowable as *mathematical* knowledge. Such a premise *is* required in a *different* argument to the effect that EL conflicts with Tarski's theorem on the indefinability of truth. Some have thought that we need this premise also on the grounds that the epistemological logicist might deny Lemma 2 because the predicate "True$_{L(K)}$" is not in the language of K. This involves tacitly assuming that the idealized mathematician contemplated by the EL thesis is for some reason confined to knowledge statable in the formal language in which mathematical knowledge is to be expressed. In that case, Lemma 2 would indeed be objectionable. However, I see no basis for such a restriction. Idealized human mathematicians have at least as much capacity for semantic ascent as we ordinary mortals. What would prevent such a mathematician from introducing a new truth-predicate, not by explicit definition of course, but by the scheme for Tarski T-sentences? One may claim that such an extension of a formal system is "trivial," in that it is a conservative extension, not allowing us to prove things that we should like to see proved (Cf. [8]: 34). Be that as it may; Lemma 2 does not presuppose more than the capacity to extend the EL system in this trivial way.

Thus, the proof of metametatheorem I will give, relying on Gödel's second incompleteness theorem and not on Tarski's theorem, has the advantage of side-stepping the question whether sentences employing truth predicates do or do not belong to "mathematics." The argument presented here arrives, via metamathematical concepts whose status can remain moot, at the conclusion that a sentence asserting the consistency of a formal system is knowable. Now this kind of sentence we already know to be statable in the language of arithmetic. No further argument over its status as mathematics is required.

8 For example, all the axioms of ZF set theory, plus any number of large cardinal axioms or other axioms of infinity, may be added.

9 It has been suggested that a logicist could get around this result by maintaining that a sentence in mathematical language may be knowable without being "mathematically knowable," and then restricting the EL thesis to this (presumably narrower) class of sentences. Then, even if one grants that first-order logical moves preserve "mathematical knowability," one may still object to lemma 2, on the grounds that truth claims belong, not to mathematics, but to metamathematics. Now while there are independent reasons why even powerful truth concepts should be seen as mathematical (cf. e.g. [8]), it seems to me quite counter to the thrust of logicism to insist on a sharp distinction between mathematics and metamathematics, especially where all that is involved is a conservative extension with stipulative axioms (Tarski biconditionals). On the other hand, one might insist that for a sentence to become mathematically known, it must be arrived at "by proof": hence the EL axioms would not be thought of as knowable in the first place. This, however, is incoherent, since proof is relative to system and systems have many equivalent formulations with different sets of axioms. Until some formulations have been singled out as privileged, a viewpoint here has not even been articulated. What basis there might be in logicism or elsewhere for such a distinction I have no idea.

Incidentally, in note 7 above I just argued that the proof of metametatheorem I has the advantage of sidestepping the question whether sentences employing truth predicates do or do not belong to mathematics, and in this note I seem to have needed to take a stand on just that question. There is no conflict because metametatheorem I concerns the EL thesis as formulated in this paper, whereas my stand in this note concerns the propriety of attaching importance to a different thesis.

10 In some cases, of course, many of us are persuaded that we have knowledge of a sentence affirming the truth of all axioms of an infinite set, without imagining ourselves capable of carrying out an infinite search. Rather we appeal to our grasp of recursive rules governing the construction of formulas, for example, all formulas of first-order arithmetic with one free variable; we add to this some further claim that the structure we intend to describe with the axioms (e.g. a standard model of arithmetic) satisfies any sentence having a certain definite form (e.g. that of an induction axiom). (We might spell this out along logicist lines, by appealing to second-order notions: we know that every wff with one free variable picks out a set of natural numbers, and we understand the numbers to be just those objects that fall in every hereditary set containing zero.) Some of us are even comfortable with the claim that all the axioms of replacement of ZF set theory are true. The point is, however, that the thesis EL by itself does not commit the logicist to the knowability of the corresponding claim for any putative logicist system K, independent of any further information about that system.

It would be nice to have a characterization of systems satisfying the move from (i) to (ii). Are they just the system all but a finite set of whose axioms can be given by a finite number of axiom schemata? If so, then, except for systems formulated in F^ω, such systems are already covered by metametatheorem I, since such schemata can be replaced by axioms at the next higher order.

11 Some have criticized this theorem as vacuous, arguing as follows: any true quantifier-free sentence of Peano arithmetic is knowable (being provable) but if one assumes the move from (i) to (ii), then any true sentence with just universal initial quantifiers is also knowable "and thus a theorem of the logicist

system, which is impossible." (Presumably, the Gödel undecidable sentence would be a counterexample.) Thus, for the relevant cases, the move from (i) to (ii) is clearly blocked.

Now a moment's reflection suffices to realize what is going on here: the move from (i) to (ii) has been shown unsound *on the assumption that the logical system exists*. As we noted at the outset, knowability of the Gödel sentence for a weaker system would only establish that that system is not EL's. The critic, moreover, needs the existential assumption implied by the phrase, "the logicist system," in order to move from knowability to provability (presumably by EL, clause (i)). Our critic has in effect sketched a proof of metametatheorem II. (With criticism like this, who needs support?)

12 It might occur to the reader that perhaps we could weaken or bypass entirely the restriction of metametatheorem II if we imposed the requirement of compactness on systems alleged to exist by EL. The compactness theorem (for consistency) states that if every finite subset of a set Γ of sentences is consistent, then the whole set Γ is also consistent. Note that this version of compactness is trivially satisfied by any system in which proofs are finite. As such, it is hardly any restriction at all on the EL thesis. Furthermore, it has the status of invariant knowledge, something we may legitimately suppose known in any of the situations relevant for determining knowability of mathematical truth. Therefore, one might reason, we could extend theorem I to the infinite case by simply applying the argument for it to each finite subset of Γ, thereby obtaining the knowability of the antecedent of compactness for K, whence knowability of the consequent follows. Tantalizingly enough, however, this reasoning is fallacious, as closer inspection will reveal.

What EL commits us to is that, for every finite subset B_i of axioms of Γ, there is some situation in which it becomes known and, therefore (by reasoning of theorem I), the consistency of it becomes known. That is, we have

(iii) $\forall i \; \Diamond \; Kn \ulcorner B_i \text{ consistent} \urcorner$

But the antecedent of the compactness theorem applied to K has the form $\ulcorner \forall i \; B_i \text{ consistent} \urcorner$. It is the knowability of this, of the claim *that* every finite subset of Γ is consistent, that must be made out if the above reasoning is to go through. That is, in order to infer the knowability of the consistency of the whole set Γ on the basis of compactness, we must first arrive at

(iv) $\Diamond \; Kn \ulcorner \forall i \; B_i \text{ consistent} \urcorner$.

But this is precisely the form of the move from (i) to (ii) that we encountered in trying to extend theorem I in the first place. Replacing talk of truth with talk of consistency alters nothing. Compactness can only go to work once the universal quantifier has crossed the intensional operators; it plays no role in the crossing. There would seem to be no way of avoiding the antecedent conditional of metametatheorem II.

13 A general incompleteness theorem for such progressions based on second order or higher functional calculi is given by Feferman in [6], p. 314: Any such consistent progression lacks as a theorem either a true Π_1^1 or a true Σ_1^1 sentence. Yet such a sentence may well count as knowable, depending on what it asserts.

14 For a good treatment exposing a number of confusions in attempts to brandish Gödel as an anti-mechanist instrument, see [13].

15 In [2], Chihara modified this second argument in order to arrive at essentially the same conclusion as that of Benacerraf's first argument. Space does not permit adequate treatment here of the issues raised by this modified second argument. Suffice it to say, there are several problems with it, some of which Chihara discusses (though most of his discussion concerns its implications). However, a weak link that he does not discuss involves passing from knowledge of a machine's program to knowledge of a formula, S(x), that arithmetically defines the machine's output, S. According to Chihara, this step "seems reasonable," but in fact it is problematic. Even given an arithmetical definition S(x) of S, one needs some method of telling which natural numbers satisfy it. A natural sufficient condition for this is that the defining formula be a representing formula in some formal system. Given such a formula we may claim that, for each n, it is knowable that the machine, T, puts out n iff n satisfies S(x); but what Chihara's argument requires is the stronger claim that it be knowable that, for all n, T puts out n iff n satisfies S(x). This has precisely the form of the step from (i) to (ii) encountered above in connection with our own argument. There is no apparent reason why the move is legitimate in the present setting. That it is not gains support from the following technical consideration, having to do with limitations on uniformity results in recursion theory (see [11], 5.5). It is well known that the recursive sets are not closed uniformly effectively under complementation. Thus, we cannot pass uniformly from r.e. indices (of recursive sets) *to* representing formulas *and back* (since the move from a formula to its negation is obviously uniformly effective). But we have a uniform method of constructing, for any representing formula, a Turing machine whose output is the extension of the formula, i.e. (codes for) all the numbers satisfying the formula. (The method just consists in describing a search for positive instances of the formula among the theorems of the formal system in which the representing formula is being used.) Therefore, we cannot go uniformly effectively from r.e. indices to representing formulas. In other words, there is no general method, given the "program" of a machine (whose output is recursive), for finding effectively a formula that represents the output.

Of course, connecting such facts with mathematical epistemology depends upon more precise specification of the epistemic notions themselves.

16 For a Turing machine M can be supplied with a new predicate to serve as a truth-predicate and appropriate axioms (Tarski biconditionals and statements that each axiom is true), whereby M will be able to derive the link between truth and consistency. M can thus carry out a Benacerraf-style consistency proof. Consistency of what? Not of its entire output as standardly specified, but of its output *stipulated to be true.* Cf. Feferman's point about the intensionality of consistency proofs which emerges clearly in this context ([6]: 260, 262, 283).

17 I wish to thank Mark Steiner, Richard Grandy, Michael Resnik, and Mic Detlefsen for helpful comments on an earlier draft of this paper. For helpful discussion I am also indebted to J. Michael Dunn.

References

[1] P. Benacerraf, "God, the Devil, and Gödel," *Monist* 51, 1 (Jan. 1967): 9–23.
[2] C. Chihara, "On Alleged Refutations of Mechanism Using Gödel's Incompleteness Results," *The Journal of Philosophy* LXIX, 17 (Sept. 21, 1972): 507–26.
[3] A. Church, *Introduction to Mathematical Logic, I* (Princeton: Princeton University Press, 1966).

[4] P. J. Cohen, *Set Theory and the Continuum Hypothesis* (New York: Benjamin, 1966).

[5] S. Feferman, "Arithmetization of Metamathematics in a General Setting," *Fundamenta Mathematicae* LXIX (1960): 35–92.

[6] —— "Transfinite Recursive Progressions of Axiomatic Theories," *Journal of Symbolic Logic*, 27, 3 (Sept., 1962): 259–316.

[7] R. G. Jeroslow, "Consistency Statements in Formal Theories," *Fundamenta Mathematicae*, LXXII (1971): 17–40.

[8] C. Parsons, "Informal Axiomatization, Formalization and the Concept of Truth," *Synthèse* 27 (1974): 27–47.

[9] J. R. Lucas, "Minds, Machines and Gödel," reprinted in *Minds and Machines*, A. R. Anderson, ed., (Englewood Cliffs, N.J.: Prentice-Hall, 1964).

[10] M. D. Resnik, "On the Philosophical Significance of Consistency Proofs," *Journal of Philosophical Logic*, 3 (1974): 133–47.

[11] H. Rogers, *Theory of Recursive Functions and Effective Computability* (New York: McGraw-Hill, 1967).

[12] M. Steiner, *Mathematical Knowledge* (Ithaca, N.Y.: Cornell University Press, 1975).

[13] J. Webb, "Metamathematics and the Philosophy of Mind," *Philosophy of Science*, 35 (1968): 156–78.

13

Epistemic Logicism and Russell's Regressive Method*

A. D. Irvine

1 Introduction

Traditional accounts of logicism invariably include an epistemic component. The reduction of mathematics to logic, it is claimed, is not just of formal or mathematical interest, but of epistemological importance as well. After all, logicism, formalism and intuitionism all arose in their modern forms partly in response to a common problem: the crisis in foundations brought about by the discovery of the antinomies.[1] Twentieth century logicism, like formalism and intuitionism, took as part of its mandate the task of restoring to mathematics the kind of certainty which could only come about through the elimination of the paradoxes. Only by accounting for and eliminating the paradoxes, it was claimed, could mathematical belief again be justified, thereby regaining the high degree of certainty which had preceded their discovery.

Because of its purported certainty, mathematics in general (and geometry in particular) had been regarded by many until well into the nineteenth and early twentieth centuries as the paragon branch of human learning. After all, the critical movement which began in the 1820s had eliminated much of the vagueness and many of the contradictions of earlier mathematics. Bolzano, Abel, Cauchy and Weierstrass had taken up the challenge of rigorizing the calculus. By 1837 Hamilton had introduced ordered couples of reals as the first step in supplying a logical basis for the complex numbers. Weierstrass, Dedekind and Cantor had all developed methods for founding the irrationals in terms of the rationals. Building upon the results of Grassmann and Dedekind, Peano[2] had gone on to develop the rationals from his now famous axioms for **N**. Thus, beginning with a few primitive notions, it was possible to derive all the magnificent results of mathematics in a rigorous, coherent fashion. Prior to the discovery of the antinomies, mathematics was seen as the quintessential branch of human learning which other disciplines strove to emulate.

Despite this, the picture was in reality not quite so simple. Work in non-Euclidean geometries, which had begun with Saccheri, Klügel, Lambert and others in the mid-1700s, culminated in the geometries of Bolyai and Lobachevski.[3] Thus, by the mid-nineteenth century the mathematical community had begun reconsidering the relationship between mathematical truth and truth in nature. At the same time, despite the initial advances of the critical movement, analysis and other branches of mathematics were still known to have their own share of difficulties. Until the mid-nineteenth century the calculus had gained its legitimacy in large measure from its analogy to, and from applications within, geometry. However, with the discovery of continuous but nowhere differentiable curves and other unexpected results, work in analysis began to outdistance geometrical intuition. With the discovery of the antinomies in set theory at the turn of the century, dogmatic certainty in mathematical results had become a thing of the past.

It was in response to these unprecedented events that Russell, Hilbert and Brouwer put forward their respective remedies. Despite their differences, all three emphasized epistemic foundations. All three shared the common presumption that mathematics required a foundation which could eliminate the antinomies and account for the putative certainty of traditional results. In the case of logicism, Russell's autobiographical comment is often cited:

I wanted certainty in the kind of way in which people want religious faith. I thought that certainty is more likely to be found in mathematics than elsewhere. But I discovered that many mathematical demonstrations, which my teachers expected me to accept, were full of fallacies, and that, if certainty were indeed discoverable in mathematics, it would be in a new kind of mathematics, with more solid foundations than those that had hitherto been thought secured.[4]

Russell was not alone in this view. Hilbert is equally blunt in his epistemic demands: "The goal of my theory is to establish once and for all the certitude of mathematical methods."[5] Later he adds the following assessment of the then current situation:

Admittedly, the present state of affairs where we run up against the paradoxes is intolerable. Just think, the definitions and deductive methods which everyone learns, teaches and uses in mathematics, the paragon of truth and certitude, lead to absurdities! If mathematical thinking is defective, where are we to find truth and certitude?[6]

One way or another, the notorious antinomies had to be accounted for and shown to be eliminable. One way or another, mathematics had to be given a secure epistemic foundation and the certainty of its results explained.

How was it that Russell's logicism would meet these goals? The received view is that, according to Russell, clear and immediate epistemic gains would result from the reduction of mathematics to logic. By reducing mathematics to logic the problem of justifying mathematical belief would be reduced to the comparatively easier problem of justifying the self-evident principles of logic. Frege's original idea had been that if the principles of logic are granted self-evidence, and that if the laws of arithmetic can be shown to be derivable from them, arithmetic will have become epistemologically justified. On such an account, arithmetic would become just as certain as logic itself. In Russell's enlarged program it was supposed that all of mathematics would acquire, in Haack's helpful phrase, this "innocence by association."[7]

This standard epistemic interpretation of Russell's logicism needs to be carefully appraised. Perhaps surprisingly, such an account is palpably inconsistent with Russell's explicitly stated views on the subject. In addition, in and of itself such an account is susceptible to a number of well-known, related objections. Briefly put, it is unlikely that mathematics should gain its sole epistemic justification via logic since parts of mathematics are themselves more certain than (and are often known independently of) the requisite body of logical belief.

In what follows, Section 2 will consider in greater detail just such common objections to any straightforward epistemic interpretation of logicism. Since Russell held that, because of this type of objection, epistemic logicism cannot provide an adequate epistemic warrant for even the very elementary parts of the discipline, the so-called standard epistemic interpretation which is so often attributed to him must be incorrect. Section 3 then goes on to consider Russell's actual epistemological views with regard to mathematics. An interpretation of Russell's mathematical epistemology which differs considerably from the standard view will be defended. In particular, it will be shown that, contrary to popular belief, Russell consistently upholds as fundamental a distinction between the epistemological and logical orders within mathematics. Section 4 builds on this interpretation of Russell's mathematical epistemology. Parallels between Russell and Gödel are discussed. It is then pointed out that Russell's mathematical epistemology is of more than simple historical interest. Despite the acknowledged failure of logicism, Russell's plausible, commonsense epistemological account lends support to recent work done in contemporary philosophy of mathematics. By highlighting important epistemic similarities between mathematics and the empirical sciences, Russell's epistemological account of mathematics should help substantiate the view that mathematics is itself a science, albeit a highly abstract one.

2 Epistemic Logicism

Russell first advocated his logicist thesis in print in 1901. In his essay "Recent Work on the Principles of Mathematics" he enthusiastically and confidently comments:

> Now the fact is that, though there are indefinables and indemonstrables in every branch of applied mathematics, there are none in pure mathematics except such as belong to general logic . . . All pure mathematics – Arithmetic, Analysis, and Geometry – is built up by combinations of the primitive ideas of logic, and its propositions are deduced from the general axioms of logic.[8]

This foreshadowed Russell's more famous 1903 statement in the Introduction to his *Principles of Mathematics*, where he makes the claim that

> all pure mathematics deals exclusively with concepts definable in terms of a very small number of fundamental logical concepts, and that all its propositions are deducible from a very small number of fundamental logical principles.[9]

Thus, in its original formulation, Russell's logicism had two goals. The first was to show that all mathematical concepts can be derived from purely logical ones via explicit definitions. To put this another way, it was to show that, in essence, the vocabulary of mathematics is a proper part of the vocabulary of logic. The second goal was to show that all mathematical theorems are capable of being deduced from purely logical axioms by means of uncontroversial rules of deductive inference. In other words, according to the logicist, the theorems of mathematics would turn out to be a proper subset of the theorems of logic. Viewed together, these two goals can be seen to define the logicist position. In Carnap's often quoted account of the doctrine, it is these two goals which together entail the thesis that "Every provable mathematical sentence is translatable into a sentence which contains only primitive logical symbols and which is provable in logic."[10] It is a position which Russell held consistently and which he repeated often. For example, over fifty years later Russell once again unhesitatingly explained that the purpose of *Principia* and of the Frege–Russell–Whitehead program "was to show that all pure mathematics follows from purely logical premises and uses only concepts definable in logical terms."[11]

Today, these famous statements of the objectives of the logicist program are regularly given an epistemological gloss. That is, they are often identified with, or thought to entail, the view that the reduction of mathematics to the more easily justified principles of logic provides a secure, otherwise

unavailable, foundation for mathematical knowledge. Under this interpretation, logicism gains epistemological significance since, in claiming
that mathematics is based upon logic, the logicist is apparently claiming
to reveal the true grounds by which mathematical knowledge can be
explained and justified. According to this view, since we are epistemically
justified in accepting the self-evident truths of logic, the successful identification of mathematics with logic would give us the same justification for
accepting the truths of mathematics. Let us baptize this commonly
espoused epistemic aspect of the logicist program *epistemic logicism*.[12]

Once logicism itself is accepted, epistemic logicism gains a *prima facie*
plausibility. Commentators, for example, regularly interpret traditional
logicists such as Russell as advocating a position which includes just this
type of epistemic component.[13] Although unlikely in the case of Russell,
for other logicists such as Frege and Hempel, this interpretation is quite
clearly correct.[14] Frege, for example, makes explicit his epistemic goal at
the beginning of his *Grundgesetze*: "In my *Grundlagen der Arithmetic*, I
sought to make it plausible that arithmetic is a branch of logic and *need not
borrow any ground of proof whatever from either experience or intuition*. In
the present book this shall now be confirmed."[15]

However, upon closer examination, even if the reduction of mathematics
to logic were unproblematic (which it is not),[16] defined as it is, epistemic
logicism is open to a series of related commonsense objections. For example, consider an elementary arithmetical proposition such as "2 + 2 = 4".
What is it that provides the requisite justification for our acceptance of
such a proposition? If it is suggested that our knowledge that such a
proposition obtains results from a formal proof from first principles,
immediate objections arise. Not everyone who knows such elementary
propositions to be true, if pressed, could come up with a satisfactory
sequence of sentences which would constitute the required proof. In fact,
most people who know many elementary arithmetical truths could not
even truthfully claim ever to have seen such a proof, let alone to being
able to reproduce one as a warrant for their belief. Additionally, unlike
children, most adults would not be content to base their claim to such
knowledge on an argument from authority. If there is one thing that we do
not need someone else to justify for us, it is that 2 + 2 = 4. Even if the
authorities began to change their minds on this issue, eventually agreeing
that such elementary arithmetical statements were false, for most of us this
fact alone would not constitute sufficient ground for changing our minds.
Most of us would continue to feel justified in our beliefs despite our
inability to provide the requisite justification by way of logical proof.

A related argument for saying that a proof from first principles does not
provide the requisite justification for such a basic arithmetical belief is that
in almost every instance we would be less certain of the proof itself than we
are of its conclusion. If asked which we feel more justified in accepting, that

such a proof is sound, or that 2 + 2 = 4, most of us (if we are prepared to answer and are not epistemically indifferent between the two) would choose the latter. After all, a complete proof from self-evident premises would have to be very detailed.[17] It seems quite unlikely that after such a lengthy proof anyone could seriously claim that it was the proof which provided the justification of our belief that 2 + 2 = 4. It is much more likely that an error has been made in the proof than that 2 + 2 does not equal 4. It follows that our knowledge of such basic arithmetical beliefs comes from some means other than mathematical proof.

This type of objection to epistemic logicism is not new. Poincaré attacked logicism on just such grounds.[18] Wittgenstein, too, argued that it is not possible to come to know mathematics on the grounds of logic alone since we can never know enough logic to make this possible.[19] Steiner makes similar points and gives them reasonably detailed discussion. His conclusion is that epistemic logicism fails since "the theory to which arithmetic is reduced – whether we call it set theory or logic – is far less certain than arithmetic itself. If so, arithmetic cannot be based on logical foundation."[20]

However, for current purposes the most important point that can be made with respect to such objections to epistemic logicism is that Russell himself accepted many of them as sound. He does so most clearly in an important but little known essay in which he attempts to resolve a number of issues concerning the epistemology of mathematics.[21] After all, admits Russell,

> There is an apparent absurdity in proceeding, as one does in the logical theory of arithmetic, through many rather recondite propositions of symbolic logic, to the "proof" of such truisms as 2 + 2 = 4: for it is plain that the conclusion is more certain than the premises, and the supposed proof therefore seems futile.[22]

For Russell, it is a simple Moorean fact that we are more certain of much of elementary mathematics than we are of many logical axioms and their derivative proofs. Despite his commitment to logicism proper, this observation alone is sufficient in Russell's eyes to vitiate *epistemic* logicism. Perhaps surprisingly, Russell concludes that it is in fact our knowledge of elementary mathematical propositions which eventually helps form the ground for many principles of logic, rather than vice versa.

3 Russell's Regressive Method

As a result of the observation that many propositions of elementary mathematics are more evident than those of logic, Russell sees two tasks as being of primary importance for any mathematical epistemology. The first is the task of explaining in what sense "a comparatively obscure and difficult proposition may be said to be a premise for a comparatively obvious proposition."[23] The second is the task of explaining how such comparatively obscure premises are ever discovered and then justified.

In response to the first of these two tasks, Russell distinguishes between two quite different types of premise. The first type is what he calls an "empirical premise", a premise "from which we are actually led to believe the proposition in question."[24] An empirical premise is a premise which is of epistemic value in that from it (usually together with other relevant premises), less certain or less commonly known results follow. The second type of premise is what Russell calls a "logical premise." A logical premise is a "logically simpler proposition [roughly speaking, a proposition with fewer logical constituents] . . . from which, by a valid deduction, the proposition in question can be obtained."[25] Most often in mathematics the empirical and logical premises coincide. It is in exactly these cases that a mathematical proof is of direct epistemological value. However, as Russell points out, this is not always the case. It is simply not true that a logically simpler idea or proposition is always more readily accepted than a more complicated one. Just as is the case with our intuitions about the physical world, Russell points out, it is the mid-range concepts (concepts which are neither extremely fundamental nor extremely complex) that are commonly comprehended most readily. In some cases, despite their logical simplicity, such premises will have less epistemic simplicity (and less certainty) than the conclusion which follows from them. Hence, there exists the possibility of a "comparatively obscure and difficult proposition" acting as a (logical) premise for a "comparatively obvious proposition."

Russell goes on to note that in these cases it is not the purpose of a mathematical proof so much to prove the conclusion as it is to prove that the conclusion *follows from* those premises. What such proofs show is that from a particular set of logically simple (but sometimes epistemologically complex) premises, other (sometimes epistemologically simple) conclusions follow deductively. This is important since such proofs help resolve the second of Russell's two tasks, that of explaining how it is that such "comparatively obscure and difficult propositions" can themselves ever be discovered and justified.

Russell's explanation is that in cases where previously accepted conclusions can be shown to follow from a particular logical premise (or set of premises) via a valid deduction, such a deduction tends to help justify, not the previously accepted conclusion, but rather the original premise (or set of premises) in question. This is a result of what Russell calls the "regressive method."[26] Russell contends that because of this "regressive" aspect of mathematics, the methodology of mathematics is closely related to that of the ordinary sciences of observation. In Russell's words,

We tend to believe the premises because we can see that their consequences are true, instead of believing the consequences because we know the premises to be true. But the inferring of premises from consequences is the essence of induction; thus the method in investigating the principles of mathematics is really an inductive method, and is substantially the same as the method of discovering general laws in any other science.[27]

Science begins with the ordinary facts of observation of which we are all quite certain. It then attempts to answer two resulting questions: First, what follows from these facts? Second, from what do these facts themselves follow? Answers to the second of these questions determine the general laws of the science, propositions which are logically simpler than the observation statements but which are often epistemologically more difficult to justify. When the initial facts are conjoined with these general laws, answers to the first question yield further observation statements and it is with these that science gains its predictive power.

According to Russell, mathematics is no exception to this general account. Epistemologically simple propositions such as elementary propositions of arithmetic are originally justified via inference from concrete, often physical, cases.[28] These observations form the basic facts within mathematics of which we are most certain. Statements describing these facts in turn follow from the logically simpler general laws which become as certain as our original empirical premises only if one of the following two cases obtains: either it must be shown that no significantly different hypotheses or general laws could lead to the same empirical premises, or (what is often the case in logic and mathematics) the general laws, once discovered, turn out to be just as obvious as the original empirical premises. As an example of the latter, Russell cites the law of contradiction. This law, Russell feels, "must have been originally discovered by generalizing from instances, though, once discovered, it was found to be quite as indubitable as the instances. Thus it is both an empirical and a logical premise."[29] In the cases where the general laws cannot be shown to be the only ones possible, and are not themselves evident to the same extent as are empirical premises, they must remain merely probable, but often probable to a very high degree. Thus, it is by answering the question, "From what do empirical premises follow?" that Russell's second task (the task of explaining how even epistemologically complex logical premises are discovered and justified) is resolved.

As a result of the above observations, the following reconstruction of Russell's account of mathematical knowledge can be given. According to Russell, mathematical knowledge begins in the first instance from particular observations, e.g., the observation that two objects together with two distinct objects are four objects. These observations form our first epistemologically relevant premises. From these empirical premises we obtain generalizations, e.g., that $2 + 2 = 4$. Such generalizations in turn are often recognized to be "sufficiently obvious to be themselves taken as empirical premises"[30] and so to have additional epistemic value.

In addition to these initial empirical premises of which we are quite certain, there exist two other classes of mathematical knowledge. The first consists of the mathematical knowledge which follows from empirical premises (or from empirical premises together with other known premises) by means of deductive proof. The second consists of that "regressively" justified mathematical knowledge (which includes the general laws of logic and mathematics) from which the original empirical premises can be shown to follow. The first of these two types of mathematical knowledge is reasonably straightforward in terms of its justification. As Russell points out, the expanded body of empirical premises "when discovered, [is] pretty certain to lead to a number of new results which could not otherwise have been known: in the sciences, this is so obvious that it needs no illustration, and in mathematics it is no less true."[31]

In contrast, the second of these two additional classes of knowledge requires a somewhat more sophisticated account for its justification. Here the general laws of mathematics are discovered "regressively" when the mathematician inquires after the fewest and logically simplest premises from which all known empirical premises can themselves be deduced. Because of the inductive method which underlies it, such knowledge is sometimes less certain than the (deductively) proven parts of mathematics. As with fundamental laws in the physical sciences, those general laws of logic which do not appear to be as obvious as the original empirical premises will be justified only to the extent that they can be shown to be the most plausible source from which those original premises may be deduced. The result is that even the most fundamental of logical laws may remain merely probable. Russell himself is explicit on this inductivist point:

In induction, if p is our logical premise and q our empirical premise, we know that p implies q, and in a text-book we are apt to begin with p and deduce q. But p is only believed on account of q. Thus we require a greater or less probability that q implies p, or, what comes to the same thing, that not-p implies not-q. If we can *prove* that not-p implies not-q, i.e. that p is the only hypothesis consistent with the facts, that settles the question. But usually what we do is to test as many alternative hypotheses as we can think of. If they all fail, that makes it probable, more or less, that any hypothesis other than p will fail. But in this we are simply betting on our inventiveness: we think it unlikely that we should not have thought of a better hypothesis if there were one.[32]

This inductivist element of Russell's mathematical epistemology differs markedly from the so-called standard account, the account which identifies Russell as a paradigm advocate of epistemic logicism. This standard view, when it notices Russell's inductivist tendencies at all, puts it off as the occasional lapses of an otherwise staunch defender of epistemic logicism.[33]

Such an interpretation is understandable. After all, other logicists have conspicuously advocated positions which are decidedly inconsistent with any inductive or "regressive" element whatsoever. Frege, for example, espouses the view that axioms are truths, as are theorems, but that "they are truths for which no proof can be given in our system, and for which *no proof is needed*. It follows that there are no false axioms, and that *we cannot accept a thought as an axiom if we are in doubt about its truth*."[34] As well, it is also true that from early youth Russell had craved after knowledge that was absolutely certain or, failing that, at least after the knowledge that such certainty was, for the most part, unattainable. His disappointment at the age of eleven at discovering Euclid's failure to prove his axioms (an appalling shortcoming in the eyes of the young Russell) has often been recounted.[35]

Tracing his development further, it is apparent that this quest for certainty accompanied Russell at least up to the writing of the first draft of his *Principles*.[36] Proudly summarizing his initial work, Russell notes: "In the whole philosophy of mathematics, which used to be at least as full of doubt as any other part of philosophy, order and certainty have replaced the confusion and hesitation which formerly reigned."[37] However, with the discovery of his famous contradiction in the spring of 1901 there appears a watershed in Russell's thought. It was with the discovery of the contradiction that his self-acclaimed "intellectual honeymoon" ended and that he began to develop the idea that much of logic would have to be justified by some method other than self-evidence. The following comment is representative and telling:

> I wrote to Frege about it [the paradox] who replied that arithmetic was tottering and that he saw that his Law V was false . . . For my part, I felt that the trouble lay in logic rather than in mathematics and that it was logic which would have to be reformed.[38]

In the end it would be that parts of logic were to be epistemologically justified as a result of their mathematical consequences; it would not be that mathematics would gain its sole justification via logic alone. In addition, a distinction between logical and epistemological order within mathematics would emphasize not only the role of the regressive method but also the close analogy that Russell saw between the epistemology of mathematics and that of the natural sciences. This distinction of Russell's between logical and epistemological order, articulated so clearly by the mature Russell in 1907 in the midst of his work on *Principia*, was then held with remarkable consistency for the remainder of his life.

Details of the view appear to have been developed during the early and mid-1900s,[39] after the discovery of his contradiction and after Russell had become convinced of the need for non-logical axioms such as the axiom of infinity.[40] Russell then appears never again to have changed his mind on this issue. In the first volume of *Principia*, the position is stated clearly:

> But in fact self-evidence is never more than a part of the reason for accepting an axiom, and is never indispensable. The reason for accepting an axiom, as for accepting any other proposition, is always largely inductive, namely that many propositions which are nearly indubitable can be deduced from it, and that no equally plausible way is known by which these propositions could be true if the axiom were false, and nothing which is probably false can be deduced from it. If the axiom is apparently self-evident, that only means, practically, that it is nearly indubitable; for things have been thought to be self-evident and have yet turned out to be false. And if the axiom itself is nearly indubitable, that merely adds to the inductive evidence derived from the fact that its consequences are nearly indubitable: it does not provide new evidence of a radically different kind. Infallibility is never attainable, and therefore some element of doubt should always attach to every axiom and to all its consequences. In formal logic, the element of doubt is less than in most sciences, but it is not absent, as appears from the fact that the paradoxes followed from premises which were not previously known to require limitations.[41]

Later, in the Introduction to the second edition in 1925, Russell's comments are to much the same effect when he mentions the "purely pragmatic justification" of the axiom of reducibility.[42]

Précis of this same position are given in several of Russell's other publications. In his *Introduction to Mathematical Philosophy* Russell observes that the propositions of simple arithmetic are more obvious than those of logic and that "The most obvious and easy things in mathematics are not those that come logically at the beginning; they are things that, from the point of view of logical deduction, come somewhere in the middle."[43] Later, in his 1924 essay "Logical Atomism," Russell again explains his position but in greater detail. His comments are worth quoting in their entirety because of their clarity:

> When pure mathematics is organized as a deductive system . . . it becomes obvious that, if we are to believe in the truth of pure mathematics, it cannot be solely because we believe in the truth of the set of premises. Some of the premises are much less obvious than some of their

consequences, and are believed chiefly because of their consequences. This will be found to be always the case when a science is arranged as a deductive system. It is not the logically simplest propositions of the system that are the most obvious, or that provide the chief part of our reasons for believing in the system. With the empirical sciences that is evident. Electro-dynamics, for example, can be concentrated into Maxwell's equations, but these equations are believed because of the observed truth of certain of their logical consequences. Exactly the same thing happens in the pure realm of logic; the logically first principles of logic – at least some of them – are to be believed, not on their own account, but on account of their consequences. The epistemological question: 'Why should I believe this set of propositions?' is quite different from the logical question: 'What is the smallest and logically simplest group of propositions from which this set of propositions can be deduced?' Our reasons for believing logic and pure mathematics are, in part, only inductive and probable, in spite of the fact that, in their *logical* order, the propositions of logic and pure mathematics follow from the premises of logic by pure deduction. I think this point important, since errors are liable to arise from assimilating the logical to the epistemological order, and also, conversely, from assimilating the epistemological to the logical order.[44]

Just what are the lessons that should be learned from such comments? The major lesson is that Russell's regressive method, emphasizing as it does the distinction between logical and epistemological order,[45] shows how closely Russell's mathematical epistemology was integrated within his general theory of knowledge. Wood, for example, emphasizes exactly this close relationship. After describing the importance of inductive reasoning for Russell, Wood concludes that the regressive method is characteristic, not only of Russell's mathematical epistemology, but of his epistemology in general.[46] Russell himself bolsters this contention when he states that throughout his academic life, epistemological concerns have been central[47] and when he notes that Wood's account "admirably clarifies various things that might otherwise cause misunderstanding."[48]

At the same time, upon careful reading it becomes clear that Russell's regressive method is not in any way inconsistent with comments of Russell's such as the claim that "Mathematics is a deductive science."[49] Read in context, it becomes clear in such cases that Russell is referring to the logical order of the discipline. Following the above quotation, for example, Russell goes on to explain that "No appeal to common sense, or 'intuition', or anything except strict deductive logic, ought to be needed in mathematics *after* the premises have been laid down",[50] leaving unanswered within the then current context the question of just how the original axioms are to be obtained.

The second major lesson that should be learned from the above observations is just how important Russell felt the analogy between epistemological concerns in mathematics and in the sciences to be. Given the number of times that Russell emphasizes this analogy,[51] together with the fact that the stated purpose of his paper on the regressive method was, in part, "to emphasize the close analogy between the methods of pure mathematics and the methods of the sciences of observation", Russell's intention should be clear: only by emphasizing this analogy can a complete and accurate picture of the acquisition and nature of mathematical knowledge be obtained.

4 Logical and Epistemological Foundations in Science and Mathematics

Russell concluded his 1907 paper on the regressive method by once again emphasizing not only the distinction between logical and epistemological order within mathematics, but also the close analogy between mathematics and the natural sciences with respect to epistemology:

> If the contentions of this paper have been sound, it follows that the usual mathematical method of laying down certain premises and proceeding to deduce their consequences, though it is the right method of exposition, does not, except in the more advanced portions, give the order of knowledge . . . The various sciences [which include mathematics] are distinguished by their subject-matter, but as regards method, they seem to differ only in the proportions between the three parts of which every science consists, namely (1) the registration of 'facts', which are what I have called empirical premises; (2) the inductive discovery of hypotheses, or logical premises, to fit the facts; (3) the deduction of new propositions from the facts and hypotheses.[52]

Both themes are repeated often by Russell and, to some extent, are mutually dependent upon one another. As Russell points out, the distinction between logical and epistemological order is so obvious in the case of the natural sciences that, after noting it in the case of mathematics, the analogy follows almost immediately.

Russell's distinction between logical and epistemological order in effect paves the way for a distinction between two types of foundational program. On the one hand, logical foundations emphasize the general but logically simple propositions from which, Russell originally hoped, all of mathematics could be deduced. Russell lists several advantages that are to be gained by the pursuit of such a program. For example, logical foundations help organize sometimes disparate knowledge, they help reduce the possibility of inconsistency and error, and they help to increase the number of consequences derivable from previously known premises.[53] In contrast, epistemological foundations emphasize the basis of those fundamental beliefs upon which arithmetical knowledge ultimately rests. Epistemological foundations show the actual justification of those beliefs which are independent of the ordinary methods of mathematical proof.

Gödel held a similar view regarding foundations.[54] It was his contention that logical investigations often do not provide epistemological foundations for our actual mathematical beliefs. As a result, he also appears to advocate that a distinction be drawn between logical and epistemological foundations. In fact, Gödel sees inductive inference along the lines of Russell's regressive method as playing a role in the justification of many logically fundamental axioms. For example, Gödel comments:

> even disregarding the intrinsic necessity of some new axiom, and even in case it has no intrinsic necessity at all, a probable decision about its truth is possible also in another way, namely inductively by studying its "success." Success here means fruitfulness in consequences, in particular in "verifiable" consequences, i.e., consequences demonstrable without the new axiom, whose proofs with the help of the new axiom, however, are considerably simpler and easier to discover, and make it possible to contract into one proof many different proofs.[55]

According to Gödel, what logical foundations do is organize mathematical knowledge, at the same time isolating errors and unifying diverse concepts. In this respect they function much as do explanatory hypotheses within a physical theory. A logical foundation for a branch of mathematics is not literally a foundation in the sense of attempting to establish once and for all the truth of all mathematical propositions. Rather, the role of foundational work in mathematics is comparable to that in the natural sciences. In short, logical foundations do their work by *explaining* rather than *proving* the truths of mathematics.[56] In contrast, epistemic foundations take as their objective the providing of an account of actual mathematical knowledge. They provide foundations in the genuine sense of the word by establishing the truth of bedrock mathematical beliefs and thereby justifying mathematical knowledge.

This distinction between logical investigations on the one hand, and epistemological ones on the other, receives further justification in part by the fact that both Russell's regressive method and Gödel's tests for inductive success are commonly used in one form or another by practising mathematicians. For example, axioms (such as the axiom of choice) have often been accepted by the mathematical community, not because of self-evidence, but because there exists a kind of inductive confirmation over a period of time. That is, when used as an axiom within the appropriate axiomatic-deductive system, they produce the required results. It was for just such reasons that Zermelo accepted the axiom of choice when proving his famous well-ordering theorem in 1904. Similarly, Fraenkel has stated that some axioms only receive their "full weight" from "the evidence of their consequences."[57]

Furthermore, according to many mathematicians, it is not always (or even usually) the case that it is the axioms of mathematics of which they are the most certain. To cite just one example, Hamming states:

> If the Pythagorean theorem were found not to follow from the postu-
> lates, we would again search for a way to alter the postulates until it was
> true. Euclid's postulates came from the Pythagorean theorem, not the
> other way. For over thirty years I have been making the remark that if
> you came into my office and showed me a proof that Cauchy's theorem
> was false I would be very interested, but I believe that in the final analysis
> we would alter the assumptions until the theorem was true.[58]

It thus appears that Russell's regressive method is, and always has been, used extensively throughout the history of mathematics.

What may prove surprising is that this type of epistemological account for mathematics resembles so closely that of the natural sciences. After all, traditional epistemology distinguishes sharply between mathematics and the natural sciences. Mathematics is popularly understood to be *a priori* and often analytic; the natural sciences are understood to be *a posteriori* and synthetic or, in short, empirical. Even the logical positivists who, more than anyone else this century, emphasized the importance of an empiricist epistemology maintained (in fact, championed) the distinction.[59]

However, if Russell and Gödel are correct, it turns out that a strong parallel between mathematics and the natural sciences will be capable of being justified, in part by the distinction between logical and epistemological foundations. After all, on this account, just as in the sciences, our most general mathematical beliefs are inferred from more ordinary pre-theoretical or pre-formal beliefs. Thus mathematical discovery can be seen to follow lines which are very similar to those of the sciences.[60] Differences between scientific and mathematical methodology are to be understood as differences of degree rather than as differences of kind. As in science, it is only from independently justified empirical premises that logical premises can be discovered via inductive reasoning or the regressive method. At the same time, in addition to its unifying and explanatory functions, a secure logical foundation assists in the discovery and justification of further knowledge.

Given that much contemporary work in the philosophy of mathematics regularly emphasizes a closer relationship between science and mathematics than has traditionally been assumed,[61] it thus turns out that Russell's often misinterpreted epistemological views regarding mathematics are of more than simple historical interest. By highlighting the important epistemic similarities between mathematics and the empirical sciences, Russell's epistemological account clearly lends support to such work. Despite the acknowledged failure of his logicism, Russell's plausible, commonsense epistemological account gives encouragement to those who desire to substantiate the view that mathematics is itself a science, albeit a highly abstract one.

Notes

* Work on this paper began while I was a Visiting Fellow at the University of Pittsburgh's Center for Philosophy of Science and continued later at the University of Toronto. During this time, financial support was gratefully received from the Social Sciences and Humanities Research Council of Canada.
1 This point holds for the logicism of Russell and Whitehead. Frege's logicism, of course, preceded the discovery of Russell's paradox by some twenty years. The idea of reducing mathematics to logic had been advocated first by Leibniz and later by Dedekind. By 1879, Frege had gone on to develop the logical apparatus necessary for such a project. Within five more years he had arrived at the appropriate logical definitions for the necessary arithmetical terms and during and after the 1890s he worked on the essential derivations. After the discovery of the antinomies, Russell and Whitehead went on to complete the project as best they could. Still, despite Frege's predating the antinomies, it is plausible to expect that he was as much motivated by epistemological concerns as were Russell, Hilbert and Brouwer. See note 15 below.
2 Despite Peano's fame, Dedekind was in fact the first to give a semi-axiomatic presentation of formal number theory. For details, see Dedekind [1901]. For historical information, see Wang [1957].
3 For details regarding the development of non-Euclidean geometry, see Bonola [1907].
4 Russell [1956b], p. 53. Reprinted in Russell [1969], p. 220. As is so often the case with Russell, essentially the same point is expressed, equally as clearly but in different words, elsewhere. In his [1924] he states: "From early youth, I had an ardent desire to believe that there can be such a thing as knowledge, combined with a great difficulty in accepting much that passes as knowledge. It seemed clear that the best chance of finding indubitable truth would be in pure mathematics" (p. 359). Reprinted in Russell [1956a], p. 323.
5 Hilbert [1925], p. 184.
6 *Ibid.*, p. 191.
7 Haack [1978], p. 10.
8 Russell [1901], p. 84. Reprinted in Russell [1918a], pp. 75f.
9 Russell [1903], p. xv.
10 Carnap [1931], p. 44. See Carnap, p. 41 and Hempel [1945], p. 378 for additional encapsulations.
11 Russell [1959], p. 74.
12 Steiner [1975] uses similar terminology. He contrasts what he calls *epistemological logicism* with *ontological logicism*, the latter being the view that the reduction of mathematics to logic is of ontological importance. In short, for the ontological logicist, logicism is understood as demonstrating some form of

ontological economy. The idea is basically that ontological comfort can be taken from the construction of mathematical entities (about whose nature there exist unresolved problems) out of other more manageable, less problematic, entities. It was along these lines that Russell attempted to develop his no-class theory. By constructing classes out of propositional functions Russell and Whitehead felt entitled to claim that "classes, so far as we introduce them, are merely symbolic or linguistic conveniences, not genuine objects . . ." (See Whitehead and Russell [1910], p. 72. Also see Hahn [1930], especially pp. 14ff.) As is well known, this aspect of the program ran into difficulties as a result of the ambiguous usage of the phrase "propositional function." Sometimes the phrase was used to mean an open sentence; at other times an attribute. See Quine [1953], pp. 122f. for details. Quine himself might be classified as an ontological logicist in the limited sense that he views the reduction of mathematics to set theory as important. For Quine, this shows how numbers can be dispensed with in favour of sets, thus lessening one's ontological commitments. According to Quine, this reduction has philosophical importance even though there may be no epistemic gain to be had; ontological economy is a goal which is in itself worth pursuing. On this point, see Steiner [1975], Ch. 2.

13 For example, Steiner [1975] comments: "It is certain that logicists attributed epistemological significance to their 'reduction.' The reduction was supposed to provide a foundation for mathematical knowledge, to the extent that Frege felt that arithmetic was 'tottering' when his logical system was proved inconsistent . . . *Principia Mathematica* itself was supposed to supply such a justification" (pp. 17f.); and again: "logicism, then, is intended by its proponents to explain mathematical knowledge" (p. 24). Also see pp. 14–16 *passim*. Similarly, Parsons [1967] notes that it is one of the purposes of logicism to "reduce the problem of giving such an account [of how there can be *a priori* knowledge in mathematics] to the corresponding problem with regard to logic . . . Thus, a reduction of mathematics to logic might make superfluous certain difficult epistemological theories" (p. 193). Later on, Parsons explicitly groups Russell together with Frege "and many later proponents" in seeking epistemic gains from the reduction of arithmetic to logic (p. 197). To cite just one additional example, Lakatos [1962], although recognizing Russell's inductivist tendencies, interprets them as just occasional lapses in Russell's otherwise deductivist epistemological program (pp. 16ff.). I mention these examples, not because they are atypical, but only because they state so clearly this common interpretation of the logicist position.

14 However, it is important to note that Hempel specifically excludes geometry from this interpretation. See Hempel [1945].

15 Frege [1893], p. 29, emphasis added. Also compare Frege's comments at the beginning of his *Grundlagen* in which he notes that a primary purpose of proof in arithmetic is to "place the truth of a proposition beyond all doubt" and in which he inquiries after the "ultimate ground upon which rests the justification for holding" arithmetical propositions (Frege [1884], pp. 2^{e}f.). In further support of this point, see Kitcher [1979], where it is argued that "Frege's motives for logicism are primarily epistemological" and that it was Frege's opinion that only through logicism could mathematical knowledge be capable of perfection (p. 239).

16 Russell had acknowledged difficulties from the outset. Initially the troublesome axioms were the multiplicity axiom (Russell's name for the axiom of choice) and the axiom of infinity. Russell (rightly) hesitated to confer upon either of them the status of a self-evident logical axiom. Instead he concluded that mathematics could make only conditional statements in certain areas, including

matters of existence. (See Russell [1919], Chs 12 and 13.) In addition, as a result of Russell's use of the ramified theory of types (introduced to avoid impredicative definitions and with them the antinomies), many fundamental theorems, particularly in the theory of real numbers, not only could not be proved, but could not even be expressed. Russell's solution was the introduction of the axiom of reducibility. This allowed for the reduction of the necessary sentences to types of a lower order. However, in none of these cases have Russell's attempted solutions proved successful. Especially in the case of the axiom of reducibility, even those sympathetic with logicism (and with Russell's postulationism) recognized its *ad hoc* nature. Russell himself eventually admitted the axiom's inadequacy and dropped it from the second edition of *Principia*. By 1960, even Church, one of the few remaining logicists, acknowledged that logicism was untenable in its original formulation. (See Mehlberg [1960], p. 74).

17 It might be recalled that it was not until proposition *110.643 on page 83 of the second volume of *Principia* that Whitehead and Russell were able to prove that 1 + 1 = 2, let alone that 2 + 2 = 4. In a book not otherwise noted for its humour, it is enjoyable to note that immediately below the proof is the following observation: "The above proposition is occasionally useful. It is used at least three times" (see Whitehead and Russell [1912], p. 83).

18 For example, see Poincaré [1905], pp. 3f.

19 For example, see Wittgenstein [1956], §65^{e}ff.

20 Steiner [1975], p. 19.

21 Russell [1907b]. The late publication date, 1973, of this essay would be one reason why the article appears to be so little known. Despite its obvious saliency, Lakatos fails to note the essay in his [1976]. In contrast, he does mention the apposite aside in the early part of Russell's [1924]. Steiner, too, despite his discussion of epistemological logicism, fails to mention the essay in his [1975]. In both cases discussion of the article would have been of advantage since, in it, Russell's position is shown to be substantially different from that of other so-called "classical logicists." For example, while Russell *may* have agreed with Steiner's ambiguous statement that classical logicism "sees logic as the epistemic ground of all mathematics" (p. 15), it is doubtful that he then would have included himself as a "classical" logicist in Steiner's sense. Russell certainly would have disagreed with Steiner's comment that even though he had observed that the propositions of elementary arithmetic are more obvious than many of those within logic, he, Russell, "was insufficiently concerned with the mechanics of such justification" (p. 18).

22 Russell [1907b], p. 272.

23 *Ibid.*

24 *Ibid.* Russell's use of the phrase "empirical premise" is somewhat misleading. Not all of his "empirical premises" need be observational, although some are. Nor need they be directly about the empirical world. Rather, what Russell means by an "empirical premise" is simply a premise which has epistemic value. A more suggestive name for such a premise would have been "epistemological premise."

25 *Ibid.*, pp. 272f.

26 In a number of respects, Russell's regressive method is similar to Peirce's abduction. I am indebted to Scott Kleiner for pointing this out to me. In contemporary terminology, it might also be termed "inference to the best explanation."

27 Russell [1907b], pp. 273f.

28 *Ibid.*, p. 272.

29 *Ibid.*, p. 274.

30 *Ibid.*, p. 275.

31 *Ibid.*, pp. 282f.

32 *Ibid.*, pp. 274f.

33 For example, Lakatos comments in his [1962]: "Russell *occasionally* despairs of Euclidean manifestness and opts for a sort of inductivism" (p. 16, emphasis added).

34 Frege [1914], p. 205, emphasis added.

35 See Russell [1944a], p. 7; Russell [1967], p. 36.

36 Russell completed the first draft of the *Principles* on December 31, 1900. Revisions (especially of Parts I, II and VII) took place throughout the following year in part as a result of his discovery of the contradiction. The book was eventually completed on May 23, 1902, and was published the following year.

37 Russell [1901], p. 88. Reprinted in Russell [1918a], pp. 79f.

38 Russell [1959], p. 76.

39 Given the following quotation from his [1907a], one might be tempted to think that Russell retained his old views regarding the certainty of mathematics even in 1907: "Too often it is said that there is no absolute truth, but only opinion and private judgment ... Of such scepticism mathematics is a perpetual reproof; for its edifice of truths stands unshakable and inexpugnable to all the weapons of doubting cynicism" (p. 43. Reprinted in Russell [1910], p. 85; [1918a], p. 71; [1985], pp. 92f.). However, despite its late publication date, the essay was in fact written much earlier, while Russell was in London in October, 1902. (See Russell [1985], p. 83.) Even as early as 1901 Russell had doubted the importance of a proposition's self-evidence. (See Russell [1901], pp. 85f. Reprinted in Russell [1918a]. pp. 77f.)

40 For example, see Russell [1907b], p. 282. Originally Russell held that the axiom of infinity was not required as a separate assumption but that it could be proved from prior principles. He was convinced otherwise in part by the mathematician C. J. Keyser. See Russell [1904].

41 Whitehead and Russell [1910], p. 59 (p. 62 of the first edition).

42 *Ibid.*, p. xiv. Despite such comments, Russell apparently never gave up the hope of deducing such axioms from other, more self-evident logical truths. For example, see the Introduction to the second edition of *Principia*, Vol. 1, p. xiv. Once it is admitted, as Russell does, that these axioms are in part empirical, such hope seems inexplicably misguided since if this is so it follows immediately that one would not expect them to be derivable from purely logical premises, whether self-evident or not.

43 Russell [1919], p. 2.

44 Russell [1924], pp. 361f. Reprinted in Russell [1956a], pp. 325f.

45 In addition to the examples already cited from Russell [1907b], [1919], [1924], and Whitehead and Russell [1910], see Russell [1906], p. 194; Russell [1911], pp. 482, 492f. (reprinted in Russell [1973], pp. 285, 293f.); Russell [1918b], pp. 498f. (reprinted in Russell [1956a], p. 180); Russell [1940], p. 16; and Whitehead and Russell [1910], pp. vf. A few general comments about the notion of epistemological order are also given in Russell [1944b], pp. 710–714.

46 Wood [1959], pp. 264–266. Wood appears to have had access to Russell's then unpublished [1907b]. On p. 265 he quotes a sentence of Russell's which begins "The inferring of premises from consequences is the essence of induction", but without giving a reference. The sentence appears on p. 274 of Russell's [1907b]. It is also possible that at times Gödel refers to the article (although without explicitly mentioning it). For example, see Gödel [1944], p. 127.

47 Russell [1959], p. 11.

48 *Ibid.*, p. 3.
49 Russell [1919], p. 144.
50 *Ibid.*, p. 145, emphasis added.
51 For example, see Russell [1906], p. 194; Russell [1907b], pp. 272, 273, 274, 275, 280 and 282f.; and Russell [1924], pp. 361f. (reprinted in Russell [1956a], pp. 325f.). Further support might come from the fact that Russell understood mathematics to be synthetic. For example, see Russell [1900], p. 24 and Russell [1903], p. 457.
52 Russell [1907b], p. 282.
53 Russell [1907b], p. 275. For example, Russell points out: "the logical premises have, as a rule, many more consequences than the empirical premises, and thus lead to the discovery of many things which could not otherwise be known. The law of gravitation, for example, leads to many consequences which could not be discovered merely from the apparent motions of the heavenly bodies, which are our empirical premises. And so in arithmetic, taking the ordinary propositions of arithmetic as our empirical premises, we are led to a set of logical premises from which we can deduce Cantor's theory of the transfinite."
54 See Gödel [1947], pp. 476ff. In fact, Gödel is aware of the strong parallel that Russell sees between mathematics and the natural sciences in the case of epistemology and may even have been influenced by it. For example, in his [1944] he comments: "The analogy between mathematics and a natural science is enlarged upon by Russell also in another respect . . . the axioms need not necessarily be evident in themselves, but rather their justification lies (exactly as in physics) in the fact that they make it possible for these 'sense perceptions' to be deduced" (p. 127).
55 Gödel [1947], p. 477.
56 Mehlberg [1960] comes to the same conclusion, commenting that for Gödel "so-called logical or set-theoretical 'foundations' for number-theory or any other well-established mathematical theory, [are] explanatory, rather than really foundational, exactly as in physics" (p. 86).
57 Translated and quoted by Lakatos in his [1962], p. 17.
58 Hamming [1980], p. 87.
59 For example, see Ayer [1936] (esp. Ch. 4) and Hahn [1929] and [1930].
60 It is true that Russell did not want to push the analogy too far. For example, in his [1907b] he notes that there are differences between many of the obvious "empirical" premises of mathematics and those of the natural sciences: "In the natural sciences, the obviousness is that of the senses, while in pure mathematics it is an *a priori* obviousness" (p. 279). However, it must be remembered that for Russell *any* general proposition is *a priori* in the sense that it goes beyond particular observations obtained through the senses. According to Russell [1911], for example, the existence of general assertions known to be true "shows that traditional empiricism is in error" (p. 292) and that "human knowledge is not wholly deduced from facts of sense" alone (p. 294). However, if this line of argument is accepted, it follows that all general *scientific* knowledge would have to be classed as *a priori* as well.
61 For example, recent work which emphasizes a close relationship between mathematical and scientific epistemology includes Maddy [1980] and [1984], Resnik [1975] and [1982], Kitcher [1983] and Lind [1984]. Other work emphasizes a parallel between science and mathematics on non-epistemological grounds. Steiner [1975], for example, holds that "mathematics is a science, whose methods differ little, in principle, from those of other sciences" but then goes on to emphasize a similarity particularly with regard to ontology: "As I see it,

mathematics studies the natural numbers as zoology studies animals (to revive a discarded Russellian position). Mathematics can be distinguished from the other sciences only by its subject matter – not on the grounds that it has none" (p. 21). In addition, see Resnik [1981] and Lakatos [1976].

References

Ayer, Alfred Jules: 1936, *Language, Truth and Logic*, second edition (New York, Dover), 1946.

Bonola, Roberto: 1907, *La Geometria Non-Euclidea*. Translated by H. S. Carslaw as *Non-Euclidean Geometry* (New York, Dover), 1955.

Carnap, Rudolf: 1931, "Die logizistische Grundlegung der Mathematik," *Erkenntnis* 2, 91–105. Translated by Erna Putnam and Gerald J. Massey as "The Logicist Foundations of Mathematics", in Paul Benacerraf and Hilary Putnam, *Philosophy of Mathematics*, second edition (Cambridge, Cambridge University Press), 1983, 41–52.

Dedekind, Richard: 1901, *Essays on the Theory of Numbers*, revised edition, translated by Wooster Woodruff Beman (New York, Dover), 1963.

Frege, Gottlob: 1884, *Die Grundlagen der Arithmetik* (Breslau, Köbner). Translated by J. L. Austin as *The Foundations of Arithmetic*, second revised edition (Oxford, Blackwell), 1980.

Frege, Gottlob: 1893, 1903, *Grundgesetze der Arithmetik*, 2 volumes (Jena, Pohle). Abridged and translated by Montgomery Furth as *The Basic Laws of Arithmetic* (Berkeley and Los Angeles, University of California Press), 1964.

Frege, Gottlob: 1914, "Logic in Mathematics," translated by Peter Long and Roger White in Frege, *Posthumous Writings* (edited by Hans Hermes, Friedrich Kambartel and Friedrich Kaulbach) (Chicago, University of Chicago Press), 1979, 203–250.

Gödel, Kurt: 1944, "Russell's Mathematical Logic," in Paul Arthur Schilpp, *The Philosophy of Bertrand Russell*, third edition, New York: Tudor, 1951, 123–153. Reprinted in Paul Benacerraf and Hilary Putnam, *Philosophy of Mathematics*, second edition (Cambridge, Cambridge University Press), 1983, 447–469. Page numbers refer to the former.

Gödel, Kurt: 1947, "What is Cantor's Continuum Problem?," *American Mathematical Monthly* 54, 515–525. Revised and reprinted in Paul Benacerraf and Hilary Putnam, *Philosophy of Mathematics*, second edition (Cambridge, Cambridge University Press), 1983, 470–485. Page numbers refer to the latter.

Haack, Susan: 1978, *Philosophy of Logics* (Cambridge, Cambridge University Press).

Hahn, Hans: 1929, "Empirismus, Mathematik, Logik," *Forschungen und Fortschritte* 5. Translated as "Empiricism, Mathematics and Logic," in Hahn, *Empiricism, Logic, and Mathematics* (edited by Brian McGuinness) (Dordrecht, Holland, Reidel), 1980, 39–42.

Hahn, Hans: 1930, "Superfluous Entities, or Occam's Razor," in Hahn, *Empiricism, Logic, and Mathematics* (edited by Brian McGuinness) (Dordrecht, Holland, Reidel), 1980, 1–19.

Hamming, R. W.: 1980, "The Unreasonable Effectiveness of Mathematics," *American Mathematical Monthly* 87, 81–90.

Hempel, Carl Gustav: 1945, "On the Nature of Mathematical Truth," *American Mathematical Monthly* 52, 543–556. Reprinted in Paul Benacerraf and Hilary

Putnam, *Philosophy of Mathematics*, second edition (Cambridge, Cambridge University Press), 1983, 377–393. Page numbers refer to the latter.

Hilbert, David: 1925, "Über das Unendliche," *Mathematische Annalen* 95 (1926), 161–190. Translated by Erna Putnam and Gerald J. Massey as "On the Infinite," in Paul Benacerraf and Hilary Putnam, *Philosophy of Mathematics*, second edition (Cambridge, Cambridge University Press), 1983, 183–201. Also translated by Stephan Bauer-Mengelberg, as "On the Infinite," in Jean van Heijenoort, *From Frege to Gödel* (Cambridge, Mass., Harvard University Press), 1967, 369–392. Page numbers refer to Benacerraf and Putnam.

Kitcher, Philip: 1979, "Frege's Epistemology," *The Philosophical Review* 88, 235–262.

Kitcher, Philip: 1983, *The Nature of Mathematical Knowledge* (Oxford, Oxford University Press).

Lakatos, Imre: 1962, "Infinite Regress and Foundations of Mathematics," *Aristotelian Society: Supplementary Volume* 36, 155–184. Reprinted in Lakatos, *Mathematics, Science and Epistemology* (edited by John Worral and Gregory Currie) (New York, Cambridge University Press), 1978, 3–23. Page numbers refer to the latter.

Lakatos, Imre: 1976, "A Renaissance of Empiricism in the Recent Philosophy of Mathematics," *British Journal for the Philosophy of Science* 27, 201–223. Reprinted in Lakatos, *Mathematics, Science and Epistemology* (edited by John Worral and Gregory Currie) (New York, Cambridge University Press), 1978, 24–42.

Lind, Richard W.: 1984, "Microphenomenology and Numerical Relations," *Monist* 67, 29–45.

Maddy, Penelope: 1980, "Perception and Mathematical Intuition," *Philosophical Review* 89, 163–196.

Maddy, Penelope: 1984, "Mathematical Epistemology: What is the Question?," *Monist* 67, 46–55.

Mehlberg, Henryk: 1960, "The Present Situation in the Philosophy of Mathematics," *Synthèse* 12, 380–412. Reprinted in B. H. Kazemier and D. Vuysje, *Logic and Language* (Dordrecht, Holland, Reidel), 1962, 69–103. Page numbers refer to the latter.

Parsons, Charles: 1967, "Mathematics, Foundations of," in Paul Edwards, *The Encyclopedia of Philosophy*, Vol. 5 (New York and London, Macmillan and The Free Press), 188–213.

Poincaré, Henri: 1905, *Science and Hypothesis* (New York, Dover, 1952).

Quine, Willard Van Orman: 1953, "Logic and the Reification of Universals," in Quine, *From a Logical Point of View*, second edition (Cambridge, Mass., Harvard University Press), 1961, 102–129.

Resnik, Michael David: 1975, "Mathematical Knowledge and Pattern Cognition," *Canadian Journal of Philosophy* 5, 25–39.

Resnik, Michael David: 1981, "Mathematics as a Science of Patterns: Ontology and Reference," *Noûs* 15, 529–550.

Resnik, Michael David: 1982, "Mathematics as a Science of Patterns: *Epistemology*," *Noûs* 16, 95–105.

Russell, Bertrand Arthur William: 1900, *A Critical Exposition of the Philosophy of Leibniz* (London, Cambridge University Press.)

Russell, Bertrand Arthur William: 1901 "Recent Work on the Principles of Mathematics," *The International Monthly* 4, 83–101. Reprinted with revisions as "Mathematics and the Metaphysicians," in Russell [1918a], 74–96. Page numbers refer to the former. (In the reprint the original article is miscited as "Recent Work in the Philosophy of Mathematics.")

Russell, Bertrand Arthur William: 1903, *The Principles of Mathematics*, second edition (London, George Allen & Unwin), 1937.

Russell, Bertrand Arthur William: 1904, "The Axiom of Infinity," *Hibbert Journal* 2, 809–812. Reprinted in Russell [1973], 256–259.

Russell, Bertrand Arthur William: 1906, "Les paradoxes de la logique," *Revue de Métaphysique et de Morale* 14, 627–650. Translated by Russell as "On 'Insolubilia' and Their Solution by Symbolic Logic," in Russell [1973], 190–214.

Russell, Bertrand Arthur William: 1907a, "The Study of Mathematics," *New Quarterly* 1, 29–44. Reprinted in Russell [1910], 71–86 (first edition only), in Russell [1918a], 58–73, and in Russell [1985], 85–93. Page numbers refer to the *New Quarterly*.

Russell, Bertrand Arthur William: 1907b, "The Regressive Method of Discovering the Premises of Mathematics," read before the Cambridge Mathematical Club, 9 March 1907. Published in Russell [1973], 272–283.

Russell, Bertrand Arthur William: 1910, *Philosophical Essays* (London, Longmans, Green & Co.)

Russell, Bertrand Arthur William: 1911, "L'importance philosophique de la logistique," *Revue de Métaphysique et de Morale* 19, 281–291. Translated by P. E. B. Jourdain (with revisions by Russell) as "The Philosophical Implications of Mathematical Logic," *Monist* 23 (1913), 481–493 and reprinted in Russell [1973], 284–294. Page numbers refer to the *Monist*.

Russell, Bertrand Arthur William: 1918a, *Mysticism and Logic* (London, Longmans Green).

Russell, Bertrand Arthur William: 1918b, 1919, "The Philosophy of Logical Atomism," *Monist* 28, 495–527; 29, 32–63, 190–222, 345–380. Reprinted in Russell [1956a], 177–281. Page numbers refer to the former.

Russell, Bertrand Arthur William: 1919, *Introduction to Mathematical Philosophy* (London, George Allen & Unwin).

Russell, Bertrand Arthur William: 1924, "Logical Atomism," in J. H. Muirhead, *Contemporary British Philosophy*, first series (London, George Allen & Unwin), 1924, 357–383. Reprinted in Russell [1956a], 323–343. Page numbers refer to the former.

Russell, Bertrand Arthur William: 1940, *An Inquiry Into Meaning and Truth* (London, George Allen & Unwin).

Russell, Bertrand Arthur William: 1944a, "My Mental Development," in Paul Arthur Schilpp, *The Philosophy of Bertrand Russell*, third edition (New York, Tudor), 1951, 1–20.

Russell, Bertrand Arthur William: 1944b, "Reply to Criticisms," in Paul Arthur Schilpp *The Philosophy of Bertrand Russell*, third edition (New York, Tudor), 1951, 679–741.

Russell, Bertrand Arthur William: 1956a, *Logic and Knowledge*, edited by Robert Charles Marsh (London, George Allen & Unwin).

Russell, Bertrand Arthur William, 1956b, *Portraits From Memory* (London, George Allen & Unwin).

Russell, Bertrand Arthur William: 1959, *My Philosophical Development* (New York, Simon & Schuster).

Russell, Bertrand Arthur William: 1967, 1968, 1969, *The Autobiography of Bertrand Russell*, 3 volumes (London, George Allen & Unwin).

Russell, Bertrand Arthur William: 1973, *Essays in Analysis* (edited by Douglas Lackey) (London, George Allen & Unwin).

Russell, Bertrand Arthur William: 1985, *Contemplation and Action, 1902–14*. (*The Collected Papers of Bertrand Russell*, Vol. 12) (London, George Allen & Unwin).

Russell, Bertrand and Alfred North Whitehead: 1910, 1912, 1913, *Principia Mathematica*, 3 volumes, second edition (New York, Cambridge University Press), 1925 (Vol. 1), 1927 (Vols 2 and 3).

Steiner, Mark: 1975, *Mathematical Knowledge* (Ithaca, N.Y. and London, Cornell University Press).

Wang, Hao: 1957, "The Axiomatization of Arithmetic," *Journal of Symbolic Logic* 22, 145–158.

Whitehead, Alfred North and Bertrand Russell: 1910, 1912, 1913, *Principia Mathematica*, 3 volumes, second edition (New York, Cambridge University Press), 1925 (Vol. 1), 1927 (Vols 2 and 3).

Wittgenstein, Ludwig: 1956, *Bermerkungen über die Grundlagen der Mathematik*. Translated by G. E. M. Anscombe as *Remarks on the Foundations of Mathematics* (edited by G. E. M. Anscombe, R. Rhees and G. H. von Wright), Oxford: Blackwell, 1956.

Wood, Allan: 1959, "Russell's Philosophy: A Study of its Development," in Russell [1959], 255–277.

14

Logic in Russell's Logicism

Peter W. Hylton

Russell, as is well known, was a logicist.[1] He believed, and attempted to demonstrate, that mathematics is reducible to logic. What is perhaps less clear is *why* Russell was a logicist – what philosophical purpose was served by his belief in this doctrine, what motive lay behind his attempt to reduce mathematics to logic. An investigation of this point will, I think, enable us to see more clearly what logicism amounts to in Russell's hands. Russell's logicism was originally intended as part of some kind of argument against Kant, and post-Kantian idealism, but how exactly does this argument go? Russell, unlike the logical positivists, does not seek to use logicism to show that mathematics is analytic; his use of logicism against Kant is quite different from that of the positivists. But how, then, does Russell think that logicism is anti-Kantian? A fairly clear answer to this question emerges from an examination of the earliest phase of Russell's logicism (i.e. that dominated by *The Principles of Mathematics*).[2] In section I, I attempt to articulate this answer. My discussion of the motivation of Russell's early logicism is intended as the starting point of a discussion of Russell's conception of logic, and this is the subject of section II. The significance of the reduction of mathematics to logic depends, of course, upon the conception of logic that is in play. An understanding of the significance that Russell attributed to logicism in the early years of this century will therefore provide us with insight into the conception of logic that he held at that period, and into his reasons for holding it. Russell's conception of logic is antithetical to one crucial element, at least, in the modern view of logic. I shall call this element the model-theoretic conception. I shall try to show that the differences between Russell's conception of logic and this modern conception are closely connected with his use of logicism as an argument against Kant (as he interpreted Kant) and against idealism. In particular, if Russell's conception of logic were the model-theoretic one, his argument against Kant would not have the force that he took it to have. Both the motivation that I attribute to Russell's early logicism, and the conception of logic upon which it relies, are threatened by the paradox which bears Russell's name. The theory of types, which was Russell's response to the paradox, undermines logicism as Russell had originally conceived it. These very complex issues will be briefly discussed in section III.

I

Russell thought of logicism as anti-Kantian. This is clear both from his discussion at the time (see *Principles, passim*) and from his later statements. Thus he says, in *My Philosophical Development*:

> The primary aim of *Principia Mathematica* was to show that all pure mathematics follows from purely logical premises and uses only concepts definable in logical terms. This was, of course, an antithesis to the doctrines of Kant, and initially I thought of the work as a parenthesis in the refutation of [Kant].[3]

(A similar passage, repeating the phrase 'a parenthesis in the refutation of Kant' is to be found in Russell's 'Autobiography', in the Schilpp volume on Russell.)[4] But how, exactly, did Russell take logicism to be part of an argument against Kant? Most fundamentally, Russell's logicism was intended as a refutation of Kant's view of mathematics. Russell, as we shall see, does not deny the Kantian claim that mathematics is synthetic *a priori*. He does, however, deny the claim that mathematics is based on what Kant had called the forms of our intuition, forms which impose spatiality and temporality upon the objects which we intuit. Russell insists that mathematics is wholly independent of space and time. Logicism was to constitute a basis for this insistence in the following way. If one accepts, as Kant did, that *logic* is independent of space and time (and of our forms of intuition), then logicism will show that the same is true of mathematics. One crucial property which logicism shows to be transferable from logic to mathematics is thus the property of being independent of space, time and the forms of intuition.[5]

Kant, according to Russell, held the opposite opinion only because of his ignorance of mathematics and, in particular, of the new logic.[6] The logic available to Kant was syllogistic logic, which lacks even the full power of monadic quantification theory. Given this logic, the theorems of Euclid, say, do not follow from Euclid's axioms by logic alone. As Russell sees the matter, this fact is at the basis of Kant's theory of mathematics:

> There was, until recently, a special difficulty in the principles of mathematics. It seemed plain that mathematics consists of deductions, and yet

the orthodox accounts of deduction were largely or wholly inapplicable to existing mathematics. Not only the Aristotelian syllogistic theory, but also the modern doctrines of Symbolic Logic . . . In this fact lay the strength of the Kantian view, which asserted that mathematical reasoning is not strictly formal, but always uses intuitions, i.e. the *a priori* knowledge of space and time. Thanks to the progress of Symbolic Logic, especially as treated by Professor Peano, this part of the Kantian philosophy is now capable of a final and irrevocable refutation (*Principles*, section 4).

A decisive advance here was Russell's development of polyadic quantification theory, and the associated understanding of quantifier dependence.[7] One result of this was a logic which, unlike syllogistic logic, could handle the reasoning which is involved in mathematics, for example, in deriving theorems from axioms. A second result concerns the understanding of the calculus. The work of Dedekind, Cantor and Weierstrass allowed the crucial notions of the calculus to be given precise definitions. These definitions require the use of nested quantifiers if they are to be put in rigorous form; quantifier dependence is crucial here. These definitions make no appeal to space, time or motion; nor do they rely upon the notion of an infinitely small quantity, or infinitesimal.[8] This second point too Russell sees as an advance which undermines Kant's theory of mathematics:

It was formerly supposed – and herein lay the real strength of Kant's mathematical philosophy – that continuity had an essential reference to space and time, and that the Calculus (as the word *fluxion* suggests) in some way presupposed motion or at least change. In this view, the philosophy of space and time was prior to that of continuity, the Transcendental Aesthetic preceded the Transcendental Dialectic, and the antinomies (at least the mathematical ones) were essentially spatiotemporal. All this has been changed by modern mathematics (*Principles*, section 249).

These results of polyadic quantification theory are impressive, especially to a mathematician educated to think that logic means syllogistic logic. Impressive as they are, however, these results do not amount to logicism. They may show that modern logic is necessary for a (non-Kantian) understanding of mathematics, but they do not show that it is sufficient; they do not amount to a reduction of mathematics to logic. For this we need to take into account the fact that logic, for Russell, is not (what we call) first-order logic but is, rather, higher-order logic, as powerful as set theory. This fact is something that I shall discuss later. The present point is that it makes possible the full reduction of mathematics to logic. Two issues in particular are worth emphasizing. First, given the Russellian analogue of set theory, the arithmetic of the real numbers can be understood in terms of the natural numbers. Second, it appears to be possible to reduce the arithmetic of the natural numbers, in turn, to logic – given Russell's generous conception of what is to count as logic. This is in contrast to the view that the natural numbers are special entities, governed by their own laws, laws which might admit of, or even require, explanation in terms of the form of our intuition. From Russell's point of view, then, modern logic and mathematics show that the reliance upon spatio-temporal notions, which is characteristic of Kant's theory of mathematics, is not required at any point for an understanding of geometry or of the calculus, or of any part of mathematics.[9] Kant's theory of mathematics is thus refuted by logicism, the view that mathematics is reducible to logic.

The use of logicism against Kant's view of mathematics may seem to be a relatively narrow point. It is not clear, on the face of it, why the success of this claim of Russell's should carry any weight as a general argument against Kantianism, or as an argument against Kant's idealist successors, most of whom were far less concerned with mathematics than was Kant himself. But in Russell's hands the refutation of Kant's view of mathematics served as the basis for a more general attack on Kantianism and on post-Kantian idealism. The attack is against what Russell at least took to be a single doctrine, crucial to both Kantianism and post-Kantian idealism. We can formulate this doctrine as follows: our ordinary knowledge (of science, history, mathematics, etc.) is, at best, true in a conditioned and non-absolute sense of truth. This formulation obscures several points, having to do in particular with the differences between Kant and the idealists, and with idealist (and Russellian) interpretations of Kant. More subtly, perhaps, the idea that this doctrine is objectionable suggests that there is an absolute or unconditioned sense of truth which can be contrasted with conditioned truth. These matters will require some discussion.

Kant held that our knowledge is not unconditioned. It is confined to the world of appearances, which cannot be thought of as ultimately real and independent of us. One important basis for this claim is embodied in the argument of the antinomies, that if the world is taken to be 'a whole existing in itself', i.e. as independent of our representations of it, then contradictions can be derived. Kant's conclusion is that the world is not such a whole. This is the doctrine of transcendental idealism, that the world is empirically real but transcendentally ideal. All of our knowledge thus has this status: it is knowledge only of the world as it appears to us, and if construed more strongly than this is contradictory. The idea of the unconditioned, or of a world of things-in-themselves, plays a purely negative role here; our knowledge is *not* unconditioned, is *not* of things-in-themselves. (This is not to deny that these ideas may play a positive role in other parts of Kant's philosophy.)

The post-Kantian idealists rejected Kant's distinction between the phenomenal world, or world of appearances, and the noumenal world, or world of things-in-themselves. This distinction is closely connected with other Kantian dualisms which the idealists rejected: that between sensibility and the understanding, and that between the analytic and the synthetic (one of the connections, at least, will emerge in our later discussion; see note 29). The fact that the idealists rejected the distinction between the phenomenal world and the noumenal world meant that they drew un-Kantian conclusions from Kant's arguments against the consistency of regarding the world we know as a thing-in-itself. The idealists claimed that these arguments (and others) show that the ways in which we ordinarily think of the world are inconsistent. Ordinary 'knowledge', if thought through with full rigour, leads to contradictions. For the idealists, these contradictions do not result from a special metaphysical way of construing our ordinary knowledge, as if it were about things-in-themselves rather than about appearances. For the idealists the contradictions simply are implicit in (what we take to be) our ordinary knowledge. For this reason, they do not infer from the contradictions that we should eschew metaphysics. They infer, rather, that the categories of thought used in ordinary 'knowledge' are inadequate, and that we must attempt to find categories of thought that are not vulnerable to such inconsistencies. The only truly consistent way of thinking – that which yields 'absolute knowledge' – is to be found in the metaphysical conception of the world as a single organic whole, every part of which is internally related to every other. (This idealist position is perhaps most obviously articulated in the Hegelian dialectic; but something like this is, I think, a distinguishing characteristic of post-Kantian idealism in general.) The idea of absolute knowledge affords the idealists a perspective from which all of our ordinary (i.e. non-metaphysical) claims to knowledge can be judged and found to be at best relatively or conditionally true.

For the idealists, then, real truth is absolute truth, which in turn means unconditioned truth. This makes it natural for the idealists to read Kant as if he too held that conditioned truth is second-rate, somehow not real truth – even though for Kant there is no other sense of true than the sense in which it refers to conditioned truth. Now the important point, from our perspective, is that Russell more or less took for granted this idealist reading of Kant. Given the idealist orthodoxy in which he was educated, this is hardly surprising. The point, however, goes deeper than Russell's reading of Kant. Russell also took for granted the conception of truth from which this reading stems. Truth, for Russell, was absolute and unconditioned. Like the idealists, but unlike Kant, he held that there is an absolute sense of truth, and that it is to this that human knowledge should aspire. Unlike the idealists, however, Russell held this to be the only sense of truth, anything else being just a polite word for falsehood. From Russell's point of view, then, the crucial doctrine common to Kant and to his successors is the claim that all of our ordinary knowledge is true in a second-rate sense.

What we call 'knowledge' is only relatively true, not absolutely true, true only from an empirical point of view, not from a transcendental point of view. (From this point I shall, where convenient, ignore the fact that this claim cannot be straightforwardly attributed to Kant. Equally, I shall sometimes speak of Kant as an idealist, as Russell does without hesitation.) Russell objects to this claim because he thinks it tantamount to saying that all of what we ordinarily take as knowledge (including mathematics) is false.

Russell uses logicism to argue against the crucial idealist and Kantian claim that our ordinary knowledge cannot be absolutely or transcendentally true. There are, I think, two rather different arguments that connect logicism to the refutation of this claim, though only one of them is explicit in Russell's texts. The first, and explicit, connection has to do with the arguments that Kant, and to some extent other idealists, used as a basis for the claim that the world as we ordinarily understand it is not wholly consistent. (I am here presupposing an idealist interpretation of Kant – in particular that for Kant it is our ordinary understanding of the world, and not only a metaphysical construal of that understanding, which is inconsistent.) For Kant, as I have already said, one important basis for this idea is to be found in the antinomies. The first two antinomies are spatio-temporal, and claim to show that if space and time are taken as real – as features of the world as it really is, rather than merely of the world as it appears to us – then contradictions follow. This claim, if accepted, seems immediately to show that the world as we take it to be cannot be fully real, for the world as we take it to be is spatial and temporal, and these features, it seems, give rise to contradictions. This point seems to have been more or less taken for granted by many of Kant's idealist successors. Hegel, for example, says:

> These Kantian Antinomies will always remain an important part of the critical philosophy; they, more than anything else, brought about the downfall of previous metaphysics and can be regarded as a main transition into more recent philosophy.[10]

More striking than this, perhaps, are the flattering terms in which Hegel refers to Zeno, calling him, for example, 'the originator of the dialectic' (*der Anfänger der Dialektik*).[11] For one post-Kantian idealist, in particular, the supposed contradictions in the notion of space were of the highest importance. This was Russell himself, who argued, in the late 1890s, that space, if considered as devoid of matter, gives rise to contradictions: 'empty space . . . gives rise to the antinomy in question; for empty space is a bare possibility of relations, undifferentiated and homogeneous, and thus wholly destitute of parts or of thinghood'.[12] This claim, which was elaborated in his *Foundations of Geometry*, was intended to be the first step in an elaborate 'dialectic of the sciences', which would take scientific knowledge as the subject of a Hegelian-style dialectic.[13] The result of this dialectic would be to show that all such knowledge is merely relative, i.e. not fully true as it stands. So when, a few years later, Russell argues against (what he took to be) Kant's claims of the inadequacy of the notions of space and time, it is perhaps with the fervour that is said to characterize recent converts.

In *Principles*, in any case, Russell's claim is that space and time are consistent, and that modern (i.e. nineteenth-century) mathematics demonstrates this beyond doubt. More accurately, perhaps, he claims that modern mathematics makes available consistent theories which may represent the truth about space and time; whether they in fact do so is a matter on which he is willing to remain agnostic. The crucial point is that mathematics makes consistent theories of space and time possible.[14] The importance of this point to Russell can be gathered from the fact that the notion of space, which is hardly an obvious subject for a book on the foundation of mathematics, is the subject of Part VI of *The Principles of Mathematics*, and occupies nearly 100 pages of that book. This part of the book concludes with a discussion of Kant's antinomies, and claims that they are 'disproved by the modern realization of Leibniz's universal characteristic' (section 436). Russell's claim that there are consistent mathematical theories of space and time draws, as one would expect, upon the treatment of real numbers and of continuity made available by Cantor, Dedekind and (especially) Weierstrass. It is important, however, to see that it also depends upon the central claim of Russell's logicism, that mathematics is wholly independent of the Kantian forms of intuition. It is only if mathematics is in this way independent of space and time that it can be used, in noncircular fashion, as an argument for the consistency of the latter notions. Russell thus takes the central claim of logicism, and the claim of the consistency of space and time, as crucial to his opposition to Kant:

> The questions of chief importance to us, as regards the Kantian theory, are two, namely, (1) are the reasonings in mathematics in any way different from those of Formal Logic? (2) are there any contradictions in the notions of space and time? If these two pillars of the Kantian edifice can be pulled down, we shall have successfully played the part of Samson towards his disciples (*Principles*, section 433).

This, then, is the first and most explicit way in which Russell takes logicism as part of a general argument against Kant and post-Kantian idealism. Logicism shows that consistent theories of space and time are available; the spatio-temporal world need not be written off as contradictory and not fully real.

Less explicit in the text of Russell's work, but hardly less important, I think, is the idea that mathematics functions as a particularly clear counter-example to the crucial idealist claim about knowledge which I briefly discussed earlier. A direct consequence of the Kantian version of the claim is that our knowledge is confined to what can be given in intuition, i.e. to actual or possible objects of sensible experience. Since these objects are partially constituted by our minds, a second consequence of the Kantian view is that our knowledge is conditioned by the nature of our cognitive faculties. The post-Kantian idealist analogue of this general claim is that all of our ordinary, non-metaphysical knowledge is at best relatively true. As against these very general idealist claims as to the inadequacy of our ordinary (non-metaphysical) knowledge, Russell sets out, in *Principles*, to show that mathematics is true – not true just as one stage in the dialectic, or more or less true, but true absolutely and unconditionally; not just true if put in a wider context, or if seen as part of a larger whole, but true just as it stands; not, to revert to the Kantian idiom, true from the empirical standpoint but false from the transcendental standpoint, but simply TRUE, with no distinctions of standpoint accepted. Mathematics, for Russell, is thus to function as a counterexample to a claim which he sees as crucial to any form of idealism, Kantian or post-Kantian.[15] The claim that mathematics is independent of space and time is again important here for two reasons. First of all, as before, space and time were themselves held by the idealists to be inconsistent or only 'relatively true'. If mathematics were based on these notions it would be subject to the same doubts. Second, if mathematics were based on space and time, it would not be *unconditionally* true; its truth would be confined to the sphere of the spatio-temporal.[16]

For Russell in the early years of this century, then, logicism was the basis for a complex argument against idealism, of both the Kantian and the non-Kantian varieties. It is worth contrasting this argument with that of the logical positivists,[17] for whom logicism also formed part of an argument against Kant, but an argument of a very different sort. For the positivists, the essential claim about logic was that it was analytic, in the sense of being true by meaning or true by convention; they held that truths which are analytic in this sense were empty of content, and made no claim on reality. Logicism, on this account, enables one to maintain the *a priori* and non-empirical status of mathematics while denying that there is any genuine *a priori* knowledge. Because mathematics is logic it is analytic, and because it is analytic it is empty of content; so one can insist that it is not genuine knowledge. This, in turn, enables one to maintain the empiricist claim that sense experience is the source of all genuine knowledge. Mathematics, which threatened to provide a counterexample to this principle, is shown by logicism not to do so. All of these points can be seen in, for example, Carnap's discussion of the impact that Wittgenstein's *Tractatus* had on the Vienna Circle.[18] Given this account of logicism and its philosophical significance, it is clear why logicism can be thought of as an anti-Kantian doctrine. Kant held that our knowledge of mathematics is *a priori* even though the truths of mathematics are synthetic rather than analytic. One of the motives of his philosophy as a whole was to explain the possibility of this (supposed) kind of knowledge – to answer the question which he at one stage described as 'the proper problem of pure reason', namely: 'How are synthetic *a priori* judgments possible?'[19] If logicism shows that mathematics is analytic, then it shows that at least in one clear case, perhaps the clearest, Kant's motivating question is simply based upon a mistake. More generally, as was indicated above, logicism seems to clear the way for the anti-Kantian view that all knowledge is straightforwardly based on a single source, and that source is sense experience.

For the positivists, then, the point at which logicism told against the Kantian view had to do with the issue of the sources of knowledge – in particular, whether knowledge must be thought of as having the mind as one of its sources. Given the Kantian assumption that knowledge is correlative with what is known, the issue is at the same time the issue of whether the world that is known must be thought of as partially constituted by the mind. Russell's use of logicism against Kant is quite different. One sign of this is the fact that he does not hold that mathematics is empty of content or analytic or tautologous. It is clearly Russell's view that mathematics is genuine knowledge, and this is essential to the use that he makes of logicism. A deeper sign of the difference between Russell and the positivists is that for the former the terms 'analytic' and 'synthetic' bear no real philosophical weight. He does say that mathematics (and logic) are synthetic,[20] but these remarks function simply as a denial of what he sees as the absurd view that the propositions of mathematics follow from the law of contradiction, and nothing else.[21] The claim that mathematics is synthetic is not, in Russell's hands, part of a theory of mathematics. Nor is it part of a theory of analytic and synthetic knowledge. Russell has no such theory, and no concern at all with the distinction between the analytic and the synthetic except to reject it as philosophically unimportant. The fundamental point here is that Russell in *The Principles of Mathematics* completely rejects the Kantian concerns with the sources of knowledge, and with anything recognizable as epistemology at all. Underlying the arguments against Kant and the idealists is a shift of focus, due as much to Moore as to Russell, from epistemology to ontology, from knowledge to truth.[22] He believes, or writes as if he believes, that in favourable cases the mind has direct and unmediated contact with abstract objects: we simply perceive them, in some non-sensuous sense of 'perceive' which is held to be unproblematic and presuppositionless. Metaphysics is no longer subservient to epistemology; knowledge now appears as merely our access to what we know, not as constitutive of it. (We can perhaps recognize in this the sort of view that Kant found objectionable in Leibniz and Wolff;

certainly it has the same results, that metaphysics proceeds without epistemological constraints, and threatens to run riot.)

First and foremost among the things with which the mind has direct contact, in Russell's view, are *propositions*. These are abstract entities, neither linguistic nor mental. The notions of truth and ontology (being) are very closely connected with that of a proposition. Propositions are the bearers of truth and falsehood; the absoluteness and objectivity of truth requires the objectivity and independence of propositions. Propositions have constituents; everything that is, is a constituent of propositions, and everything that can be a constituent of a proposition must have some sort of ontological status (in Russell's words, it *is*, even if it does not exist). The notion of a proposition is thus central to Russell's philosophy. Elsewhere I have discussed its general role in his break with idealism,[23] and I shall not repeat this discussion here. In the next section, however, we shall see that this notion plays a role both in the use that Russell wishes to make of logicism and in his conception of logic.

II

Given that Russell's use of logicism as part of an argument against Kant and the idealists is as I have described it, what does this imply about Russell's conception of logic? To play the philosophical role that Russell had in mind, logic must, above all, be *true*. Its truth must be absolute, unconditioned and unrestricted. These features may appear to be uncontroversial, even trivial, but in fact they mark a crucial difference between Russell's conception of logic and what I have called the model-theoretic conception. Logic, for Russell, was a universal language, a *lingua characteristica*, not a mere calculus which can be thought of as set up within a more inclusive language.[24] He thus conceives of logic as universal and all-inclusive. I shall endeavour to explain both this conception of logic and its connection with Russell's use of logicism against the idealists.

The idea of logic as made up of truths already marks a difference between Russell's conception and the model-theoretic conception. According to the latter, logic is made up of a formal system which contains schemata which are subject to interpretations, where each schema has a truth-value in each interpretation. The crucial notion is thus *truth in all interpretations* or validity. For Russell, by contrast, the crucial notion is simply truth. Logic on his conception does not consist of schemata whose truth-values wait upon the specification of an interpretation; it consists of propositions which have a content and a truth-value on their own account.[25] Propositions, as we have already said, are taken to be objective non-linguistic and non-mental entities; they have their truth-values independently of our language, of our acts of synthesis or of any interpretation.

The propositions of logic, as Russell constantly implies, contain variables and logical constants, and nothing else (see e.g. *Principles*, Ch. I); this implies, and Russell clearly accepts, that variables and logical constants are themselves non-linguistic entities.

The notion of an interpretation, and the correlative idea of an uninterpreted formalism, are wholly alien to Russell's thought at this period. He simply never mentions such ideas; the conception of logic as universal is not something that Russell articulates and defends, but something that he seems to take entirely for granted. He does, however, defend one feature of his conception. On Russell's conception of logic, there is no question of our specifying what the variables are to range over; they range over everything. It is thus a part of his conception that there is no room for the specification of a universe of discourse. (We might say that the only universe of discourse, on Russell's conception of logic, is *the* universe, the actual universe, comprising everything that there is. To say this, however, is to reject the notion of a universe of discourse within which the range of the variables is confined.) Thus the propositions of logic are wholly general: they contain variables, and the variables range over everything. Russell's argument against the idea of (restricted) universes of discourse is revealing, and I shall examine it at some length.

The basic argument is one that Russell repeats several times in his work in the first decade of the century. One version goes as follows:

> it is quite essential that we should have some meaning of *always* which does not have to be expressed in a restrictive hypothesis as to x. For suppose 'always' means 'whenever x belongs to class i'. Then 'all men are mortal' becomes 'whenever x belongs to the class i, then, if x is a man, x is mortal; i.e. 'it is always true that if x belongs to the class i, then, if x is a man, x is mortal'. But what is our new *always* to mean? There seems no more reason for restricting x, in this new proposition, to the class i, than there was before for restricting it to the class *men*. Thus we shall be led on to a new wider universe, and so on *ad infinitum*.[26]

The point of this argument is that if we are to have a restricted universe of discourse (i.e. something other than simply *the* universe), then we must establish this universe of discourse by means of a statement which says what the variable is to range over. But in *that* statement there is no reason to suppose that we are using a restricted universe of discourse. Nor, indeed, can we be doing so unless there is yet another statement in which the restrictions on the first statement are made explicit; and then, of course, exactly the same point will apply to the second statement. Thus it is, on this view, possible to use restricted variables, but the use of such variables presupposes the use of unrestricted variables, which simply range over everything that there is. Thus we can conclude that it is the unrestricted

variable which is fundamental. We can also conclude that only propositions using such variables should be thought of as propositions of logic, at
least by Russell's standards of what is to count as logic. A proposition
which uses a restricted variable is made within the context of some other
statement which establishes the universe of discourse. Its meaning, and its
truth if it is true, are thus conditional upon that other statement. To say
this, however, is to say that it is not unconditionally true. By Russell's
standards it thus has no right to be thought of as a proposition of logic;
such propositions must be unconditionally true, and this in turn requires
that they contain all their conditions within themselves.

This argument of Russell's takes it for granted that the statement which
establishes the universe of discourse is on the same level as the assertion
which is made once the universe of discourse is established. Thus the
former can be taken as antecedent and the latter as consequent in a single
conditional statement. Russell, that is, assumes that all statements are on
the same level; this contrasts with the model-theoretic view that we must
distinguish some as object-language statements and some as metalanguage
statements. Intrinsic to Russell's conception of the universality of logic is
the denial of the metalinguistic perspective which is essential to the model-
theoretic conception of logic. This makes a crucial difference to the way in
which one thinks of logic. Consider, for example, the question of the
completeness of a system of logic, which is so natural for us. This question
relies upon the idea that we have, independently of the logical system, a
criterion of what the system ought to be able to do, so that it relies upon
the essentially meta-theoretic notion of an interpretation, and of truth in
all interpretations. These meta-theoretic ideas, however, are foreign to
Russell's conception of logic; the question of the completeness of a system
in the modern sense simply could not arise for him.[27] Logic for him was not
a system, or a formalism, which might or might not capture what we take
to be the logically valid body of schemata; logic for him was, rather, the
body of wholly general truths.

The fact that Russell does not see logic as something on which one can
take a meta-theoretical perspective thus constitutes a crucial difference
between his conception of logic and the model-theoretic one. Logic, for
Russell, is a systematization of reasoning in general, of reasoning as such. If
we have a correct systematization, it will comprehend all correct principles
of reasoning. Given such a conception of logic there can be no external
perspective. *Any* reasoning will, simply in virtue of being reasoning, fall
within logic; any proposition that we might wish to advance is subject to the
rules of logic. This is perhaps a natural, if naive, way of thinking about logic.
In Russell's case, however, we can say more than this to explain why he
should have held such a conception. Given the philosophical use that
Russell wishes to make of logicism, no other conception is available to
him. If logic is to be unconditionally and unrestrictedly true, in the sense

that Russell must require it to be, then it must be universally applicable. This in turn implies that statements about logic must themselves fall within the scope of logic, so the notion of a meta-theoretical perspective falls away. If this were not so, if logic were thought of as set up within a more inclusive metalanguage, then by the standards which Russell and the idealists share, it would appear that logic is not absolutely and unconditionally true. Logic, on this modern picture, is not unrestricted, for it is set up in a more inclusive language which must fall outside its scope. Nor can the truth of logic, conceived of in this way, be thought of as absolute and unconditioned, for it is dependent upon the metalanguage within which it is set up. There is no reason to believe that Russell ever considered anything like the model-theoretic conception of logic – at least as a conception of *logic* – but if he had done so, the use he wishes to make of logicism would have given him reason to reject it in favour of the conception of logic as universal.

My claim here, of course, is a claim about Russell and about the argumentative situation that he found himself in. Given that situation, I want to say, he would have found this view of logic necessary to sustain his attack on the idealists.[28] We can reinforce this idea by seeing that the conception of logic as universal, and some arguments for it, have analogues in certain idealist lines of thought. What I have particularly in mind here is the argument which the post-Kantian idealists used against the Kantian notion of the thing-in-itself. The Kantian thing-in-itself, as the idealists understood the notion, provides a contrast with all knowledge that is possible for us. What we know are appearances, which are conditioned by our forms of sensibility and by the (schematized) categories of the understanding. The thing-in-itself is, by definition, that which is independent of us and our cognitive faculties; it is therefore something of which we can have no knowledge. Kant's claim, of course, is that although we can – almost by definition – have no knowledge about things-in-themselves, we can nevertheless think of them, and may, indeed, have rational grounds for belief about them. He does, moreover, presuppose that we can at least know that there are things-in-themselves, even though we can have no (other) knowledge about them. These views of Kant's were widely attacked by his idealist successors; it is the basis of the attack that is of concern to us. If things-in-themselves are really wholly beyond the reach of our knowledge, how could we know even that there are such things? More broadly, since the categories of the understanding are surely conditions of *thought* as well as of knowledge, how can we even have thoughts or beliefs about things-in-themselves?[29] These objections are clearly expressed by McTaggart:

> The thing-in-itself as conceived by Kant, behind and apart from the phenomena which alone enter into experience, is a contradiction. We cannot, we are told, know what it is, but only that it is. But this is itself an important piece of knowledge relating to the thing. It involves a

judgment, and a judgment involves categories, and we are thus forced to surrender the idea that we can be aware of anything which is not subject to the laws governing experience.[30]

McTaggart is attacking Kant for being insufficiently serious and literal about the idea of generality. If the categories really are the categories, then they must apply to everything. There is nothing that we can conceive of as being exempt from them, and no position from which we think without employing them. In particular, they must apply to the critical philosophy, and thereby to the very statement of the categories themselves.

Russell, I wish to suggest, might have accepted similar arguments against the idea of a perspective external to logic, from which we can establish logic. On Russell's conception, logic applies to everything – including the very statements which establish logic. This point can be very clearly seen in certain passages in *Principles*. Russell denies that we can prove the independence of a truth-functional axiom by finding an interpretation for the negation of that axiom together with the other axioms. The general technique is clearly well-known to him, but he argues that it is not available in this specific case. If we deny an axiom of this sort, reasoning itself becomes impossible:

> it should be observed that the method of supposing an axiom false, and deducing the consequences of this assumption, which has been found admirable in such cases as the axiom of parallels, is here not universally available. For all our axioms are principles of deduction; and if they are true, the consequences which appear to follow from the employment of an opposite principle will not really follow, so that arguments from the supposition of the falsity of an axiom are here subject to special fallacies (*Principles*, section 17).

This view, moreover, seems to be one that Russell held not only in *Principles* but also later, at the time when he was completing *Principia*.[31]

Russell's conception of logic as universal is connected with another crucial feature of his view of the subject. For Russell, logic has direct and immediate metaphysical or ontological implications. If the propositions of logic are indeed general truths, then certain things follow from them about what the world must be like. To put it another way: logic has metaphysical implications, which must be correct if logic is true. This is suggested by an important passage in the Preface of *Principles*, where Russell acknowledges his indebtedness, in metaphysical issues, to G. E. Moore:

> On fundamental questions of philosophy, my position, in all its chief features, is derived from Mr G. E. Moore. I have accepted from him the

non-existential nature of propositions (except such as happen to assert existence) and their independence of any knowing mind; also the pluralism which regards the world, both that of existents and that of entities, as composed of an infinite number of mutually independent entities, with relations between them which are ultimate, and not reducible to adjectives of their terms or of the whole which these compose. Before learning these views from him, I found myself unable to construct any philosophy of arithmetic, whereas their acceptance brought about an immediate liberation from a large number of difficulties which I believe to be otherwise insuperable. The doctrines just mentioned are, in my opinion, quite indispensable to any even tolerably satisfactory philosophy of mathematics . . . Formally my premises are simply assumed; but the fact that they allow mathematics to be true, which most current philosophies do not, is surely a powerful argument in their favour (*Principles*, p. xviii).

The 'philosophy of arithmetic' which Russell found himself able to construct after (but only after) accepting certain metaphysical views from Moore is of course logicism; logicism has these presuppositions because they are presuppositions of logic itself.

Russell, then, sees logic as requiring the existence of propositions as non-spatio-temporal and non-mental entities; the existence of infinitely many distinct and independent entities; and the existence of non-reducible relations holding among these entities. These claims are fundamental to a whole metaphysics, which is sketched by Russell and Moore in conscious opposition to idealism. Why should logic have any such implications? This question can be approached through the technical considerations that we have already touched on. The propositions of logic, for Russell, contain only variables and logical constants; and the variables range over everything in the (actual) universe. So the letter 'p' in (say) '$p \vee q$' and the letter 'F' in 'Fx' are treated as free variables, in the same way as 'x' is treated as a free variable in 'Fx'. This has the immediate implication that the propositions of logic assert not merely that there are objects over which the objectual variables range, but also that there are propositions over which the propositional variables range, and predicates or their analogues over which the predicate variables range. The truth-functional part of logic requires that each proposition be determinately true or false; if the truth of logic is to be absolute, objective and completely general, then all true propositions must be objectively and absolutely true. Russell, I think, took this to imply that propositions themselves must be non-mental entities, which exist independently of any mind.[32] The quantificational part of logic, similarly, requires that there are predicates which are determinately true or false of objects (and never both); if logic is to be wholly general, each predicate must be determinately true or false of *each* object. These implications are, as Russell fully realized, claims which would be rejected by his idealist opponents. His position is that the power of logic, and the insight that it affords us into mathematics, ought to persuade us to accept the metaphysical presuppositions on which logic rests.

Russell's position here is closely connected with another issue which I have mentioned in passing: the fact that for him logic is (what we would call) higher-order logic, and first-order logic not even a natural fragment of logic. To put the point a different way: for Russell, higher-order logic is implicit in first-order logic, and involves nothing new in principle. In its mature form, in *Principia Mathematica*[33] or in 'Mathematical Logic as Based on the Theory of Types', Russell's logic quantifies over propositional functions as well as over individuals. It is, of course, because of this fact that Russell is able to achieve the power of set theory without assuming that there are sets; it is also because of this fact that some commentators have claimed that Russell's mature logic is not more logic properly so-called than is set theory.[34] From the present perspective, the question is whether the universality of logic is compatible with, or even implies, the idea that we can, as a part of logic, quantify over propositional functions. Such quantification involves us in existential claims; do such claims introduce a new and special subject matter (the theory of propositional functions)? My claim is that from Russell's point of view the introduction of quantification over propositional functions into logic is, in itself, quite compatible with the universality of logic, and arguably even implied by it. The necessity for avoiding the paradoxes, however, leads, as we shall see in section III, to steps which are not compatible with the universality of logic. My emphasis here, however, will be on the first and positive claim, that if one grants Russell the conception of logic as universal, and waives the issues raised by the paradoxes, then one can argue that the theory of propositional functions is indeed part of logic, whereas set theory, say, is not. In the end Russell may be wrong to think that he has a coherent conception of logic according to which *Principia* is logic, for in the end the paradoxes cannot be ignored. But there is, I think, more to be said for this Russellian view than most of his critics acknowledge.

Let us begin by taking it for granted that what we call first-order logic is indeed logic. Presupposing the Russellian notion of a proposition, we can say that first-order logic requires that we analyse propositions in a certain way. We must show that there is something shared by the propositions that Caesar killed Caesar and that Brutus killed Brutus, which is not shared by the proposition that Caesar killed Brutus. This much is necessary to show e.g. that the first two imply '$(\exists x)(x$ killed $x)$' whereas the third does not (although all three imply '$(\exists x)(\exists y)(x$ killed $y)$'). But what is this 'something shared'? Given the non-linguistic nature of a Russellian proposition, it can hardly be a merely linguistic entity (an open sentence); it is, rather, what Russell calls a propositional function.[35] What the first two propositions have in common, which the third does not, is that they are values or instances of the propositional function $\hat{x}$ killed $\hat{x}$. It is for these sorts of reasons, not simply because of a need for an analogue of set theory, that Russell's logic requires that there be propositional functions. The crucial point is that even doing first-order logic requires that we accept that there are propositional functions. The formal reflection of this fact is that the primitive proposition (axiom) of *Principia* which assures us of the existence of propositional functions is laid down as part of the transition from truth-functional logic to quantification theory. (The primitive proposition states: 'If, for some *a*, there is a proposition ϕa, then there is a [propositional] function $\phi \hat{x}$, and vice versa. Pp.' Since the transition from truth-functional logic to quantification theory is done twice over, in different ways, this proposition has two different numbers: *9.15 and *10.122.) The transition from first-order logic to higher-order logic in *12, by contrast, requires no primitive propositions concerning the existence of propositional functions, and, indeed, no new primitive propositions at all. (The axiom of reducibility does occur in *12 but, as we shall see in section III, it is not required for Russell's higher-order logic; the need for it arises from the project of reducing mathematics to this logic.) Hence from Russell's point of view the distinction between first-order and higher-order logic is of no particular significance. Since quantification over objects of any sort requires that we accept that there are propositional functions, introducing quantification over these latter entities does not, by Russell's lights, involve any new principle; higher-order logic merely makes explicit what is in fact implicit in first-order logic.[36]

Let us contrast this Russellian view with that of a modern logician, who thinks that the distinction between first-order and higher-order logic is an important distinction of principle. Quine sees the schemata of first-order logic as made up of schematic predicate letters and quantified (or quantifiable) variables. The latter have true generality. When the schema is interpreted, they become variables ranging over some specified domain of entities (the universe of discourse of the interpretation in question). The former, however, do not have this sort of generality. When the schema is interpreted, each predicate letter is replaced by a particular predicate. The generality which seems to attach to a predicate letter, unlike that of a genuine variable, is simply a matter of the multiplicity of possible interpretations which are available; within any given interpretation, however, the predicate letter is simply interpreted as a particular predicate, which is in turn thought of as a linguistic entity. Quine has emphasized the importance of the contrast between a schematic letter and a true variable in a passage which deprecates the use of the notation of higher-order logic, rather than that of set theory:

This notation has the fault . . . of diverting attention from major cleavages between logic and set theory. It encourages us to see the general theory of classes and relations as mere prolongations of quantification theory, in which hitherto schematic letters are newly admitted into quantifiers and other positions that were hitherto reserved for 'x' and 'y' etc. . . . The existence assumptions, vast though they are, can become strangely inconspicuous; they come to be implicit simply in the ordinary rule of substitution for predicate letters in quantification theory, once we have promoted these letters to the status of genuine quantifiable variables . . . along with somewhat muffling the existence assumptions of the theory of types, [the notation] fostered a notion that quantification theory itself, in its 'F' and 'G', was already a theory about classes or attributes and relations. *It slighted the vital contrast between schematic letters and quantifiable variables.*[37]

The contrast which is crucial to Quine's position is, however, not available to Russell. The notion of a schematic letter is an essentially meta-theoretic one, which relies upon the idea that logic consists of schemata which are subject to interpretation. Given Russell's conception of logic as universal, and as consisting of propositions which have a meaning and a truth-value just as they stand, the notion can make no sense to him. To understand Russell's position we therefore have to invert all of Quine's points. Given Russell's conception of logic, higher-order quantification theory – and thus the Russellian analogue of set theory – really *is* a mere prolongation of quantification theory, and the existence assumptions of this theory really *are* implicit in the ordinary rules for quantification theory. Quine's remarks occur in the context of a discussion of Russell's use, in *Principia* and elsewhere, of propositional functions rather than classes as fundamental entities. Quine's position is that it would be on every score preferable to assume classes or sets as fundamental, rather than to define them in terms of propositional functions. From the perspective afforded by a Russellian conception of logic, however, Quine's implicit attack on Russell is misdirected. Given this conception, the ontology of propositional functions (or at least of some entities corresponding to predicate variables) really is implicit in ordinary quantification theory and, indeed, in all ordinary propositions. The ontological assumptions here may indeed be vast, but they are not special assumptions about some special subject matter, as the assumption of the existence of classes would be. This, from a Russellian point of view, provides a reason to think that the theory of propositional functions is logic, as the theory of classes would not be.

This contrast between Russell and Quine enables us to see more clearly what is involved in Russell's conception of logic. Russell's conception of logic cannot be characterized simply in terms of the rejection of what I have called the model-theoretic conception of logic, for Quine's position does not depend upon his holding that conception. Quine, indeed, does not appear to hold this conception; he does not, that is to say, accept that logic consists of a formalism which is subject to various interpretations.[38] One salient feature of Russell's conception of logic is thus not merely its rejection of the view of logic as formalism and interpretation, but its insistence upon the unconditional and presuppositionless character of logic. For Russell, anything whose existence must be presupposed in order to establish or state logic is itself a part of logic. If logic demands that there be propositions, or relations, then as a matter of logic there are; so also for propositional functions.[39] In discussing Russell's use of logicism against idealism we saw something of the basis for this idea of presuppositionlessness. It is, perhaps, a matter of indifference whether one thinks of this as intrinsic to the universalist conception of logic, or as merely a feature of Russell's universal conception of logic. A second salient feature of Russell's conception of logic is that he takes it for granted that our concern is not with language. The 'entities corresponding to predicate variables', on Russell's account, are not linguistic entities. This assumption stems from Russell's general attitude that it is propositions which are of real concern, and that the study of language (as distinct from the propositions which it expresses) is of no intrinsic philosophical significance. (This attitude is seen most clearly in *Principles*. It is somewhat modified by the rejection of the *Principles* theory of denoting, which leads to the view that certain expressions must be understood as incomplete *symbols*; and by the theory of types, according to which certain *symbols* lack significance. Even in *Principia*, however, this attitude survives. It is manifest in the explicitness and emphasis with which Russell says he is talking about symbols when he is, as if he sees talking about symbols as an odd thing to do. See e.g. vol. I, pp. 11, 48n. and 66–7.) This Russellian attitude is connected with a further feature of his early logic, to which I now turn.

Logic, for Russell, is not a subject to be studied syntactically. Russell, indeed, shows no sign of having a conception of syntax as a tool which might be used for this task. There is, of course, a contrast here with what I have called the model-theoretic conception of logic. According to that conception, logic consists of a formalism subject to various interpretations, and a formalism is an object defined and studied by syntactic means. One does not, however, have to hold the model-theoretic conception of logic in order to think that logic can be studied syntactically. Even on something like a universalist conception, one might think that at any rate certain significant fragments of logic could be set up and studied by syntactic means, and results proved which would show something about logic in the universal sense. This suggests that the contrast between the universalist conception of logic and the model-theoretic conception is too crude. Many philosophers, I suspect, hold both and are more or less conscious of the differences and the connections between them. Certainly it seems reasonable to attribute something like this twofold attitude to Quine. The use of syntactic methods in the way that I have suggested appears, moreover, to be compatible with the view that in the fundamental sense logic is universal and presuppositionless. A philosopher who comes close to exemplifying this twofold approach is Frege, and at this point it will be helpful briefly to compare Frege's view of logic with that of Russell.

Much of what I have said of Russell's conception of logic as universal could also, I think, be said of Frege's conception of logic (although the motivation of Frege's logicism is, as I have already remarked, quite different from Russell's). What I have said of Russell's propositional functions, for example, could equally well be said of Fregean *Begriffe*. (There is of course a difference arising from the presence, within Frege's system, of a sharp distinction between *Begriffe* and *Gegenstände*. This has the consequence that no analogue of set theory, and hence also no danger of paradox, arises for Frege until we add to his system the statement that to every *Begriff* there is a corresponding *Gegenstand* – axiom V of *Grundgesetze*. For Russell, by contrast, no such axiom is necessary.) There is, however, one general difference between Russell's conception of logic and Frege's. Russell's conception of logic is based on a metaphysical view which could be, and to some extent was, articulated quite independently of logic. Russell, as we have seen, held himself to be indebted to Moore for the metaphysics of propositions and their constituents, of being and truth. This metaphysics is independent of the logic which Russell erected upon it (which is not to say that it has any plausibility when considered apart from Russell's logic). For Russell, then, the metaphysics was independent of and prior to the logic. For Frege, at least according to the interpretation that I find most compelling,[40] the opposite is true. For Frege, logic, in the sense of the inferences that we do in fact acknowledge as correct, is primary; metaphysics is secondary, and articulated in terms which presuppose logic.

What is the significance of this difference for the conceptions of logic held by Frege and by Russell? Since Frege took logic, the body of correct inferences, as prior to metaphsysics, he was bound to be concerned to delimit this body in terms which made no metaphysical presuppositions. It is for these reasons, I think, that Frege gives something very like a modern syntactic account of logic. Frege's standards of formal rigour approach those of the more rigorous of modern logicians. For this reason the notion of a formal system seems to be at least implicit in Frege's work. (If one takes this notion to imply a meta-theoretic perspective, then of course Frege does not have it. His concern with rigour was an internal concern, an object–language concern: he wanted to do deductions and assure himself that they were gap-free.) For these reasons too it is easy to suppose that Frege holds something like the modern conception of logic, implying at least the possibility of a meta-theoretic approach. This, I think, is a mistake. Frege's use of syntax has a different origin from that of a modern logician; although his work seems to exhibit similar standards of rigour, the reason for the rigour is different.

To look at Russell's work with the expectation of finding anything like syntactic rigour, however, is to be disappointed. As Gödel has said of *Principia*:

> It is to be regretted that this first comprehensive and thoroughgoing presentation of mathematical logic . . . is so greatly lacking in formal precision in the foundations . . . that it presents [*sic*] in this respect a considerable step backwards as compared with Frege. What is missing, above all, is a precise statement of the syntax of the formalism. Syntactical considerations are omitted even in cases where they are necessary for the cogency of the proofs, in particular in connection with the 'incomplete symbols'.[41]

Our earlier discussions suggest that Russell's lack of concern with syntactic rigour is not a matter of carelessness. Why should Russell have any concern with syntax? Not in order to define an uninterpreted formalism which can then be subject to various interpretations, or to be able to treat a system of logic meta-theoretically, as itself the object of mathematical study. Both of these reasons are ruled out, for Russell, by his lack of a genuinely meta-theoretical perspective. Nor, on the other hand, does Russell have a reason of Frege's sort. Russell's philosophical–logical views do not need to be based on a neutral, and therefore syntactic, notion of correct logical inference, for Russell's metaphysics is independent of logic and therefore available for use in defining the notion of logic. The definition is given in terms of the notion of a proposition, of the constituents of a proposition, and of truth. These notions are, as we have already seen, ones to which we have direct and immediate access, through a non-sensuous analogue of perception. Thus there is no need for a syntactic approach, from Russell's point of view. This is not to say that anything in Russell's conception of logic in fact rules out such an approach, though this conception of logic does show something about the significance of the results which can be obtained in this way. What it does indicate is that the syntactic approach is not a natural one for someone with Russell's conception of logic; there is no particular reason why it should have occurred to Russell. Nor, indeed, do I think that it did. From Russell's point of view, therefore, there is no reason that the proofs of *Principia* should obey standards of rigour at all different from those of any ordinary working mathematician. By these standards the proofs of *Principia* can be faulted, but the faults are confined. The view of *Principia* as pervasively lacking in rigour stems from the assumption that the appropriate standards of rigour are syntactic. But this is not the authors' view of the matter – otherwise it would be wholly inexplicable that they should claim that their proofs are in fact unusually rigorous.[42] The fact that Whitehead and Russell employ standards of rigour which are not those of either Frege or of the modern logician is not something that we have to accept as inexplicable (or explicable only by the dubious supposition of Russell's carelessness). Once we have a correct understanding of Russell's conception of logic we shall also understand what his standards of rigour are, and why they are not those of Frege, or of the modern logician.

What I have said above about Russell's standards of rigour in logic can, I think, be generalized. Much of what Russell says about logic differs from what a modern logician would say. But we do Russell an injustice, and impede our own understanding, if we do not see that these differences are explicable in terms of a coherent (if perhaps ultimately untenable) conception of logic which is quite different from the modern one. This conception of logic, in turn, is directly connected with the philosophical motivation of Russell's logicism. When we see why logicism mattered so much to Russell, we see also that his conception of logic *must* have been quite different from ours.

III

Although I have, in the preceding sections, drawn to some extent on *Principia Mathematica*, what I have said of Russell's conception of logic, and especially of the motivation of his logicism, is clearly more inspired by *Principles* than by *Principia*. How does the picture change when we focus on the later work? One important general shift is that the anti-idealist motivation ceases to play any overt role. Russell was as much of an anti-idealist in 1910 as in 1902, but the issue no longer seems urgent to him; he looks on that battle as long since won. A second change is philosophically more interesting. In *Principia* Russell expounds, and relies upon, the theory of types; this alters the picture suggested by *Principles* in ways that are extremely complex. In what follows I shall simply attempt to indicate some of the changes most relevant to the present perspective.

The theory of types has two effects which are worth distinguishing. First, it threatens the conception of logic that I have attributed to Russell; here the crucial facts are that Russell's logic after 1907 has to contain explicit type restrictions, and the axiom of reducibility. Second, it makes it dubious, at best, whether what Russell attempts to reduce to logic is indeed mathematics; here the chief difficulty is the necessity, in *Principia*, for what Russell calls (misleadingly, as we shall see) the axiom of infinity and the axiom of choice (I shall largely confine my discussion to the former.)[43]

Let me begin with the axiom of reducibility. There is a clear contrast here between *Principles* and *Principia*; in the earlier work no such axiom is mentioned. In *Principles* there is no need for the axiom of reducibility or

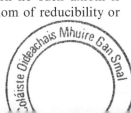

any analogue of it. The axiom of reducibility is required in *Principia* because of two features of that work, which conflict if the axiom is not assumed. First, propositional functions are employed to do the work of classes, whose existence need not be presupposed (in this respect *Principia* is unlike *Principles*). Second, to avoid the threat of paradox, there are complex distinctions of category among propositional functions; in particular, these distinctions prevent us from generalizing over all the propositional functions which are true or false of a given entity. The two features threaten to conflict because if propositional functions are to play the role of classes, it is essential that we be able to generalize over all propositional functions which are true or false of a given entity; otherwise the reduction of mathematics to logic (including the theory of propositional functions) becomes quite impossible. The axiom of reducibility removes this difficulty, more or less by stipulation. The crucial consequence of the axiom is that distinctions of ontological category among propositional functions true or false of a given object – i.e. distinctions of order – can be ignored for mathematical purposes.[44] The axiom achieves this effect by stipulating that for every propositional function, of whatever order, there is a *co-extensive* propositional function of the lowest order.[45] Thus in mathematics, where only the extensions of propositional functions concern us, we can achieve the effect of generalizing over all propositional functions true or false of a given object simply by generalizing over those of the lowest order. By this method, the needs of mathematics are reconciled with Russell's type theory.

If *Principia* is to count as a reduction of mathematics to *logic* then the axiom of reducibility must, of course, be a logical truth. It is, however, very far from clear that counting this axiom as logically true is consistent with the conception of logic that I have attributed to Russell. In one sense the axiom is so consistent: it can be stated using only logical expressions. It is, however, very hard to see how the sort of rationale that I gave for thinking that the theory of propositional functions is part of logic could be extended to show that this axiom is a truth of logic. That rationale was, roughly, that the assumption that there are propositional functions is required to make sense of logical relations in which any proposition stands, whatever its subject matter; thus this assumption is required not to explain some special class of statements – those about classes, say – but to explain the possibility of propositions and their logical relations in general, regardless of their subject matter. Clearly, however, no such rationale will justify the idea that the axiom of reducibility is a truth of logic. The truth of the axiom is not required to explain the possibility of propositions, and of logical relations between propositions, of all kinds, without regard to subject matter. On the contrary: the existence assumption embodied in the axiom is clearly required only for the special purposes of mathematics and the theory of classes. Counting the axiom of reducibility as part of logic thus seems quite inconsistent with the conception of logic that I have attributed to Russell.

A similar difficulty arises in rather a different way from the fact that *Principia* contains, and must contain, explicit statements of type restrictions. The difficulty here does not arise from the mere fact that there are type restrictions. I have suggested that it is a truth of logic (on the Russellian conception) that there are propositional functions; it is also a truth of logic that no contradiction is true. If propositional functions must, to avoid contradiction, be subject to type restrictions, then it must also be true (and presumably also a truth of logic) that there are type distinctions among propositional functions. The difficulty arises not from the mere fact that there are type distinctions; it arises from the fact that these distinctions have to be stated within *Principia*. The crucial fact here is that according to the conception of logic which I have attributed to Russell there can be no genuine meta-perspective on logic: logic applies to every statement, and thus also to statements which are intended to limit the scope of the variables used in other statements.

We saw this point stated explicitly in 'Mathematical Logic as Based on the Theory of Types' (see p. [206] above). The point recurs in the introduction to *Principia*, where Russell again argues that the unrestricted variables is fundamental, but goes on to qualify the claim:

> We shall find that the unrestricted variable is still subject to limitations imposed by the manner of its occurrence, i.e. things which can be said significantly concerning a proposition cannot be said concerning a class or relation, and so on. But the limitations to which the unrestricted variable is subject do not need to be explicitly indicated, since they are the limits of significance of the statement in which the variable occurs, and are therefore intrinsically determined by this statement (*Principia*, p. 4).

The picture that this suggests is that the limitations imposed by type theory do not need to be stated but will, in a later terminology, make themselves manifest. Certainly this is what *Principia* requires, for statements of the limitations imposed by restrictions of type are, as we shall see, liable to be in violation of type theory.[46] But the expectations aroused by this statement are not fulfilled. *Principia* does contain statements of type restrictions. These statements, moreover, do not occur merely in the expository prose, which has perhaps a purely heuristic function. On the contrary: the numbered sentences which are the heart of *Principia* themselves contain notions which are required to set up type theory, and which threaten to violate it. Thus *9.131 is a definition of 'being the same type as'; and the primitive proposition (axiom) *9.14 makes essential use of the notion, asserting 'If "ϕx" is significant, and if a is of the same type as x, "ϕa" is significant, and vice versa' (for reasons already noted, p. [212] above, the proposition stated in *9.14 occurs again, with the number 10.121).

It is important to see clearly exactly why a statement establishing type theory – indeed the very notion 'is of the same type as' – violates type restrictions. If the clause '*a* is of the same type as *x*' is not to be wholly otiose (and in fact it is not), then it must sometimes be true and sometimes false. That is, there must be an object, call it *b*, of which it makes sense to say that it is of the same type as some given object *a*, but where this is not true; and there must be another object, *c*, which is of the same type as *a*, and where this can also be said. But then there is one propositional function, that expressed by '*x* is of the same type as *a*' which can be significantly applied both to *b* and to *c* (truly in one case, falsely in the other). But by a crucial tenet of type theory itself (expressed in the 'vice versa' clause of *9.14) it ought to follow from this that *b* and *c* are of the same type. Since 'is of the same type as' is transitive, this conclusion is directly contrary to the initial assumption that *b* is different in type from *a* but that *c* is of the same type as *a*.

The difficulty here clearly arises from the attempt to state type theory within type theory. The argument above constitutes a *reductio ad absurdum* of the idea that we can treat 'is of the same type as' as expressing a propositional function which must itself be subject to the restrictions of type theory. Yet the universality of logic, as I have articulated it, seems to demand that *every* proposition fall within the scope of logic, and that every propositional function be subject to type theory. Once again, the demands of type theory seem to be inconsistent with the conception of logic that I have attributed to Russell. On this issue there is a clear contrast between Russell's conception of logic and the model-theoretic conception. On the latter conception we have available a metalanguage in which we can state type distinctions for the object language; the question whether our statements in the metalanguage violate the type distinctions of the object language simply does not arise. It is also worth noting that the difficulty that I raised for Russell might be resolved by combining the universalist conception of logic with a syntactic approach to type theory, so that type restrictions would not state anything about (non-linguistic) entities, but would simply lay down conditions of well-formedness on combinations of symbols. I shall not, however, investigate this possibility here.[47]

I turn now to the issues raised by the so-called axiom of infinity. Again, it is worth noting that no such axiom is mentioned in *Principles*. The main body of that work advances a view which lacks any distinctions of logical category. It is, according to that view, thus provable that there are infinitely many entities: 'if *n* be any number, the number of numbers from 0 up to and including *n* is *n* + 1, whence it follows that *n* is not the number of numbers. Again, it may be proved directly, by the correlation of whole and part, that the number of propositions or concepts is infinite' (section 339). The first of these arguments is directly analogous to that used by Frege to show that his definition of natural number ensures that there are infinitely many natural numbers.[48] The correctness of this argument in Frege's logic, however, is directly connected with those features of that logic which make it contradictory. So also in the case of Russell's *Principles*. One way to make this point is to say that it is only because of the lack, in the view conveyed in most of *Principles*, of any type distinctions that the argument works; once type distinctions are introduced to avoid paradox, the argument fails. Unlike Frege, Russell is aware of the need for type distinctions, or some analogous way of avoiding the paradox. He is, however, not satisfied by the systems of types that he considers, and most of *Principles* proceeds as if Russell had never discovered the paradox. Certainly this is true of the present point. The issue of the axiom of infinity does not arise in *Principles* because Russell believes – or is willing to write as if he believes – that the infinitude of entities is provable by the general methods of logic.

In *Principia*, by contrast, type theory makes it impossible to prove that there are any infinite classes unless there are infinitely many *individuals*. This matter Russell insists, cannot be settled by logic: 'This assumption [the axiom of infinity] . . . will be adduced as a hypothesis whenever it is relevant. It seems plain that there is nothing in logic to necessitate its truth or falsehood, and that it can only be legitimately believed or disbelieved on empirical grounds' (*Principia*, vol. II, p. 183). Russell does not, however, assume the infinitude of individuals as an axiom (although he does use the expression 'the axiom of infinity'). He says, rather, that both this so-called axiom and the axiom of choice are to be taken 'as hypotheses', i.e. as antecedents to conditionals, wherever they are needed (besides the passage from *Principia* vol. II, p. 183, quoted above, see also vol. I, p. 482).

Russell's attitude towards the axiom of infinity does not threaten the conception of logic that I have attributed to him. It does, however, threaten the fundamental project of logicism: it might be said that *Principia* represents not so much the culmination of Russell's logicism as Russell's abandonment of logicism. It is, however, a subtle question, whether a form of (pseudo) logicism that is forced to take the axiom of infinity as an extralogical assumption can play the philosophical role that I claimed Russell's early logicism played. One of the arguments that I attributed to Russell was simply that mathematics is an example of a body of absolute truth, whose truth was in no way dependent upon (or conditioned by) the spatiotemporal; this example undermines a crucial idealist doctrine. Stated like this, the argument no longer holds. Mathematics will no longer stand as an undeniable example of knowledge which is absolute, valid beyond the realm of the spatio-temporal, and non-trivial (i.e. obviously genuine knowledge). Mathematics, i.e. logic plus the axiom of infinity, is presumably dependent upon whatever evidence we may have for there being an infinitude of individuals, and individuals presumably exist in space and time (hence the statement in the passage quoted above that the infinitude of individuals is an empirical matter). It is, however, possible that the basic point of Russell's claim would still hold. Logic (not including the axiom of infinity) is not shown by the need for the axiom of infinity to be other than wholly general and absolutely true. It is perhaps less obvious than before that logic is an example of genuine knowledge, rather than being analytic in Kant's sense, but the point is at least arguable. It is thus possible that logic, including the theory of propositional functions but excluding the axiom of infinity, could play the anti-idealist role for which Russell originally cast mathematics. The fate of the other argument that I attributed to Russell is equally unclear. This argument had to do with the crucial role of mathematics in showing that consistent theories of space and time are available. Now if it were thought that the consistency of the infinite, and indeed the transfinite, depended simply upon the fact that their existence is a truth of logic, then clearly the need for an extra-logical assumption of infinity would be fatal. Or again, it might be thought that the crucial question posed by the need for an extra-logical assumption of the infinite is the consistency of this assumption (given the truths of logic); to this question Russell clearly has no answer. An interpretation somewhat more sympathetic to Russell, however, might claim that the power of his position comes from the fact that he is able to show that particular arguments purporting to show the inconsistency of the infinite are one and all erroneous. This fact continues to hold. The logic of *Principia*, though it cannot prove that there are infinitely many entities, can define the notion of the infinite; the understanding embodied in this definition is sufficient to show that traditional philosophical arguments against the infinite are misconceived.

The details of the impact of type theory upon Russell's conception of logic and of logicism are very complex. But even from the outline given above it is clear that the picture which I sketched of the motivation of Russell's logic and of the Russellian conception of logic is seriously threatened by the introduction of type theory. Should we infer from this that Russell's views on these matters shift between *Principles* and *Principia*? Is it incorrect to attribute the earlier picture to Russell at the time of *Principia*? I suggest that it is wrong in principle to insist that there must be a definite answer to a question of this sort. In the case of this particular question I suspect that no clear-cut answer would emerge, even if all the facts were known. The most significant facts in this case are, first, as we have seen, that the development of type theory does undermine Russell's earlier conception of logic and his philosophical claims for logicism; second, he does at times show at least some awareness of this; third, within the relevant period Russell does not find any other conception of logic, or any other view of the significance of logicism, which is remotely plausible. This third fact is in some ways the most significant, for it means that Russell continues, at least when his attention is not fully focused on the issue, to talk as if he still held the old conception of logic, and the old view of logicism. In so far as any general philosophical conception of logic influences him at this time it is this one. He does not really discard the old picture, for he has nothing with which to replace it; on the other hand, he cannot continue to hold this picture with a clear conscience.

One way of thinking about this situation is as an example of what is, I think, a more general truth. When philosophy takes on a technical guise there is always the danger that the technical endeavour will take on a life of its own. One may become caught up in the technical endeavour, and cease to think very hard about whether it will still serve the purposes that originally motivated it, or any others. When the resulting mathematical achievement is *Principia Mathematica*, the neglect of philosophy may be pardonable, even laudable; commentators, however, should be wary of assuming that so great an achievement, simply in virtue of its magnitude, *must* have a clear philosophical point. It is entirely possible that changes in the enterprise, perhaps dictated by technical needs, cause it to lose contact with the considerations that gave it its original point. Something like this, I think, happened to Russell's logicism.

One piece of evidence in favour of the general reading that I am advancing is that Russell never attempts, in *Principia*, to give an account of logic, even when such an acount seems to be called for. Thus his statement of the conditions that a logical system must satisfy, the analogues of completeness and consistency, reads like this:

> The proof of a logical system is its adequacy and its coherence, that is: (1) the system must embrace among its deductions *all those propositions which we believe to be true and capable of deduction from logical premises alone . . .* and (2) the system must lead to no contradictions (*Principia*, pp. 12–13, my italics; cf. also pp. v, 59–60).

The first of these two criteria is the analogue of completeness: our system of logic must be powerful enough. But Russell has no characterization of what *powerful enough* comes to, because he has no way of characterizing logic (which the system is presumably trying to capture). He cannot characterize it semantically, as suggested by the model-theoretic conception, for this conception is still wholly alien to his thought. Yet neither can he characterize it in terms of the universalist conception, for these terms do not fit the type-theoretic system of *Principia*. Instead he offers a statement of what a system of logic ought to be able to prove which is completely without content; as an account of logic it would be absurd. Taken quite literally it makes any (axiomatizable) theory at all reducible to logic, provided we can persuade ourselves to believe that that theory is reducible to logic or that its axioms are principles of logic; given our belief, logic just expands (so to speak) to embrace the relevant axioms. But what, then, is the content of the *belief* that such a theory is reducible to logic? What is it that we are trying to persuade ourselves to believe? Russell, so determinedly anti-psychologistic, would hardly advance a view according to which the scope of logic is dependent upon the beliefs which we have; what the passage indicates, I think, is that he simply has no account of logic which he can accept.[49] He realizes, more or less clearly, that his previous view of logic will not do, and so realizes that some alternative account is required, but he simply has no coherent alternative to offer.

A second piece of evidence for the reading that I am advancing is the eagerness with which Russell later adopts a new view of logic – a view which he admittedly does not fully understand at the time. In the final chapter of his *Introduction to Mathematical Philosophy*,[50] written in 1918, Russell discusses the nature of logic (and thus, given logicism, of mathematics) as follows:

> All the propositions of logic have a characteristic which used to be expressed by saying that they were analytic, or that their contradictories were self-contradictory. This mode of statement, however, is not satisfactory . . . Nevertheless, the characteristic of logical propositions that we are in search of is the one which was felt, and intended to be defined, by those who said that it consisted in deducibility from the law of contradiction. This characteristic, which, for the moment, we may call tautology . . . (*Introduction to Mathematical Philosophy*, p. 203).

Russell eagerly claims that logic consists of tautologies (he is influenced in this by his earlier conversations with Wittgenstein; at the time he wrote this, however, he had not read the *Tractatus Logico-Philosophicus*). He insists upon this in spite of the fact that, as he says, he does not know how to define 'tautology' (p. 205). It ought to be a puzzle to us that so great a thinker as Russell can insist, in diametrical opposition to his earlier views, that logic has an essential characteristic which he cannot define, and cannot explain in a fashion which is at all illuminating. Without a clear understanding of the notion of tautology, how could he possibly have reason to believe that logic consists of tautologies? Part of the answer to this puzzle no doubt lies in the impact that Wittgenstein's personality had on Russell before the First World War, an impact that was evidently not dependent upon Russell's understanding of Wittgenstein's views. But a crucial part of the answer also must be Russell's recognition that his thought about the nature of logic was bankrupt: his old view will no longer work, he has nothing to take its place, and yet his work crucially depends on logic having some kind of special philosophical status. Under these circumstances he clutches at the word 'tautology', hoping, perhaps, that Wittgenstein will emerge from the trenches with a definition of the word which will enable it to play the role that Russell needs it for.

My conclusion, then, is not straightforward. If one focuses on *The Principles of Mathematics* a rather clear picture emerges of Russell's conception of logic and of the general philosophical motivation of Russell's logicism; the two are connected in complex ways which I have tried to indicate. This clear picture is, however, only possible because the main doctrines of *Principles* ignore the difficulties posed by Russell's paradox and related paradoxes. No doubt Russell thought that he would find a solution to the paradoxes which did not threaten anything which he took to be philosophically fundamental. This hope, however, was misplaced; the theory of types, I have argued, *does* undermine philosophically crucial aspects of Russell's early conception of logic. The magnificent structure of *Principia* is thus left without a clear and coherent philosophical motivation.[51]

Notes

1 Given the length of Russell's active philosophical life, and the multiplicity of positions that he held, few claims about his views can be made without qualification as to time. I mean primarily his views in the first decade of this century, when he did all of his serious work on logicism – *The Principles of Mathematics*, 'Mathematical Logic as Based on the Theory of Types' and the *Principia* itself.

2 Cambridge University Press: 1903; 2nd edn, George Allen and Unwin, London: 1937. Abbreviated in the text simply as *Principles*.

3 George Allen and Unwin, London: 1959, pp. 74–5.

4 'My Mental Development', in *The Philosophy of Bertrand Russell*, ed. P. A. Schilpp (Evanston, Illinois: 1944), p. 13.

5 The contrast between Kant and Russell here is complex; their agreement on the synthetic status of mathematics masks two points of disagreement (as well as a more basic conflict over the significance of the distinction between the analytic and the synthetic, which I shall discuss later). Kant holds that being analytic and being independent of space and time are co-extensive properties of judgements (see especially *Critique of Pure Reason*, A 158 = B 197, where Kant makes it clear that all synthetic judgements are dependent on intuition and thus on space and time; analytic judgements, by contrast, are repeatedly said to be dependent only on concepts, and thus not on intuition). Logic, for Kant, has these two properties: it is independent of space and time and it is analytic. For Kant, however, the status of logic is different from that of mathematics, which lacks both properties. Russell, by contrast, argues that logic and mathematics have the same status. Both, he insists, are independent of space and time. For Russell, however, being independent of space and time is not co-extensive with being analytic; he denies that either logic or mathematics has this latter property.

6 Russell's general view of Kant is largely endorsed by Michael Friedman in his 'Kant's Theory of Geometry' (*Philosophical Review*, vol. XCIV, no 4, October 1985, pp. 455–506). Friedman's work is, however, far more sympathetic to Kant than is Russell's.

7 I say 'Russell's development' because, in spite of what Russell says in the passage quoted, this notion is not to be found in any explicit form in Peano's work. On the other hand, Russell's treatment is itself less explicit than that of Frege, but I assume that it is independent of the latter. The best source for Russell's development of (a theory equivalent to) quantification theory is 'The Logic of

Relations', first published in French in Peano's journal, *Rivista di Mathematica*, vol. VII (Turin, 1900–1), pp. 115–48; reprinted in *Logic and Knowledge*, ed. R. C. Marsh (George Allen and Unwin, London: 1956), pp. 3–38.

8　Since our concern is with the post-Kantian idealists, as well as with Kant, it is important to note that the use of the infinitesimal in mathematics was explicitly discussed by Hegel, who found it to be contradictory. See especially *Hegel's Science of Logic* (George Allen and Unwin, London: 1969), which is a translation by A. V. Miller of Hegel's *Wissenschaft der Logik*, section 2, ch. 2, C.

9　The case of geometry deserves special mention. The argument that geometry is logic requires the distinction between pure geometry and applied geometry: the former is simply a branch of mathematics, whereas the latter, for Russell, is part of physics (roughly, it tells you which geometry in the first sense is applicable to the real world). No such distinction was accepted by Kant, for example: his view is that there is only one sense of geometry, and that it gives knowledge of the real (physical) world.

　　The issue of geometry makes it clear that Russell's logicism is not exactly the same as Frege's. Frege was also willing to accept a version of Kant's claim that geometry depends upon the forms of our intuition. This difference in content stems in part from a difference in philosophical context and motive. Frege was not concerned with post-Kantian idealism; his target was naturalism and psychologism. See Hans D. Sluga, *Gottlob Frege* (Routledge and Kegan Paul, London: 1980), especially ch. I.

10　Hegel op. cit., p. 190; cf. also pp. 197–8.

11　The context of this quotation is as follows: 'Zeno's distinctive characteristic is the dialectic. He is the master of the Eleatic school, in which pure thought comes into its own in the movement of the concept in itself, and in the pure spirit of inquiry; he is the originator of the dialectic.' Hegel, *Vorlesungen über die Geschichte der Philosophie* (*Lectures on the History of Philosophy*), vol. I (p. 295 of the edn by Suhrkampf Verlag, Frankfurt am Main: 1971; the translation is my own).

12　*An Essay on the Foundations of Geometry*, Cambridge University Press: 1897, p. 191. It is worth noting that Russell sees nothing new in the idea that there are contradictions in space; it is, he says 'an ancient theme – as ancient, in fact, as Zeno's refutation of motion' (p. 188). One of Russell's arguments (on pp. 189–90) closely resembles F. H. Bradley's discussion on pp. 31–2 of *Appearance and Reality* (2nd edn, Oxford University Press: 1897; ninth impression, 1930), and has more distant affinities with Zeno's argument and with Kant's second antinomy.

13　Besides *Foundations of Geometry*, see also 'On The Idea of a Dialectic of the Sciences', notes of Russell's dated 1 January, 1898. These were not published at the time, but are in *My Philosophical Development* (see n. 3), pp. 43–53.

14　Russell puts forward this claim in opposition to Kant. The idea that it conflicts with Kant's view relies, as I have indicated, upon an interpretation of Kant which I do not wish to endorse. The alternative interpretation sees Kant as claiming that the mathematical theories of space and time are, on their own terms, consistent, and that inconsistency arises only from the metaphysical interpretation given to these theories. The important point here, however, is *Russell's* interpretation of Kant.

15　At this point we can see that it is in fact crucial to Russell's purposes that mathematics be genuine knowledge; this is one of the reasons that he insists that mathematics and logic are both synthetic in character. Kant holds logic to be analytic, and not genuine knowledge; he asserts, for example, 'no one can venture with the help of logic alone to judge regarding objects, or to make any assertion' (*Critique of Pure Reason*, A 60B 85). Since Kant holds logic to apply beyond the spatio-temporal, he might be thought to hold it to be (in his sense) 'unconditioned' (as Parsons points out, the applicability of logic to things-in-themselves is implicit in Kant's view that we can *think* of things-in-themselves; see 'Kant's philosophy of arithmetic', reprinted in *Mathematics in Philosophy*, Cornell University Press, Ithaca, New York: 1983, pp. 115–19). But since logic is analytic, it is not unconditioned *knowledge*, and so not a counterexample to his general position.

16 Russell sometimes offers a different sort of argument, which I do not emphasize, against Kant's view of mathematics. If mathematics depends upon the forms of our intuition, and this is a psychological feature of the human mind, then it looks as if mathematics is dependent upon psychology. Russell does not always clearly distinguish this anti-psychologistic argument from his anti-idealist arguments. See e.g. *Principles*, section 430.

17 At this point I am of course simplifying a very complex story. In particular, the view of Carnap in *Logical Syntax of Language* (Routledge and Kegan Paul, London: 1937) does not depend on logicism in anything like the sense which I am presupposing. See Michael Friedman, 'Logical truth and analyticity in Carnap's *Logical Syntax of Language*, in eds W. Aspray and P. Kitcher, *Essays in the History and Philosophy of Mathematics* (University of Minnesota Press: 1987).

18 Carnap's 'Autobiography', in *The Philosophy of Rudolf Carnap*, ed. P. A. Schilpp (La Salle, Illinois: 1963), pp. 46–7:

> Wittgenstein formulated . . . [the view] that all logical truths are tautological, that is, that they hold necessarily in every possible case, therefore do not exclude any case, and do not say anything about the facts of the world . . . [T]o the members of the Circle, there did not seem to be a fundamental difference between elementary logic and higher logic, including mathematics. Thus we arrived at the conception that all valid statements of mathematics are analytic in the specific sense that they hold in all possible cases and therefore do not have any factual content.
>
> What was important in this conception from our point of view was the fact that it became possible for the first time to combine the basic tenet of empiricism with a satisfactory explanation of logic and mathematics.

19 Section VI of the introduction to the *Critique of Pure Reason*. This section was added in the second or 'B' edn of the Critique, but contains nothing that is not consistent with the 1st edn text; the passage is at B 19.

20 See e.g. *Principles*, 434. This view was one which Russell held consistently throughout the period leading up to *Principia* (and, in fact, until he came under the influence of Wittgenstein's new views on the status of logic; see p. 224). For a later reference, see *The Problems of Philosophy* (Williams and Norgate, London: 1912; new edn, Oxford University Press: 1946), pp. 79, 83–4. In the former of these passages, Russell makes clear his view that deduction can give *new* knowledge, i.e. knowledge not contained in the premises.

21 The notion of analyticity is not discussed at all in *Principles*, which is one sign of the lack of importance that it had in Russell's thought. He does discuss it, as one could hardly avoid doing, in his book on Leibniz (*The Philosophy of Leibniz*, Cambridge University Press: 1900; new edn, Allen and Unwin, London: 1937).

His discussion there contains a number of arguments against the philosophical significance of the notion.

22 It must seem paradoxical to speak of the author of *Our Knowledge of the External World*, the advocate of reduction of physical object-statements to sense-data statements, as anti-epistemological in his orientation. Various considerations mitigate this paradox. One is that all of Russell's work in the epistemological vein is written after the completion of *Principia*; there was a shift in his concerns around this time, perhaps traceable in part to the lectures that Moore gave in 1910–11 (later published as *Some Main Problems of Philosophy*, George Allen and Unwin, London: 1953). A second is that the notion of a sense-datum can be seen, in a curious way, as the natural outcome of the view that we have a direct and unproblematic relation to the objects of our knowledge. If one holds this view then it may seem obvious, upon reflection, that the objects of our knowledge are not such things as tables and trees. The fact of sensory illusion seems to show this (it may be said, indeed, that one who holds the view of knowledge that I have mentioned is the appropriate target for the argument from illusion). Thus one searches for suitable objects of knowledge–relata which can preserve the relation of knowing as a direct and unproblematic one. The result is the notion of a sense-datum, as conceived by Russell and Moore – not as a subjective or mental entity, but as an objective non-mental thing with which our minds are in direct and unmediated contact. The non-mental nature of Russellian sense-data is of course crucial to this way of understanding matters, and is often overlooked. A third fact is probably most important of all from the present perspective. Russell's epistemological worries do not rapidly extend themselves to serious questions about our knowledge of abstract objects. Here the answer that we simply are in direct contact with them, that we 'perceive' them in some non-sensuous fashion, continues to satisfy him at least until the 1920s. This is the point which is most relevant to the discussion of logicism and also, although less obviously, to his anti-Kantianism.

23 See 'The nature of the proposition and the revolt against idealism', in *Philosophy in History*, eds R. Rorty, J. Schneewind and Q. Skinner, Cambridge University Press: 1984.

24 For discussions of this conception of logic, see van Heijenoort, 'Logic as language and logic as calculus', *Synthèse*, vol. 17 (1967), pp. 324–30; and Goldfarb, 'Logic in the twenties: the nature of the quantifier', *Journal of Symbolic Logic*, vol. 44, no. 3, September 1979, pp. 351–68.

25 This point is closely connected with that made by Frege, when he insists that his logic *expresses a content*. See especially 'On the aim of the "conceptual notation" ', trans. in ed. T. W. Bynum, *Conceptual Notation and Related Articles*, Oxford University Press, Oxford: 1972: 'my aim [in the *Begriffsschrift*] was different from Boole's. I did not wish to present an abstract logic in formulas, but to express a content through written symbols'. To say that a statement of logic expresses a content is presumably also to say that it is true or false on its own account, without the need for an interpretation.

26 This version is from 'Mathematical logic as based on the theory of types', reprinted in ed. Marsh, *Logic and Knowledge* (George Allen and Unwin, London: 1956), p. 71. For other versions see e.g. 'On "insolubilia" and their solution by symbolic logic', reprinted in ed. Lackey, *Essays in Analysis* (George Allen and Unwin, London: 1973), pp. 190–214, and *Principles*, section 7.

27 For the development of the issue of (semantic) completeness in its modern sense, see the paper of Goldfarb's cited in n. 24, and also the introductory note by Burton Dreben and Jean van Heijenoort to Gödel's proof of completeness, in

vol. I of *Gödel's Collected Works*, ed. Solomon Feferman *et al.*, Oxford University Press: 1986.

28 I say 'would have' rather than 'did' because there is no reason at all to believe that Russell articulated the sorts of considerations that I am giving. In particular, there is, as I have said, no reason to think that he considered any other conception of logic as possible.

29 At this point the idealist interpretation of Kant is again arguably mistaken. In particular, the view that things-in-themselves are independent of all our cognitive faculties seems to neglect Kant's distinction between sensibility and the understanding, and between the schematized and the unschematized categories. At least in some places, Kant's view seems to be that things-in-themselves are independent of sensibility (and therefore of the schematized categories), but not of the understanding (and the unschematized categories). See especially *Critique of Pure Reason*, A 253–4 = B 309–10.

30 *Studies in Hegelian Dialectic*, Cambridge University Press: 1896, 2nd edn, 1922, p. 27. I cite McTaggart not only because he is clear and (on this point) representative, but also because we know that Russell took him seriously, read his work, and was influenced by his interpretation of Hegel. See e.g. *My Philosophical Development* (cited, n. 3), p. 38.

31 See Russell's letter to Jourdain, dated 28 April 1909: 'I do not prove the independence of primitive propositions by the recognised methods; this is impossible as regards principles of inference, because you can't tell what follows from supposing them false: if they are true, they must be used in deducing consequences from the hypothesis that they are false, and altogether they are too fundamental to be treated by the recognised methods.' This portion of the letter is printed in *Dear Russell–Dear Jourdain*, edited by I. Grattan Guinness (Duckworth, London: 1977), p. 117.

32 See *Our Knowledge of the External World* (London: George Allen and Unwin, 1914; revised edition 1916) for some discussion of this point.

33 A. N. Whitehead and B. Russell, *Principia Mathematica*, vol. I, Cambridge University Press: 1910; 2nd edn 1927. All my references are to material printed in the 1st edn and reprinted 'unchanged except as regards misprints and minor errors' in the 2nd (introduction to the 2nd edn, p. xiii); my pagination, however, is that of the 2nd edn. I make the simplifying assumption that it is Russell, rather than Whitehead, who is responsible for the parts of *Principia* that are my concern.

34 See Quine, *Philosophy of Logic* (Prentice-Hall, Englewood Cliffs, N.J.: 1970), pp. 64–8. Elsewhere Quine argues at some length that Russell's strategy of taking propositional functions as fundamental, and classes as defined, has no advantages (and some disadvantages) compared with that of taking classes as fundamental outright. See especially *Set Theory and its Logic* (Harvard University Press, Cambridge, Mass.: 2nd edn, 1969), ch. XI.

35 Here I presuppose that propositional functions are not linguistic entities, a claim that has been doubted by a number of commentators. See *Principia*, vol. II, p. xii, where a distinction is made between a propositional function and the *symbolic form* of a propositional function. The context of this passage may make it less than conclusive. The general tenor of Russell's discussions of propositional functions, both in *Principles* and in *Principia*, however, is that they have the same status as propositions, and are indeed exactly like propositions except that propositional functions have variables in one or more places where the corresponding proposition has an entity.

36 It is important to note that propositional functions are not *constituents* of

propositions (see *Principia*, vol. 1 pp. 54–5); this fact is crucial to the basis of type theory. But we must acknowledge propositional functions if we are to have any account of generality.

37 *Set Theory and Its Logic*, pp. 257–8; my italics.

38 See for example Quine's *Philosophy of Logic*, Prentice-Hall, Englewood Cliffs, N.J.: 1970.

39 Here again there is a clear contrast between Russell and Kant (and equally between Frege and Kant). For Kant, logic has no objects of its own, and does not even deal with objects; its concern is with the understanding and its form (see especially *Critique of Pure Reason*, preface to the 2nd edn, at B ix). Russell's propositions and propositional functions, by contrast, are logical objects (as are Frege's *Wertverlaüfe*). One way to understand the significance of Russell's paradox, and related paradoxes, is as showing that Kant was right on this issue, and Russell and Frege wrong. The assumption that there are logical objects, when combined with the generality which both Russell and Frege took as characteristic of logic, leads to paradox; see section III.

40 See especially T. G. Ricketts, 'Objectivity and objecthood', in *Synthesizing Frege*, eds L. Haaparanta and J. Hintikka (Reidel, Dordrecht: 1986).

41 'Russell's Mathematical Logic', in ed. P. A. Schilpp, *The Philosophy of Bertrand Russell*, The Library of Living Philosophers, Evanston, Illinois: 1946, p. 126.

42 In the preface to the 1st edn of *Principia*, Whitehead and Russell say that '[t]he proofs of the earliest propositions are given *without the omission of any step*' (p. vi; my italics). The reasons they give for this care are also important. They do not appeal to any abstract standards of syntactic rigour, but to more practical considerations: 'otherwise it is scarcely possible to see what hypotheses are really required, or whether our results follow from our explicit premisses', and 'full proofs are necessary for the avoidance of errors, and for convincing those who may feel doubtful as to our correctness' (ibid.). How far they are from wishing to put forward a formal system in the modern sense may also be gathered from the Preface and from the discussion, in the introduction to the 1st edition, of their use of symbolism. They say in the introduction, for example, 'In proportion as the imagination works easily in any region of thought, symbolism (except for the express purpose of analysis) becomes only necessary as a convenient shorthand writing to register results obtained without its help' (p. 3).

43 Like the so-called axiom of infinity, the so-called axiom of choice is not mentioned in *Principles* but is recognized in *Principia* as required for mathematics; like the axiom of infinity, again, it is not in fact taken as an axiom of *Principia* but is used as an hypothesis as required (see above, pp. [220–222]). I shall not discuss the axiom of choice for two reasons. First, the philosophical issues which the need for this 'axiom' raises are raised also by the need for the axiom of infinity, which is perhaps more interesting for our purposes. Second, the fact that the axiom of choice is not discussed in *Principles* is not due to some difference between that work and *Principia* which implies that the issue does not arise in the former. It is, rather, simply that Russell was not aware, when he wrote *Principles*, that the axiom had to be assumed as an independent principle. As he himself says in the introduction to the 1937 edn, he 'did not become aware of the necessity for this axiom until a year after the *Principles* was published' (p. viii). I see no reason to doubt his later statement on this point. By contrast, the need for the axiom of infinity in *Principia* but not in *Principles* indicates a crucial difference between these works, as we shall see.

44 The word 'order' is consistently used in this sense in the introduction to the 2nd edn of *Principia*. Ramsey adopts this usage, and confines the word 'type' to

distinctions among propositional functions which are based on distinctions among the entities to which they can be significantly applied; see 'The Foundations of Mathematics' (first published in the *Proceedings of the London Mathematical Society*, series 2, vol. 25, and reprinted in *The Foundations of Mathematics and other Logical Essays*, ed. R. B. Braithwaite, Littlefield, Adams and Co., Totowa, N.J.: 1965), especially pp. 23–8. In his usage, there is thus a clear distinction between type and order, and many later authors have followed him in making this distinction. In the first edition of *Principia*, however, Russell's use of the words 'type' and 'order' does not consistently follow this rule. In particular, he often uses 'type' for both kinds of distinctions among propositional functions (e.g. in 9.14, which is discussed on pp. [219–220]). Although I follow Ramsey's use of the word 'order' here, my later discussion, like that of the 1st edn of *Principia*, uses the word 'type' in a non-Ramseyan way to include distinctions of order.

45 Two propositional functions are said to be co-extensive if they are true of exactly the same things; the extension of a propositional function consists of those things of which it is true. If the notion of the extension of a propositional function were taken as fundamental, it would provide us with an analogue of set theory with no more ado. Russell's method of dispensing with the assumption that there are classes (or sets or extensions) is to define class symbols in such a way that a sentence involving such a symbol expresses a (more complex) proposition about propositional functions.

46 This point was perhaps first made by Wittgenstein; see 'Notes on logic' (printed as appendix I to *Notebooks 1914–16*, University of Chicago Press: 1961, 2nd edn: 1979), pp. 98, 101.

47 A syntactically specified version of *Principia* would also be clearly inadequate for mathematics because of Gödel's incompleteness theorem, which states that any (consistent) formalism fails to prove some arithmetical truth. *Principia* is not syntactically specified, and it is by no means evident that one should think of it as a (rather careless) formalism at all. It is thus by no means clear that *Principia*, as its authors intended it, is vulnerable to an argument based on Gödel's theorem.

48 Compare Frege, *Foundations of Arithmetic* (trans. J. L. Austin, Blackwell, Oxford: 1950, 2nd edn: 1953), section 82.

49 The question of the nature and status of logic occupied Russell after the completion of *Principia*. It appears that this was to have been one of the issues discussed in the unwritten third portion of Russell's projected 1913 book, 'The Theory of Knowledge'. See *The Collected Papers of Bertrand Russell*, vol. 7, ed. E. R. Eames (George Allen and Unwin, London: 1984) which contains as much as Russell wrote of the book, and also discusses his plans for the remaining portions.

50 George Allen and Unwin: 1919.

51 I should like to express my gratitude to the organizers of the conference in Munich where this paper was read, and to the Volkswagen Stiftung for making the conference possible. I cannot mention all those at the conference who gave me criticism, advice and encouragement, but I should like to thank them all, and especially Peter Clark and Bill Hart. For criticism of earlier drafts of this paper I am indebted to Francis Dauer, Michael Friedman, Warren Goldfarb, Leonard Linsky, Thomas Ricketts and, especially, Burton Dreben.

15

Russell's Reasons for Ramification

Warren D. Goldfarb

I

Russell introduced a form of ramification in his 1906 paper "On 'Insolubilia' and Their Solution by Symbolic Logic."[1] There it is applied to propositions. Extended and somewhat modified, ramification is the central component of the theory of types as it is presented in "Mathematical Logic as Based on the Theory of Types" in 1908 and in *Principia Mathematica*.[2] That is, Russell did not separate the theory of orders, which embodies the ramification of propositional functions, from the theory of types. A disentanglement of these two notions was first urged by Ramsey in 1925, when he formulated a simple theory of types.[3] Ramification could then, and only then, be seen as a superposition of a theory of orders on a basic type-theoretic structure.

For over sixty years now, ramification has elicited an intriguing bipolar reaction. Those who have most shared Russell's motivations in the philosophy of mathematics have thought it confused or misguided (thus Ramsey, and also Carnap, Gödel, and Quine).[4] Yet many whose basic outlook is rather more distant from Russell's have found the notion alluring, have continued to study its nature and consequences (although often in settings removed from the theory of types), and have argued for its importance in foundational studies.[5]

Ramification of a domain of abstract entities is the result of requiring that legitimate specifications of such entities be predicative. Briefly put, a specification is predicative if it contains no quantifier that ranges over a universe to which the entity specified belongs.[6] (Obviously, we speak of specifications in an interpreted language.) The predicativity requirement allows a specification to license an existence claim only if the entity whose existence is inferred lies outside the universes of the quantifications in the specification. Thus, the requirement will yield a hierarchy of entities: those at any given level of the hierarchy are just those that are specifiable using quantifiers that range only over lower levels of the hierarchy. Ramification is just this division of entities into levels.

There is a particular philosophical cast that, it seems, has to be put on the nature of the entities under discussion in order for the predicativity requirement, and hence for ramification, to be justified. This philosophical cast, roughly put, is nonrealist and in a sense constructivist: these entities do not subsist independently of us, but are created or legitimized by our being able to specify them. (I have said "in a sense constructivist" because the specifications need not be constructive in the ordinary sense. There is no constraint of effectiveness, and no prohibition of quantifiers with infinite ranges.) It is, to be sure, not an easy matter to spell out such a constructivist view, particularly if the legitimacy of classical (truth-functional) logic is also to be supported. Yet it does seem clear that some such view will entail the predicativity requirement. Since it is first the specification that legitimizes the entity specified, that specification can in no way depend on the existence of the entity. Therefore, the ranges of the quantifiers in the specification cannot include the entity.[7]

My interest, however, is in the converse claim, namely, that ramification is justified *only* on such a constructivist view (and hence that, implicitly at least, Russell held such a view). This claim was forwarded by Gödel in "Russell's Mathematical Logic":

> If, however, it is a question of objects that exist independently of our constructions, there is nothing in the least absurd in the existence of totalities containing members which can be . . . uniquely characterized only by reference to this totality (p. 136).

The point is echoed by Quine in *Set Theory and Logic*, speaking of classes as the entities in question:

> For we are not to view classes literally as created through being specified . . . The doctrine of classes is rather that they are there from the start. This being so, there is no evident fallacy in impredicative specification. It is reasonable to single out a desired class by citing any trait of it, even though we chance thereby to quantify over it along with everything else in the universe (p. 243).

Given this analysis, by now enshrined as the common wisdom, the bipolar attitude toward ramification that I have mentioned becomes most understandable. The sort of constructivism that Gödel and Quine impute to Russell is, it seems, simply out of place in a logicist. For constructivism bespeaks a shift in the very conception of existence, a shift away from realism; whereas one point of logicism, and other classical theories of mathematics – including that which Gödel espoused – is to vindicate, in one way or another, our full-bloodedly realistic talk about mathematical entities. What work and attention ramification has received over the past sixty years has issued from authors with markedly proof-theoretic leanings.

Now the claim that a constructivist view must underlie ramification is not implausible, and it is even possible to read some of Russell's remarks as pointing to such a view. Yet constructivism does seem inconsonant with Russell's usual overarching manner of talking about existence.[8] In the period of the *Principles of Mathematics*, Russell espoused a strong variety of realism.[9] Subsequently, he became ontologically more and more parsimonious. This parsimony is achieved by elimination and reduction, using the devices of incomplete expressions and logical constructions. That is, statements apparently about certain entities are systematically paraphrased, so that they can be held true without any commitment to those entities. Thus Russell is able to shrink the class of things whose existence must be assumed. But, throughout, his conception of what it is to be an entity does not change. There is no notion of a sort of existence, different from the full-blooded kind in being reliant on our specifications.

Thus, it seems to me that the imputation of constructivism to Russell stands in need of refinement. Gödel and Quine make Russell out to have a general vision of what the existence of abstract entities comes to, and thus to be adopting constructivism as a fundamental stance toward ontology. That does not seem accurate to Russell. Rather, the justification for ramification rests on the particular sorts of entities to which it is applied, namely, propositions and propositional functions. To understand this, we must see more clearly why these entities are central to Russell's logical enterprise and what special features of their structure Russell exploits. The results might have the appearance of constructivism, but Russell's most basic reasons for ramification are not the outgrowth of such a general position; rather, they are far more particular to the nature of the entities he treats.

Attention to the importance of propositions in Russell's conception of logic will also clarify the other widely recognized root of the predicativity requirement. Russell's logical theorizing always proceeds in response to the paradoxes, both set-theoretic and semantic. Now, Ramsey pointed out that the former are blocked by simple type theory alone. The others are not, but they involve notions like truth, expression, and definability (indeed, that is why we call them "semantic"). Therefore, Ramsey argued (as had Peano before him), their solution need not come from the logical theory itself. Thus, it appears, it was a misguided desire on Russell's part that the logical system do more than is appropriate that led to ramification. However, it seems to me that Russell's treating the two sorts of paradoxes as one is not a gratuitous blunder: his view of the aims of logic precludes any sharp separation of them.

In what follows, I shall examine Russell's conception of logic and the theories of propositions that it spawns. The general themes of this conception, canvassed in section II, explain the centrality of propositions and propositional functions to logic and support Russell's view that logical structures must preclude the possibility of semantic paradox. In section III, I examine those features of propositions and propositional functions – features that arise from their intensionality – that undercut any immediate link between ramification and constructivism. Russell's particular theories of propositions, sketched in section IV, exhibit the mechanisms through which ramification is generated, and cast some light on various oddities in *Principia Mathematica*.

Russell's reasons for ramification rest on a wealth of rather intricate views; they cannot be accurately summarized by a label or a quick diagnosis. I hope here to be making a first step towards the fuller treatment that they demand.

II

Russell took logic to be completely universal. It embodies all-encompassing principles of correct reasoning. Logic is constituted by the most general laws about the logical furniture of the universe: laws to which all reasoning is subject. The logical system provides a universal language; it is the framework inside of which all rational discourse proceeds.

For Russell, then, there is no stance outside of logic: anything that can be communicated must lie within it. Thus there is no room for what we would call metatheoretic considerations about logic. Logic is not a system of signs that can be disinterpreted and for which alternative interpretations may be investigated: such talk of interpretations would presuppose just the sort of exterior stance that Russell's conception precludes. In particular, the range of the quantified variables in the laws of logic is not subject to change or restriction. These ranges must be fixed, once for all, and fixed as the most general ranges possible.

The conception of the universality of logic that I have just outlined is intrinsic to Russell's logicism.[10] Although prior to his coming under the influence of Wittgenstein Russell did not have much to say about the status of the laws of logic, he did draw strong philosophical consequences from the reduction of mathematics to logic. These consequences rest on the complete generality that Russell took logic to have. For logic, on his conception, is not a special science. It invokes no concepts or principles peculiar to one or another particular area of knowledge. Rather, it rests only on assumptions that are involved in any thinking or reasoning at all. In this way, Russell could take the logicist reduction to show that no special faculties (such as Kantian intuition) need be postulated in order to account for mathematics.

This conception points also to what has to figure among the "logical furniture of the universe" whose laws are at issue. Logic is the universal framework of rational discourse; this suggests that its primary objects of study will be the vehicles of judgment, that is, the entities to which a person who judges is primitively related. For Russell (in his earlier period), the vehicles of judgment are propositions.[11] Logic will provide laws that govern all propositions, and will thus exhibit the bounds of discourse: the bounds, so to speak, of sense. Now, that there are general laws of propositions depends essentially on the fact that propositions are complex. Hence part of the task of logic is to display what this complexity consists in. The branch of logic that Russell sometimes calls "philosophical logic" provides the general framework for the analysis of propositions: the categories of building blocks from which propositions are made, and the ways in which they are fitted together. In this way propositional functions – functions whose values are propositions – also come to figure centrally among the entities that logic treats.

The centrality of propositions underlies Russell's view that the logical system must treat the semantic paradoxes. Now Russell did recognize a distinction between these and the set-theoretic paradoxes. In "On 'Insolubilia'," he presents a "simple substitutional theory" that eliminates classes, relations, and propositional functions. He goes on to say:

> The above doctrine solves, as far as I can discover, all paradoxes concerning classes and relations; but in order to solve the *Epimenides* we seem to need a similar doctrine as regards propositions (p. 204).

(This "similar doctrine" is his earliest form of ramification, discussed in section IV.) The distinction, then, is simply a distinction of subject matter. Just as the set-theoretic paradoxes are about classes and relations, and to solve them logic must inquire into the nature of these entities, the Epimenides paradox and its ilk are about propositions and propositional functions, and logic must inquire here too. Indeed, given Russell's conception of logic, the semantic paradoxes are more important to it. Since the structure of propositions is the very center of logic's attention, the semantic paradoxes pose a greater threat.

Although Ramsey shared Russell's view of the centrality of propositions to logic, he denied that logic bears the responsibility for solving the semantic paradoxes. In "The Foundations of Mathematics," Ramsey gives an account of propositions, using infinitary truth-functions, that supports the simple – rather than ramified – theory of types. He claims that this system need not concern itself with the semantic paradoxes, in so far as

[they] are not purely logical, and cannot be stated in logical terms alone; for they all contain some reference to thought, language, or symbolism, which are not formal but empirical terms. So they may be due not to faulty logic or mathematics, but to faulty ideas concerning thought and language (p. 21).[12]

Thus the semantic paradoxes are to be blocked not by laws about the structure of propositions but rather by special features of the notions like truth and definability that are invoked in them.

A brief look at Ramsey's solution of the Grelling paradox (that of the adjective "heterological") will show why his position would be unacceptable to Russell. Ramsey notes that the paradox depends upon a relation of expression between a word (an adjective) and a propositional function. He then urges that "expression" is ambiguous, and that there is a hierarchy of expression relations. Once this is taken into account, the definition of "heterological" leads to no contradiction. Now Russell, I think, would ask why there is no relation that sums up (is the union of) the different expression relations that Ramsey postulates. (Such a union would reintroduce the paradox.) Since in the absence of ramification the propositional functions expressed are all of the same type, nothing in the nature of the relata of these relations would preclude such a union. Particularly given his acceptance of arbitrary infinitary truth-functions, Ramsey must take the impossibility of summing the relations to be merely factual, perhaps of a natural or empirical sort. Given his notion of proposition, this position is of doubtful coherence – particularly in view of the a priori reasoning that engenders it.

In fact, the ramified theory of types, even with the axiom of reducibility, does prevent precisely this summation. As Church has rigorously substantiated, ramification – in particular, the differing orders of the propositional functions involved – precludes the existence of a single expression relation that could generate Grelling's paradox.[13] The impossibility here flows from the nature of the entities at issue, not from any *ad hoc* restriction. Thus the hierarchical structure of semantic relations arises from purely logical considerations; it is not a fact of a special science. No conclusion of a special science could block a union of levels of a hierarchy; only a logical impossibility could do so.

There is another criticism that Russell could make of Ramsey's diagnosis of the semantic paradoxes – one specific to the Epimenides. In this paradox, Ramsey would presumably take the notion of truth to be the culprit, and claim that special features of that notion – perhaps some ambiguity in the phrase "is true" – forestall the reflexivity that yields contradiction. (This would be similar to a Tarskian approach.) However, Russell's view of propositions enables one to dispense with all explicit mention of truth in logic. The proposition, e.g., that no proposition having property φ is true can be expressed as

(1) $(p)(\varphi p \supset \neg p)$.

Hence this proposition does not contain the notion of truth. Now, the acceptability of this manner of expression rests on the construal of truth as a property of propositions (rather than of sentences, as in Tarski), and, to some extent, on Russell's view that propositions are both nameable and assertible by sentences; i.e., propositions both are complex entities on all fours with other objects and are the objects of judgment. As a result of these views, the notion of truth simply disappears, through formulations like (1). Moreover, Ramsey agrees with Russell, at least to the extent of accepting formulations like (1); this forms the basis of his redundancy theory of truth.[14]

The Epimenides paradox can then be generated with no use of semantic notions. All that is required is a value for the propositional function φ in (1) that is uniquely satisfied by the proposition expressed by (1). Such a propositional function, it seems, would not be hard to imagine. Thus, it appears, a Ramseyan solution to the paradox is simply not available. The weakness of the extralogical assumptions needed for the paradox makes it clearer why for Russell the nature of propositions themselves must figure in any solution. (In fact, ramification blocks the paradox by precluding the proposition expressed by (1) from being a member of the range of the quantified variable in (1).)[15]

I have been talking of the central role of propositions in Russell's logic, and have so far ignored the other principal sort of entity Russell considers; namely, classes. Now the system of *Principia* makes no class-existence assumptions; rather, Russell eliminates classes in favor of propositional functions. He sees this "no-class theory" as the solution to the problems that had vexed him for many years. For mathematics, it seems, requires classes; yet the paradoxes had raised pervasive questions about their existence. Such questions could not be solved merely by devising a consistent theory of classes and leaving it at that. For this would make the theory a special science, whereas Russell sought to justify classes as *logical* objects: as objects guaranteed by principles implicit in all reasoning. Only thus could the reduction of mathematics to class theory be a logicist reduction, and bear more weight than a mere interpretation of one branch of mathematics in another.[16]

For this reason Russell worries not just about which classes exist but about the very nature of a class. In the *Principles of Mathematics* a central issue is that of how a class is a unity: what logical operation binds the members together into a single object, so that the class can serve as a logical subject. In the *Principles'* theory there is a general feature of discourse that is of help here; namely, the quantifier-words. For at that time, Russell took *all* φ's to be a denoting concept that denotes the class of φ's. Since "all" is a logical word if anything is, the logical nature of classes is thereby vindicated. However, this route is not open to Russell after the demise of the *Principles'* theory of denoting concepts in 1905.

Given all this, the attractions of the no-class theory for Russell are obvious. The paradoxes show that the straightforward naive views fail for both propositional functions and classes. But whereas Russell's fundamental conception of logic demands an account of propositions and propositional functions, classes are additional, and pose further questions. The no-class theory enables Russell to be agnostic about the existence of classes and to say nothing about their nature.

III

Important consequences about the nature of ramification follow from the fact that Russell's logic treats propositions and propositional functions rather than classes. Indeed, Russell never envisaged a ramification of classes. When in "Mathematical Logic as Based on the Theory of Types" or in *Principia* he speculates about the existence of classes, he treats them as all of the same order, and he asserts that the existence of classes would imply the axiom of reducibility. Now the claim that ramification necessarily bespeaks constructivism is, it seems to me, most plausible if ramification of classes is at issue. If all the members of two classes are of like logical category, then the intrinsic nature of these classes can provide no ground for a difference in *their* logical category. To support any such distinction, some feature extrinsic to the identity of the classes would have to be brought in. To support ramification in particular, this extrinsic feature would have to reflect something about how the classes are characterized. But to justify in turn the role that a feature extrinsic to the identity of the class is now taken to play, it would have to be maintained that the feature is essential to the existence of the class. The constructivism implicit in such a view is clear.[17]

Thus it appears that the close connection between ramification with respect to classes and constructivism depends on the fact that we have a conception of the nature of the class that works "from below." The identity of a class is determined by its membership; yet ramification would demand that categorical distinctions be made among classes on grounds over and above membership.

Matters are different, however, with propositions and propositional functions. For these are intensional entities. The identity of a propositional function is not determined by the objects of which it is true, nor is the identity of a proposition determined by its truth-value. This opens the possibility that intrinsic features of propositions and propositional functions could support the categorical distinctions that ramification demands. If so, the immediate link between ramification and constructivism that exists for classes would be severed.

Our conception of the nature of a proposition or propositional function comes not "from below" but rather by way of the manner in which the proposition or propositional function is expressed. This points to a distinction in the notion of specification when applied to propositions and propositional functions, as opposed to classes. To specify a class is to give a propositional function that is true of all and only the members of that class. The specification can be understood on its own; given such an understanding, it is a further question whether or not a given class is the one specified. That is, the specification by itself does not tell us which entity *is* the one specified. This space between the specification and the entity specified does not exist in the case of propositions and propositional functions. Here, to understand the specification is to understand the proposition or propositional function specified. That is, the specification immediately tells us which entity is the one meant.

For Russell, understanding is – like judging – a relation to the propositions and propositional functions expressed by our words. To understand a sentence is to grasp the proposition expressed by the sentence.[18] Thus, for propositions and propositional functions, it makes no sense to speak of first understanding a specification and then going on to investigate which entity is specified; for that entity is given in the understanding of the specification. With classes, clearly, matters are different: a specification can be understood, that is, a propositional function can be grasped, yet there can still be a question as to which class is specified.

Indeed, for this reason I find the terminology of "specification" completely misleading in the realm of propositions and propositional functions. The closest analogue to class specifications here would be descriptions like "the last proposition conjectured by Fermat," descriptions the understanding of which is independent of the particular propositions specified. Such "indirect" specifications do not figure in Russell's logical system. Rather, the comprehension axioms for propositions and propositional functions that are implicit in the system involve not so much the specification of these entities as the presentation of them. One is not characterizing a proposition or propositional function: one is giving it. I shall therefore use "presentation" rather than "specification" in this connection.

This helps explain, I think, why no comprehension axioms are explicit in *Principia*. When Russell talks about the existence of classes, he clearly recognizes that the issue concerns which principles of the form

$$(\exists\alpha)(x)(x\epsilon\alpha \equiv Fx)$$

are to be accepted.[19] From a modern perspective, a theory of propositions and propositional functions would have to answer the analogous questions: for which formulas F and Gx (and for what orders of the variables p and φ) are

$$(\exists p)(p = F)$$

and

$$(\exists \varphi)(\varphi \hat{x} = G \hat{x})$$

to be accepted?[20] But Russell never comes close to formulating this or to having axioms of this form. The mathematical power of such axioms is obtained by means of generalization and instantiation, as in

$$\frac{H(G\hat{x})}{(\exists\varphi)H(\varphi\hat{x})} \qquad \text{and} \qquad \frac{(\varphi)H(\varphi\hat{x})}{H(G\hat{x}).}$$

The absence of such axioms springs from the idea that, once the presentation $G\hat{x}$ is given, one needs no special principle to yield the existence of the propositional function. Rather, in using the formula $G\hat{x}$ in our sentences at all, we are using that propositional function in our propositions. Thus, inferences like the preceding appear to be purely logical, and not the result of special existence assumptions.

The role of presentations of propositions and propositional functions also lies behind Russell's not distinguishing among the various formulations of the vicious-circle principle. One formulation is "no totality may contain members that are definable only in terms of that totality"; the others use "presuppose" and "involve" instead of "are definable only in terms of." Gödel points out that, prima facie, these are three distinct principles, and he claims that only the first yields ramification, whereas only the second and third are plausible without recourse to constructivism ("Russell's Mathematical Logic," p. 135). But if definitions are not external to the entities under consideration, as they are to classes but are not – if they are presentations in my sense – to propositions and propositional functions, then the distinction among these formulations seems to collapse. For, in that case, to say that a totality is necessarily involved in any presentation of a proposition is to say that the totality is involved in the proposition.

In pointing to what I have called the lack of space between the intrinsic nature of a proposition or propositional function and the manner in which it is presented, I do not mean to be suggesting that the existence of such an entity is dependent on its having been presented. That would lead to an extreme constructivism involving a notion of temporality, of the sort to which Quine alludes (*Set Theory and Its Logic*, p. 243). It may appear, however, that every such entity must be in some sense presentable. Indeed, Ramsey and Gödel speak of Russell's system as treating only "nameable" entities. Yet the terms "presentable" and "nameable" must be approached with caution; they cannot be used here in any ordinary sense. Certainly, presentability construed as nameability in the language of *Principia* is not at issue. Indeed, Russell never tells us – nor does he think he needs to tell us, in the logical writings – what the basic building blocks of presentations are. The logical vocabulary of *Principia* is a mere skeleton: any notions the special sciences (or epistemology) might arrive at are to be added to its vocabulary. Logic does not set any limits on which predicates and relations (i.e., elementary propositional functions) exist. Even to speak of propositions as "in principle presentable" is somewhat misleading. This is shown by a claim Russell makes concerning a consequence of the hypothesis that classes exist: he says that if α is a class, then $\hat{x} \in \alpha$ is an elementary propositional function (*Principia*, vol. 1 p. 166). Now, if classes exist, there are too many of them to be even potentially nameable; thus these elementary propositions also fail to be nameable. In short, the notion of "presentability" that is at issue does not involve even the notion of a possible language. It is, so to speak, an ontological rather than a linguistic notion. Thus it provides no ground for the sort of criticisms that Ramsey and Gödel make.

Since logic sets no limits to the elementary functions, it may appear that it can provide no information at all about presentations of propositions. This appearance is deceptive. Consider, for example, the Epimenides paradox. Here we present (or so it seems) a proposition like:

Every proposition hereby asserted is false.

Now our understanding of this proposition is *as* a universal one, with a quantifier over propositions. That is, the complexity represented by the quantifier is built into the proposition. Since logic does tell us what sorts of complexity can figure in the structure of propositions, this proposition and ones like it can be treated by logic, even in ignorance of what the basic building blocks of propositions generally – that is, what the elementary propositions and propositional functions – are.

I have been arguing that the intensional nature of propositions and propositional functions makes it in principle possible to justify ramification without reliance on a constructivist view of these entities. This does not yet provide any justification. The substantive constraints on the complex structures of propositions and propositional functions that comprise ramification rely on the details of the theory of these entities that Russell adopts. To those details I now turn.

IV

Unfortunately, in *Principia* and the writings leading up to it, Russell never lays out any comprehensive theory of propositions. (This is in marked contrast to the *Principles*, in which the nature of propositions is investigated at length.) One clear reason for this absence is that, during this period, Russell's views frequently shift. Often, several different theories seem to be espoused simultaneously. Hence I shall here be engaging in somewhat speculative reconstruction.

One rather startling view that Russell expresses in *Principia* is that propositions simply do not exist. On page 44 (vol. 1) he writes,

> What we call a "proposition" . . . is not a single entity at all. That is to say, the phrase which expresses a proposition is what we call an "incomplete" symbol; it does not have meaning in itself, but requires some supplementation . . . when I judge "Socrates is human" the meaning is completed by the act of judging.

This view is of a piece with Russell's "multiple-relation" theory of judgment, about which Russell subsequently writes at length. It does not appear that this view is consistent with the logic of *Principia*.[21] Luckily, the view seems to play no real role in Russell's explanations of his logical system. In what follows, I shall take the charitable course of ignoring it.

As background, let me recall Russell's early view of propositions. A proposition is a complex of entities; ordinarily, it is that complex which, if true, is identical with the fact that makes it true. Thus the constituents of a proposition are, ordinarily, the entities that the proposition is about; for example, the proposition that Mont Blanc is higher than the Zugspitze literally contains two mountains, as well as the relation *higher than*. I have said "ordinarily" since, in the *Principles of Mathematics*, there are exceptions that arise in connection with denoting concepts. As a result of "On Denoting," the exceptions disappear.[22]

The theory of descriptions of "On Denoting," and, indeed, the general notion of incomplete expression there introduced, puts into prominence the role of quantified variables. In line with the early view of propositions, Russell takes variables to be actual constituents of propositions; that is, to be entities underlying the use of a letter "x" or "φ" in the same way that an object underlies the use of its name. To the obvious question of what these entities are, Russell has no answer, but does not seem overly perturbed by this. In "On Denoting" he says, "I take the notion of the *variable* as fundamental," and explains no further (p. 104). Note that Russell speaks of "the variable" as though there were only one. In this period Russell took variables to be completely unrestricted: all variables range over everything. Since every variable confers the same generality, the particular identity of a variable is needed only for its role in cross-referencing. Thus, in a sense, there is only *the* variable – that is, the notion of unrestricted variation – to explain.

Indeed, during this period Russell stresses the complete generality of variables. He takes the lack of restrictions on range to arise from the universality of logic, especially from the idea that anything expressible at all can be expressed inside its framework. (See, e.g., "On 'Insolubilia'," p. 206. Such reasons also seem to underlie his dissatisfaction with the primitive theory of types discussed in Appendix B of the *Principles of Mathematics*.) The retention of unrestricted generality is a great advantage he sees in the "substitutional theory" he develops in 1906. In that theory, classes and propositional functions are eliminated in favor of propositions and a primitive notion of substitution of one entity for another in propositions.[23] The set-theoretic paradoxes are avoided, even though the basic language contains no type restrictions, because of the form of the contextual definitions through which class variables can be introduced. Were the basic language to be extended by means of these definitions, the class variables so introduced *would* have to be restricted as to type. In other words, any putative formula in the extended language that violates type restrictions could not be reduced by means of the contextual definitions to a formula of the basic language.

However, Russell recognizes in the third section of "On 'Insolubilia'" that the theory as he had so far laid it out does not block the semantic paradoxes. Hence he takes it a step further and denies that any but elementary propositions exist: that is, he suggests, there are no propositions that contain bound variables. Thus paradox-engendering forms like $(p)(\varphi p \supset \neg p)$ do not express propositions; *a fortiori*, there is nothing they express that can instantiate the universal variable, and paradox is blocked. Of course, Russell then has to show how to make sense of quantified statements at all. He does this by talking of ambiguous statements:

> "For all values of *x*, $x = x$" I take to be an ambiguous statement of any one of the various propositions of the form "$x = x$." There is thus not a new proposition, but merely an unlimited undetermined choice among a number of propositions (p. 207).

It is hard to extract a coherent theory from Russell's sketchy remarks here, but I take it that what he has in mind is, roughly, that judgment, assertion, truth, and so on relate only to elementary propositions. The force of applying such notions to quantified statements is captured by more complex ways in which the notions can be related to elementary propositions. Thus, he says:

> If we want to say what is equivalent to "I am making a false statement containing *n* apparent variables," we must say something like: "There is

a propositional function $\varphi(x_1 x_2, \ldots, x_n)$ such that I assert that $\varphi(x_1, x_2, \ldots, x_n)$ is true for any values of $x_1, x_2, \ldots, x_n$ and this is in fact false" (p. 208).

Statements are logical fictions, and "there is no way of speaking of statements *in general*: we can speak of statements of propositions, or statements containing one, two, three . . . apparent variables, but not of statements in general" (p. 207).

Russell does not give the contextual definitions needed here (and there may well be serious problems in this, particularly with regard to alternating quantifiers and nonprenex statements). But it seems clear that what he envisages still preserves the virtues of the substitutional theory. In the basic language, all variables range over the whole universe; now, though, the universe contains none but elementary propositions. If the contextual definitions are used to extend the language by introducing variables for quantified propositions, the form of those definitions would require a hierarchy of such variables. Indeed, his remarks suggest that to quantify over n-quantifier statements is really to use $n + 1$ quantifiers in the basic language; thus, one cannot quantify over all statements, and, more particularly, one cannot in an n-quantifier statement quantify over n-quantifier statements. A ramified structure is thereby induced by the contextual definitions, although none exists in the basic language.[24]

The sort of ramification that results, however, is more finely grained than that which would arise from a constraint of predicativity. *Any* additional quantifier affects the order of a statement; that is, order is determined by the number of quantifiers, not by their range. To be sure, the constraint of predicativity is obeyed, but as a special case. No statement can contain a quantifier that ranges over a domain of which that statement is a member, since that would require a statement to contain simultaneously n and $n + 1$ quantifiers.

Russell seems to jettison this theory: there is no hint of it in "Mathematical Logic as Based on the Theory of Types," and no subsequent assertion that elementary propositions are real while others are logical fictions. (This may be due to difficulties in giving the appropriate contextual definitions or in finding a satisfactory account of judgment and other propositional attitudes; more likely, Russell may feel that his later official view that *no* propositions exist supersedes it.) None the less, as we shall see, remnants of the 1906 view persist in *Principia*.

In "Mathematical Logic," Russell's view is quite different from that exhibited in the substitutional theory. Propositional functions are now taken as legitimate entities; with their reappearance, the realistic view of propositions as complexes also returns. Moreover, variables no longer have unlimited generality; rather, a variable ranges only over the entities of one order. These two points are closely related. Once propositional functions are allowed, with the concomitant idea that every well-formed open formula of the language expresses one, paradoxes like the Russell paradox will immediately arise unless some restrictions are put on the variables. Fortunately, the admission of propositional functions allows Russell to think that restrictions in the ranges of variables are consonant with the universality of logic. For, he argues, those restrictions come from the ranges of significance of the propositional functions. That is, inherent in a propositional function is a range of arguments to which the propositional function can be applied with sense. In this way, the restrictions on variables are intrinsic rather than stipulated *ad hoc*; they do display the bounds of sense.

I shall not examine Russell's tenuous arguments for the coincidence of ranges of significance and orders. I wish only to point to a consequence of having variables that lack complete generality. Once such variables are used, the question of the nature of the variable (as an entity) becomes far more urgent. Different variables can have different ranges; it then appears that our understanding of a proposition or a propositional function that contains quantified variables will depend quite heavily on an understanding of what those ranges are. The variable must carry with it some definite information; it must in some way represent its range of variation. Therefore, I would speculate, Russell takes a variable to presuppose the full extent of its range. Now, since the identity of a proposition or propositional function depends on the identity of the variables it contains, and the variables presuppose their range of variation, even the weakest form of the vicious-circle principle suffices to yield ramification. Indeed, Russell may perhaps even think of the variable as *containing* all the entities over which it ranges; in that case, the only principle needed is that a complex entity cannot contain itself as a proper part. In any case, the ramification engendered is just the sort required by the constraint of predicativity. In short, in this theory ramification springs from the strongly realistic picture Russell has of propositions and propositional functions, and in particular of the nature of variables.

In *Principia Mathematica* it is by and large this theory of 1908 that is put to work. However, in both the philosophical discussions and the technical work there are remnants of the 1906 view. For example, in the Introduction, chapter II, part III, Russell distinguishes between first truth, which elementary propositions can have, and second truth, the truth of propositions that contain one quantified variable. He takes second truth to be parasitic on first truth. This leads him to a distinction of orders of propositions on the basis of the number of quantifiers they contain, a clear shadow of the 1906 view. Yet in part IV of the same chapter, he distinguishes orders of propositions on the basis of the sorts of variables they contain, in the standard ramified manner. Both views are reflected in subsequent technical work. The more finely grained ramification that stems from 1906 motivates his grounding quantificational logic in *9 by *defining* the truth-functions of quantified propositions in terms of quantifications of truth-functions of elementary ones. This is unnecessary on the 1908 view; and in *10, he starts quantificational logic over again, giving what he calls an "alternative method." This method is a more standard axiomatic approach, consonant with the fully realistic view of quantified propositions of 1908. There are other curiosities in the text that exhibit the presence of two distinct theories.[25] Thus, it seems to me that the murky beginning sections of *Principia* will be illuminated if the influence of these competing theories is traced through.

Conclusion

I have been emphasizing how the issues surrounding ramification look when we bear in mind the conception of logic that focuses on propositions and propositional functions. Russell's logicism comes down to the idea of trying to obtain mathematics from the laws of these intensional entities; in this way, his basic conception of logic is less mathematical than Frege's. Russell's logicist enterprise fails, as is shown by the need for the axiom of reducibility (which cannot be justified on any grounds but expediency); this failure may indeed show, as Gödel says, that there is irreducibly mathematical content in mathematics.

Many features of the project give rise to ramification. Russell is no constructivist, although a semblance of constructivism can arise from the tight connection between how these intensional entities are presented and what they are. In fact, Russell tends toward realism, but a realism modified by his concern to investigate how intelligible claims on reality could function. Criticisms of ramification from a "Platonist" point of view simply ignore this concern. However muddled Russell sometimes gets, he seems to have grasped the extremely subtle points that such a concern can unearth.[26]

Notes

1 B. Russell, "On 'Insolubilia' and Their Solution by Symbolic Logic," in Russell, *Essays in Analysis*, ed. D. Lackey (New York: Braziller, 1973), pp. 190–214.
2 B. Russell, "Mathematical Logic as Based on the Theory of Types," (1908), in J. van Heijenoort (ed.), *From Frege to Gödel: A Sourcebook in Mathematical Logic* (Cambridge, Mass.: Harvard University Press, 1967), pp. 150–82. A. N. Whitehead and B. Russell, *Principia Mathematica*, vol. 1 (Cambridge: Cambridge University Press, 1910).
3 F. P. Ramsey, "The Foundations of Mathematics" (1925), in F. P. Ramsey, *The Foundations of Mathematics and Other Logical Essays* (London: Routledge & Kegan Paul, 1931), pp. 1–61.
4 R. Carnap, "On the Logicist Foundations of Mathematics" (1931), in P. Benacerraf and H. Putnam (eds.), *Philosophy of Mathematics: Selected Readings*

(Cambridge: Cambridge University Press, 1983), pp. 41–52. K. Gödel, "Russell's Mathematical Logic," in P. A. Schilpp (ed.), *The Philosophy of Bertrand Russell* (LaSalle, Ill.: Open Court, 1944), pp. 125–53. W. V. Quine, *Set Theory and Its Logic* (Cambridge, Mass.: Harvard University Press, 1969).

5 See, e.g., H. Weyl, *Das Kontinuum* (Leipzig: Veit, 1918), S. Feferman, "Systems of Predicative Analysis," *Journal of Symbolic Logic*, 29 (1964), pp. 1–30, and I. Hacking, "What is Logic?" *Journal of Philosophy*, 76 (1979), pp. 285–319.

6 In the Russellian setting, the notion of predicativity has to be amplified to preclude quantifiers that range over universes containing anything that "pre-supposes" the entity specified. For the amusing history of the word "predica-tivity," see Quine, *Set Theory and Its Logic*, p. 242.

7 Clearly, this argument relies upon a premise to the effect that the sense of a specification depends in some way on the ranges of the quantifiers it contains. Interestingly enough, it is this premise – rather than the thesis that certain entities are first legitimized by their specifications – that Carnap denies in "Logicist Foundations."

8 I do not use Russell's ontological terminology. For him, existence means existence in space and time. Abstract entities thus do not exist; they have Being (they *are*). Since I prefer to avoid the grammatical awkwardness, and am not concerned with any contrast between concreta and abstracta, I use "existence" for Russell's "Being."

9 B. Russell, *The Principles of Mathematics* (London: Allen & Unwin, 1903).

10 Fuller accounts of this conception can be found in J. van Heijenoort, "Logic as Calculus and Logic as Language," *Synthèse*, 32 (1967), pp. 324–30; W. Goldfarb, "Logic in the Twenties: The Nature of the Quantifier," *Journal of Symbolic Logic*, 44 (1979), pp. 351–68; and P. Hylton, "Russell's Substitutional Theory," *Synthèse*, 45 (1980), pp. 1–31. Hylton also discusses in more detail the relation between this conception and the philosophical upshot Russell took logicism to have.

11 This move, although natural, is not inevitable. Although Frege had a similar conception of logic, he distinguished between the vehicles of judgment (thoughts) and the entities that logical laws are about (objects, including the truth-values, and functions). Russell, of course, rejected the basic points on which Frege's distinction rests: the theory of sense and reference and the notion that sentences refer to truth-values.

12 Ramsey continues, "If so, they would not be relevant to . . . logic, if by 'logic' we mean a symbolic system, though of course they would be relevant to logic in the sense of the analysis of thought": and, in a footnote: "These two meanings of 'logic' are frequently confused." This rather glib distinction suggests that Ramsey is not, in the end, in agreement with key features of Russell's conception of logic. Perhaps it explains how Ramsey could introduce infinitary truth-functions so cavalierly, a step justly criticized by Gödel as undercutting the whole point of a logicist reduction ("Russell's Mathematical Logic," p. 142).

13 A. Church, "Comparison of Russell's Resolution of the Semantical Antinomies with That of Tarski," *Journal of Symbolic Logic*, 41 (1976), pp. 747–60.

14 See F. P. Ramsey, "Facts and Propositions" (1927), in *The Foundations of Mathematics and Other Logical Essays*, p. 143.

15 Cf. *The Principles of Mathematics*, p. 527, where Russell considers a paradox that, as far as I know, does not reappear in his writings. This paradox would be classified as semantic, from our point of view: but it is engendered by means that, for Russell, involve no nonlogical notions. (I am grateful to Leonard Linsky and to C. Anthony Anderson for calling my attention to this passage.)

16 An interest in showing classes to be logical objects also lies behind Frege's criticizing Cantor at the same time as adopting the notion of extension (and, later, course-of-values) of a concept in order to obtain classes. Of course, Frege and Russell have different conceptions of what it is to be a logical entity.

17 Even the simple theory of types looks unnatural if taken directly as a theory of classes. While there might be arguments from our conception of classes to the need for a cumulative hierarchy, I see none for a noncumulative hierarchy of classes, one that precludes all mixed-level classes.

18 Sentences and, in general, words and symbols play no role in Russell's characterizations of understanding, judgment, assertion, and inference. That is why such use-mention errors as exist in his writings rarely turn out to have vicious effect.

19 See B. Russell, "On Some Difficulties in the Theory of Transfinite Numbers and Order Types" (1906), in *Essays in Analysis*, pp. 135–64, especially section II.

20 Russell uses the circumflex as an abstraction operator: if Fx is an open sentence, then $F\hat{x}$ expresses the propositional function that, for each argument a, yields as value the proposition expressed by Fa. He discusses this operator in the Introduction to *Principia*, p. 15; but in the body of that work it is introduced almost on the sly, in *9.131. Cf. Hylton, "Russell's Substitutional Theory," p. 27.

21 See Church, "Comparison," p. 748.

22 B. Russell, "On Denoting" (1905), in *Essays in Analysis*, pp. 103–19.

23 Details of this theory are given in Hylton, "Russell's Substitutional Theory." Note that it is entities that are substituted one for another, not words or names. Hence this theory is quite distinct from what is currently called "the substitutional theory of quantification."

24 Here I disagree sharply with Hylton's reading of this section of "On 'Insolubilia'" ("Russell's Substitutional Theory," pp. 22–6).

25 A more minor example is his definition of predicative function. In the Introduction (p. 51), Russell identifies the predicative functions with the first-order ones. Thus a predicative function of individuals is one whose quantifiers, if any, range only over individuals. This is in keeping with standard ramification. But in *12 he calls a propositional function predicative only if it is elementary, a definition that the more finely grained ramification of 1906 would support.

26 I am greatly indebted to Peter Hylton for many illuminating conversations and much useful advice. I would also like to thank Burton Dreben, Leonard Linsky, and Thomas Ricketts for helpful discussions.

16

Was the Axiom of Reducibility a Principle of Logic?

Bernard Linsky

The title of this paper is in the past tense to indicate that the question it will address is whether the Axiom of Reducibility is a principle of logic according to the view of logic that Russell had when writing the first edition of *Principia Mathematica*.[1] It is often said that Logicism was a failure because when it avoided the Scylla of contradiction in Frege's system it fell into the Charybdis of requiring obviously non-logical principles at Russell's hands. The axiom of reducibility is cited along with the axiom of infinity as a non-logical principle which Russell had to add to his system in order to be able to develop mathematics.

I want to consider this criticism of the axiom from several points of view. Why is it thought that the axiom of reducibility is not a principle of logic? What reasons does Russell actually give for doubting its logical status? Are they good reasons?

Objections to the Axiom

The Ramified Theory of Types of the first edition of *Principia* goes beyond the divisions of a "simple" theory between individuals, first-order propositional functions which apply to individuals, second-order functions which apply to first-order functions, etc. It further subdivides each of those groups according to the range of the bound variables used in the definition of each propositional function. Russell often used the example of the predicate "x has all the properties of a great general" which will itself be a property of great generals, but not one within the range of that particular quantifier "all." It will thus define a propositional function of a higher type than any of the variables bound by that quantifier. Similarly a difference of type would have to be marked in the theory of the real numbers between the property of "belonging to the set X" and "being the least upper bound of the set X," as the latter is defined in terms of a quantifier ranging over *all* members of X. The consequent division of numbers, and types generally, into different orders makes much ordinary reasoning seemingly invalid. The axiom of reducibility eases this difficulty. It asserts that for any propositional function, of whatever type, there is a *coextensive* propositional function of the lowest type compatible with its arguments, called a "predicative" propositional function.[2] Thus there will be a propositional function true of just those individuals with all the properties of a great general, which itself is of the same type as those properties quantified by "all." There will be a propositional function true of the least upper bound of a set X of the same type as the function "is a member of X," and so on. The ready availability of predicative propositional functions, guaranteed by the axiom of reducibility, allows them to substitute for classes in Russell's famous "no-class" theory of classes.[3] Sentences seemingly about "the class of ϕs" are to be analyzed as existential sentences asserting that some predicative propositional function coextensive with ϕ has the given properties. The axiom of reducibility thus both avoids some of the stringency of the ramified theory of types and guarantees the existence of the predicative propositional functions that replace classes. It is these very virtues that have been the source of doubt about the axiom.

Objections to the axiom of reducibility often combine several related points, in particular, that it makes an existence claim that is not purely logical, that it seems *ad hoc* and so lacks the obviousness of genuine logical principles, that the whole ramified theory of types of which it is a part is itself not purely logical, and, indeed, borders on incoherence since it seems to take back with the axiom of reducibility all of the ramification of types which is its hallmark. I consider these objections in turn.

It is often suggested that the axiom of reducibility is like the axiom of infinity in making an existence claim and as such is not a principle of logic. Viewed as a comprehension scheme, or perhaps like the axiom of separation, the axiom would look like the axioms of Zermelo–Fraenkel set theory, which are seen as rivals to logicism as a foundational scheme.[4] Set theory is viewed as having given up the project of reducing mathematics to logic, and instead as having resorted to just postulating the existence of those distinctively mathematical entities that are needed to develop the rest of mathematics. The axiom of reducibility also seems to postulate the existence of peculiarly mathematical entities, predicative propositional functions, and so would seem to be of a piece with set theory.

Russell himself was suspicious of a priori existence proofs. He often claimed that logic cannot prove the existence of certain things, such as God, or how many things there are in the world.[5] But this is not a very good reason to say that logicism with the axiom of reducibility is a failure. One could have known that no logicist program could work if the problem lies in proving existence claims. In arithmetic we can prove many existence claims; for example, that there is an even number between 4 and 8. Since we could prove an existence claim, if logicism were correct, then logic could prove an existence claim, which is impossible, QED. There is no need to find the particular source of the existence claim to disqualify the logicist program, we know it must be there from the start. (One might provide an analysis of mathematical existence claims that gives them some other logical form, just as Russell's theory of descriptions analyzes descriptions as not really singular terms. For Frege and Russell, however, there were legitimately *logical* objects, whether courses of values or propositional functions, and quantification over mathematical objects was to be reduced to quantification over them.) Surely then, it is no objection to the status of the axiom of reducibility as part of a logicist program, that it asserts an existence claim. The objection must rely on the nature of the existence claim which is made. One might argue that logic should make no assumptions about the number of *individuals*, or lowest level entities, that there are. While one might be allowed to avoid a free logic, and assume that there is at least one, the assumption of a countable infinity of objects, as made by the axiom of infinity, might lie outside of purely logical principles. As merely a claim about the existence of propositional functions, however, this restriction does not bar the axiom of reducibility from logic.

Another, related, objection is that the axiom of reducibility simply undoes the construction of the hierarchy of propositional functions that is the very purpose of ramifying the theory of types.[6] If the higher type propositional functions of a given order are seen as constructed from those of lower type, then adopting the axiom of reducibility would be self-defeating. If all the classes there are have been already constructed at the first level, then all the convoluted ways of producing defining conditions for classes out of simpler classes do not really accomplish anything. Doesn't this make the constructions pointless? Quine has argued that the axiom of reducibility is a Platonistic existence assertion and so violates the constructivist motivation for the ramification of the theory of types. Quine's objection thus combines the two lines of criticism I am discussing. He charges that the axiom both undoes the effect of the ramification and commits the theory to a Platonistic view of propositional functions (which, when its use/ mention confusions are cleared up, amounts to a theory of sets).

Criticism of the axiom of reducibility is sometimes more indirect. Following Ramsey, it is often charged that the ramified theory of types involves an unnecessary complication of the simple theory of types, one introduced in order to deal with semantic paradoxes that are not properly logical paradoxes.[7] The axiom of reducibility then inherits the non-logical character of the system to which it belongs. Accordingly, a defence of the axiom will require a defence of the ramified theory of types itself as a system of logic. The answer to these questions comes in seeing the ramified theory of types as a system of intensional logic which includes the "no-class" account of sets, and indeed the whole development of mathematics, as just a part. A defence of the axiom of reducibility, then, leads to a defence of the whole ramified theory of types and the logicist project to which it belongs.

The Origin of the Axiom

Although this paper is concerned with the justification of the axiom of reducibility within Russell's views at the time of writing *PM*, a look at the earlier history of the principle will help to explain its role in his thinking. One stereotype of the evolution of Russell's thought is that he first had a simple theory of types, designed to handle his original paradox of sets, later adding the "ramification" in order to handle the semantic paradoxes, and then, realizing that the ramification made impossible the project of reducing mathematics to logic, introduced the axiom of reducibility, undoing the effect of the ramification.

This account is quite wrong. It may follow a natural ordering of topics in a presentation of the theory of types, which Russell himself uses, but it does not present any historical development of the theory. To begin with, type theory was effectively ramified from its earliest formulations around 1905–6. The distinctive feature of ramification is to distinguish propositional functions which take arguments of the same type by the ranges of the bound or "apparent" variables that occur in them. Russell's early attempts at solving the paradoxes deliberately avoided any division of types. This was in part due to his desire to see all quantifiers as unrestricted, which was in turn due to belief in the universal character of logic.[8] But once Russell accepted Poincaré's analysis of the paradoxes as due to a vicious circle, he immediately saw that the ranges of universal quantifiers in propositional functions needs to be restricted to a specific totality, in other words, the need for ramification.

Just before accepting the need for types Russell held his "substitutional" theory according to which all quantifiers are unrestricted but the (seeming) quantifiers over propositional functions *are* restricted. This is not a real restriction of quantifiers, however, because expressions for propositional functions are "incomplete symbols" which can be eliminated by contextual definitions. The real range of quantifiers is all objects and all propositions. The next stage of development for Russell was to see the need for type distinctions among propositions. In the paper "On 'Insolubilia' and Their Solution by Symbolic Logic,"[9] Russell adopts the vicious-circle principle as the analysis of the paradoxes and the consequent need for at least type distinctions among propositions, while still denying the reality of propositional functions with his "substitutional" view. Yet he immediately acknowledges that "for every statement containing x and an apparent variable is *equivalent*, for all values of x, to some statement ϕx containing no apparent variable" (p. 212). Thus for example, propositions about *all* propositions of a given sort, say all those asserted by Epimenides, must be (materially) equivalent to some proposition which does not include such quantification. This claim amounts to an axiom of reducibility.

What reason did Russell give for believing such a claim? This passage appears in response to the criticisms of the logicists' account of induction that Poincaré based on the vicious-circle principle. For a logicist, the principle of induction says that *all* properties possessed by 0 and hereditary with respect to the successor relation are possessed by all numbers. The vicious-circle principle requires that the quantification over "all" proper- ties must be restricted to avoid reference to any impredicative properties defined with apparent variables ranging over numbers.[10] As this is required in so many uses of the induction principle, adopting the vicious-circle principle seems to "destroy many pieces of ordinary mathematical reason- ing" (p. 211). Thus Russell saw that the adoption of a type theory with the consequent restriction of bound variables to ranges of significance under- cuts those principles which seem to rely on unrestricted quantification (even when the real quantifiers are only those ranging over objects and propositions). The definition of identity, that x and y are identical if and only if they share *all* properties, is another such example, which will be discussed more below.

The simultaneous appearance of types and the axiom of reducibility is all the more remarkable for the fact that at the time Russell did not even see the hierarchy of types as one of properties or propositional functions, but rather simply of propositions. In the "Insolubilia . . ." paper he was still in the grip of the "substitutional" theory which attempted to define away propositional functions with contextual definitions and the notion of replacing one object by another in a proposition. The axiom of reducibility, then, did not make its appearance as a view about the existence of proposi- tional functions, but rather as a necessity given the need to restrict quanti- fiers to types. Given that restriction, generalizations over all properties must be replaceable by quantifiers ranging over only a certain type of properties. The axiom of reducibility guarantees that restricting attention to properties of only one type will not invalidate standard patterns of reasoning about *all* properties because if any property does not apply to an object, one of that chosen type will not. Thus induction says that any property possessed by 0 and hereditary with respect to the successor relation will be possessed by all numbers. The axiom of reducibility says that any property of numbers will be coextensive with a predicative prop- erty so that if a number lacks a property it will lack a coextensive pre- dicative property and if it has a property it will have a coextensive predicative property. Consequently Russell is able to use as his definition of identity the weaker claim that $x = y$ if and only if x and y have all the same predicative properties (*13.01 $x = y . = : (\phi): \phi!x: \supset . \phi!y$ Df). The axiom of reducibility allows one to restrict attention to the predicative properties of x and y. A justification of the axiom of reducibility, then, must consist in a reason to believe that one can so restrict attention to the properties of one preferred type, the predicative functions.

In what follows I wish to explain the role of the axiom of reducibility in Russell's thinking at the time of *Principia Mathematica* when his ontology was considerably different. In fact, I believe, the ontology he had in the background in *PM* is what provided the justification for the axiom at that time. What can be learned from its earlier appearance, however, is that the axiom was an integral part of the notion of a theory of types, not some afterthought used to patch up a defect resulting from the addition of ramification to an earlier, simpler theory of types with reducibility that needs justification, not the axiom on its own.

Russell's Doubts About the Axiom

Let us turn, then, to Russell's views in *Principia Mathematica*. To evaluate those it is instructive to look at his reasons for later *abandoning* the axiom of reducibility which marks one of the characteristic differences between the systems of the first and second editions. What reasons did Russell himself give for doubting that the axiom is logical? He says very little about it in the Introduction to the second edition of *PM*. All he says is:

> One point in regard to which improvement is obviously desirable is the axiom of reducibility (*12.1.11). This axiom has a purely pragmatic justification: it leads to the desired results, and to no others. But clearly it is not the sort of axiom with which we can rest content (p. xiv).

Russell's objection is hardly explicit. We know what the objection doesn't amount to by looking at the argument *for* the axiom in the Introduction to the first edition:

> That the axiom of reducibility is self-evident is a proposition which can hardly be maintained. But in fact self-evidence is never more than a part of the reason for accepting an axiom, and is never indispensable. The reason for accepting an axiom, as for accepting any other proposition, is always largely inductive, namely that many propositions which are nearly indubitable can be deduced from it, and that no equally plausible way is known by which these propositions could be true if the axiom were false, and nothing which is probably false can be deduced from it (vol. 1, pp. 59–60).

He goes on to say that the inductive evidence for the axiom of reducibility is good so the real problem is that:

> although is seems very improbable that the axiom should turn out to be false, it is by no means improbable that it should be found to be deducible from some other more fundamental and more evident axiom. It is possible that the use of the vicious-circle principle, as embodied in the above hierarchy of types, is more drastic than it need be, and that by a less drastic use the necessity for the axiom might be avoided (vol. 1, p. 59).

In the second edition Russell says that by following Wittgenstein's example in making the logic extensional one can avoid the axiom of reducibility but still prove many useful theorems.[11] So this objection to the axiom of reducibility was that it should be proved from more self-evident axioms, or avoided in the proof of the desired theorems by adopting a different axiom. Russell then does not require that the axiom be self-evident, and does not express any doubt about its truth; rather he thinks it redundant. (It is important to note that Russell includes *logical* axioms among those that need not be self-evident, as long as they have the right deductive strength.) At the time of the first edition he thought that the axiom might be redundant because an excessively strong form of the vicious-circle principle had introduced too many types which then had to be integrated with the axiom of reducibility. The vicious-circle principle forbids the existence of any entity such as a totality, or propositional function, which depends on itself in the wrong way. If a propositional function depends on a totality, then it cannot be a member of that totality, and hence belongs to a new type, thus ramifying the type theory. But with the principle of extensionality anything true of one propositional function will be true of every coextensive one, so the *only* thing on which a propositional function can depend is its members, and so the type theory cannot be ramified. Extensionality thus weakens the force of the vicious-circle principle by limiting what a propositional function can depend on, and thus what it could depend on viciously. Other principles limiting the dependence of propositional functions by identifying some which are distinguished in the full ramified theory would have the same effect. It is clear that even at the time of writing the Introduction to the second edition Russell thought that the principle of extensionality was too strong. Thus this doubt about the axiom of reducibility was a doubt about the vicious-circle principle and the number of type distinctions it introduces, rather than a doubt about the existence claim made by the axiom.

A richer guide to Russell's thinking about the axiom of reducibility, however, is in the *Introduction to Mathematical Philosophy*, written in 1918 between the two editions of *PM*. There he expresses doubts about whether the axiom has the character of a regular principle of logic. One worry is that the axiom is not general or widely enough applicable. Thus: "This axiom, like the multiplicative axiom and the axiom of infinity, is necessary for certain results, but not for the bare existence of logical reasoning" (p. 191). He goes on to explain that it does not have the universal applicability of, for example, the quantifier laws and so *could* be just added as a special hypothesis whenever it is used. Here, obviously, Russell is concentrating on the use of the axiom of reducibility in the construction of the natural and real numbers. It is not so clear that the axiom would seldom be used outside of the theory of classes and mathematics, as can be seen from its role in proofs about identity. The need for impredicative definitions in mathematics, in particular for the notion of the *least upper bound* of a set of real numbers, has led many to see the "certain results" to which Russell alludes, to be only a limited part of higher mathematics. Indeed, the appeal of developing a "predicative" analysis has suggested that the axiom is in fact debatable. But of course Russell's project was to develop mathematics and so his attention was precisely on the role of impredicative definitions in mathematics. Attention to the identity of indiscernibles should remind us of the frequency of talk of all properties of a thing within metaphysics. Since without the axiom of reducibility such talk is banned, we see that the axiom is not just needed for the development of higher mathematics.

Russell goes on to question the *necessary* truth of the axiom of reducibility, demanding that a logical truth be true in "all possible worlds" and not just in this "higgledy-piggledy job-lot of a world in which chance has imprisoned us" (p. 192). So Russell has qualms about both the generality of the axiom and its necessary truth, features he took to be characteristic of logical truths. It is these remarks that are most likely the source of many of the claims that the axiom of reducibility is not a principle of logic because it is not intuitively obvious enough, or a general enough principle of reasoning.

Russell's objections here are a mixed lot. He has a theoretician's concern that the axiom is *ad hoc* and could be replaced by more basic principles. He is also concerned that the axiom is not a *necessary* truth, another feature which does not distinguish logic from a very general metaphysical theory of the world. Russell's concern that the axiom is only of use in mathematics, and not a general principle of reasoning, shares this character. Given Russell's earlier remarks that axioms need not be directly evident, it is hard to attribute to him a view of the nature of logic which marks it off from a more substantive, metaphysical theory other than by differences of degree.

These, then, were Russell's various qualms about the axiom of reducibility. What can be said in defence of the axiom of reducibility? Should Russell have had such qualms about it given its role in his logic?

Principia Mathematica as Intensional Logic

I wish to argue that in fact the axiom plays a crucial role in the logic of *PM* because of the nature of propositional functions, in particular, the distinctive role of predicative propositional functions. It is a realist view about propositional functions in particular, a view about predicative propositional functions as encapsulating the real features of objects, which serves as a justification for the axiom within the philosophical system of *PM*.

First it is important to get clear about the role of the axiom of reducibility in Russell's theory of classes. It does not just undo the effects of the ramification as the "constructivist" reading suggests. Here I refer to the recent work of Alonzo Church and Leonard Linsky on what might be called the "intensional interpretation" of *Principia Mathematica*.[12] They have argued that despite the central project in *PM* of developing mathematics, which is a thoroughly extensional subject, the logic of *PM* is fundamentally intensional. The intensional nature of the logic explains many otherwise puzzling features of its presentation. One example is the role of scope in the theory of definite descriptions. In extensional contexts the scope differences do not have any logical effect, as long as the descriptions are proper. Why then, are they introduced with such care? Likewise several features of the "no-class" theory also depend on the intensionality of propositional functions. In particular the significance of the axiom of reducibility depends on the logic being intensional. Linsky's argument goes like this. Russell's contextual analysis of classes, the "no-class" theory, is very similar to the analysis of definite descriptions, including the possibility of scope distinctions. Just as it is true, and *proved* in *PM* (*14.3) that scope distinctions for definite descriptions make no difference in extensional contexts, it is true that scope distinctions make no difference in extensional contexts for sets. That this is not proved, Linsky argues, shows that Russell had in mind the application of *PM* to mathematical contexts where extensionality rules. That it *could be* expressed and proved shows that the logic was set up to handle intensional contexts. Furthermore, there are two conditions to be met for descriptions such as "the *F*" to behave like names with regard to scope and substitution. It is not only necessary that one restrict oneself to extensional contexts, but that the description be proper (i.e. that there be one and only one *F*). A similar requirement that class abstracts behave like names is that, in addition to occurring in extensional contexts, the requisite predicative propositional function must exist. But that is precisely what the axiom of reducibility says. It is, as Gödel remarked, a comprehension principle, but this is in the context of an intensional logic, one capable of expressing much more than just the extensional sentences of mathematics. So, Linsky's argument goes, Russell's ignoring of scope indicators for class abstracts, unlike his use of them with descriptions, shows that he saw himself as restricting his talk of classes to talk of *extensional* mathematical contexts, but not so restricting the logic of *PM*.

My interest is not in establishing the intensional character of the logic of *PM* but rather the logical character of the axiom of reducibility. The axiom clearly plays a crucial role in the theory of classes, given Russell's *particular* contextual definition of classes. While having the force of a comprehension principle, it does not assert the existence of some new, non-logical category of entity, but rather just of a *predicative* propositional function coextensive with an arbitrary propositional function. Because the extensional theory of classes is only part of the whole of logic, the axiom of reducibility does not just undo the ramification of the theory of types. It is crucial in the reduction of classes to logic, and unless one assumes that logicism is false and so automatically any talk of classes is not part of logic, it seems to be a quite legitimate logical notion for Russell – provided, of course, that a claim about the existence of a *predicative* propositional function with a given extension can be seen as a logical principle.

What of the charge that the axiom of reducibility undoes the whole point of the hierarchy of types of propositional functions? That assumes that the only point of the hierarchy of types is to represent the possible constructions of propositional functions and hence of classes. What view could hold, rather, that all the classes have been constructed at the level of predicative functions? The answer is that the propositional functions of higher types are needed to capture intensional phenomena. The predicative functions are needed to reconstruct the extensional part of logic, that part which deals with the extensions of predicates, or classes. The higher types are needed for purely intensional phenomena, cases where the same class is picked out by distinct intensions, i.e. propositional functions. This view requires seeing the ramified hierarchy of *PM* not as a constructivist theory of classes but rather as a theory of propositional functions which includes as a part the theory of classes, but which does much more. Of course predicative propositional functions are not extensional. They can be distinct, yet coextensive. Rather, all extensional talk about classes is analyzed as a general (existential) claim about predicative propositional functions.

What then is so special about predicative propositional functions that one can adopt a "comprehension" principle asserting the existence of a coextensive predicative propositional function for every arbitrary propositional function?

The Axiom of Reducibility and the Identity of Indiscernibles

The distinctive character of predicative propositional functions can be seen in the details of Russell's charge that the axiom of reducibility is not a necessary truth. Russell says that

The axiom, we may observe, is a generalised form of Leibniz's identity of indiscernibles. Leibniz assumed, as a logical principle, that two different subjects must differ as to predicates. Now predicates are only some among what we called "predicative functions," which will include also relations to given terms, and various properties not to be reckoned as predicates. Thus Leibniz's assumption is a much stricter and narrower one than ours.

(Introduction to Mathematical Philosophy, p. 192)

Russell goes on to say that the axiom *seems* to hold of the actual world, for

there seems to be no way of doubting its empirical truth as regards particulars, owing to spatio-temporal differentiations: no two particulars have exactly the same spatial and temporal relations to all other particulars. But this is, as it were, an accident, a fact about the world in which we happen to find ourselves.

(Ibid.)

How is the axiom of reducibility a "form" of the identity of indiscernibles? The identity of indiscernibles says that $x = y$ just in case all the same predicates (propositional functions) apply to x and y. The axiom of reducibility allows one to restrict the principle to only requiring the sharing of all the same *predicative* propositional functions. For suppose that ψx but not ψy where ψ is not predicative. Then there is a predicative function ϕ coextensive with ψ, and thus true of x, which distinguishes it from y with predicative functions alone. Accordingly, Russell's definition of identity at *13.01 is this "restricted" form of the identity of indiscernibles, and the above reasoning is equivalent to the proof of theorem *13.101 ($\vdash: x = y. \supset .\psi x \supset \psi y$), one "half" of the more familiar identity of indiscernibles. (The more controversial half of the principle, that if x and y have all the same properties, then $x = y$, follows immediately from the fact that if they share *all* properties, they share all predicative properties.) The axiom of reducibility is possibly a stronger principle than is needed to prove the identity of indiscernibles from the definition of identity, for the proof only requires that objects sharing all predicative properties share all properties of any type, whereas the axiom of reducibility accomplishes this by providing a predicative property which is coextensive with each arbitrary property. This may have been one of the points where Russell suspected that the axiom of reducibility might be replaced by a simpler principle. Still, however, he accepts the axiom to the extent of calling it a "generalized form" of the identity of indiscernibles. Reasons for accepting that generalized principle would, for Russell at least, provide a justification for the axiom of reducibility.

What then is the reason for accepting the axiom of reducibility and its accompanying definition of identity? I believe that for Russell it was not just a matter of stipulation that made classes coincide with predicative propositional functions. Rather, he thought that predicative propositional functions really characterize the genuine properties which individuate things in the world. Objects don't always differ in their monadic qualities, as Russell had argued against Leibniz. It was a distinctive feature of Russell's philosophy that he argued for the reality of relations and hence the irreducibility of some relational properties. Thus "being two miles from x" is a perfectly good relational property, not reducible to any monadic properties of x. It is the original stock of one-place properties, then added to it all the possible relational properties, and boolean combinations of them, which constitute the predicative propositional functions. It is because Russell saw predicative propositional functions as expressing more than just monadic qualities that he speaks of the axiom as a "generalized" version of Leibniz's principle. Leibniz, according to Russell's account, would presumably endorse an even stronger "axiom of reducibility" to the effect that every propositional function is equivalent (by analysis and not just coextensiveness) with some conjunction of monadic qualities.

Russell feared that it might be a matter of arbitrary postulation, or at least contingent, that the predicative propositional functions should suffice to distinguish all objects. Why shouldn't some higher-type property allow us to distinguish objects? Russell considers examples like "having all the qualities of a great general" and "being a typical F" (where the latter seems to mean something like having all the properties shared by *most* Fs). The answer can be seen in the very nature of these examples. Higher-type propositional functions do not really introduce new properties of things. They may characterize new ways of thinking of things or of classifying them, but they don't introduce any new real properties. Russell himself did not keep clear enough the distinction between propositional functions and these real properties of things, universals. That he sometimes made such a distinction is clear. It is certainly necessary to make such a distinction for him to be able to argue, as he did in the Introduction to the first edition of *PM*, both that propositional functions depend on their values, propositions, in a way that makes the vicious-circle principle applicable, and that propositions are to be analyzed according to the "multiple relation" theory into universals and particulars which are the real furniture of the world. Thus propositional functions and universals are separated by propositions in the hierarchy of dependence which the vicious-circle principle enjoins us to observe. A simpler way of seeing that Russell was committed to such a distinction is to observe that it is of the essence of propositional functions that they allow compounding by logical connectives; thus "being red or blue" is a perfectly acceptable propositional function.[13] Yet universals are only discovered as the end result of analysis – they can be objects of acqaintance, but are simple. They correspond with the primitive predicates of a fully analyzed language, not with the arbitrarily complex propositional functions. This distinction is not very clear in *PM*, however, especially as Russell did not ever explicitly mark it or even observe it at all times.[14]

If one grants that Russell had in mind some distinction between propositional functions and universals that have a metaphysically important role as what underlies the real qualities of things, then it is clear that predicative propositional functions inherit some of that character. One need not argue that any two objects will be distinguished by some universal that one has and the other lacks. That would be to claim that all objects have a unique *nature*, an implausible metaphysical assumption. But one might hold that *something* accounts for the particularity of objects, if not their qualities or natures, then perhaps their locations. If one holds a relational view of space, then the view that it is spatio-temporal location which individuates particulars is one which allows a relation to individuate.[15] If one were only interested in individuating objects two at a time then universals or relational properties might be sufficient. One could say of objects with different natures that one has *F* and the other does not, where *F* is one universal in the nature of the object. For objects with the same nature one could use relational properties as one does with spatio-temporal relations with concrete particulars. When whole classes of objects are involved one may require boolean combinations of universals as well as relational properties. Some of the objects may be distinguished by being *F*, others by being *G*, others by *not* being *H*, and so on, so that the *predicative* propositional function "being *F* and *G* but not *H* . . ." is needed to mark off the class. Russell's qualms about the axiom of reducibility being contingent amount, then, to the worry that such a scheme of spatio-temporal relations is merely contingent.

As I have presented it, the axiom of reducibility marks out the special role of predicative propositional functions, which coincide with classes, and indicates the properties which individuate things in the world. One still needs the whole hierarchy of ramified propositional functions to handle all the things that can be said of the world, or thought of it, the whole realm of intensional phenomena. This makes the axiom of reducibility out to be a metaphysical principle. It is one of great generality, however, certainly unlike any principle about numbers as abstract entities or of the sort that might occur in any special science. Still, this accounts for Russell's qualms about it. While it is a very general principle of metaphysics does it have the necessity required of a principle of logic? Is it *logically* necessary? Russell was not sure. Ultimately it was the lure of doing without the ramified theory by adopting the principle of extensionality that made him give up the principle. But giving up on intensional phenomena was an extreme solution. It undid the whole relation between classes and propositional functions that was at the heart of the first edition of *Principia Mathematica*.

The axiom of reducibility was an integral part of the theory of types. From the beginning it was clear that if a theory of types requires restricting the ranges of bound variables to a given range of significance, or type, then those principles which seem to require quantifying over *all* properties must be stronger than necessary. Identity, while seeming to require the sharing of all properties, really only requires the sharing of properties of the lowest, predicative order; and the existence of sets, which should allow a set for all predicates, really only requires sets for all predicative properties. As well, all numbers, and properties of numbers, to which the induction principle will apply, are already represented at the lowest type. Some criticisms of the axiom and its role seem to require forgetting the intensional nature of the logic, and hence the use for all those additional, non-predicative propositional functions. Russell was aware of the need for an independent justification for the principle, one that showed how conclusions about numbers, classes and identity could be settled by only considering predicative propositional functions. That predicative functions are all that is needed for the theory of classes and numbers follows directly from the "no-class" theory and the definition of numbers as classes. The adequacy of predicative propositional functions for the definition of identity and other more "metaphysical" or non-mathematical applications of the logic of *PM*, comes from the distinction between propositional functions and universals, and the proximity of predicative propositional functions to universals. Predicative propositional functions mark the real kinds in the world. That this is so, is a fairly substantive metaphysical claim about the world, and so not obviously of the same generality or as clearly "necessary" as the other principles of Russell's logic. It was, however, also not obviously out of place in the logic of *Principia Mathematica*.[16]

Notes

1 Page references will be to A. N. Whitehead and B. Russell, *Principia Mathematica to *56* (Cambridge: Cambridge University Press, 1962).

2 Strictly speaking there are an infinite number of axioms of which the following applies to one-place propositional functions *12.1 $\vdash$: $(\exists f): \phi x. \equiv_x. f!x$. Thus for every propositional function ϕ there is a materially equivalent *predicative* function f of the lowest order compatible with arguments of the same type. I follow the formulation of the ramified theory of types of Alonzo Church, "Comparison of Russell's Resolution of the Semantical Antinomies with That of Tarski," *J. of Symbolic Logic*, 41 (1976): 747–60. The following brief sketch will be enough for what follows. Variables and constants are assigned *(r-)types*, i for individuals and $(\beta_1, \beta_2, \ldots, \beta_m)/n$ for m-ary propositional functions of *level n* with arguments of types $\beta_1, \beta_2, \ldots, \beta_m$. (Propositional variables will have r-type $(\,)/n$.) $n \geq 1$ is the *level* of the expression (when $n = 1$ it is *predicative*). $(\alpha_1, \ldots, \alpha_m)/k$ is *directly lower* than $(\beta_1, \ldots, \beta_m)/n$ if $\alpha_1 = \beta_1, \ldots, \alpha_m = \beta_m$ and $k < n$. The *order* of an individual variable (type i) is 0, the *order* of a variable of type $(\beta_1, \ldots, \beta_m)/n$ is $N + n$ where N is the maximum of the orders of $\beta_1, \ldots, \beta_m$. The force of the division of types is felt in the restriction on well-formed formulas: $f(x_1, x_2, \ldots, x_m)$ is a *wff* iff f is a variable or constant of type $(\beta_1, \ldots, \beta_m)/n$, x_1 is a variable or

constant of type β_1 or directly lower, . . ., and x_m is a variable or constant of type β_m or directly lower. That propositional functions defined with quantifiers will have a raised type is made explicit by comprehension schemas including: $\exists f^{(\beta_1, \cdots, \beta_m)/n} f(x_1, \ldots, x_m) \equiv_{x_1, \ldots, x_m} P$ where the bound variables of P are of order *less* than the order of f and the free variables and constants are not greater. The axiom of reducibility is very similar: $(\phi^{(\beta_1, \cdots, \beta_m)/n}) (\exists f^{(\beta_1, \cdots, \beta_m)/1}) \phi(x_1, \ldots, x_m) \equiv_{x_1, \ldots, x_m} f(x_1, \ldots, x_m)$.

3 The "theory" is stated as an axiom schema very like the contextual definition of definite descriptions: *20.1 $f\{\hat{z}(\psi z)\}. \equiv: (\exists \phi): \phi!x. \equiv_x .\psi x: f\{\phi!\hat{z}\}$.

4 Gödel says that in the realist, simple, theory which ought to replace the ramified theory of types, "the place of the axiom of reducibility is now taken by the axiom of classes, Zermelo's *Aussonderungsaxiom*," in "Russell's Mathematical Logic," in P.A. Schilpp, ed., *The Philosophy of Bertrand Russell*, The Library of Living Philosophers (Evanston, Ill.: Northwestern University Press, 1944), pp. 140–1.

5 See *Introduction to Mathematical Philosophy* (London: Allen and Unwin, 1919), p. 141.

6 Quine presents this objection in his *Set Theory and Its Logic* (Cambridge, Mass.: Harvard University Press, 1969), pp. 249–58. See also Myhill, cited in note 11.

7 F.P. Ramsey, "The Foundations of Mathematics (1925)," in his *The Foundation of Mathematics and Other Logical Essays* (London: Routledge & Kegan Paul, 1931), pp. 1–61. Quine makes this objection as well. On his account, the set-theoretic nature of the axiom is hidden by its quantification over propositional functions which are creatures of the confusion of use and mention, of semantics and ontology.

8 See Peter Hylton, "Russell's Substitutional Theory", *Synthèse*, 45 (1980): 1–31.

9 Reprinted in *Essays in Analysis*, ed. Douglas Lackey (New York: Braziller, 1972), pp. 190–214.

10 Poincaré would seemingly ban all impredicative properties, while Russell would restrict them to a distinct type.

11 Russell even claims this about the ramified theory of types in the first edition. This claim is shown incorrect in John Myhill, "The Undefinability of the Set of Natural Numbers in the Ramified *Principia*," in George Nakhnikian, ed., *Bertrand Russell's Philosophy* (London: Duckworth, 1974).

12 See Alonzo Church, *op. cit.*, note 2, and Leonard Linsky, *Oblique Contexts* (Chicago: University of Chicago Press, 1983), Appendix, as well as Warren Goldfarb, "Russell's Reasons for Ramification," in C. W. Savage and C. A. Anderson, eds, *Rereading Russell: Essays on Bertrand Russell's Metaphysics and Epistemology*, Minnesota Studies in the Philosophy of Science, Vol. XII (Minneapolis: University of Minnesota Press, 1989).

13 See *Principia Mathematica*, vol. 1, p. 56.

14 See my "Propositional Functions and Universals in *Principia Mathematica*," *Australasian Journal of Philosophy*, 66 (Dec. 1988): 447–60, for a discussion of this point. See Nino Cocchiarella, "Russell's Theory of Logical Types and the Atomistic Hierarchy of Sentences" in *Rereading Russell*, pp. 41–62, for an explicit argument that Russell *identified* propositional functions and universals.

15 See D. M. Armstrong's *Universals and Scientific Realism* (Cambridge: Cambridge University Press, 1980), Ch. 11 for a discussion of spatio-temporal location and particularity.

16 This paper was written while I was a visiting scholar at the Center for the Study of Language and Information at Stanford University. I would like to thank the Center for the use of its facilities, and those affiliated with the Center for discussions which led to this paper.

17

The Advantages of Honest Toil over Theft

George Boolos*

> He [Russell] had a secret craving to have proved *some* straight mathematical theorem. As a matter of fact there *is* one: "$2^{2^a} > \aleph_0$ if a is infinite." Perfectly good mathematics.
>
> J. R. Littlewood[1]

In the section of his and Martha Kneale's *Development of Logic* called "Russell's Theory of Logical Types," William Kneale writes:

> It is essential for mathematics that there should be no end of the sequence of natural numbers, and so Russell finds himself driven to introduce a special Axiom of Infinity, according to which there is some type with an infinity of instances, and that presumably the type of individuals, which comes lowest in the hierarchy. Without this axiom, he tells us, we should have no guarantee against the disastrous possibility that the supply of numbers would give out at some highest number, i.e., the number of members in the largest admissible set.
>
> There is something profoundly unsatisfactory about the axiom of infinity. It cannot be described as a truth of logic in any reasonable use of that phrase, and so the introduction of it as a primitive proposition of logic amounts in effect to abandonment of Frege's project of exhibiting arithmetic as a development of logic. . . . But even if we abandon all hope of carrying out Frege's programme in full and say boldly that Russell's axiom is required as an extralogical premiss for mathematics, how can we justify our acceptance of it? What are the individuals of which Russell speaks, and how can we tell whether there are infinitely many of them? . . . [H]e even suggests that there may be [no individuals] because everything which appears to be an individual is in fact a class or complex of some kind. With regard to [this] possibility, which seems very mysterious, he adds cheerfully that if it is realized, the

axiom of infinity must obviously be true for the types which there are in the world. But he does not profess to know for certain what the situation is, and he ends by saying that there is no known method of discovering whether the axiom of infinity is true or false. [Footnote in Kneale and Kneale: *Introduction to Mathematical Philosophy*, p. 143.][2]

The irritated tone of Kneale's commentary is noticeable, but one might well think that something more like utter exasperation with Russell's procedure is called for. In *Principia Mathematica*,[3] a work supposedly intended to show arithmetic to be a part of logic, more than *950* pages of text[4] precede the official introduction of the axiom of infinity. Just once in volume 1 is the axiom mentioned, in the introduction to the second edition, on page xxiv. On page 335, Russell states:

We might, of course, have included among our primitive propositions the assumption that more than one individual exists, or some assumption from which this would follow, such as

$$(\exists \phi, x, y) . \phi!x . \sim \phi!y.$$

But very few of the propositions which we might wish to prove depend upon this assumption, and we have therefore excluded it. It should be observed that many philosophers, being monists, deny this assumption.

The wisecrack may distract the reader from the outrageous claim that few of the propositions we might wish to prove depend on the assumption that there are at least two individuals.

Perhaps there are only a few propositions that depend *just* on that assumption and on nothing stronger; but the existence of the cardinal number 2, equivalent in *Principia* to the existence of at least two individuals, is one of those, and without its truth the development of arithmetic is impossible. The importance of the propositions depending on this axiom that we might wish to prove may offset the smallness of their number.

And of course a much stronger statement is needed than that of the existence of at least two individuals. The first two Peano postulates, in the order given them by Russell in *Introduction to Mathematical Philosophy*, assert that zero is a (natural) number and that the successor of a number is a number; the fourth states that zero is not the successor of a number; the fifth is the principle of mathematical induction. These are very easily proved in *Principia* without the assumption of any special axiom. The third, however, states that different numbers have different successors; together with the first three and Russell's definitions of *zero, successor,* and *natural number,* it implies the truth of the axiom of infinity, which asserts there are infinitely many individuals. The first four Peano postulates are theorems of every formal system for arithmetic that I know of; it is hard to see how any development of *arithmetic* could fail to deliver them.

Three axioms of *Principia* have struck commentators as having diminished claims to *logical* truth: those of reducibility, choice, and infinity. (Russell calls the axiom of choice the "multiplicative axiom.") Of these only the axiom of infinity is required for a *Principia*-style development of the arithmetic of the natural numbers, basic to all mathematics, but it is the only one of the three of which no mention is made in the first edition of volume 1, where indeed not a word is spoken of the need to assume a special axiom guaranteeing the truth of the third Peano postulate.

In order to determine whether Russell has unjustifiably minimized the role of the axiom of infinity by thus tucking it away, to raise certain further worries, to point out certain perhaps underappreciated virtues of his procedure, and to compare his with the sublime (and therefore consistent) account of number found in Frege's *Grundlagen der Arithmetik*, we shall have to race over some all too familiar material: the development of arithmetic in the modernized theory of types *TT*, which, for the sake of simplicity and ignoring Russell's own strenuous efforts to dispense with classes, we shall pretend was the theory Russell was expounding. The version we shall explain is essentially the one given in Gödel's "On formally undecidable propositions of *Principia Mathematica*, etc." but without symbols for zero and successor, and without the assumption that the natural numbers are individuals.

In *TT*, the objects of type 0 are the *individuals*, whatever they are; those of type $n + 1$ are the classes of objects of type n, n a natural number. Objects of types 1, 2, and 3 we shall call *sets*, *classes*, and *class-classes*, respectively. Variables $x_n, y_n, z_n, \ldots$ range over objects of type n; for every natural number n, there is an axiom

$$\forall x_{n + 1} \forall y_{n + 1} (\forall z_n (z \in x \leftrightarrow z \in y) \rightarrow x = y)$$

of extensionality and infinitely many comprehension axioms

$$\exists y_{n + 1} \forall x_n (x \in y \leftrightarrow \phi)$$

ϕ a formula not containing $y_{n + 1}$ free.[5]

We shall frequently use $a, b, c, \ldots$ as variables ranging over individuals (in addition to $x_0, y_0, z_0, \ldots$); $x, y, z, \ldots$, over sets; $m, n, A, B, C, \ldots$, over classes; and $X, Y, Z, \ldots$, over class-classes.

Λ is the null set; V is the universal set, that is, the set of all individuals. $\varnothing$ is the null class; 0, alias zero, is $\{\Lambda\}$. Like those that follow, these sets and classes all exist by comprehension and are unique by extensionality. $x - a$ is $\{b: b \in x \land b \neq a\}$, $y + a$ is $\{b: b \in y \lor b = a\}$, and sA, alias the successor of A, is $\{x: \exists a(a \in x \land x - a \in A)\}$.

À la Frege and Russell, *n* is a number if and only if

$$\forall X \, (0 \in X \wedge \forall A(A \in X \to sA \in X) \to n \in X)$$

that is, iff *n* belongs to every class-class to which zero and the successor of every member belong; *m*, *n*, . . . range over (natural) numbers.

The first, second, and fifth Peano postulates are trivial to prove. (*Applications* of induction of course require comprehension.) And it is very easy to prove the fourth, that 0 is not the successor of a number: every member *x* of *sn* is non-empty but 0 has an empty member. The difficulty is to see that different numbers have different successors. This will turn out to be the case iff ∅ is not a number.

Infin ax, introduced in section 120 of *Principia Mathematica*, reads

$$\alpha \in \text{NC induct.} \supset_\alpha . \exists! \, \alpha$$

In our terminology, for all *n*, *n* has at least one member; equivalently, ∅ is not a number.

Not only is it more than dubious whether any version of the axiom of infinity can be regarded as a logical truth, this formulation disguises what is being asserted more than need be. As usual, define a set *x* to be finite if and only if

$$\forall A(\Lambda \in A \wedge \forall y \, \forall a(y \in A \to y + a \in A) \to x \in A)$$

A less *ad hoc* formulation of the axiom of infinity is V, the set of individuals, is not finite. Of course, the two versions are fairly easily inter-derivable. Thus it might be thought a matter of "taste" which one assumes. Perhaps so, but it would be absurd to claim that "∅ is not a number" expresses the statement that there are infinitely many individuals as directly as does "V is not finite."

However that may be, I shall want to argue that this lapse from perspicuity is the only charge against Russell mentioned in this essay that can be made to stick and that in *Principia Mathematica* Russell has in no way given us grounds for complaint that he has disguised, obscured, or minimized the role of the axiom of infinity.

If, following Russell, we say that *x* sm *y* if and only if there is a one-to-one function with domain *x* and range *y*, then with the aid of a lemma provable by induction on *n*, and asserting that if *x* ∈ *n*, then *x* sm *y* iff *y* ∈ *n*, it is easy enough to show that ∅ is not a number if and only if the third Peano postulate holds, that is, iff different numbers have different successors.

The proofs, found in Appendix I, are short and routine. They show how short the logical distance is between the axiom of infinity and the third Peano postulate. One could well think it not much less of a cheat for

Russell to have assumed the axiom of infinity and then derived the third Peano postulate from it than it would have been for him to proclaim the postulate a truth of logic outright.

Russell once wrote, sarcastically, I believe, that "The method of 'postulating' what we want has many advantages; they are the same as the advantages of theft over honest toil. Let us leave them to others and proceed with our honest toil."[6]

Russell's procedure may seem to suffer further when compared with the account of number found in Frege's *Grundlagen der Arithmetik*. It will be recalled that in sections 74–83 of that work, Frege outlines a derivation of (second-order) arithmetic in the logical system given in his *Begriffsschrift* from the principle that the number belonging to the concept *F* is the same as that belonging to the concept *G* if and only if the objects falling under *F* are in one–one correspondence with those falling under *G*. Frege derives this principle, sometimes called the number principle, or Hume's principle, from an inconsistent theory of objects, extensions (a species of object), and concepts of various levels. A number is defined as the extension of some second-level concept under which falls some first-level concept along with all and only those first-level concepts that are equinumerous with it. Being extensions, numbers are objects. Frege's criterion for the identity of extensions, that extensions of concepts (of the same level) are identical if and only if the same entities fall under them, is inconsistent, not only with respect to extensions of first-level concepts, as Russell showed, but also with respect to extensions of concepts of any higher level. Thus it is clear that the theory Frege implicitly employed in *Grundlagen* to define *number* is inconsistent.

Suitably formalized, however, Hume's principle can be shown to be equiconsistent with the arithmetic that Frege wished to derive from it: a proof of a contradiction in the system that results when Hume's principle is adjoined to the logic of the *Begriffsschrift* can (easily) be turned into a contradiction in second-order arithmetic, and, as Frege in effect showed, vice versa.[7] The derivation of arithmetic from Hume's principle that Frege sketched can be elaborated into formal deductions of the (infinitely many) axioms of second-order arithmetic. The most remarkable part of Frege's argument is his proof that every natural number has a successor. It utilizes a much more interesting mathematical idea than any found in Russell's derivation of the Peano postulates: *zero*, *successor of*, and *natural number* having been defined, and *less than* being defined as the ancestral of the relation an object bears to any of its successors, the number of objects less than or equal to any given natural number *a* can be shown to be a successor of *a*.

Recall also that Frege wished to show how numbers could be "conceived as logical objects." It is clear enough that before Russell's communication to him of the Contradiction, Frege supposed that the identification of numbers with certain sorts of *extensions* expressed a recognition of numbers as logical objects, and that the mere recognition of the truth of Hume's principle did not. As many commentators have noted, what is perhaps not clear is why Frege should have supposed this. Questions of consistency aside (!), what is there about extensions that makes *them*, and not numbers, logical objects in the absence of an account such as Frege tried to give? Extensions of concepts are supposed to be the same if and only if the objects falling under one of the concepts are identical with those falling under the other. To say when numbers are the same, simply change "extensions of" to "numbers belonging to" and change "identical" to "in one–one correspondence" in the foregoing sentence. Although it certainly requires a somewhat more complex formula to express that some objects are in one–one correspondence with others than to express that some objects are identical with others, one may reasonably doubt whether that difference entitles us to conclude that extensions are logical objects, but numbers are not.

Frege, it is also well known, failed to find a way out: his proposed solution to the difficulty turned out to be inconsistent with the assertion that there are at least two numbers. There is a modification of the notion of an extension that works, however. Say that a concept F is *small* iff the objects falling under F cannot be put in one–one correspondence with all the things there are. Say that F equiv G if and only if, if either F or G is small then the same objects fall under both. Equiv is an equivalence relation. Introduce subtensions by assuming that the subtension $*F$ of the concept F is identical with $*G$ if and only if F equiv G. This assumption can be shown to be consistent relative to second-order arithmetic, and can be used to define numbers: let $0 = *[x: x \neq x]$, that is, let $0 = *F$, where $\forall x(Fx \leftrightarrow x \neq x)$; let $sy = *[x: x = y]$; and let x be a number iff, as usual, $\forall F(F0 \land \forall y(Fy \rightarrow Fsy) \rightarrow Fx)$. The development of arithmetic then proceeds smoothly enough. (Peano three is no problem since $\exists x\; x = x$; thus $0 \neq *[x: x = x]$; thus there are at least two objects; thus for every y, $[x: x = y]$ is small.)

If subtensions are logical objects, then we have a way of recognizing numbers as logical objects; if not, despite their resemblance to extensions and the consistency of the axiom governing them, then we have even less reason than before to agree with the view that extensions, "had Rule V been consistent," would be logical objects.

Whether extensions, subtensions, or numbers are logical objects or not, it may seem, from a Fregean point of view, that Russell's definition of the numbers as certain sorts of class fails in two respects: invoking the axiom of infinity invalidates a claim to have shown numbers to be *logical* objects; defining them as certain classes (of sets of individuals) forbids him from thinking he has shown them to be logical *objects*. To show numbers to be objects, Russell would have had to show which individuals they are.

My aim so far has been to depict Russell's account of number in the worst possible light, as a series of tedious definitions and deductions in an inadequate theory to which an inelegantly formulated axiom has been surreptitiously adjoined with no justification other than to derive an indispensable but otherwise unobtainable theorem, and in which the definitions, moreover, obviously fail to satisfy one basic requirement of the enterprise of setting up a theory of number at all.

What, then, did Russell achieve? The answer may be found by reflecting on the "perfectly good" piece of mathematics mentioned in Littlewood's remark. This proposition and its proof, found in Volume II at *124.57, constitute, I want to claim, the mathematical core of the theory of natural numbers given in *Principia Mathematica*.[8]

Never forget that the natural numbers form not merely an infinite totality, but one that is *Dedekind* infinite. Assuming now some theory of sets such as ZF, we say that a set is *finite* if and only if (as in the definition given previously) it belongs to all classes (here = sets) that contain the null set and contain all results of adjoining to any member any one object. Equivalently, a set x is finite if and only if there is a natural number i such that x can be put into one–one correspondence with the set of natural numbers less than i. A set is *Dedekind infinite* if and only if it can be put in one–one correspondence with a proper subset of itself. Equivalently, a set x is Dedekind infinite if there is a one–one correspondence between the set of all natural numbers and a subset of x (not necessarily a proper subset). The set of natural numbers is, trivially, Dedekind infinite according to either of these equivalent definitions. A set is infinite if and only if it is not finite, Dedekind finite if and only if not Dedekind infinite. It is easy to show that no finite set is Dedekind infinite; it requires some assumption that is not a theorem of ZF such as the axiom of choice to show that no infinite set is Dedekind finite. Russell, who was admirably clear on the distinction, called the finite sets "inductive" and the Dedekind infinite sets "reflexive"; it is a pity that this excellent terminology has not become standard.

According to the theorem Littlewood ascribed to Russell, if a is an infinite number, then $2^{2^a} > \aleph_0$. What does the theorem mean? Theorems about cardinal numbers are often best understood as encrypted theorems about one–one correspondences. After decoding, the theorem states that if x is an infinite set (with cardinal number a), then the set of natural numbers (which has cardinal number $\aleph_0$) can be mapped one–one into the power set $\mathscr{P}\mathscr{P}x$ of the power set $\mathscr{P}x$ of x (which thus has cardinal number 2^{2^a}; thus $\aleph_0 \leq 2^{2^a}$), that is, that $\mathscr{P}\mathscr{P}x$ is Dedekind infinite; but that there is no one–one correspondence between the set of natural numbers and the power set of the power set of x (thus $\aleph_0 \neq 2^{2^a}$, and so $2^{2^a} > \aleph_0$). The more interesting half of the theorem is thus that if x is an infinite set, then $\mathscr{P}\mathscr{P}x$ is Dedekind infinite.

How, then, may this half of the theorem be proved? Let x be an infinite set. The null set is a subset of x of cardinality 0. If y is a subset of x of cardinality n, then since y is a finite subset of the infinite set x, y is not identical with x; thus there is some element a of x not in y and $y \cup \{a\}$ is a subset of x of cardinality $n + 1$. By mathematical induction, for every natural number n, there is a subset of x of cardinality n. Thus for each finite n the set S_n of subsets of x of cardinality n is nonempty, and if $m \neq n$, S_m and S_n are disjoint and hence distinct. Each S_n is a subset of the power set $\mathscr{P}x$ of x. Thus $n \mapsto S_n$ is a one–one function from the set of natural numbers into $\mathscr{P}\mathscr{P}x$.

(The other half of the theorem, according to which $2^{2a} \neq \aleph_0$, is immediate: if $2^{2a} = \aleph_0$, then since $a < 2^a < 2^{2^a}$ by Cantor's theorem, $a < \aleph_0$, a is finite, and then so are 2^a, 2^{2^a}, and $\aleph_0$, impossible. I am not sure whether Littlewood had this, the "*strictly*-less-than," half of the theorem in mind when he made his remark.)

Thus, although one can point to a specific place in *Principia* where Russell proved the theorem ascribed to him by Littlewood, it would not be unreasonable to give: "*PM*, passim" as a citation for the theorem. To belabor the obvious: call the members of the infinite set x *individuals*. Then $\mathscr{P}\mathscr{P}x$ comes to type 2 and S_n to the Russellian version of n; the Dedekind infinity of $\mathscr{P}\mathscr{P}x$ is witnessed by S_0 and the function, which assigns S_{n+1} to each S_n and A itself to each member A of $\mathscr{P}\mathscr{P}x$ not of the form S_n.

Put in Russellian terminology, the point is that Russell did not assume the type of individuals to be reflexive. He supposed it non-inductive and showed that it follows from that weaker supposition that type 2 is reflexive, and thus includes a subcollection similar to the set of natural numbers.

Not only can it not be proved in set theory without choice that there are no infinite Dedekind finite sets, it cannot even be proved that there do not exist infinite sets *whose power set* is Dedekind finite. And by adapting to the theory of types the Fraenkel–Mostowski method for showing the independence of various forms of the axiom of choice from set theory with individuals it can be shown that it is consistent with the theory of types supplemented with the axiom of infinity that the type of all individuals is infinite whereas the type of sets, that is, all classes of individuals, and hence the type of all individuals as well, is Dedekind finite.[9]

The idea of the proof is simple. Working in the theory of types, we shall build a model $\{T_0, T_1, T_2, \ldots\}$ of the theory of types in which T_0 is infinite, but in which there is no one–one mapping of the Russell numbers into T_1.

Begin with an infinite (Dedekind infinite if you like) set T_0, of individuals. Define a permutation π to be a one–one function whose domain and range are T_0. Say that π fixes a set x of individuals if for every $a \in x$, $\pi a = a$. Now suppose T_n defined, and $\pi \alpha$ defined for all α in T_n. If β is a subset of T_n, let $\pi \beta = \{\pi \alpha : \alpha \in \beta\}$, and let T_{n+1} be the set of those subsets β of T_n

such that for some *finite* set x of individuals, $\pi\beta = \beta$ for all π that fix x. Thus each T_n is a subset, in general a proper subset, of type n.

It is easy to see that T_1 consists of the sets of individuals that are either finite or have a finite complement (relative to T_0). If n is a Russell number, then $\pi n = n$, for *every* π, and thus n is in T_2 (take $x = \Lambda$); similarly for the set N of Russell numbers: $\pi N = N$ for every π, and therefore N is in T_3.

The sets T_n, together with the sets belonging to them, turn out to form a model $\mathcal{M}$ of the theory of types and the statements that there are infinitely many individuals but Dedekind finitely many classes of individuals. The details of the proof are given in Appendix II.

Russell showed that there are Dedekind infinitely many classes of classes of individuals from the assumption that there are infinitely many individuals. But, as we have just observed, Dedekind infinity could not have been found any lower: without the aid of some such assumption as the axiom of choice it cannot be proved from the axiom of infinity that the individuals or the classes of them form a Dedekind infinite totality.

Of course there is a simpler reason why the numbers must first appear two types up if only the axiom of infinity is assumed. In the theory of types there is no way to define the numbers as sets of individuals and hence no way to define them as individuals. More precisely, for every formula $\phi(x)$ containing exactly the (set) variable x free, the sentence $\exists!\,3x\phi(x)$[10] expressing the existence of exactly three sets satisfying $\phi(x)$ is not a theorem of the theory of types. Thus there are no formulae $0(x)$, $1(x)$, and $2(x)$ such that $\iota x0(x)$, $\iota x1(x)$, and $\iota x2(x)$ can be proved to exist and differ from one another; otherwise $\exists!\,3x(0(x) \vee 1(x) \vee 2(x))$ would be provable.

In fact, it can be shown more generally that for any formula $\phi(x)$ of *TT* and any integer $i > 2$, the sentence

$$[\exists!\,ix\phi(x) \rightarrow \bigvee \{\exists!\,na\ a = a: n \leq i \text{ and for some } \sigma \subseteq \{0, \ldots, n\},$$
$$i = \Sigma\,\{nCr: r \in \sigma\}\}]$$

is provable in *TT* (*nCr* is the binomial coefficient). As the only rows of Pascal's triangle from which 3 can be obtained by summing entries are 121 and 1331, for any formula $\phi(x)$, $\exists!\,3x\phi(x) \rightarrow \exists!\,2a\ a = a \vee \exists!\,3a\ a = a$ is provable in *TT*. Since $\exists!\,2a\ a = a \vee \exists!\,3a\ a = a$ is not a theorem, neither is $\exists!\,3x\phi(x)$. Thus, if our resources are confined to those of the theory of types with the axiom of infinity, the natural numbers cannot be classes of individuals. (The mod 2 numbers could be, however.)

In his first proof that every set can be well ordered, Zermelo in effect showed how to extend the theory of types plus the axiom of infinity to make it possible to define the numbers as individuals. It will be instructive to examine the extension and definition, which it is perhaps not too farfetched to take to formalize the theory of arithmetic of Frege's interlocutor at the beginning of *Die Grundlagen der Arithmetik*, who, according to Frege, will likely invite us to "*select* something for ourselves – anything we please – to call one."

Let us add to the language of the theory a symbol θ for a function f whose values for arguments of type 1 are of type 0. And now let us take as a new axiom a strengthened version of the axiom of choice for type 1:[11]

$$\exists a\; a \in x \to \theta x \in x \;(*)$$

We can now define 0 as $f T_0$, 1 as $f(T_0 - 0)$, 2 as $f(T_0 - 0 - 1)$, etc. (Had we asked Frege's man on the street to tell us what two was, he would surely have invited us to select something *else* – anything *else* we please – and call it two.)

By the argument of Zermelo's proof, there is a unique well-ordering R of T_0 in which $f(T_0 - A)$ is the R-least element of $T_0 - A$, for any proper initial segment A of R. We may then define b to be the successor of a if aRb and for no c, $aRcRb$, and a to be a natural number if every b such that bRa or $b = a$ is zero or a successor. The axiom of infinity here guarantees that every natural number has a successor.

Thus, simply by adding a new function symbol to the language of the theory of types and a suitable axiom governing the function denoted by it, we have found a way to "recognize" the numbers as individuals. Of course, there was no need to bring in a *function* symbol; we could have adhered more closely to the syntactic style of the theory of types by introducing a constant $\mathscr{C}$ of type 4, along with the axiom

$$\exists a\; a \in x \to \exists!\, a(a \in x \wedge \{\{x\}, \{x, \{a\}\}\} \in \mathscr{C})$$

"But," it may be objected, "isn't that cheating? We are trying to find individuals with which to identify the natural numbers. However, not any old means of finding them is allowed. We have to use means that are recognizably logical. I don't see that the importation of a brand-new function sign, designating who knows what function (or the use of a higher-type constant: there's no difference), counts as a logical means of finding individuals that can serve as the natural numbers. We don't know which function θ denotes; you've just pulled something out of thin air to do the work you wanted to have done."

Let us note this objection for now and examine another means of recognizing the numbers as individuals.

Suppose that we add to the theory of types a function sign $^{\#}$ whose values for arguments of type 1 are of type 0 and take as a new axiom

$$^{\#}x = {}^{\#}y \leftrightarrow x \text{ sm } y$$

("sm" abbreviates "is similar to," defined as usual).

Then, as Frege showed in *Grundlagen*, if, *working without axioms of extensionality, the axiom of infinity or any version of the axiom of choice,* we define 0 as

$$\iota a\, \exists y (\forall c\ c \notin y \wedge a = {}^{\#}y)$$

define c to succeed b iff

$$\exists a\, \exists y\, \exists z (z = y + a \wedge a \notin y \wedge b = {}^{\#}y \wedge c = {}^{\#}z)$$

and define a to be a natural number iff

$$\forall x (0 \in x \wedge \forall b \forall c (b \in x \wedge c \text{ succeeds } b \rightarrow c \in x) \rightarrow a \in x)$$

then we can prove the Peano postulates, together with all necessary existence and uniqueness assumptions. It is an immediate consequence that the individuals form a Dedekind infinite totality, and that the axiom of infinity therefore holds after all. Moreover, the numbers have indeed been defined as individuals.

For all its excellences, this method of obtaining the natural numbers at the lowest level of the type hierarchy is as much subject to the objection that we have no idea which function the new symbol refers to as was the postulation previously described of a *particular* choice function f for type 1 (e.g., if π is a permutation of T_0, then where a is the value of ${}^{\#}x$ and b that of ${}^{\#}y$, $\pi a = \pi b$ iff x sm y holds).[12] It can be said with equal justice in both cases that nothing establishes, determines, fixes the function to which the newly introduced function symbol refers. No one struggled harder than Frege to overcome the apparent lack of fixity of the function referred to by "the number of (belonging to)." But it has often been remarked that whatever other problems may have beset Rule V of *Grundgesetze*, for Frege to use that axiom to introduce extensions and then to define a number as a certain sort of extension, is to advance little if at all in settling the question to which items number words refer: if we are uncertain whether numbers are conquerors, we are not going to be helped out of the slough by being told that numbers are extensions. (I think Michael Dummett pointed this out to me more than thirty years ago.)

It may be thought that we know what it is for one item to bear the relation indicated by "$\in$" to another better than we know which particular function is designated by "the number of," and certainly better than we know which function is designated by θ. To the extent that this is so, or supposed so, Russell's treatment of the numbers will be, or seem, *ideologically* superior to Frege's in the sense of Quine, superior in respect to the clarity of determinacy of the notions of which it avails itself. Russell may assume as an axiom a statement that Frege can prove, but Frege utilizes a notion that can neither be expressed in Russell's language, a sublanguage of Frege's, nor, apparently, freed from a very familiar sort of indeterminacy.

Of course, there is indeterminacy aplenty in the theory of types. As in the theory of complex numbers, i and $-i$ are indiscernible – any truth remains true in which "i" and "$-i$" are everywhere interchanged – so in the theory of types "ϵ" and "$\notin$" may be uniformly interchanged at any one type (thanks to the existence of a unique complement in its type for every item not of the type of individuals). More exactly, for any n, if ϕ is a theorem of the theory of types, then so is the result of replacing every atomic formula of the form $x_n \epsilon y_{n+1}$ in ϕ with its negation. (In set theory we cannot perform this sort of switch: $\exists y \forall x \neg x \epsilon y$ is, but $\exists y \forall x x \epsilon y$ is not, a theorem of set theory.) Moreover, such interchange can be performed at any other type independently of whether it is performed at any others. Thus the theory of types is indeterminate in at least $2^{\aleph_0}$ ways.

But this sort of indeterminacy also infects the theory of objects and first- and higher-level concepts that was employed by Frege: we are free to interpret the predication Fx as asserting that the value of x fails to fall under the concept denoted by F. Thus, in any event a *new* sort of indeterminacy arises with the introduction of either $^\#$ or θ.

Of course the axiom $^\#x = {}^\#y \leftrightarrow x$ sm y (Hume's principle) is not to be regarded as a *definition* of number; it is merely a consistent principle whose addition to a suitable higher-order (indeed, second-order) logic yields a system in which the basic notions of the arithmetic of natural numbers can be defined and their most familiar properties proved. Thus, with the aid of a familiar-seeming principle, Frege has given a remarkably simple axiomatization of arithmetic whose consistency is not at present subject to doubt. (The tragedy of Russell's paradox was to obscure from Frege and from us the great interest of his actual positive accomplishment.) It has been my aim these last few pages to point out a number of respects in which Russell's account of arithmetic stands comparison with the one Frege is now known to have provided.

The construction of the numbers with the aid of a choice function, which was sketched earlier, shows, I think, that Hume's principle cannot be thought to be *the* foundation of arithmetic. One of zero's properties, and a very important one too, is that it is the number of things there are that are not self-identical; but, as our discussion of Frege's man in the street showed, there is also a perfectly sensical alternative development of the idea that 0, or 1 (if you prefer to begin the number series there), is the "typical object." It is also to be noted that there is no trace in the construction of the idea that 2, for example, is the class of all couples; nor is use made in the construction of a function injecting Russell numbers into the individuals.

Moreover, by the trick of reserving 0 for the number of things that are self-identical and "pushing each natural number up one," we can define $^\#$

so as to prove Hume's principle in the theory of types plus the axiom of infinity and our strengthened version (*) of choice.

I now want to take up the question whether Russell's introduction of the axiom of infinity in volume II of *Principia Mathematica* amounts, as Kneale put it, "to abandonment of Frege's project of exhibiting arithmetic as a development of logic." Of course the axiom of infinity cannot be counted as a truth of logic, and no one was clearer on that score than Russell himself.

From the fact that the infinite is not self-contradictory, but is also not demonstrable logically, we must conclude that nothing can be known *a priori* as to whether the number of things in the world is finite or infinite. The conclusion is, therefore, to adopt a Leibnizian phraseology, that some of the possible worlds are finite, some infinite, and we have no means of knowing to which of these two kinds our actual world belongs. The axiom of infinity will be true in some possible worlds and false in others; whether it is true or false in this world we cannot tell. . . .

We may take the axiom of infinity as an example of a proposition which, though it can be enunciated in logical terms, cannot be asserted by logic to be true. . . . We are left to empirical observation to determine whether there are as many as *n* individuals in the world. . . . There does not even seem any logical necessity why there should be even one individual [Footnote in original: The primitive propositions in *Principia Mathematica* are such as to allow the inference that at least one individual exists. But I now view this as a defect in logical purity.] – why in fact there should be any world at all.[13]

In *Principia Mathematica*, Whitehead and Russell say:

If, for example, Nc'Indiv = v, then this proposition is false for any higher type; but this proposition, Nc'Indiv = v, is one which cannot be proved logically; in fact it is only ascertainable by a census, not by logic. Thus among the propositions which can be proved by logic, there are some which can only be proved for higher types, but none which can only be proved for lower types. . . .

"Infin ax," like "Mult ax," is an arithmetical hypothesis which some will consider self-evident, but which we prefer to keep as a hypothesis, and to adduce in that form whenever it is relevant. Like "Mult ax," it states an existence theorem. . . .

It seems plain that there is nothing in logic to necessitate its truth or falsehood, and that it can only be legitimately believed or disbelieved on empirical grounds.[14]

And in volume III:

> Great difficulties are caused, in this section ["Generalization of number"], by the existence-theorems and the question of types. These difficulties disappear if the axiom of infinity is assumed, but it seems improper to make the theory of (say) 2/3 depend upon the assumption that the number of objects in the universe is not finite. We have, accordingly, taken pains not to make this assumption, except where, as in the theory of real numbers, it is really essential, and not merely convenient. When the axiom of infinity is required, it is always explicitly stated in the hypothesis, so that our propositions, as enunciated, are true even if the axiom of infinity is false.[15]

But if Russell made it plain that he did not consider the axiom of infinity to be a truth of logic, "asserted by logic to be true," what becomes of the project of showing arithmetic to be a development of logic, of logicism? Russell was a logicist, wasn't he?

To determine whether or not he was, it might just be advisable to consult his writings instead of common opinion. It turns out that Russell was rather more cautious in certain works than in others in proclaiming that mathematics can be reduced to logic, or is identical with it. The question whether Russell was or was not a logicist cannot, I think, be given a direct answer, and ought to be replaced with a question of the form, "Was Russell a logicist in work *X*?" What can be said is that he expressed logicist views in certain works and refrained – significantly, it seems to me – from expressing them in others, notably *Principia Mathematica*, in which, as it happens, there are rather few remarks on the relation between logic and mathematics; perhaps Whitehead and Russell considered it unnecessary to supply many, for the work is, after all, an extended disquisition upon just that subject. Those there are, however, make it doubtful that the authors should be considered logicists, that is, defenders of the view that mathematics, or arithmetic, or at least the Peano postulates, can be derived by logical means alone from statements true solely in virtue of logic and appropriate definitions of mathematical notions. *Principia* is not quite 2,000 pages long, and it is hard to be perfectly certain that one has not overlooked a significant remark or failed to put together separated comments that would make it plain that its authors do after all count as logicists. However, there appears to be only one section of *Principia* that explicitly deals with the relation between logic and mathematics, at the beginning of the introduction to the first edition. There Russell and Whitehead list three aims of the logic that occupies part I of *Principia*. They are, in reverse order, the avoidance of the contradictions, the precise symbolic expression of mathematical propositions, and the one that concerns us:

effecting the greatest possible analysis of the ideas with which it deals and of the processes by which it conducts demonstrations, and . . . diminishing to the utmost the number of the undefined ideas and undemonstrated propositions (called respectively *primitive ideas* and *primitive propositions*) from which it starts.[16]

Later, the first aim is described, rather differently, as "the complete enumeration of all the ideas and steps in reasoning employed in mathematics".[17]

It is evident that one who claims to have enumerated all the ideas and steps involved in mathematical reasoning need not imply that that reasoning is logical reasoning, or even that the third Peano postulate is a truth of logic. However justly, it might well be said that Zermelo–Fraenkel set theory provides such an enumeration; to say so is, obviously, not to be committed to the view that its axioms are logical truths. Russell's second description of his first aim provides no reason to take him to be committed to the central thesis of logicism.

Nor does his first description. The most thorough analysis possible of mathematical ideas and argumentation might well have as its outcome that the third Peano postulate is equivalent to the axiom of infinity, but leave entirely open the question whether the latter is a truth of logic. Russell repeatedly states that it is not one, and he did not take it to be a primitive proposition; moreover, he claimed to have proved from primitive propositions only the conditional with consequent Peano three and antecedent Infin ax.

One may distinguish, as Carnap has usefully done,[18] two theses of logicism, the first of which states that the concepts of mathematics can be explicitly defined from logical concepts; the second, that the theorems of mathematics can be deduced from logical axioms by logical means alone. We may call these the *definability thesis* and the *provability thesis* of logicism.

Establishing the definability thesis will show that all truths of mathematics can be expressed in the vocabulary of pure logic. But it is important to distinguish truths expressed in the vocabulary of pure logic from truths that are true "by virtue of logic alone," that is, *logical truths* or *truths of logic* properly so called. Russell's way of making this distinction was between propositions that are "enunciated in logical terms" and those that are "asserted by logic to be true."[19] "$\exists x \; \exists y \; x \neq y$" is a truth, and expressed in logical vocabulary, which Russell, correctly in my view, did not regard as a logical truth. One who accepts the theory of types will almost surely regard Infin ax as true and in logical vocabulary, but one who so regards it need not therefore take it to be a logical truth. Establishing both theses would certainly show the truths of mathematics to be logical truths, but establishing the definability thesis alone does not suffice to do this, and hence certainly does not establish the provability thesis. No one, I take it, counts as a full-fledged logicist who does not endorse the provability thesis as well as the definability thesis.

It seems fair to take Russell's aim in *Principia* to have been the systematic exposition of a sufficiently large portion of mathematics to enable the reader to see that, and how, the whole of the subject could be treated in its system, in the sense that every concept of mathematics could be defined in terms of the primitive ideas of the system and every theorem of mathematics either proved from its primitive propositions, *or suitably related* to other propositions of mathematics. In *Principia*, then, Russell was an advocate of the definability thesis, but not of the provability thesis of logicism. It was never part of his aim there to show that (say) Peano three, as opposed to "If Infin ax then Peano three," could be derived from the primitive propositions of the system. Whitehead and Russell might have paraphrased Boole and called their work *The Logical Analysis of Mathematics.* To provide such an *analysis*, however, it is not requisite to derive from logic the whole of elementary mathematics.

Once the idea is abandoned that the aim of *Principia* is to vindicate full-fledged logicism, to exhibit arithmetic as a development of logic, there is little to object to in Russell's *modus operandi*. The axiom of infinity is introduced at the appropriate point: in subsection *120 "Inductive cardinals," of section C, "FINITE AND INFINITE," of part III, "CARDINAL ARITHMETIC" (with which volume II begins). Part I of *Principia* is entitled "MATHEMATICAL LOGIC"; part II, "PROLEGOMENA TO CARDINAL ARITHMETIC." Where else should the axiom of infinity have been introduced?

When pronouncing on the relation of logic to mathematics, Russell is significantly less circumspect in the exoteric *Introduction to Mathematical Philosophy* than he is in *Principia*:

> Pure logic, and pure mathematics (which is the same thing), aims at being true, in Leibnizian phraseology, in all possible worlds, not only in this higgledy-piggledy job-lot of a world in which chance has imprisoned us. . . .

> The consequence is that it has now become wholly impossible to draw a line between the two; in fact, the two are one. . . . The proof of their identity is, of course, a matter of detail. . . . If there are still those who do not admit the identity of logic and mathematics, we may challenge them to indicate at what point in the successive definitions and deductions of *Principia Mathematica* they consider that logic ends and mathematics begins. It will then be obvious that any answer must be arbitrary. . . .

> Assuming that the number of individuals in the universe is not finite, we have now succeeded not only in defining Peano's three primitive ideas,

but in seeing how to prove his five primitive propositions, by means of primitive ideas and propositions belonging to logic.[20]

These remarks and others that might be cited might well lead one to take Russell to be advocating a position he himself has given the best of reasons for rejecting, since he has elsewhere been as explicit as possible that he does not regard the axiom of infinity as a logical truth. To the challenge Russell lays down, one may respond that every proposition deduced in *Principia* is indeed a truth of logic, but Peano three; a proposition of mathematics if any is, has not been deduced there.

The last quotation, however, suggests a more charitable reading of *Introduction to Mathematical Philosophy*, under which one may interpret Russell to be claiming the identity of the concepts of mathematics with those of logic, the derivability of all the Peano axioms but the third, and the provability of "if Infin ax then Peano three." On this reading, the frequent omissions of an important qualification of the logicist thesis must be thought careless, if not propagandistic. In *Introduction to Mathematical Philosophy*, then, Russell can perhaps be considered to espouse the definability thesis of logicism, but to hedge significantly on the question whether the provability thesis holds. It is therefore arguable that Russell does not significantly change his mind between the writing of *Principia Mathematica* and *Introduction to Mathematical Philosophy*, and that in neither work should he be seen as fully committed to logicism.

Appendix I

Lemma. If $x \in n$, then x sm y iff $y \in n$.

Proof. Induction: The lemma is trivial if $n = 0$, since Λ sm y iff $y = \Lambda$. Suppose $x \in sn$. Then for some $a \in x$, $x - a \in n$. Suppose x sm y via f. Then $fa \in y$, $x - a$ sm $y - fa$, $y - fa \in n$ by the i.h., and $y \in sn$. Conversely, suppose $y \in sn$. Then for some $b \in y$, $y - b \in n$. By the i.h., $x - a$ sm $y - b$ via some f, and thus x sm y via g, where domain $(g) = x$, $gc = fc$ for $c \in x - a$, and $ga = b$.

Theorem: $\varnothing$ is not a number iff different numbers have different successors.

Proof: Suppose that $\varnothing$ is a number. $\varnothing$ is empty; 0 is not empty. By induction we may assume that for some number n, n is not empty, but sn, which is a number, is empty. Thus $n \neq sn$. Since sn is empty and $ssn = \{x: \exists a(a \in x \wedge x - a \in sn)\}$, ssn is also empty, and by Ext, $sn = ssn$. Since ssn is also a number, n and sn are different numbers with the same successor. Conversely, assume that $\varnothing$ is not a number, m, n are numbers and $sm = sn$. Since sm is a number, $sm \neq \varnothing$, and for some x, $x \in sm = sn$. Then for some a, b, $a \in x$, $b \in x$, $x - a \in m$ and $x - b \in n$. Then $x - a$ sm $x - b$ via f, where domain $(f) = x - a$, $fb = a$ if $b \in x - a$, and $fc = c$ for $c \in x - a$, $c \neq b$. If $z \in m$, z sm $x - a$ by the lemma, whence z sm $x - b$, and $z \in n$ by the lemma again. Similarly, if $z \in n$, $z \in m$. By Ext, $m = n$.

Appendix II

In $\mathcal{M}$, T_0 satisfies the formula "x is infinite": since there is in fact no one–one function from any finite set of natural numbers onto T_0, no function in $\mathcal{M}$ witnesses the finitude of T_0.

We now show that T_1 does not satisfy "x is Dedekind infinite" in $\mathcal{M}$.

Suppose that f, $\in \mathcal{M}$, witnesses the Dedekind infinity of T_1. Abbreviate "$\iota z\{\{n\}, \{n, \{z\}\}\} \in f$" by "$fn$." Then f is a one–one function with domain N such that for every n in N, $fn \in T_1$. Since $f \in \mathcal{M}$, there is some finite $x \subseteq T_0$, such that $\pi f = f$ for every π that fixes x. There are only finitely many y such that $y \subseteq x$ or $T_0 - y \subseteq x$. Thus, for some n in N and some finite $y \subseteq T_0$, y is not a subset of x, and either $fn = y$ or $fn = T_0 - y$. Let a be an individual in $y - x$, and let b be an individual in neither y nor x (some such b exists since x and y are finite and there are infinitely many individuals). Let π permute a and b but do nothing else. π fixes x; so $\pi f = f$. Then if $fn = y$, $\pi y = \pi fn = \pi f \pi n = fn = y$, and if $fn = T_0 - y$, then $y = T_0 - fn$, and since $\pi T_0 - T_0$, $\pi y = \pi(T_0 - fn) = \pi T_0 - \pi fn = T_0 - \pi f \pi n = T_0 - fn = y$. In either case $\pi y = y$, $a \in y$, whence $b = \pi a \in \pi y = y$. But $b \notin y$, contradiction.

We now show that $\mathcal{M}$ is a model of the theory of types.

That extensionality holds in $\mathcal{M}$ is clear: if x, $y \in T_{n+1}$, $x \neq y$, then for some z, $z \in x$ or $z \in y$. But then $z \in T_n$.

As for comprehension, let $x^1, \ldots, x^n$ be a list containing all variables free in a formula ψ; each x^i ranges over some one type or other. By induction on ψ, for any π, any objects $o^1, \ldots, o^n$ of the appropriate types, $\mathcal{M} \vDash \psi(o^1, \ldots, o^n)$ iff $\mathcal{M} \vDash \psi(\pi o^1, \ldots, \pi o^n)$.

Now let x_n be a variable ranging over type n, x_n, $x^1, \ldots, x^m$ be a list containing all variables free in a formula ϕ. We must see that for any objects $o^1, \ldots, o^m$ in $\mathcal{M}$ of the appropriate types $\{o \in T_n: \mathcal{M} \vDash \phi(o, o^1, \ldots, o^m)\} \in T_{n+1}$. Notice that for each n, T_n is a definable subset of type n, and therefore for each formula ϕ, "$\mathcal{M} \vDash \phi(o, o^1, \ldots, o^m)$" defines a definable relation. It thus suffices to show that if $q = \{o \in T_n: \mathcal{M} \vDash \phi(o, o^1, \ldots, o^m)\}$, then for some finite $z \subseteq T_0$, $\pi q = q$ for every π that fixes z.

For each i, $1 \leq i \leq m$, let z_i be a finite subset of T_0 such that $\pi o^i = o^i$ for every π that fixes z_i. Let $z = z_1 \cup \ldots \cup z_m$. Suppose π fixes z. We show that $\pi q = q$. π fixes $z_1, \ldots, z_m$, and so $\pi o^i = o^i$, $1 \leq i \leq m$, $\pi T_n = T_n$. Suppose $o \in \pi q$. Then $\pi^{-1} o \in q$; $\pi^{-1} o \in T_n$ and $\mathcal{M} \vDash \phi(\pi^{-1} o, o^1, \ldots, o^m)$; $o \in \pi T_n$ and $\mathcal{M} \vDash \phi(o, \pi o^1, \ldots, \pi o^m)$; $o \in T_n$ and $\mathcal{M} \vDash \phi(o, o^1, \ldots, o^m)$, and so $o \in q$. Thus $\pi q \subseteq q$. And if $o \in q$, then $\pi^{-1} o \in \pi^{-1} q$, whence, similarly, $\pi^{-1} o \in q$, and $o \in \pi q$. So $q \subseteq \pi q \subseteq q$, done.

Notes

* I am grateful to Tony Anderson, David Auerbach, Richard Cartwright, Philippe de Rouilhan, Michael Hallett, Elliott Mendelson, Michael Resnik and Linda Wetzel for helpful comments. Research for this paper was carried out under grant no. SES-8808755 from the National Science Foundation.
1 Littlewood (1986), 128.
2 Kneale and Kneale (1984), 657–672, esp. 669.
3 Whitehead and Russell (1927).
4 More than 800 in the first edition.
5 We will often drop type subscripts when the type of a variable is clear from context.
6 Russell (1919), 71.
7 Cf. Boolos (1990) and (1987).
8 The theorem is erroneously ascribed to Tarski in one well-known excellent text: Lévy (1979), 80.
9 Cf. Jech (1973), Ch. 4, and Felgner (1971), Ch. 3.
10 That is, $\exists x \, \exists y \, \exists z (\phi(x) \wedge \phi(y) \wedge \phi(z) \wedge x \neq y \wedge x \neq z \wedge y \neq z \wedge \forall \, w(\phi(w) \rightarrow w = x \vee w = y \vee w = z))$.
11 By replacing items with their singletons, we can see that "choice drops down"; thus, if we had introduced a function sign ρ and a strengthened version of choice for type $n + 1$:

$$\exists x_n \, x_n \in x_{n+1} \rightarrow \rho x_{n+1} \in x_{n+1}$$

we could then have defined a suitable θ and proved (*).
12 The "Irving Caesar" problem.
13 Russell (1919), 141, 202–203.
14 Quotations from Whitehead and Russell (1927), vol. II, x, 203, 183, respectively.
15 Whitehead and Russell (1927), vol. III, 234.
16 Whitehead and Russell (1927), vol. I, 1.
17 Whitehead and Russell (1927), vol. I, 2–3.
18 Carnap (1983).
19 Russell (1919), 202–203.
20 Quotations from Russell (1919), 192, 194–195, 24–25, respectively.

References

Boolos, G. 1987. The consistency of Frege's *Foundations of Arithmetic*. In J. J. Thomson, ed., *On Being and Saying*. Cambridge, Mass., MIT Press, 3–20.

—— 1990. The standard of equality of numbers. In *Meaning and Method: Essays in Honor of Hilary Putnam*. Edited by G. Boolos. Cambridge University Press, 261–277.

Carnap, R. 1983. The logicist foundations of mathematics. In P. Benacerraf and H. Putnam, eds., *Philosophy of Mathematics: Selected Readings*, 2nd edn. Cambridge University Press, 41–52.

Felgner, U. 1971. *Models of ZF-Set Theory: Lecture Notes in Mathematics*, vol. 233. Berlin, Springer-Verlag.

Frege, G. 1879. *Begriffsschrift*. Halle, Verlag von Louis Nebert.

—— 1884. *Die Grundlagen der Arithmetik*. Breslau, W. Koebner.

—— 1893, 1903. *Grundgesetze der Arithmetik*, Vols. I, II. Jena, Hermann Pohle.

Jech, T. 1973. *The Axiom of Choice*. Amsterdam, North-Holland.

Kneale, W., and M. Kneale. 1984. *The Development of Logic*. Oxford University Press.

Lévy, A. 1979. *Basic Set Theory*. Berlin, Springer-Verlag.

Littlewood, J. E. 1986. *Littlewood's Miscellany*. Edited by B. Bollobás. Cambridge University Press.

Russell, B. 1919. *Introduction to Mathematical Philosophy*. London, Allen and Unwin.

Whitehead, A. N., and B. Russell. 1927. *Principia Mathematica*, 2nd edn. Cambridge University Press.

18

Russell's "No-Classes" Theory of Classes

Leonard Linsky

I

Russell found classes to be creatures of darkness beginning with his earliest discussions of them in 1903 in *The Principles of Mathematics* (second edition, 1937). The *Principles* antedates any conception of philosophy as linguistic analysis, so Russell does not express his misgivings about classes as an inability to fix a clear meaning of the word "class." He expresses his qualms as a failure to "see" a kind of object clearly. He takes the notion of class to be "indefinable." This means that the concept cannot be broken down into a number of constituent concepts of which it is composed. The concept is a "simple" one – like Moore's yellow. We can come to know it only through a kind of direct acquaintance and not through analysis or definition. Russell says: "The discussion of indefinables – which forms the chief part of philosophical logic – is the endeavour to see clearly, and to make others see clearly, the entities concerned, in order that the mind may have that kind of acquaintance with them which it has with redness or the taste of a pineapple" (1937, p. xv). Such passages are reminiscent of things Plato says about seeing the Forms with "the eye of the soul." Indeed the epistemological Platonism here expressed by Russell seems to be an almost inevitable accompaniment to the ontological Platonism (realism) that is a central feature of both Plato's dialogues and Russell's *Principles of Mathematics*. Russell goes on to say: "In the case of classes, I must confess, I have failed to perceive any concept fulfilling the conditions requisite for the notion of *class*" (1937, p. xvi). In a letter to Frege dated 8 August 1902, Russell writes: "I still lack a direct intuition, a direct insight into what you call a range of values: logically it is necessary, but it remains for me a justified hypothesis" (Frege 1980, pp. 144–145).

Of course, a principal reason for Russell's qualms about classes is his discovery of the antinomy about the class of all classes that are not members of themselves. So long as he saw no resolution for this, he could not believe himself to have an adequate conception of the nature of classes. But this is not the whole explanation. Russell also discovered an analogous antinomy about properties (or propositional functions). Yet this did not cause him to be skeptical about attributes and propositional functions. He never expressed an inability to "see" these things clearly – to doubt that he knew them in the way he did the taste of pineapple.

How can we account for this asymmetry in Russell's attitude toward classes on the one hand and properties (attributes, concepts, propositional functions) on the other? For one thing there is what Russell refers to as "the ancient problem of the One and the Many" (Whitehead and Russell 1910, p. 72).

> Is a class which has many terms to be regarded as itself one or many? Taking the class as equivalent simply to the numerical conjunction "*A* and *B* and *C* and etc.', it seems plain that it is many; yet it is quite necessary that we should be able to count classes as one each, and we do habitually speak of *a* class. Thus classes would seem to be one in one sense and many in another.
>
> (Russell 1937, p. 76)

What we see here is not a passing aberration or early confusion that Russell will soon see through. The same reason for skepticism about the existence of classes is expressed in Russell's most mature writing about classes in *Principia Mathematica*. "If there is such an object as a class, it must be in some sense *one* object, yet it is only of classes that *many* can be predicated. Hence, if we admit classes as objects, we must suppose that the same object can be both one and many, which seems impossible" (Whitehead and Russell 1910, p. 72n). In *Our Knowledge of the External World* (1914), Russell gives yet another version of the "ancient problem." "In the third or fourth century BC there lived a Chinese philosopher named Hui Tzu, who maintained that 'a bay horse and a dun cow are three; because taken separately they are two, and taken together they are one: two and one make three'" (1929, p. 224). Russell concludes that what is shown here is that "collections of things" are not things. "It is only because the bay horse and the dun cow taken together are not a new thing that we can escape the conclusion that there are three things wherever there are two" (1929, p. 224). Hence classes are not things; they are a *façon de parler*.

The quotations from *Our Knowledge of the External World* reflect the "no-classes" theory of *Principia*: "collections of things" (classes) are not things. In *Principles* Russell resolves the difficulty by distinguishing the class *as one* from the class *as many*. For example, "*class of all rational animals* which denotes the human race as one term, is different from *men*, which denotes men, i.e. the human race as many" (1937, p. 76). Russell's conclusion is that the class as one is different from the class as many. We are not dealing with two different ways of viewing the *same* thing. "But it is more correct, I think, to infer an ultimate distinction between a class as many and a class as one, to hold that the many are only many, and not also one. The class as one may be identified with the whole composed of the terms of the class i.e., in the case of men, the class as one will be the human race" (1937, p. 76).

This solution leads only to another difficulty. In his account of the constituents of propositions, Russell has committed himself to the view, opposed to Frege, that every constituent of a proposition can play the role of logical subject. It is in this way that he avoids Frege's paradox about the concept "horse." But now, if we hold "that the many are only many and not also one," the following problem arises: "But can we now avoid the contradiction always to be feared, where there is something that cannot be made a logical subject?" (Russell 1937, p. 76). Russell resolves *this* difficulty by deciding that assertions need not be about single subjects; they may be about many subjects. He concludes: "[T]his removes the contradiction which arose, in the case of concepts, from the impossibility of making assertions about them unless they were turned into subjects. This impossibility being here absent, the contradiction which was to be feared does not arise" (1937, p. 77). What Russell is saying here is that there is no difficulty in making assertions about classes as many so long as we recognize that an assertion need not be about a single logical subject. "In such a proposition as '*A* and *B* are two', there is no logical subject: the assertion is not about *A*, nor about *B*, nor about the whole composed of both, but strictly and only about *A* and *B*" (1937, pp. 76–77).

If the class as one is always to be distinguished from the class as many, another perplexity arises in the case of the null class and unit classes. The null class has no members, so there can be no such thing as the null class as many; and a unit class has only one member so there is no distinction between a unit class as one and as many. Russell concludes: "The first consequence is that there is no such thing as the null-class, though there are null class-concepts. The second is, that a class having only one term is to be identified, contrary to Peano's usage, with that one term" (1937, p. 68).

The rejection of the null class and of unit classes (as distinct from their members) in turn creates a problem in the theory of cardinal numbers. Russell holds that "numbers are . . . applicable essentially to classes" (1937, p. 112). More specifically, he says, "Mathematically, a number is nothing but a class of similar classes" (1937, p. 116). The rejection of the null class brings with it, accordingly, the rejection of the cardinal number 0. If unit classes are to be identified with their unit members, the cardinal number 1 (the class of all unit classes) becomes wrongly identified with the universal class – the class of everything.

Besides these difficulties about the One and the Many and about "the contradiction," there is another argument for skepticism about classes in *Principles of Mathematics*. Russell gives the argument briefly in *My Philosophical Development*. Like "the contradiction," it is closely associated with Cantor's theorem: "[A] class of *n* terms has 2^n sub-classes. This proposition is still true when *n* is infinite. What Cantor proved was that, even in this case, 2^n is greater than *n*. Applying this, as I did, to all the things in the universe, one arrives at the conclusion that there are more classes of things than there are things. It follows that classes are not 'things'" (Russell 1959, pp. 80–81). At the time of *Principles* then, Russell was already well on the way to his later no-classes theory. "The conclusion to which I was led was that classes are merely a convenience in discourse" (Russell 1959, p. 81). "A class is . . . only an expression. It is only a convenient way of talking about the values of the variable for which the function is true" (1959, p. 82).

II

The difficulties here are not peculiar to Russell. Cantor's 1895 definition of class leads to its own perplexities. Cantor's celebrated definition runs as follows: "Unter einer 'Menge' verstehen wir jede Zusammenfassung *M* von bestimmten wholunterschiedenen Objekten *m* unserer Anschauung oder unseres Denkens (welche die 'Elemente' von *M* gennant werden) zu einem Ganzen" [By an aggregate we are to understand any collection into a whole *M* of definite and separate objects *m* of our intuition or our thought] (Cantor 1895–1897, p. 282). The use of the words "intuition" and "thought" gives the whole definition a psychological cast, and leaves the implication that the "collection" is itself a mental act. The suggestion of psychologism is soon reenforced, and it becomes explicit in Cantor's account of the cardinal numbers. "We will call by the name 'power' or 'cardinal number' of *M* the general concept which by means of our active faculty of thought, arises from the aggregate *M* when we make abstraction of the nature of its various elements *m* and the order in which they are given" (Cantor 1915, p. 86). The results of this double act of abstraction are the cardinal numbers or powers associated with each set. But the double act of abstraction will never produce zero. No act of our intuition or our thought can collect "definite and separate" objects into the null class. In the case of the null class, there is no element to be the target even of the first act of abstraction. This, perhaps, explains why, when Cantor turns to his account of "the finite cardinal numbers," he begins his construction with the cardinal number 1 and not with 0 (Cantor 1895–1897, section 5).

Cantor now provides us with a more detailed account of the double act of abstraction that gives us the cardinal numbers.

We denote the result of this double act of abstraction, the cardinal number or power of M, by $\bar{\bar{M}}$. Since every single element m, if we abstract from its nature, becomes a 'unit', the cardinal number $\bar{\bar{M}}$ is a definite aggregate composed of units, and this number has existence in our mind as an intellectual image or projection of the given aggregate M.

(Cantor 1915, p. 86)

If we abstract from the nature of the units, how, Frege asks, do they remain distinguishable? What distinguishes one from another? In whose mind does the number exist? Is my number 2 the same as yours? This line of criticism is, of course, inspired by Frege's attack on abstraction, the idea of the unit, and psychologism in section III of *Die Grundlagen der Arithmetik*. Abstraction, Frege remarks, is a powerful lye. Is it really necessary, he asks, to first "collect" together all the citizens of Germany before we can assign them a cardinal number?

None of these perplexities attend Russell's conception of classes. Psychologism in logic was never a temptation for him. For Russell the concept of class is indefinable. It can be correctly characterized only with the use of terms synonymous with it. For the Russell of *Principia*, what is logically prior is the class concept (propositional function). A class is the extension of a class concept. In this he agrees with Frege. With Cantor, on the one hand, and the Russell of *Principia* and Frege on the other, we have two quite different conceptions of the nature of classes. Here I follow Charles Parson's discussion in his paper "Some Remarks on Frege's Conception of Extension" (Parsons 1976). Parsons describes the difference as follows:

One appeals to intuitions associated with ordinary notions such as 'collection' or 'aggregate'. According to it, a set is 'formed' or 'constituted' from its *elements*. The axioms of set theory can then be motivated by ideas such as that sets can be formed from given elements in a quite arbitrary way, and that *any* set can be obtained by iterated application of such set formation, beginning either with nothing or with individuals that are not sets. According to the other, the paradigm of a set is the extension of a *predicate*. Terms denoting sets are nominalized predicates and sets are distinguished (e.g., from attributes), by the fact that predicates true of the same objects have the same set as their extension. Generally, the axioms of set theory are viewed as assumptions as to what predicates have extensions.

(Parsons 1976, p. 265)

It is Cantor who is the founder of the iterative conception according to which a class (set) is formed or constituted from its elements. It is this conception that is formulated in his celebrated 1895 definition. Whatever the perplexities about abstraction, psychologism, the cardinal number 0, associated with Cantor's account, it does not lead to antinomy. The class of all classes that are not members of themselves cannot be constituted from its elements. On this conception the elements are logically prior; a class arises by collecting them "into a whole," and self-membership is excluded. Frege and the Russell of the *Principia* are the founders of the other, logical conception that makes the class concept logically prior. A class is the extension of a concept. This conception presents no difficulties about the null class, the unit class as distinct from its unit member, 0 and 1, and the ancient problem of the One and the Many. But in its naive form, it leads swiftly and directly to Russell's antinomy. It is no accident that Russell, not Cantor, discovered it; it is remarkable that Frege did not also discover it independently, especially as he expressed some uncertainty about the consistency of his fifth axiom, which embodies his theory of extensions.

Following Wang and Gödel we may speak of Cantor's iterative concept as the mathematical concept of sets and of Frege's concept of extensions as the logical concept (Wang 1983, p. 537). We have, in the last paragraphs associated Russell with Frege as cofounder of the logical concept. This is true for the Russell of the no-classes theory of *Principia*, but the Russell of *Principles* is uneasily divided between the two conceptions. When, in *Principles*, he writes about the class as one and the class as many, of classes as "plural objects," and the problem of the One and the Many, he shows the influence of Cantor, including the use of Cantor's own Platonic terminology. In 1883 Cantor defined a set as follows: "Unter einer 'Mannigfaltigkeit' oder 'Menge' verstehe ich nämlich allgemein jedes Viele, welches sich als Eines denken lässt, d. h. jeden Inbegriff bestimmter Elemente, welcher durch ein Gesetz zu einem Ganzen verbunden werden kann" [every Many, which can be thought of as One, i.e. every totality of definite elements that can be united into a whole by a law] (Cantor 1932, p. 204n).

Russell, however, also writes about "the genesis of classes from an intensional standpoint" (1937, p. 67). According to this standpoint, "every predicate (provided it can be sometimes truly predicated) gives rise to a class" (1937, p. 67). He contrasts this with the mathematical concept that, he says, has an "extensional genesis" (1937, p. 67). Here he clearly has in mind the class as constituted by its members. "Here it is not predicates and denoting that are relevant, but terms connected by the word *and*, in the sense in which this word stands for a *numerical* conjunction. Thus Brown and Jones are a class, and Brown singly is a class. This is the extensional genesis of classes" (1937, p. 67). It is this conception that leads Russell to the problem of the One and the Many, while the intensional conception, according to which "every predicate . . . gives rise to a class" leads Russell to "the contradiction." The fact that Russell attempts, in *Principles*, to maintain both standpoints explains, in part, I believe, his inability "to perceive any concept fulfilling the conditions requisite for the notion of *class*" (1937, pp. xv–xvi). In a celebrated letter to Dedekind, dated "Halle, 28 July 1899" (not published until 1932), Cantor formulated the earliest attempt to resolve the antinomies of the theory of sets. His language recalls the 1883 definition and his solution anticipates future developments. Cantor's discussion turns entirely on the interplay between the class as one and the class as many. (This connection between Russell and Cantor was suggested to me by William Tait.)

> If we start from the notion of a definite multiplicity [*Vielheit*] (a system, a totality) of things, it is necessary, as I discovered, to distinguish two kinds of multiplicities (by this I always mean definite multiplicities). For a multiplicity can be such that the assumption that *all* of its elements 'are together' leads to a contradiction, so that it is impossible to conceive of the multiplicity as a unity, as 'one finished thing'. Such multiplicities I call *absolutely infinite* or *inconsistent* multiplicities. . . . If, on the other hand, the totality of the elements of a multiplicity can be thought of without contradiction as 'being together', so that they can be gathered together into '*one* thing', I call it a *consistent multiplicity* or a 'set'. (In French and in Italian this notion is aptly expressed by the words 'ensemble' and 'insieme'.)
>
> (Van Heijenoort 1967, p. 114)

Cantor's "multiplicities" are, intuitively, the same as Russell's classes as many. Cantor's "consistent multiplicities" are those that can be gathered together as *one* thing. These are, intuitively, the same as Russell's "classes as one." Inconsistent multiplicities are those that cannot be gathered together as one on pain of contradiction. Cantor does not consider the Russell antinomy in his letter, although he does discuss the antimony first published by Cesare Burali-Forti in 1897 and since known by his name. He concludes his discussion of the contradiction as follows: "The system Ω of all [ordinal] numbers is an inconsistent, absolutely infinite multiplicity" (Van Heijenoort 1967, p. 115). Although Cantor does not consider Russell's contradiction, his resolution is near to hand. The class of all classes that are not members of themselves is an inconsistent multiplicity that cannot be gathered together as one finished thing. Cantor's criterion as to when a multiplicity can be considered as one thing is not given with precision. The idea becomes sharply defined in subsequent developments when it is specified that a multiplicity is a set ("one thing") whenever it is an element of another multiplicity. The class of all classes that are not members of themselves is not an element. In contemporary terms, it is not a set.

It is remarkable that Russell had the same idea as Cantor, quite independently. In a letter to Frege dated 10 July 1902 Russell writes:

> Concerning the contradiction, I did not express myself clearly enough. I believe that classes cannot always be admitted as proper names. A class consisting of more than one object is in the first place not *one* object but many. Now an ordinary class does form *one* whole; thus soldiers for example form an army. But this does not seem to me to be a necessity of thought, though it is essential if we want to use a class as a proper name. I believe I can therefore say without contradiction that certain classes . . . are mere manifolds [*nur Vielheiten*] and do not form wholes at all. This is why there arise false propositions and even contradictions if they are regarded as units.
>
> (Frege 1980, p. 137)

The class of all classes that are not members of themselves is one such "manifold" that does not form a "whole," it must not be regarded as a "unit." In his first letter to Frege of 16 June 1902, in which Russell informs him of his discovery of the contradiction, Russell also proposes this resolution of it. "[T]here is no class (as a whole) of those classes which, as wholes, are not members of themselves. From this I conclude that under certain circumstances a definable set does not form a whole" (Frege 1980, p. 131).

Russell is led to this line of thought when considering classes in their "extensional genesis," which leads to the mathematical or iterative concept of sets and which he explicitly opposes to Frege's logical conception. In a letter to Frege dated 24 July 1902, he writes:

> And in general, if one connects ranges of values closely with concepts, as you do, it seems doubtful whether two concepts with the same extension have the same range of values or only equivalent ranges of values. I find it hard to see what a class really is if it does not consist of objects but is nevertheless supposed to be the same for two concepts with the same extension. Yet I admit that the reason you adduce against the extensional view . . . seems to be irrefutable.
>
> (Frege 1980, p. 139)

What is striking about this passage is Russell's claim that the most basic characteristic of classes, their extensionality, follows immediately from the concept according to which classes "consist of objects" – Cantor's conception. At the same time, he is unable to see how the extensionality of classes follows from Frege's logical conception "which connects ranges of values closely with concepts." Russell's ultimate resolution of his antinomy, however, abandons this direction in favor of the logical conception of classes in the form of his no-classes theory.

It would be wrong to suppose that either intuitive conception, the mathematical or the logical, was held in its pure form and totally to the exclusion of the other conception by either Cantor or Russell. Rather, what is found is a mixture of the two with one conception tending to dominate. In Russell's case it is different conceptions that dominate the mixture at the time of *Principles* and at the time of *Principia*. In Cantor's case the presence of the logical conception is indicated by his reference to laws ("every totality of elements that can be united into a whole by a law") in his 1883 definition. The only purist is Frege who does seem to hold exclusively to the logical conception in a pure undiluted form.

III

For Russell the concept of class was beset with difficulties, and most of these difficulties seemed to him not to afflict class concepts (attributes, propositional functions). The class concept "even prime number" is readily distinguished from the number 2, which is the only object falling under that concept, and the class concept "present king of France" is as unobjectionable as any other even though nothing falls under it. Also, each class concept is a single logical subject, however many objects fall under it. Hence Russell's asymmetry of skepticism. The one remaining difficulty is, of course, "the contradiction."

Russell formulates "the contradiction" both in terms of predicates and in terms of classes (1937, p. 102). Thus from the start he held the view that there is a single contradiction capable of appearing in various forms. Given his general skepticism about classes, which rests on considerations apart from those connected with the contradiction, it was natural for Russell to assume that the most fundamental form of the antinomy was the intensional form concerning predicates. In Russell's celebrated letter of 16 June 1902, in which he informs Frege of the existence of the antinomy, he gives both formulations (Frege 1980, pp. 130–131). For Frege, of course, it is the extensional formulation in terms of classes that is most important, because it brings with it the downfall of his system. Predicates (concepts, functions) for Frege are arranged in a simple type hierarchy, but classes are all "objects" without distinction of type. This leads directly to the inconsistency of his set theory.

Russell writes in his intellectual autobiography, *My Philosophical Development*, that his discovery of the theory of descriptions was his first real insight into the solution of the antinomy about classes. "Throughout 1903 and 1904, my work was almost wholly devoted to this matter [the contradiction], but without any vestige of success. My first success was the theory of descriptions, in the spring of 1905" (1959, p. 79). Now, nothing in Russell's "On Denoting" of 1905 directly concerns the antinomies or the theory of logical types, so just what in the theory of descriptions did Russell find to lead to his final resolution of the antinomies? The answer must be that the key to Russell's solution to his problem about denoting lies in his use of the idea of an incomplete symbol. An incomplete symbol, such as a definite description, is one that has the superficial grammar of a singular term but functions logically as a syncategorematic expression that contributes to the sense of the whole proposition containing it while having no independent meaning of its own. Class abstracts on this view have no independent meaning and they refer to nothing. In particular, they do not stand for classes. If such a theory of classes can be carried through, it will treat classes as logical constructions whose real existence need not be assumed. This is what Russell accomplishes in his no-classes theory. It does not rest on an explicit denial of the reality of classes, but it proceeds without having ever to explicitly commit itself to their reality. The no-classes theory that Russell finally adopts implements his initial skepticism about classes. It treats them as a mere *façon de parler.*

The logical construction of classes out of propositional functions is effected by definition *20.01.

$$*20.01 \quad f\{\hat{z}(\psi z)\}. = : (\exists \varphi) : \varphi!x . \equiv_x .\psi x: f\{\varphi!\hat{z}\} \quad \text{Df.}$$

This provides a contextual definition of the class abstract $\hat{z}(\psi z)$ in the propositional context $f\{\hat{z}(\psi z)\}$; hence it provides for the elimination of class abstracts from any atomic propositional context containing them. Classes differ from propositional functions solely on the ground of extensionality. Classes are extensions, whereas propositional functions are intensions. This means that coextensive propositional functions need not be identical, but classes whose members are the same are themselves the same. In order to justify definition *20.01 therefore, we see that it is necessary that it should secure the extensionality of classes. Extensionality is expressed as

$$\vdash:. \hat{z}(\varphi z) = \hat{z}(\psi z). \equiv :\varphi x. \equiv_x .\psi x.$$

The proof is as follows: $\hat{z}(\varphi z) = \hat{z}(\psi z)$ expands, by definition *20.01 (and Russell's convention, which accords to the first occurring incomplete symbol the largest scope), to

$$(\exists \chi) :\varphi x. \equiv_x . \chi!x:\chi!\hat{z} = \hat{z}(\psi z).$$

Another application of definition *20.01 effects the elimination of the remaining class abstract:

$$(\exists \chi):.\varphi x. \equiv_x .\chi!x:.(\exists \theta): \psi x. \equiv_x .\theta!x:\chi!\hat{z} = \theta!\hat{z}.$$

This is equivalent to

$$(\exists\chi.\ \theta):\ \varphi x.\ \equiv_x .\chi!x:\ \psi x.\ \equiv_x .\theta!x:\chi!\hat{z} = \theta!\hat{z}.$$

This, by laws of identity is equivalent to

$$(\exists\chi)\ :\varphi x\ .\ \equiv_x .\chi!x:\psi x.\ \equiv_x .\chi!x.$$

$(\exists\chi)\ :\varphi x.\ \equiv_x .\chi!x$ is an axiom of reducibility; hence the last displayed formula is equivalent to

$$\psi x.\ \equiv_x .\varphi x \qquad \text{Q.E.D.}$$

(All of this proof is taken from Whitehead and Russell (1910, p. 78).)

A second definition, *20.02, introduces ϵ contextually as a relation between an individual and a propositional function:

$$*20.02 \quad x\epsilon\ (\varphi!\hat{z}).\ =\ .\varphi!x \quad \text{Df.}$$

The only role for this definition is to enable Russell to introduce ϵ in its usual meaning as the relation of class membership – $x\ \epsilon\ \hat{z}(\varphi z)$. Definition *20.02 does this together with definition *20.01 by securing the law of class comprehension.

$$*20.3 \quad \vdash:x\ \epsilon\ \hat{z}(\psi z).\ \equiv\ .\psi x.$$

It is of interest to examine the proof of this theorem in order to see how crucial the axiom of reducibility is to Russell's entire construction. (We have already seen one example of this in the proof of the extensionality of classes.)

The proof for theorem *20.3 is as follows:

$$x\ \epsilon\hat{z}(\psi z).\ \equiv\ :.(\exists\varphi):.\psi y.\ \equiv_y .\varphi!y:x\ \epsilon\ (\varphi!\hat{z})$$

is a theorem by definition *20.01. This, by definition *20.02, is equivalent to

$$x\ \epsilon\hat{z}(\psi z).\ \equiv\ :.(\exists\varphi):.\psi y\ .\ \equiv_y .\ \varphi!y\ :\varphi!x,$$

which, by second-order logic, is equivalent to

$$x\ \epsilon\hat{z}(\psi z).\ \equiv\ :.(\exists\varphi):.\psi y\ .\ \equiv_y .\ \varphi!y\ :\psi x.$$

Again, by quantifier laws, this is equivalent to

$$x \in \hat{z}(\psi z). \equiv :. \ (\exists \varphi): \psi y. \equiv_{\,y} .\varphi! y :. \psi x.$$

The left conjunct of the right-hand side of this biconditional is an axiom of reducibility. Hence the biconditional itself is equivalent to

$$x \in \hat{z}(\psi z). \equiv .\psi x, \qquad \text{Q.E.D.}$$

We can now return to our discussion of Russell's resolution of his antinomy about classes in *Principia Mathematica*. The antinomy arises from consideration of the class of all classes that are not members of themselves:

$$\hat{a}\ (\alpha \notin \alpha).$$

Suppose first that this class is a member of itself:

$$\hat{a}\ (\alpha \notin \alpha) \in \hat{a}(\alpha \notin \alpha).$$

Then, by the appropriate form of the law of class comprehension proven in what follows,

$$\hat{a}\ (\alpha \notin \alpha) \notin_{\alpha} (\alpha \notin \alpha).$$

Conversely, if $\hat{a}\ (\alpha \notin \alpha)$ is not a member of itself, then by the same law it does not satisfy its own defining condition, that is,

$$\hat{a}\ (\alpha \notin \alpha) \in \hat{a}(\alpha \notin \alpha).$$

Hence "the contradiction."

To see how Russell resolves the antinomy, we must first reformulate it within his no-classes theory of classes. Because the existence of classes is not assumed in the *Principia*, the antinomy must make its appearance in its predicative form if it is to be dealt with at all. First, an explanation is required of the use of the lower-case Greek letters α and β in the formulation of the antinomy. These are explained as schematic letters that hold places for class abstracts. "The representation of a class by a single letter α can now be understood. For the denotation of α is ambiguous, in so far as it is undecided as to which of the symbols $\hat{z}(\varphi z)$, $\hat{z}(\psi z)$, $\hat{z}(\chi z)$, etc. it is to stand for, where $\varphi \hat{z}$, $\psi \hat{z}$, $\chi \hat{z}$, etc. are the various determining functions of the class" (Whitehead and Russell 1910, p. 80). Accordingly, Russell introduces the expression $\hat{a}(f\alpha)$ for the class of classes that satisfies the condition $f\alpha$, and he provides a contextual definition for it with definition *20.08, which is an analogue of *20.01:

$$\text{*20.08} \quad f\{\hat{a}(\psi\alpha)\}. = :(\exists\varphi):\psi\alpha. \equiv_\alpha .\varphi!\alpha: f(\varphi!\hat{a}) \quad \text{Df.}$$

(see also Whitehead and Russell 1910, p. 79). Similarly, he introduces an analogue of definition *20.02:

$$\text{*20.081.} \quad \alpha \, \varepsilon \, \psi \, !\alpha. = .\psi \, !\alpha \quad \text{Df.}$$

(see also Whitehead and Russell 1910, p. 79). This, in turn, enables Russell to prove the required form of the law of class comprehension:

$$\gamma \in \hat{a}(f\alpha). \equiv .f\gamma.$$

We can now turn our attention to the class of all classes that are not members of themselves, $\hat{a}(\alpha \notin \alpha)$. To formulate the antinomy we must consider the purported proposition

$$\hat{a}(\alpha \notin \alpha) \in \hat{a} \, (\alpha \notin \alpha).$$

But, if this collection of symbols were to have a meaning, it would mean, by double application of definition *20.08,

$$(\exists g): \alpha \notin \alpha. \equiv_\alpha .g!\alpha: g!\hat{\gamma} \notin g!\hat{\gamma}.$$

This, in turn, by definition *20.081 expands to

$$(\exists g): \sim (\alpha \in \alpha). \equiv_\alpha .g!\alpha: \sim \{g!(g!\hat{\gamma})\}.$$

Here the expression $g!(g!\hat{\gamma})$ occurs, and it assigns a propositional function as argument to itself. This is prohibited by the theory of logical types, and this is Russell's resolution of his antinomy about classes.

The definition *20.08 uses the letter α as a subscript to express universal quantification, and indeed Russell feels free to use lower-case Greek letters as apparent (bound) variables. This will perhaps puzzle contemporary readers familiar with Quine's dictum: *to be is to be a value of a bound variable*. The use of lower-case Greek letters as bound variables ranging over classes is prima facie incompatible with Russell's explicit program of treating classes as logical fictions. Two more definitions set the matter straight:

$$\text{*20.07} \quad (\alpha).f(\alpha). = .(\varphi)f\{\hat{z}(\varphi!z)\} \quad \text{Df.}$$

$$*20.071 \quad (\exists\alpha).f(\alpha). = .(\exists\varphi).f\{\hat{z}(\varphi!z)\} \quad \text{Df.}$$

By eliminating the class abstract, we see that *20.07 becomes

$$(\alpha).f(\alpha). = .(\varphi):(\exists\psi).\varphi!x \equiv_x \psi !x.f\{\psi\hat{z}\} \quad \text{Df.}$$

In similar fashion, definition *20.08 effects the elimination of the class abstract from *20.071. Thus there is no real quantification over classes. It also is a mere *façon de parler* (Whitehead and Russell 1910, p. 81). Russell concludes, "Accordingly, in mathematical reasoning, we can dismiss the whole apparatus of functions and think only of classes as 'quasi-things', capable of immediate representation by a single name" (Whitehead and Russell 1910, p. 81). Classes are quasi-things and quantification over them is quasi-quantification. The schematic letters α, β do not really play the role of bound variables. Definitions *20.07 and *20.071 expose the fiction.

Definitions *20.07 and *20.071 introduce lower-case Greek letters as bound (apparent) variables that range over classes, but the classes are all determined by predicative functions. Nevertheless, there is no real loss of generality here in view of the theorem

$$*20.151 \quad \vdash.(\exists\varphi).\hat{z}(\psi z) = \hat{z}(\varphi!z).$$

Russell remarks: "In virtue of this proposition, all classes can be obtained from predicative functions. This fact is especially important when classes are used as apparent variables" (Whitehead and Russell 1910, p. 192). He notes that definitions *20.07 and *20.071 make reference only to classes determined by predicative functions, but then he observes, "In virtue of *20.151 this places no limitations upon the classes concerned" (Whitehead and Russell 1910, p. 192).

IV

Russell's resolution of his antinomy about classes turns on the rejection of the expression $g!(g!\hat{\gamma})$ as not well formed. The justification for this is that a function cannot take itself as argument according to the theory of types. This is also Russell's resolution of the antinomy in its predicative form; thus Russell has vindicated his original conviction that we are dealing essentially with just one antinomy. The rejection of $g!(g!\hat{\gamma})$ does not turn on any specific consideration about the internal structure of the propositional function. *No* function whatever can take itself as argument. In particular, this prohibition does not depend on the range of values of the quantifiers occurring in the propositional function. Considerations of quantifiers do not enter into the resolution of this antinomy. The resolution invokes only the simple type hierarchy that consists of a ground level of "individuals," propositional functions from individuals to propositions, functions of *these* functions to propositions, and so on up to any finite iteration. Transfinite types are disallowed.

According to the ramified theory of types a propositional function that contains quantifications over propositional functions of order n or that contains free variables whose values are propositional functions of order n is itself at least of order $n + 1$. The range of significance of a propositional function must always be restricted to a given order, and the range of any bound variable must be confined to functions of a given order. Consequently, no function can fall within the range of one of its own bound variables. A function that falls within the range of one of its own quantifiers is said to be *impredicative*, and the ramified theory of types excludes this kind of impredicativity. It is clear that this kind of impredicativity is not, on Russell's analysis, the source of the antinomy about classes. Consequently, his resolution of the antinomy does not depend on the exclusion of this kind of impredicativity by the ramified theory of types.

Impredicative propositional functions are excluded by what Russell calls the "vicious-circle" principle. Russell's analysis of the antinomies finds them as arising, in one way or another, from violations of the vicious-circle principle and as thus committing a kind of fallacy of circularity. Gödel claims that there are actually three forms of the principle involved in Russell's analysis. "This led to the formulation of a principle which says that no totality can contain members definable only in terms of this totality, or members involving or presupposing this totality" (Gödel 1983, p. 454). What is prohibited by these forms of the principle is the definition or specification of any object with the use of a quantifier within whose range there falls the very object being defined or specified. Gödel notes that none of these forms of the vicious-circle principle inhibits the predicative form of Russell's antinomy. "In order to make this principle applicable to the intensional paradoxes, still another principle had to be assumed, namely that 'every propositional function presupposes the totality of its values' and evidently also the totality of its possible arguments" (Gödel 1983, p. 454). Gödel adds, in explanation, "Otherwise the concept of 'not applying to itself', would presuppose no totality (since it involves no quantifications), and the vicious circle principle would not prevent its application to itself" (Gödel 1983, p. 454). If every propositional function presupposes the totality of its arguments, it evidently cannot itself be one of its arguments, for such a propositional function would circularly presuppose itself. We have seen that on Russell's theory of classes the extensional form of the antinomy (about classes) reduces to the intensional form involving self-predication. Hence it is this last form of the vicious-circle principle, which prohibits a propositional function from being among its own arguments, that is the only form involved in the resolution of the antinomy about classes.

The importance of the vicious-circle principle, for Russell, is that it constitutes his analysis of the fallacy that lies at the root of the logical and set-theoretic antinomies. Therefore it is Russell's philosophical justification for the ramified theory of types. But what justifies the vicious-circle principle in its turn? We ask our question in the present context, specifically, about that form of the principle, as distinguished by Gödel, that prohibits any propositional function from taking itself as argument. It is granted, of course, that any well-determined function must have both a well-determined domain and a well-determined range. But why can't a function belong to its own domain? The obvious answer is that this threatens antinomy. But this was not Russell's answer, for, because the vicious-circle principle is his justification for the theory of types, he cannot in turn call on the theory of types to justify the vicious-circle principle. Russell believed that this form of the vicious-circle principle followed from the very nature of propositional functions.

"It would seem," Russell says, "that the essential characteristic of a function is *ambiguity*" (Whitehead and Russell 1910, p. 39). When we assert a propositional function, Russell holds that there is no one thing that is the object of our assertion. "When we speak of 'φx', where x is not specified, we mean one value of the function, but not a definite one. We may express this by saying that 'φx' *ambiguously denotes* φa, φb, φc, etc., where φa, φb, φc, etc. are the various values of 'φx'" (Whitehead and Russell 1910, p. 39). The use of the expression "ambiguously denotes" here indicates that what Russell is referring to is a *concept* and not an open sentence, in spite of the quotation marks, "φx". "When we say that 'φx' ambiguously denotes φa, φb, φc, etc., we mean that 'φx' means one of the objects φa, φb, φc, etc. though not a definite one, but an undetermined one" (Whitehead and Russell 1910, p. 39). Russell then observes that the function φx is well defined only if the objects φa, φb, φc, etc. are well defined. "It follows from this that no function can have among its values anything which presupposes the function, for if it had, we could not regard the objects ambiguously denoted by the function as definite until the function was definite, while conversely, as we have just seen, the function cannot be definite until its values are definite" (Whitehead and Russell 1910, p. 39).

Let us briefly summarize the argument of the last few paragraphs. Russell analyzes the antinomy about classes as arising from a vicious-circle fallacy. In particular, no function can apply to itself as argument. In order for this to be a genuine explanation, there must be an argument for it that is independent of the consideration that allowing functions to apply to themselves leads directly to the intensional form of the antinomy. Russell provides that argument in the considerations that lead him to conclude that the relevant prohibition arises from the very nature of propositional functions.

> A function is what ambiguously denotes some one of a certain totality, namely the values of the function; hence this totality cannot contain any members which involve the function, since, if it did, it would contain members involving the totality, which by the vicious-circle principle, no totality can do.
>
> (Whitehead and Russell 1910, p. 39)

For Russell, then, a function is an object whose essence is to be ambiguous. It is this that explains, perhaps, why the "ancient problem of the One and the Many," which so puzzled Russell about classes, does not produce in him a corresponding skepticism about propositional functions. One can hardly raise the question of whether an ambiguity is one or many. In particular, classes, if they exist, are supposed to be full-fledged objects with a clear ontological status. A propositional function, by contrast, seems to be somewhere between being and nonbeing. It was in just such considerations of the attenuated and insubstantial character of propositional functions that Russell, early on, sought a solution for his antinomy. In section 85 of *Principles*, written shortly after his discovery of the antinomy in early 1901, he writes:

> It is to be observed that, according to the theory of propositional functions here advocated, the φ in φx is not a separate and distinguishable entity: it lives in propositions of the form φx and cannot survive analysis. . . . If φ were a distinguishable entity, there would be a proposition asserting φ of itself, which we denote by $\varphi(\varphi)$; there would also be a proposition not-$\varphi(\varphi)$, denying $\varphi(\varphi)$.
>
> (Russell 1937, p. 88)

Russell then goes on to derive the intensional (predicative) form of his antinomy. He resolves the antinomy as follows: "The contradiction is avoided by the recognition that the functional part of a propositional function is not an independent entity" (Russell 1937, p. 88). From this it follows that propositional functions cannot be logical subjects. Russell expresses a doubt as to whether this view is itself consistent (1937, p. 88). He does not tell us what contradiction it is to which he fears this view of propositional functions may lead, but he had earlier discovered Frege's paradox of the concept "horse" (Russell 1937, p. 46). He concludes from this that "this results from the previous argument that every constituent of every proposition must, on pain of self-contradiction, be capable of being made a logical subject" (1937, p. 48).

Russell's view, at the time of *Principles*, is much like Frege's idea of functions as "incomplete" and "unsaturated" entities that cannot play the role of logical subjects. But Russell is, unlike Frege, unwilling to embrace the paradox to which it leads, and in *Principia* he finds another reason to deny that functions can take themselves as arguments. Russell retains his view of the attenuated and insubstantial nature of propositional functions, but it leaves the actual logic of *Principia Mathematica* unaffected. So far as that logic is concerned, propositional functions are as solid as rocks. They fall within the range of values of *Principia*'s higher-order quantifiers, and expressions for them have uninhibited access to the identity predicate. To be a value of a bound variable is to be, to reverse Quine's dictum. No identity without an entity, to reverse another. Identity is, after all, *idem-entity*, to invoke yet a third.

Propositional functions cannot take themselves as arguments because, on Russell's *Principia* view, their arguments and values are logically prior to them. Given a collection of objects and one of propositions, we can make sense of functions whose domain is the collection of objects and whose range is the collection of propositions. This gives us a new collection to be the domain of a new collection of functions. What we have is an iterative concept of functions, which is formally similar to Cantor's original iterative concept of sets. Just as Cantor's concept excludes self-membership, Russell's concept excludes self-predication.

V

In his introduction to the first edition of *Principia Mathematica*, Russell explicitly rejects the extensional interpretation of propositional functions:

> [T]wo functions may well be formally equivalent without being identical; for example
>
> $x = \text{Scott}. \equiv_x .x = \text{the author of Waverley}$
>
> but the function "$\hat{z} = $ the author of Waverley" has the property that George IV wished to know whether its value with the argument "Scott" was true, whereas the function "$\hat{z} = $ Scott" has no such property, and therefore the two functions are not identical.
>
> (Whitehead and Russell 1910, pp. 83–84)

It is evident from this quotation that Russell requires propositional functions to be intensional in order to enable him to provide a solution to the problem of informative statements of identity. In *Principles* he asks, "Why is it ever worthwhile to affirm identity?" (1937, p. 64), and it is clear that his problem is the same as Frege's. If it is true that $a = b$, how can this tell us anything other than just that $a = a$? How can $\hat{x}(\varphi x) = \hat{x}(\psi x)$ ever differ in "cognitive value," to use Frege's expression, from $\hat{x}(\varphi x) = \hat{x}(\varphi x)$, provided that the former is true? "Creatures with a heart are creatures with a kidney" is informative, whereas "Creatures with a heart are creatures with a heart" is not.

The Russellian solution to this form of Frege's puzzle is exactly the same as his solution to the form of the puzzle involving definite descriptions. Classes are regarded as logical constructions and their names – class abstracts – are incomplete symbols, just as are definite descriptions. Classes are not part of the ultimate logical furniture of the world. The basic definition is given in definition *20.01. The informative identity $\hat{x}(\theta x) = \hat{x}(\psi x)$ is, in accordance with this definition, an abbreviation for

$$(\exists \varphi) :. \varphi! x. \equiv_x .\psi x:. (\exists \pi): \pi! x. \equiv_x .\theta x: \pi! \hat{x} = \varphi! \hat{x}. \tag{1}$$

The trivial identity $\hat{x}(\theta x) = \hat{x}(\theta x)$, on the other hand, is an abbreviation of

$$(\exists \varphi) :. \varphi! x. \equiv_x .\theta x:. (\exists \pi): \pi! x. \equiv_x .\theta x: \pi! \hat{x} = \varphi! \hat{x}. \tag{2}$$

If Russell is to have a solution to Frege's puzzle on his no-classes theory, formulas (1) and (2) must differ in cognitive value. But formulas (1) and (2) differ only in that formula (1) contains a reference to the propositional function $\psi\hat{x}$, whereas (2) contains a reference to the propositional function $\theta\hat{x}$. On the extensional interpretation $\psi\hat{x}$ and $\theta\hat{x}$ are the *same* propositional function, because by formula (1) they are coextensive with propositional functions identical with each other. On the extensional interpretation, coextensiveness is the principle of individuation for propositional functions. On Russell's denotational theory of meaning, formulas (1) and (2) cannot differ in meaning on this extensional interpretation of propositional functions. The conclusion is that propositional functions must be intensions on pain of depriving Russell of his solution to this form of Frege's paradox about identity. The no-classes theory constructs extensions out of intensions.

Our discussion of Russell's no-classes theory applies only to the first edition of *Principia Mathematica*. In the second edition (1925), Russell adopts Wittgenstein's thesis of extensionality.

There is another course recommended by Wittgenstein for philosophical reasons. This is to assume that functions of propositions are always truth-functions, and that a function can only occur in a proposition through its values. . . . It involves the consequence that all functions of functions are extensional. . . . We are not prepared to assert that this theory is certainly right, but it has seemed worthwhile to work out its consequences in the following pages.

(Whitehead and Russell 1925, p. xiv)

One consequence, not noted by Russell, is that the no-classes theory is abandoned in the second edition of *Principia*. If all functions are extensional, there ceases to be any difference between classes and propositional functions. Classes then, are assumed outright in the second edition. They are not logical constructions.[1]

Note

1 This section is an elaboration of pages 27–28 of Linsky (1983).

Bibliography

Cantor, George. 1895–1897. "Beiträge zur Begündung der transfiniten Mengenlehre," in his *Gesammelte Abhandlungen Mathematischen und Philosophischen Inhalts*, 282–356.

Cantor, Georg. 1915. *Contributions to the Founding of the Theory of Transfinite Numbers*, trans. P. E. B. Jourdain, New York: Dover.

Cantor, Georg. 1932. *Gesammelte Abhandlungen Mathematischen und Philosophischen Inhalts*, ed. Ernst Zermelo, Hildesheim: Georg Olms Verlagsbuchhandlung.

Frege, Gottlob. 1885. *Die Grundlagen der Arithmetik*. Breslau: Verlag von Wilhelm Koebner.

Frege, Gottlob. 1980. *Philosophical and Mathematical Correspondence of Gottlob Frege*, ed. Brian McGuinness, trans. Hans Kaal, Chicago: University of Chicago Press.

Gödel, Kurt. 1983. "Russell's mathematical logic," in *Philosophy of Mathematics*, eds Paul Benacerraf and Hilary Putnam, Cambridge: Cambridge University Press, 447–469.

Linsky, Leonard. 1983. *Oblique Contexts*. Chicago: University of Chicago Press.

Parsons, Charles. 1976. "Some remarks on Frege's conception of extension," in *Studien zu Frege*, ed. Matthias Schirn, Stuttgart–Bad Cannstadt: Frommann Verlag, vol. 1, 265–277.

Russell, Bertrand. 1929. *Our Knowledge of the External World*. Chicago: Open Court. (First edition, 1914.)

Russell, Bertrand. 1937. *Principles of Mathematics*, Second edition. New York: Norton. (First edition, 1903.) Cambridge: Cambridge University Press.

Russell, Bertrand. 1959. *My Philosophical Development*. New York: Simon and Schuster.

Van Heijenoort, Jean. 1967. *From Frege to Gödel*. Cambridge, Mass.: Harvard University Press.

Wang, Hao. 1983. "The concept of set," in *Philosophy of Mathematics*, eds Paul Benacerraf and Hilary Putnam, Cambridge: Cambridge University Press, 530–570.

Whitehead, A. N., and Russell, Bertrand. 1910. *Principia Mathematica*. Cambridge: The University Press. (Second edition, 1925.)

19

New Evidence concerning Russell's Substitutional Theory of Classes*

Gregory Landini

Introduction

It is well known that Russell regarded his new theory of denoting (of 1905) as the conceptual breakthrough that 'made it possible to see, in a general way, how a solution of the contradictions might be possible' (Schilpp 1944, p. 14). The solution, of course, was the non-assumption of classes as single logical subjects. The theory of denoting was an important first step because it showed the way to provide a treatment of classes *as if* they were single logical subjects. In his 1908 article, 'Mathematical Logic as Based on the Theory of Types', we find the following contextual definition effecting this solution:

$$f\{x : \psi x\} = df(\exists \phi)((x)(\phi!x \equiv \psi x) \& f(\phi!\hat{z})).$$

The contextual definition appears to make the assumption of propositional functions as single logical subjects; and this has come to be the accepted view. But, according to Russell, the non-assumption of classes realized here employs only the 'technical convenience' of using symbols for propositional functions in subject positions. The convenience was supposed to be eliminable by using a technique of substitution (Russell 1908, p. 89).

Just what substitutional technique Russell had in mind remained a mystery for some time, however. On 14 December 1905 Russell had read an article entitled "On Some Difficulties in the Theory of Transfinite Numbers and Order Types" before the London Mathematical Society. (The article was subsequently published in the proceedings of the society on 7 March 1906.) In it he set out the main alternatives for avoiding the contradiction. The preferred alternative was a substitutional theory according to which neither classes nor propositional functions were assumed as single logical subjects. Because the contradiction was formulable in terms of functions,

Russell felt that 'the assumption of propositional functions is open to the same arguments, pro and con, as the admission of classes' (Russell 1905, p. 154). It was this early theory of substitution which was the direct result of Russell's studies on the new theory of denoting. The theory was able to treat classes as if they were single logical subjects, and it allowed what would be quantification over classes. Moreover, by assuming propositions (true or false) as single logical subjects instead of propositional functions or classes, the theory built homogeneous typing into the logical form of propositions whose grammatical form suggested that they were about classes. In this way, Russell avoided having types of logical subjects, and the univocity of being of all logical subjects was preserved.

None the less, the subsequent articles in which Russell went on to elaborate a substitutional theory of classes and relations went largely unnoticed. Russell himself was partly the cause. Its first detailed public elaboration in 'On the Substitutional Theory of Classes and Relations' (1906a) was read before the London Mathematical Society in May of 1906, but the article was withdrawn from publication. Russell's decision to withdraw the article seems to be related to his desire to include a solution of what are now called 'semantic' paradoxes such as the Liar Paradox. In a letter to Jourdain dated 14 June Russell wrote:

> I feel more and more certain that this theory is right. In order, however, to solve the *Epimenides*, it is necessary to extend it to *general* proposi-tions, i.e., to such as $(x) . \phi x$ and $(\exists x) . \phi x$. This I shall explain in my answer to Poincaré's article in the current *Revue de Métaphysique*.
> (Quoted from Grattan-Guinness 1977, p. 89)

Poincaré's article was 'Les Mathématiques et la Logique'. It contained criticisms of the new mathematics of the infinite and a proposed solution – namely, the Vicious Circle Principle. Russell was eager to address the criticisms and explain that his substitutional theory is what is required by adherence to the Vicious Circle Principle. In September Russell published his reply entitled 'Les Paradoxes de la Logique' (1906b). (The English title is: 'On "Insolubilia" and Their Solution by Symbolic Logic'.) In it he espoused the substitutional theory, and as promised in his letter to Jourdain, it was now extended to account for the Liar Paradox.

In Russell's mind, Poincaré's Vicious Circle Principle revealed the source of the paradoxes. According to the principle, 'whatever involves an appar-ent [bound] variable must not be among the possible values of the variable' (Russell 1906b, p. 204). Since the variable is to be unrestricted, Russell's conclusion is that no single entities involve apparent variables. In the Paradox of the Liar we have the statement: 'There is some proposition I am now asserting and it is false.' If this statement itself expresses a pro-position, then it would be a value of its own apparent variable; and the contradiction ensues. Russell's solution was to maintain that there are no generalized propositions – that is, there are no propositions which contain apparent variables. Only those statements that do not contain quantifier phrases express propositions. Thus, the statement of the Liar does not express a single proposition and so cannot be within the range of its own variable.

Russell realized there were difficulties in abandoning propositions containing apparent variables. In particular, since quantifiers could only range over propositions not containing apparent variables, he had to introduce a 'reducibility axiom' so that what would amount to quantification over generalized propositions could be effected. But in so far as his article indicates, Russell thought he had reconciled the substitutional theory with the Liar Paradox.

His published article notwithstanding, Russell's unpublished manuscripts from the period are filled with criticisms of the theory's commitment to propositions as single logical subjects, and to all appearances quantification over propositional functions is reintroduced. It seems, therefore, that the semantic paradoxes such as that of the Liar led Russell to abandon the substitutional theory late in 1906. The accepted view has come to be that by 1908 it is propositional functions and not propositions that are the values of the variables of quantification. Indeed, this interpretation seems to be encouraged by Russell himself. For in the article 'The Theory of Logical Types' published in 1910 he proclaims that 'there are no propositions'; and says he is explaining the views he set out in his earlier 1908 article (Russell 1910, p. 215).

It is difficult, however, to reconcile this view with the fact that Russell explicitly endorses a substitutional technique in his 1908 article. In a recent paper I have argued that the substitutional theory played a more central role in the historical development of the mature theory of types than has been thought (Landini 1987). Behind the technical conveniences of the notation of propositional functions, Russell was espousing a modified version of the substitutional theory in 1908.

Although Russell says he is explaining the 1908 theory in 'The Theory of Logical Types', it would be a mistake to conflate these two theories (Cocchiarella 1980, pp. 95ff.). For in 1908 Russell does allow quantification over propositions. To deal with the semantic paradoxes such as the Liar, he introduced a hierarchy of 'orders' of propositions based upon the admissible ranges of apparent variables for propositions. Moreover, the ramified hierarchy of orders of propositional functions is defined by reference to this propositional hierarchy (Russell 1908, p. 77). Thus, propositions are assumed as single logical subjects in 1908.

Further, I have discovered that from a historical standpoint the substitutional theory is inseparably linked with the 1908 hierarchy of propositions. The possibility of there being such a link came to my attention by examining Cocchiarella's observation that the substitutional theory is in conflict with Cantor's power-class theorem (Cocchiarella 1980, p. 90). The conflict yields a paradox which stems from the assumption of propositions as entities. The paradox is intensional in nature, since its formulation turns on the identity of propositions and Russell held that equivalent propositions need not be identical. In this respect, the paradox is like that of the Liar. Indeed, Russell considered it to be among the 'paradoxes of propositions' which are all of the same sort as the Epimenides. But the paradox does not depend upon semantic notions such as 'designation' or 'truth' and thus it should not be characterized as a 'semantic' paradox. None the less, Russell's 1908 hierarchy of 'orders' of propositions blocks this paradox no less so than the Liar, and the addition of the axiom of reducibility does not change this.

There seems to be no explicit acknowledgement of the conflict and its connection with the hierarchy of propositions in Russell's published writings on type-theory. However, I have recently discovered evidence in unpublished manuscripts that Russell was aware of the conflict. Most important is the manuscript entitled 'The Paradox of the Liar'. (The manuscript is dated September 1906, but seems to have been written after the article 'Les Paradoxes de la Logique'.) Here Russell not only points out the *syntactic* conflict, he uses a 1908-style hierarchy of 'orders' of propositions to avoid it.[1] This new evidence is revealed in what follows.

Classes in the Substitutional Theory

In order to see the conflict we must briefly present a sketch of how the substitutional theory (of April–May 1906) uses matrices to represent propositional functions of individuals. Russell introduces the notation 'p/a' which he calls a 'matrix'. (Both 'p' and 'a' are taken to be names of logical subjects, and Russell calls the proposition named by 'p' the "prototype".) Next he introduces the notation '$p/a;b$' which abbreviates the expression 'the result of substituting b for every occurrence of a in p'. As with all definite descriptions, the expression '$p/a;b$' is an incomplete symbol and can never occur in isolation. It is to be contextually defined in accordance with the 1905 theory of definite descriptions as follows:

$$\psi(p/a;b) = df(\exists q)(p/a;b!q \ \& \ (r)(p/a;b!r \supset r = q) \ \& \ \psi(q)).$$

The notation '$p/a;b!q$' abbreviates 'q results from substituting b for every occurrence of a in p'. Thus, while '$p/a;b$' is an incomplete symbol, '$p/a;b!q$' expresses a proposition. Russell goes on to define the negation of a proposition as follows:

$\sim p = df\ p$ is false.

He then defines ' $\sim (p/a\dot{}b)$' as '$(\exists^1 q)(p/a\dot{}b!q\ \&\ \sim q)$'. Here we use '$(\exists^1)$' to abbreviate 'exactly one' and define it in the usual way.

Russell expresses quantification by means of the notation '$(x)(p/a\dot{}x$ is true)', which would be contextually defined as '$(x)((\exists^1 q)(p/a\dot{}x!q\ \&\ q$ is true))'. Quantification should be interpreted objectually. Since Russell explicitly says that it is an entity which is to be substituted for the entity a in the proposition p, the values of the quantifiers must range over logical subjects (i.e., all 'entities' including propositions), not over constants and sentences. Any inclination to interpret the substitutional theory of 1906 as akin to the modern substitutional interpretation of quantification should, therefore, be avoided.[2]

As we can see, the substitutional theory assumes that there are primitive object-language predicates 'truth' and 'falsehood' which stand for properties of propositions. His 1905 theory of definite descriptions, elaborated in 'On Denoting', also reflects this view. Russell set out the basis of the view in his 1904 review of Meinong's Theory of Complexes and Assumptions. He wrote: 'It may be said, and this I think is the correct view, that there is no problem at all in truth and falsehood; that some propositions are true and some are false, just as some roses are red and some white' (p. 75). On this early view, 'truth' is not a semantic relation between a sentence (or mental entity) and a proposition, but is rather an unanalysable property of propositions themselves.

By 1910, however, Russell came to develop a 'correspondence' theory of truth, and his new view acknowledged that 'truth' involves what we now call 'semantic' elements. But the substitutional theory should not be thought to be committed to a semantic truth predicate in its object-language. The truth-predicate need not appear when a context is given which would complete the symbol '$p/a\dot{}b$'. We can see this, for example, in the definition of the coextensivity of propositional functions of individuals:

$$p/a = p'/a' \ = df(x)\{(\exists^1 q)(\exists^1 r)([p/a\dot{}x!q]\ \&\ [p'/a'\dot{}x!r]\ \&\ (r \equiv q))\}.$$

Moreover, where Russell wrote '$(p/a\dot{}b$ is true)', which he contextually defined as '$(\exists^1)(p/a\dot{}b!q\ \&\ q$ is true)', we can simply write '$(\exists^1 q)\ (p/a\dot{}b!q\ \&\ q)$'. There is, therefore, no essential dependency on an object-language truth-predicate in the substitutional theory.[3]

Now Russell's motivation for using matrices to represent propositional functions was quite clear. In a notation reflecting the assumption of propositional functions as single logical subjects, propositional functions would be represented by the expression '$\phi\hat{x}$'. But in Russell's view, the variable 'x' in 'ϕx' is logical or formal and thus must be wholly unrestricted; it ranges over all logical subjects. The laws of logic do not have a restricted scope. They are universally valid for all logical subjects. The unrestricted variable of logic reflects what Russell had called in *The Principles of Mathematics* the doctrine of the 'univocity of being of all logical subjects', and he never gave up this fundamental view. So if propositional functions are indeed logical subjects, then there should be nothing which prevents them from applying to themselves; and yet this is what led to the paradox. The theory of homogeneous types was to avoid this. But because of the doctrine of the univocity of being of all logical subjects, a theory of types of logical subjects is philosophically impossible.

However, if the symbols for propositional functions are taken to be incomplete, and to be contextually defined, then it is possible to build the theory of types into the logical form of their contextual definitions. Russell's matrices do just this. Matrices of the form 'p/a' go proxy for propositional functions of individuals. Dyadic relations of individuals are represented in terms of matrices of the form '$q/(a,b)$'; triadic relations are represented in terms of matrices of the form '$q/(a,b,c)$', and so on. Propositional functions of functions of individuals are next constructed in terms of matrices of the form '$q/(r/c)$', or alternatively '$q/(r,c)$, where 'r/c' is understood to form a function of individuals. To express what would be the predication of the one function of the other Russell writes '$\{q/(r/c)'p/a\}$ is true' or alternatively '$\{q/(r,c)'p,a\}$ is true'. The notation '$q/(r,c)'p,a$' abbreviates 'the result of simultaneously substituting p for every occurrence of r and a for every occurrence of c in q'.

Higher types of functions are constructed in accordance with this pattern. Relations between individuals and functions of individuals can also be represented. The matrices for such relations are of the form '$q/\{b, p/a\}$'. A relation between two functions of individuals would be of the form '$q/\{p/a, r/c\}$', etc. In this way, homogeneous stratification is built into the very logical form; no function can meaningfully apply to itself.

Classes are still to be understood as the extensions of propositional functions in so far as a class is what is common to coextensive propositional functions. Where $p/a = r/c$, for instance, the functions define the same class. Thus, a matrix of the form '$q/(p,a)$' defines a class of classes (of individuals) if the following holds:

$$(r,c)(r',c')([r/c = r'/c'] \supset [q/(p,a)'r,c = q/(p,a)'r',c']).$$

This applies for higher types as well, so that we are assured that where $q/(p,a) = q'/(p',a')$ the propositional functions define the same class. (Note that Russell used '(r,c)' to abbreviate '$(r)(c)$', and '$(\exists r,c)$' to abbreviate '$(\exists r)(\exists c)$'.) To illustrate how the theory works consider the definition of the number 0_1. Recall that in Russell's type theory, 0_1 is the class of all empty classes of individuals. In the substitutional theory the matrix '$(x) \sim (p/a'x)/p,a$' goes proxy for 0_1. The matrix '$(c \neq c)/c$' goes proxy for the empty class Λ (of individuals). Thus, $\Lambda \ \varepsilon \ 0_1$ is represented by asserting that $\{(x) \sim (p/a\dot{\cdot}x)/p,a\dot{\cdot}(c \neq c), c\}$ is true. That is, it is represented by asserting that the result of simultaneously substituting the proposition ($c \neq c$) for p and c for a is true. Since $(x)(x = x)$, we know that this holds. What would be quantification over classes is then straightforwardly effected by means of quantifying over propositions. For example, $(\exists y)(y \ \varepsilon \ 0_1)$ is represented by asserting that $(\exists p',a')(\{(x)\sim(p/a\dot{\cdot}x)/p,a\dot{\cdot}p',a'\}$ is true). By using matrices in this way, mathematics was to be constructed without the assumption of classes or propositional functions as logical subjects.

The Substitutional Theory Without Generalized Propositions

Russell never published the April–May version of the substitutional theory. As his letter to Jourdain indicates, it was his desire to apply the theory to the Paradox of the Liar that played a role in his withdrawing the article from publication. Russell thought that the solution of the Liar requires that there are no 'generalized propositions' – i.e., no single logical subject (proposition) is expressed by a statement containing a quantifier phrase. Statements without quantifier phrases, on the other hand, do express single propositions, whether true or false. And only propositions are in the range of the quantifiers. The non-assumption of generalized propositions, however, imposes serious difficulties for the substitutional theory. But by September of 1906 Russell thought that these difficulties could be overcome. His article 'Les Paradoxes de la Logique', which espoused the substitutional theory without assuming generalized propositions, was to explain this.

Russell tells us that a statement containing a quantifier phrase, such as '$(x)(x = x)$', is to be interpreted as asserting indeterminately all the propositions $x_1 = x_1$, $x_2 = x_2$, $x_3 = x_3$, etc. Similarly, a statement such as '$(\exists x)(x = x)$' is interpreted as asserting an ambiguous proposition from among these.

'Truth' and 'falsehood' are still primitive properties of propositions, but 'truth' or 'falsehood' applied to a statement has a different meaning. A generalized statement is 'true' just when the proposition(s) it asserts are true. Russell interprets the Liar as making the statement 'There is some proposition I am now asserting and it is false.' Since statements are not propositions, the statement of the Liar cannot apply to itself and is therefore 'false'.

While this avoids the Liar Paradox it poses difficulties for the substitutional theory. In particular, Russell had defined '$p/a\dot{\cdot}b!q$' to be 'q results from substituting b for every occurrence of a in p'. But if 'p' is a statement containing a quantifier phrase, then it does not express a single proposition and so there is no single proposition q which would result from the substitution. Thus, the contextual definition of '$p/a\dot{\,}b$' requires amendment.

But how are we to understand the notation '$\phi/a\dot{\,}b$', where ϕ is a statement containing a quantifier phrase? One suggestion, which I adopted in my earlier article, is to begin by reading the notation '$p/a\dot{\,}b$' as an assertion of the proposition q such that $p/a\dot{\,}b!q$. Then we could read notation such as '$(y)(Fy \supset Fa)/a\dot{\,}b$' as an assertion of all the propositions got by substituting b for a at each of its occurrences (if any) in the propositions asserted by the statement '$(y)(Fy \supset Fa)$', i.e., in $(Fy_1 \supset Fa)$, $(Fy_2 \supset Fa)$, $(Fy_3 \supset Fa)$, and so on. This interpretation enables us to state Russell's 1906 reducibility axiom (in the monadic case and for functions of individuals), as follows:

$$(\exists p,a)(x)(p/a\dot{\,}x \equiv \phi/a\dot{\,}x),$$

Where 'ϕ' is a metalinguistic variable ranging over sentences containing quantifier phrases. This formulation is attractive since it parallels Russell's notes in manuscript. The 1906 axiom says that for any matrix whose prototype is a statement there is a coextensive matrix whose prototype stands for a proposition. This enables Russell to capture all that would have been captured if there were generalized propositions within the range of the quantifiers. But the interpretation strays from Russell's claim that '$p/a\dot{\,}b$' is an incomplete symbol to be contextually defined. Here I wish to make a different suggestion which remains closer to Russell's own original reading.

Russell's 1906 axiom of reducibility assures (in the monadic case) that for any statement 'ϕ' which contains a quantifier phrase, there is a single proposition p containing the entity a which is such that $(x)(p/a\dot{\,}x \equiv \phi x)$. By contextual definition, the axiom is,

$$(\exists p,a)(x)\{(\exists'q)(p/a\dot{\,}x!q \ \& \ (q \equiv \phi x))\}.$$

Again 'ϕ' is to be understood as a metalinguistic variable for sentences containing quantifier phrases.

The axiom of reducibility assures, for example, that $(\exists p,a)(x)(\exists^1 q)$ $(p/a\dot{\,}x!q \ \& \ [q \equiv (y)(Fy \supset Fx)])$. That is, for any entity x there is a single proposition q such that $p/a\dot{\,}x!q$ and q is true if and only if all the propositions $(Fy_1 \supset Fx)$, $(Fy_2 \supset Fx)$, $(Fy_3 \supset Fx)$, . . . and so on, are true. Thus, instead of the matrix '$(y)(Fy \supset Fa)/a$', which is problematic since '$(y)(Fy \supset Fa)$' does not name a single proposition, Russell can use 'p/a'. Of course, Russell will also have to deal with cases which would have allowed the substitution of a generalized proposition. Without generalized propositions as single entities Russell cannot allow '$\{q/(r,c)\dot{\,}(y)(Fy \supset Fa), a\}$ is true'. Reducibility is again called into play. The axiom assures that '$\{q/(r,c)\dot{\,}p,a\}$ is true' will suffice as a replacement. Finally, Russell must handle cases which would have involved the substitution of a generalized proposition singly, such as in '$\{(p = p)/p'(y)(y = y)\}$ is true'. The axiom of reducibility assures that there is a proposition which is equivalent to any statement, so that we have $(\exists r)(r \equiv (y)(y = y))$. Hence, '$\{(p = p)/p'r\}$ is true' is the closest replacement.

As we can see, the denial of generalized propositions greatly increases the complexity of the substitutional theory. But given the reducibility axiom is formulable and extendable to higher types, the elimination of generalized propositions seems well underway. If this is a plausible account, then we have a reconstruction of Russell's reasons for claiming that his solution of the Liar Paradox does not undermine the construction of classes and of mathematics in the substitutional theory. Moreover, the reducibility axiom does not reintroduce the Paradox of the Liar. For the actual statement made in the Liar is relevant, and although reducibility assures that there is an equivalent proposition within the range of its quantifier, this will not suffice for the paradox (p. 212).

Russell's New Paradox of p_0/a_0

Russell's doctrine of the univocity of being of all logical subjects was realized in both the April–May 1906 and the September 1906 substitutional theories by allowing the substitution of a proposition for an individual. Propositions were individuals at this time in so far as Russell used the term 'individual' to mean 'logical subject' or 'entity'. Because all logical subjects were on a par, it was possible to form a matrix representing a universal class of all entities, propositions or otherwise. The matrix '$(a = a)/a$' goes proxy for the class of all entities, for the result of substituting any entity for the entity a in the proposition $a = a$ is clearly a true proposition. Moreover, the substitutional theory involves an intensional logic of propositions in so far as the equivalence of propositions does not assure their identity. This feature allowed Russell to prove that the universal class is infinite (Russell 1906b, p. 203). Unfortunately, allowing all propositions to be classed together in this way leads to a conflict between the technique of substitution and Cantor's power-class theorem.

The conflict with Cantor's power-class theorem arises in the following way. Supposing the class of all logical subjects (propositions or otherwise) is denumerable, we can assign every logical subject x a natural number, $\#x$. Since every subclass of the class of logical subjects is represented in terms of a matrix of the form p/a where p and a are logical subjects, we can assign each a rational number $\#p/\#a$. As is well known, the natural numbers have the same cardinality as the rational numbers. Thus, the class of all logical subjects will have the same cardinality as its power-class. (A similar argument can be formed no matter what infinite cardinality the class of all logical subjects has.) But Cantor's power-class theorem says that there is no function from any class onto its power-class; the power-class of any class always has greater cardinality!

We are now in a position to see that Russell was aware of the conflict. In a manuscript entitled 'Logic in which Propositions are not Entities', dated April–May 1906, Russell wrote:

> The above theory comes to this: that we can substitute any entity for any entity, and any proposition for any proposition, but never an entity for a proposition or a proposition for an entity.
>
> But if we don't have a hierarchy of propositions, it looks as if we should get into difficulties from the fact that there are more classes of propositions than propositions, and that, to all appearances, we can establish a 1–1 function from all classes of propositions to some propositions (p. 15).

In the first paragraph we see that originally Russell thought it was only necessary to prevent propositions from being substitutable for entities – i.e., those entities which are on a par with concrete individuals. But then he realizes that this will not do by itself; if we can class all propositions together, then the conflict with Cantor's power-class theorem will just repeat on a higher level.

In a manuscript entitled 'On Substitution', also dated April–May 1906, Russell devoted his attention almost exclusively to this contradiction in the substitutional theory. It is to this contradiction that he refers in his manuscript 'Paradox of the Liar' of September 1906:

> A second-order proposition is one in which either 'all values' or 'any value' of p occurs, or a complex $p/a\dot{}x!q$ occurs. I think the latter above is sufficient: all second-order propositions that arise contain $p/a\dot{}x!q$.
>
> We shall need a notation, say p^2, for any second-order proposition. Then we have $p^2/a\dot{}x!q^2$ and also $p^2/p\dot{}q!q^2$. Both are significant. The former substitution will affect only origin and argument in $p/a\dot{}x!q$; the latter will affect only prototype and resultant. Both these substitutions are third-order propositions. Thus $p/\alpha\dot{}\beta!q$ is always of higher order than any of its constituents; this disposes of the fallacy which led to the abandonment of substitution before, i.e.,
>
> $$p_0. \ = \ : (\exists p,a) : a_0 \ . \ = \ . \ p/a\dot{}b!q \ : \ \sim (p/a\dot{}a_0) :.$$
>
> $$\supset \ : \ p_0/a_0\dot{}(p_0/a_0\dot{}b!q) \ : \ \sim (p_0/a_0\dot{}[p_0/a_0\dot{}b!q])$$
>
> for here we substitute for a_0 the proposition $p_0/a_0\dot{}b!q$, which is necessarily of higher grade than a_0 (p. 72).

By translating the notation, we see that Russell has formulated a matrix p_0/a_0 – i.e.,

$$(\exists p,a)(a_0 \; . \; = \; . \; p/a\dot{}b!q \; \& \sim (p/a\dot{}a_0))/a_0$$

Next Russell considers the proposition $p_0/a_0\dot{}b!q$, and derives

$$p_0/a_0\dot{}[p_0/a_0\dot{}b!q] \equiv \sim (p_0/a_0\dot{}[p_0/a_0\dot{}b!q]),$$

which is a contradiction.

Of course, in the September 1906 substitutional theory of 'Les Paradoxes de la Logique', there are no generalized propositions. Since p_0 is generalized, there is no proposition $p_0/a_0\dot{}b!q$. Thus, it cannot be substituted for a_0. None the less, Russell's early Axiom of Reducibility will reintroduce the p_0/a_0 paradox. So the denial of generalized propositions which blocks semantic paradoxes will not block this intensional paradox.[4] This shows that Russell was aware in 1906 that the substitutional theory conflicts with Cantor's power-class theorem. Moreover, he was aware that the denial of generalized propositions, coupled with a reducibility axiom collapsing statements to propositions, causes grave difficulties for the substitutional theory.

If classes of logical subjects are to be represented in terms of matrices, then classing together all logical subjects must form an 'illegitimate totality'. In particular, Russell's formulation of the matrix p_0/a_0 reveals that if classes of propositions are represented in terms of matrices, then classing all propositions together has to be ruled out. (As we saw, this is so even if there are no generalized propositions – given the 1906 axiom of reducibility.) 'All propositions' must, therefore, be an illegitimate totality. Thus, he concludes that propositions must be divided into 'orders'.

Russell suggests that the hierarchy of 'orders' of propositions is based upon the legitimate range of their bound variables. The lowest order is that of individuals which are now said to be without complexity so that no proposition is an individual. Next are the 'first-order propositions', which are those propositions with no quantifiers together with those whose quantifiers range over individuals. Then there are 'second-order propositions', which contain quantifiers ranging over first-order propositions; and so on.

With the new hierarchy of propositions, a new Axiom of Reducibility is needed. The new axiom assures that for any matrix we can always find a coextensive matrix that is 'predicative' – i.e., its prototype is a proposition whose order is next above the highest order of its argument(s). The new axiom does not reintroduce the p_0/a_0 paradox. It does not collapse the orders of propositions to one order. But it does recapture, in extensional contexts, all that is lost by limiting quantification to propositions of a given order.

It should be noted that the orders are to be reflected in what is to count as a proper substitution. The class represented by the matrix '$(a = a)/a$' is now confined to all 'individuals', where no proposition is to be regarded as an individual; the class represented by the matrix '$(p^1 = p^1)/p^1$' contains all 'first-order' propositions; the class represented by the matrix '$(p^2 = p^2)/p^2$' contains all second-order propositions, and so on. No proposition can be substituted for an 'individual', and no second-order proposition can be substituted for a first-order proposition, etc. Thus, there can be no class of all propositions irrespective of their order.

Russell's actual restrictions on what counts as a proper substitution are, however, even more severe than is necessary. As we can see in the above quote, he says that '$p/\alpha'\beta!q$ is always of a higher order than any of its constituents'. But why not allow both the prototype and the argument to be of the same order? Perhaps Russell worried that a contradiction would arise if it is possible to represent every subclass of the class of (say) first-order propositions by means of matrices q/p, where both q and p are first-order propositions. To be safe, he seems to think that the prototype must always be of a higher order than the argument.

But there is no difficulty in allowing the proposition that results from a substitution to have constituents that are of the same order as it is.[5] That is, we can allow matrices of the form q/p, where both q and p are of the same order. Hence, we can take the order of $p/\alpha'\beta!q$ to be the order of q. All that seems essential is that the order of the entity substituted should be the *same* as the order of the argument for which it is being substituted. Let the propositional quantifier in p_0 range over propositions of order n. The order of p_0 will then be $n + 1$, and the order of $p_0/a_0'b!q$ is the same as the order of p_0. But for $p_0a_0'b!q$ to be admissibly substituted for a_0 in p_0 it would have to be of order n. This follows from the fact that whatever is substituted for a_0 in p_0 must have the same order as a proposition $p/a'b!q$ which is obtained from the existential instantiation of the quantifiers in p_0. Thus, a substitution such as $p_0/a_0'[p_0/a_0'b!q]$ is improper.

In any case, Russell is clearly using the hierarchy of 'orders' of propositions to avoid the syntactic conflict with Cantor's theorem. In Russell's view, the introduction of a 1908-style hierarchy of 'orders' of propositions is essential to the consistency of the substitutional theory.[6] The ramified theory of types which this hierarchy imposes would, therefore, seem to be an inescapable consequence of the framework of the substitutional theory.

I believe that this evidence makes a very strong argument for interpreting the 1908 theory of logical types as embodying the substitutional theory. The interpretation explains Russell's continued endorsement of the technique of substitution, and his return in 1908 to propositions as single logical subjects. (After all, even assuming Russell could make the view workable, the non-assumption of generalized propositions did not succeed in solving the 'paradoxes of propositions'.) In addition, it reveals a deep source for Russell's well-known conviction that the paradoxes of propositions (including that of the Liar) stem from a source in common with syntactic paradoxes and require a solution if Logicism is to proceed.

If the 1908 theory assumes propositional functions as single logical subjects outright, then, as Quine argues, ramification is entirely out of place (Quine 1941). Poincaré's Vicious Circle Principle can only apply if propositional functions are conceived as dependent upon the constructive powers of the mind, or upon their linguistic representation. The whole predicative/impredicative distinction is ill-motivated when functions are assumed outright as subsisting independently of thought and linguistic representation. As Quine says, Russell must have confused use with mention – a confusion of propositional functions with the linguistic symbols representing them. For propositional functions are not 'defined' at all, much less is one ever 'defined in terms of a totality to which it belongs'.

In the context of the substitutional theory, however, we can see that this interpretation is mistaken. Propositional functions are not in any sense 'defined', but they are 'dependent' upon propositions (in so far as functions are treated as if they are single logical subjects by means of the theory of incomplete symbols). And as we have just seen, the orders of propositions and the ramification that this imposes on type theory became an essential part of this dependency.

Notes

* Research for this paper was supported by a grant from The American Philosophical Society.
1 The manuscript raises many criticisms of the substitutional theory and responds only to some of them. But Russell added a note to the manuscript in June of 1907 which indicated that he doubted whether the remaining criticisms were telling against the theory. This shows that he then believed that a substitutional theory was still possible. In fact, he wrote in a manuscript entitled 'Fundamentals' (dated 1907) that 'types won't work without no-classes. Don't forget this' (p. 47).
2 It has been argued that, while in earlier 'no-class' theories Russell operated substitution and free variables simultaneously, in the substitutional theory of 1906 free variables were eliminated (see Grattan-Guinness 1977, p. 75). I disagree. Readers should not interpret *substitution* as the same as the *replacement* of a linguistic symbol in a sentence by a constant.
3 Peter Hylton (1980) has argued that an object-language truth-predicate is essential to the substitutional theory, and that *semantic* paradoxes led Russell to abandon the theory in 1906. Hylton suggests that every class of propositions will be correlated one-to-one with a unique proposition asserting that every proposition in the class is true. He formulates a matrix $q*/r$,

$$(\exists q,p)(r = (x)(q/p\dot{:}x \supset x \text{ is true}) \ \& \ \sim (q/p\dot{:}r))/r.$$

Then he derives a contradiction by substituting the proposition $(x)(q*/r\dot{:}x \supset x$ is true) for r. However, Hylton fails to see that a semantic 'truth'-predicate is not essential to the viability of the theory. But even with the assumption of a truth-predicate, Hylton neglects Russell's published solution of 'semantic' (and non-extensional) paradoxes in 'Les Paradoxes de la Logique'. Since there are no generalized propositions, a statement expressing the identity of a proposition with what would be a generalized proposition is not well formed, and equivalence will not suffice.

4   The contradiction follows from contextual definitions and Russell's 1906 Axiom of Reducibility. By the 1906 Reducibility Axiom we have:

$$(\exists t,a_0)\{(x)(t/a_0\dot{:}x \equiv (\exists p,a)(x = p/a\dot{:}b!q \ \& \ \sim (p/a\dot{:}x)))\}$$

Then assume, for the left-to-right direction of the contradiction, that $(\exists^1 r)(t/a_0\dot{:}[t/a_0\dot{:}b!q]!r \ \& \ r)$. The right-to-left direction is equally straightforward.

5   There would be a contradiction if every class in the power-class of the class of first-order propositions could be represented by a matrix q/p, where q and p are both first-order propositions. (A similar contradiction would arise for the power-class of the class of second-order propositions, and so on.) But these contradictions only show that one cannot represent every class in the power-class by matrices q/p, where q and p are of the same order. Moreover, a matrix q/p, where q is second-order and p is first-order, is 'predicative'. (A matrix is 'predicative' when its prototype is next above or equal to the highest order of its arguments.) Thus, Russell's axiom of reducibility does not reintroduce the paradox.

6   It might be objected that with the introduction of 'orders' of propositions the doctrine of the univocity of being of all logical subjects is lost. But it is not clear that Russell thought so. The 'limitations' on the range of the variables of quantification are built into the meaning of a proper substitution. The order of the argument is given with the matrix, and a proper substitution requires that the entity substituted is to be of the same order as the argument for which it is being substituted. Russell held that only *external restrictions* on the quantifiers, and not 'limitations' based on admissible range of significance, violate the doctrine of the univocity of being (Russell 1908, p. 72).

References

Cocchiarella, Nino B. (1980) 'The Development of the Theory of Logical Types and the Notion of a Logical Subject in Russell's Early Philosophy', *Synthèse*, 45: 71–115. Reprinted in his *Logical Studies in Early Analytic Philosophy* (Columbus: Ohio State University Press, 1987).

Grattan-Guinness, I. (1977) *Dear Russell – Dear Jourdain* (London: Duckworth).

Hylton, Peter. (1980) 'Russell's Substitutional Theory', *Synthèse*, 45: 1–31.

Landini, Gregory. (1987). 'Russell's Substitutional Theory of Classes and Relations', *History and Philosophy of Logic*, 8: 171–200.

Quine, W.V.O. (1941) 'Whitehead and the Rise of Modern Logic', in *The Philosophy of Alfred North Whitehead*, ed. P.A. Schilpp (LaSalle, Ill.: Open Court), pp. 125–63.

Russell, Bertrand. (1905) 'On Some Difficulties in the Theory of Transfinite Numbers and Order Types', in Russell 1973, pp. 135–64. First published in

Proceedings of the London Mathematical Society, 4 (March 1906): 29–53. Read before the Society on 14 December 1905.

—— (1906a) 'The Substitutional Theory of Classes and Relations', in Russell 1973, pp. 165–89. The paper was read before the London Mathematical Society on 10 May 1906.

—— (1906b) 'On "Insolubilia" and Their Solution by Symbolic Logic', in Russell 1973, pp. 190–214. First published as 'Les Paradoxes de la Logique', *Revue de Métaphysique et de Morale*, 14 (Sept. 1906): 627–50.

—— 'Logic in which Propositions are not Entities', Unpublished manuscript in the Russell Archives dated April–May 1906 (McMaster University). File RA 230.030720.

—— 'On Substitution', Unpublished manuscript in the Russell Archives, dated April–May 1906 (McMaster University). File RA 220.101950–F1–3.

—— 'The Paradox of the Liar', Unpublished manuscript in the Russell Archives, dated September 1906 (McMaster University). File RA 220.010930–F1–3.

—— 'Fundamentals', Unpublished manuscript in the Russell Archives, dated 1907 (McMaster University). File RA 230.030760–F1–2.

—— (1908) 'Mathematical Logic as Based on the Theory of Types', in R.C. Marsh, ed., *Logic and Knowledge: Essays 1901–1950* (London: Allen and Unwin, 1956), pp. 59–102.

—— (1910) 'The Theory of Logical Types', in Russell 1973, pp. 215–52.

—— (1973) *Essays in Analysis*, ed. D.P. Lackey (New York: Braziller).

Schilpp, P.A. (1944) *The Philosophy of Bertrand Russell* (Evanston and Chicago: Northwestern University).

20

Russell, Gödel and Logicism*

Francisco Rodríguez-Consuegra

In this paper I discuss three assertions, which are sometimes taken for granted: 1 Russell did not understand Gödel's celebrated results, which he interpreted as implying that arithmetic is inconsistent, and also as new 'puzzles' to be solved through the theory of types; 2 Russell was unable to handle the distinction between theory and metatheory; 3 Russell's logicism collapsed after Gödel's incompleteness results. After taking into consideration relevant – published and unpublished – materials, I will show that the three assertions are either false or considerably open to doubt.

Assertion 1: *Russell did not understand Gödel's celebrated results, which he interpreted (i) to imply that arithmetic is inconsistent, and also (ii) as new 'puzzles' to be solved through the theory of types.*

The supposed basis for (i) is a letter from Russell to L. Henkin of April 1, 1963 (now in the Russell Archives) in which he wrote:

> I realized, of course, that Gödel's work is of fundamental importance, but I was puzzled by it. It made me glad that I was no longer working at mathematical logic. If a given set of axioms leads to a contradiction, it is clear that at least one of the axioms must be false. Does this apply to school-boy's arithmetic, and, if so, can be believe anything that we were taught in youth? Are we to think that 2 + 2 is not 4, but 4.001? Obviously, this is not what is intended.

Also, Russell asked Henkin to tell him about the way in which ordinary mathematics is affected by Gödel's work. In his response (July 17; also in the Russell Archives), Henkin wrote: 'Gödel did *not* show (what seems to be suggested by your first paragraph) that the systems he investigated were inconsistent. Rather he showed these systems to be incomplete'. As for ordinary mathematics, he added: 'every working mathematician has heard of Gödel's work, but (except in the field of logic) there have been no discernible consequences on mathematical practice'. As a whole this interchange has been interpreted by Dawson 1984 to show Russell as believing that Gödel's results imply that arithmetic leads to contradiction. However, Dawson told me in a personal communication (February 23, 1990) that more charitable interpretations are possible. Let me then attempt one of these charitable interpretations.

For one thing it is of course possible that Russell misinterpreted Gödel's incompleteness theorem and also the unprovability of consistency. At any rate he would not be the only one in so doing, especially after a first impression (see Ladriere 1957 and Dawson 1984 for details about many more misinterpretations). But if we suppose that for Russell Gödel proved arithmetic to lead to contradictions, I think we are forced to provide some line of argument leading from Gödel's incompleteness theorem to some form of particular contradiction. The most similar line I have found in the literature probably known to Russell is Black's account of Gödel's results in his 1933 book. Black wrote that, in his 1931 article, Gödel showed that a proposition, which we will call *G*, although obviously true, could not be formally demonstrated, and that any demonstration of *G* 'would lead to a contradiction' (p. 167). This could be interpreted as saying that the truth of *G* leads to a contradiction, for it implies that its provability is equivalent to the provability of its negation. But this is not so. If we suppose arithmetic to be consistent then neither *G* nor its negation are provable, so *G* is undecidable, and this is not to say that it is the truth of *G* that leads to a contradiction. More precisely, what leads us to a contradiction is the belief that, as *G* is true, *G* has also to be provable, for *G* is provable only if its negation is provable too. Thus, if *G* is provable, arithmetic would be inconsistent. And the fact that *G* is true leads us, not to its provability, but precisely to its unprovability.

As a whole, it is hard to believe that Russell might have developed this line of misinterpretation, which openly starts from a confusion between truth and provability. It is true that Russell referred to Gödel's incompleteness theorems as 'a new set of paradoxes' (1945), and also as 'a new set of puzzles' (1950), but it is also true that he added: Gödel 'proved that in any formal system it is possible to construct sentences of which the truth or falsehood cannot be decided within the system', which seems to show that Russell did not confuse truth and provability. Therefore, even in case Russell actually did not understand Gödel's results, I think that the letter to Henkin is not enough to show that he thought that those results lead to the inconsistency of arithmetic. Rather, in writing the lines I have quoted above, he must have thought simply that his (and Whitehead's) lack of care in *Principia* about consistency was due to his belief that if arithmetic can be reduced to a few logical axioms, then any contradiction we find in further development must be due to the falsehood of at least one of those axioms, which can hardly be the case if the axioms are evidently and absolutely true. And this can be further interpreted as showing that after all Gödel's results have little to do with ordinary mathematics, which as is evidently true, is then consistent.

On the other hand Russell recognized in the same letter to Henkin that although Gödel had shown that their carelessness about consistency was a mistake, he thought 'that it must be impossible to prove that any given set of axioms does *not* lead to contradiction'. And Henkin, in his response, wrote precisely that Gödel gave a rigorous demonstration that this intuitive belief was absolutely true. The fact that Russell's original letter, no matter how old-fashioned it can be, contained interesting elements, was also admitted by Gödel himself, when a copy of the letter reached him (thanks to A. Robinson according to their correspondence now in Gödel's *Nachlaß*). Gödel wrote to Robinson on July 2, 1973, the following: 'Russell evidently misinterprets my result; however he does so in a very interesting manner.' Unfortunately he did not clarify the particular misinterpretation nor the interesting element he had in mind, so we cannot know whether he shared Henkin's and Dawson's interpretation.

In addition, Gödel did not take into consideration the fact that in the 1971 edition of his Schilpp [1944] volume (pp. xviii f.), Russell wrote a very little-known addendum which I think can be regarded as his final word on this matter. The main parts of that addendum are: (i) a correct exposition of the essentials of the incompleteness result; (ii) the insistence that this result cannot be regarded as a fatal objection against the truth of mathematical logic, and especially against the absolute and general truth of everyday arithmetic: 'It is maintained by those who hold this view that no systematic logical theory can be true of everything. Oddly enough, they never apply this opinion to elementary everyday arithmetic'; (iii) a further statement of his belief that proving the lack of contradictions among the consequences of a system is impossible, 'since the number of consequences of any given set of axioms is infinite'.

I think this text makes clear that my interpretation seems to be correct, as it shows that his 1963 reference to everyday arithmetic was intended merely to reinforce our intuitive confidence in the truth of self-evident elementary axioms. Also, the further appearance of his old belief about the impossibility of proving consistency shows once again that for him at least one of Gödel's results was not that surprising. At the same time, it shows the importance of an 'empirical' viewpoint for Russell's philosophy of mathematics, which can doubtless be regarded as an important point of coincidence with Gödel's.

I come now to (ii), namely the assertion that according to Russell Gödel's 'new puzzles' can be solved through the theory of types. The main evidence in print can be found in Russell 1959, where we read that he was convinced of his suggestion in the introduction to the *Tractatus* that a hierarchy of languages may allow us to dispose 'of Wittgenstein's mysticism [his thesis of the ineffability of logical form], and, I think, also of the new puzzles presented by Gödel'. This is not clearly referred to in Russell's theory of types, in spite of the fact that the hierarchy of languages was doubtless inspired by it. However, I have found further evidence in an unpublished letter of April 6, 1960, to 'Monsieur Morgenstern' (now in the Russell Archives), where we read: 'As regards your contradiction derived from the principle that a law cannot be applied to itself, I think that the doctrine of types will deal with it as well as with Gödel's problems.' Then our task has to be first to make more precise the sense in which for Russell there was something in Gödel's arguments, probably related to self-reference, which could perhaps violate the theory of types, and the sense in which this has to do with the hierarchy of languages.

According to the only author I know who has taken into consideration in print Russell's 1959 passage, Diaz 1975, Russell's mistake must have been the belief that every circular expression (an expression which is referred to itself) is a nonsense. And, as Gödel's proposition *G*, although circular, does not violate the theory of types, through the well-known device of representing the syntactical metatheory in the theory itself (the Gödel numbering), then there is not any nonsense in Gödel's argument. But I think this line is very open to doubt. For one thing it is very hard to accept that Russell merely believed that there cannot be acceptable self-reference (i.e., 'this statement has five words'). Second, it is even harder to believe that Russell did not understand the fact that *G*, the famous undecidable statement, was a metamathematical statement asserting that *G* is not provable and, at the same time, an arithmetical statement constructed through the arithmetization of syntax in the same language. Besides, there is a passage in Russell 1940 where he shows his mastering of some of the possibilities of Gödel-numbering to refer to some statement without repeating it. Therefore, there must have been something else in Russell's mind.

Nicholas Griffin wrote to me about that particular point:

> I think he would have thought that Gödel-numbering violated the sort of prohibitions on self-reference that type theory was intended to impose. At the same time, he probably would not have felt confident that his version(s) of type theory or those actually articulated by anyone else were actually capable of ruling out Gödel-numbering.

But as I said above, Russell himself was well aware of the correct use of Gödel-numbering when he wrote that his theory of types (or his distinction between several languages) was able to deal with 'Gödel's problems'. I think in so doing he was probably thinking not of his classical theory of types in the sense of 1908 or 1910, but rather in an ideal 'extended theory of types' as it was somehow intended in the Introduction to the *Tractatus*. If this were so, then he would be thinking of the possibility of languages of different orders to solve Wittgenstein's mysticism and Gödel's problems, in the precise sense that he was interpreting Gödel as falling down in the 'paradox' of expressing syntax (Wittgenstein's 'form') in the same language (apart from Gödel-numbering in itself). So, the ultimate source of his misinterpretation of Gödel might lie in his impression that Gödel's methods supposed a violation of the requirement that the syntax of a language, although it can be expressed (against Wittgenstein), this can be done only in a higher-order language (against Gödel). If this is correct, then we need now to examine Russell's difficulties in handling the difference between theory and metatheory.

Assertion 2: *Russell was unable to handle the distinction between theory and metatheory.*

On this point several accusations can be found in the literature: that Russell was unable to distinguish between logic and metalogic, between system and metasystem, between axioms and rules of inference, etc. (see the articles by Kreisel [1980], Goldfarb [1979], and van Heijenoort [1985]). As for textual evidence, §17 from 1903 is usually mentioned, as well as the corresponding place in 1910. There Russell says that for primitive (undemonstrable) propositions the method of proving independence is not applicable, because this method consists in supposing an axiom to be false and deducing the consequences. But 'all our axioms are principles of deduction; and if they are true, the consequences which appear to follow from the employment of an opposite principle will not really follow, so that arguments from the supposition of the falsity of an axiom are here subject to special fallacies'. Also, in 1910 (p. 92), Russell wrote that we have the same difficulty with primitive ideas.

The ultimate reason for that attitude seems to be Russell's belief in the absolute truth of primitive propositions, and in their also being rules of inference. As for the main consequence, it is doubtless Russell's empirical approach to logic, in which the reasons for accepting axioms are inductive, and the method of discovering them 'regressive', namely that which is based on their true consequences. However, although Russell's non-distinction between axioms and rules of inferences is undeniable, there exist places in which he tried to distinguish between true logical laws and rules of inference (i.e. general logical schemes) in a way that seems to me to depend on some application of metalinguistic distinctions, and also on deeper philosophical reasons. For instance, in the same §17 of 1903 Russell states the axiom 'A true hypothesis in an implication may be dropped, and the consequent asserted', then he adds: 'This is a principle incapable of formal symbolic statement, and illustrating the essential limitations of formalism'. A little later this sentence is somewhat clarified and Russell admits that with that he was trying to solve Carroll's puzzle in 'What the tortoise said to Achilles', which may lead us to an endless regress of more and more premises.

Then Russell introduces (§38) a distinction between mere conditional implication, lacking genuine assertion and truth, and the connective 'therefore', which, in asserting the truth of the antecedent, would be able to avoid the endless regress: only in that way could the hypothesis actually be dropped and the conclusion asserted by itself. I think with that Russell was somehow referring to something similar to what today we call a scheme or rule of inference, in the sense that it would sum up many cases of true logical laws. If this is so, Russell would be solving the puzzle with the standard distinction between language and *meta*language. And this is very interesting, because one of Russell's main reasons in being careful with these kinds of problems was his caution with Bradley's paradox against relations (and with Carroll's puzzle) that requiring the acceptance of ever more explicit relations doubtless leads us to a similar relational endless regress.

I always wondered whether someone sometime dared to ask Russell frankly about his difficulties in applying metalinguistic distinctions. Fortunately, when I asked Irving Copi about this, he told me he actually asked Russell in 1939 about it. Copi explained the results this way:

> Here I have in mind the difference between Primitive Propositions '*1.1 Anything implied by a true elementary proposition is true. Pp' and '*1.3 $q. \supset .p \vee q.$' At my first conference with Russell I inquired if the difference wasn't that one was a Rule *for* the language (and therefore *in* the *meta*language) whereas the other was a statement *of* the language and therefore *in* the object language. Russell answered 'Yes', and explained that in 1910 he and Whitehead hadn't yet 'got on to that way of talking'. He was not at all that comfortable at having to reply thus to my questions.

The fact that Russell referred to the whole matter as a new way of talking seems to me to be a sign that for him the new talk did not solve the deep question of the relationship between levels of language, as far as it can be related to the danger of some form of endless regress. But at any rate it can be also a sign that for him the distinction was well known, although obviously the later jargon was not.

Finally, I would like to insist that it was precisely Russell who introduced a hierarchy of languages of higher and higher order in his introduction to the *Tractatus*, and did so precisely in order to overcome Wittgenstein's thesis that we cannot refer with sense to logical forms. According to Russell we can actually refer to a logical form present in a language, but only from a language of higher order. Ultimately, however, this actually amounts to very little, for although Russell accepted and sometimes used metalinguistic distinctions, he still seemed to accept Wittgenstein's dictum that we cannot express the syntax of a language in the same language, so he had great trouble in accepting Gödel's devices.

Gödel's famous 1931 results were possible precisely because of his new idea according to which, as truth and provability are so different, while the truth of the propositions of a language cannot be expressed in the same language (recall the paradox of the Liar), provability can, without thereby falling into any paradox. Thus, while for the early Wittgenstein the syntax of a language cannot be expressed at all, and for the later Russell it can only be expressed in a higher language, Gödel discovered how it can be done even in the same language, with which he showed the way to over-come one of the deepest beliefs of most of the members of the Vienna Circle, who had been influenced by Wittgenstein on this particular point. Perhaps Russell's strange position is reflected in this rather obscure passage from 'On verification' (1937):

> It is true, as Tarski (*Der Wahrheitsbegriff in den formalisierten Sprachen*, Lvov, 1935) and Carnap (*Logical Syntax of Language*, Kegan Paul, 1937. – German, 1934) have proved, that in any given language there are things that cannot be said, but they can be said in a language of higher order. To say something about what cannot be said at all is not necessarily self-contradictory, but there is no reason known to me for supposing that there is any actual significant statement of this sort.

If so, Russell, although accepting the possibility of using higher-order languages without contradiction, continued to feel uncomfortable about its practical usefulness. Thus, perhaps his difficulty in accepting Gödel's devices was a consequence of his suspicious attitude toward the actual possibility of saying something really 'significant' about what cannot be said, and Gödel's celebrated undecidable proposition seemed to be a per-fect example of this situation.

Assertion 3: *Russell's logicism collapsed after Gödel's incompleteness results.*

The canonical position about the impact of Gödel's results on Russell's logicism is well represented by Henkin's 'Are mathematics and logic iden-tical?' First, *Principia Mathematica*, as any other system incorporating arithmetic, is necessarily incomplete; second, if that system is consistent, no sound proof of this fact can be produced in the system. The conclusion is that any effort to establish a close relation between logic and mathematics is a failure. Thus the only sense in which we can continue to speak of reducibility of mathematics to logic is by understanding logic as embracing set theory, as was Russell's original intention. But, 'no fixed system of axioms for set theory is adequate to comprehend all of those principles which would be regarded as "mathematically correct" '. Hence: 'A true understanding of mathematics must involve an explanation of which set-theory notions have "mathematical content", and this question is manifestly not reducible to a problem of logic, however broadly conceived' (Henkin 1962).

However, some arguments can be made in defense of Russell's original logicist intentions, even after Gödel's results (I follow here Sternfeld 1976 and Rodríguez-Consuegra 1991). First, although Russell spoke of reducibility of all mathematical propositions to logic, he did so in an informal sense; namely without explicitly stating that the logistic thesis entails the provability or disprovability of *every* well-formed mathematical statement, while Gödel did not actually show any absolutely undecidable statement, but only a relative one. Second, Russell did not maintain a conception of logic according to which logical axioms are limited in content and can be clearly distinguished from mathematical axioms. Thus, there is no justification for saying that logicism is necessarily limited to a certain set of axioms which are not rich enough to found mathematics, as the writings by Carnap and Quine have later shown. Therefore, 'since the logistic thesis presumed to show only that mathematics was derivable from logic, the fact that from no single axiom set can all the mathematical truths be proved reveals the limitations of mathematics which is perfectly consistent with the logistic thesis as similarly limited to what is possible mathematically' (Sternfeld 1976). And that means that what was actually a catastrophe for Hilbert, who explicitly looked for completeness and decidability, is not necessarily so for Russell.

Besides, the fact that a logicist reduction cannot be complete does not affect its truth, namely the fact that the instances of reduction which were actually done remain quite correct and are philosophically interesting in themselves (as was already pointed out by Putnam 1967). I think that is why Russell, who did not assume any completeness goal, maintained a much more empirical attitude to mathematics, and insisted that he was always convinced about the existence of undecidable axioms, like infinity and choice, which have to be accepted mainly because of their usefulness and 'empirical' acceptable consequences, while he always thought that the consistency of an interesting axiom system cannot be proved at all (see above).

I have no room here to refer to the literature about saving certain 'weaker' forms of logicism (Carnap, Hellman, Musgrave, Sainsbury), but I think as a whole they all are enough to show that some form of philosophical logicism, which was the only interesting one for Russell, can still be maintained, by simply accepting and incorporating Gödel's results as mere mathematical limitative results. I also think that it would be sufficient for Russell himself, who was never able to understand that, after Gödel, many logicians (although not certainly Gödel himself) regarded his magnum opus, *Principia Mathematica*, as only of historical interest. Let me then finish by quoting the following letter, in which Russell's attitude can contribute to partially explain his strange position before Gödel (1968, p. 224):

> In particular, I am grateful for the nice things you say about *Principia Mathematica* and about me. The followers of Gödel had almost persuaded me that the twenty man-years spent on the *Principia* had been wasted and that the book had better been forgotten. It is a comfort to find that you do not take this view.

Acknowledgements

I am very grateful to Ken Blackwell (the Russell Archivist, McMaster University) for the help and information provided, as well as to Elliot Shore (Institute for Advanced Study, Princeton), for his permission to study – and quote from – the Gödel correspondence. My thanks are also due to Irving Copi, John Dawson, Solomon Feferman, Ivor Grattan-Guinness, Nick Griffin and Greg Moore, who helped and encouraged me about the topics of this paper. Finally, I thank the organizers of this wonderful conference on the Philosophy of Mathematics for their kind invitation, and also an anonymous referee for useful suggestions.

Note

* Due to limitations of space . . ., I was forced to delete the first section of the original paper, as it was actually read. That section dealt with the reasons why Russell never published a reply to Gödel's contribution to Schilpp 1944 . . .

References

Black, M. 1933 *The Nature of Mathematics.* London: Routledge.
Carnap, R. [1934] 1937 *The Logical Syntax of Language.* London, Routledge.
Dawson Jr., J. W. 1984 'The reception of Gödel's incompleteness theorems'. In Shanker 1988. (Originally in PSA, vol. 2.)
Diaz, E. 1975 *El teorema de Gödel.* Pamplona: EUNSA.
Gödel, K. 1931 'On formally undecidable propositions of *Principia Mathematica* and related systems I'. In Gödel 1986 (originally in German).

Gödel, K. 1986. *Collected Works. Volume I. Publications 1929–1936*, edited by S. Feferman *et al.*, New York and Oxford: Oxford University Press.

Goldfarb, W. D. 1979 'Logic in the twenties: the nature of the quantifier'. *Jrn. Symb. Log.* 44: 351–368.

Hellman, G. 1981 'How to Gödel a Frege–Russell: Gödel's incompleteness theorems and logicism'. *Noûs* 15: 451–468.

Henkin, L. 1962 'Are mathematics and logic identical?' *Science* 138: 788–794.

Kreisel, G. 1980 'Bertrand Arthur William Russell, Earl Russell. 1872–1970'. *Biographical Memoirs of Fellows of the Royal Society*, vol. 28: 583–620.

Ladriere, J. 1957 *Les limitations internes des formalismes*. Louvain: Nauwelaerts.

Musgrave, A. 1977 'Logicism revisted'. *British Jrn. Phil. Sci* 28: 99–127.

Putnam, H. 1967 'The thesis that mathematics is logic'. In Schoenman 1967: 273–303.

Rodríguez-Consuegra, F. A. 1991 'El logicismo russelliano: su significado filosó-fico'. *Crítica* 67: 15–39.

Russell, B. 1903 *The Principles of Mathematics*. Cambridge: Cambridge University Press.

Russell, B. 1908 'Mathematical logic as based on the theory of types'. *Amer. Jrn. Maths.* 30: 222–262.

Russell, B. 1910 (with A.N. Whitehead) *Principia Mathematica*, vol. 1. Cambridge: Cambridge University Press.

Russell, B. 1937 'On verification'. *Proc. Arist. Soc.* 38: 1–20.

Russell, B. 1940 *An Inquiry into Meaning and Truth*. London: Allen & Unwin.

Russell, B. 1945 'Logical positivism'. *Polemic* 1: 6–13.

Russell, B. 1950 'Logical positivism'. *Rev. des mathématiques*. Rep. in 1956: 367–382.

Russell, B. 1956 *Logic and Knowledge*. R.C. Marsh (ed.). London: Allen & Unwin.

Russell, B. 1959 *My Philosophical Development*. London: Allen & Unwin.

Russell, B. 1968 *The Autobiography of Bertrand Russell*, vol. 2. London: Allen & Unwin.

Sainsbury, R.M. 1979 *Russell*. London: Routledge.

Schilpp, P. (ed.) 1944 *The Philosophy of Bertrand Russell*. La Salle, Ill.: Open Court, 1971.

Schoenman, R. (ed.) 1967 *Bertrand Russell – Philosopher of the Century*. London: Allen & Unwin.

Schrin, M. (ed.) 1976 *Studien zu Frege/Studies on Frege*, 3 vols. Stuttgart u. Bad Canstatt: Fromman.

Shanker, S. 1988 *Gödel's Theorem in Focus*. London: Croom Helm.

Sternfeld, R. 1976 'The logicist thesis'. In Schrin 1976, vol. 1: 139–160.

van Heijenoort, J. 1985 'Système et métasystème chez Russell'. Logic Colloquium 85. North-Holland, 1987.

Wittgenstein, L. 1922 *Tractatus logico-philosophicus*. London: Kegan Paul.

21

Mathematics and Logic

Alonzo Church

As the title indicates, this paper concerns, not a contemporary trend in the sense of something that is presently in process, but an old question in regard to which developments have come to a conclusion, or at least a pause. It is not true that opinions now agree. But the cessation of active development means that the matter can be summed up and even that some attempt may be made at adjudication.

There are two senses in which it has been maintained that logic is prior to mathematics. One of these, which I shall call the strong sense, is the doctrine which has come to be known as logicism. And the other, the weak sense, is the sense in which the standard postulational or axiomatic view of the nature of mathematics requires the priority of logic as being the means by which the consequences of a particular system of mathematical postulates are determined.

To take the strong sense first, the logicistic thesis is that logic and mathematics are related, not as two different subjects, but as earlier and later parts of the same subject, and indeed in such a way that mathematics can be obtained entirely from pure logic without the introduction of additional primitives or additional assumptions.

To make this definite, we first require an answer of some sort to the question: What is meant by logic? Certainly not merely traditional logic, i.e. the logic of Aristotle plus further developments in this same immediate context – else the logistic thesis is obviously false. If we are to take the logicists seriously, we must concede them a broad sense of the term "logic".

As a descriptive account rather than a definition, and assuming the notion of deductive reasoning as already known, from experience with particular instances of it, let us say that logic consists in a theory of deductive reasoning, plus whatever is required in object language or meta-language for the adequacy, generality, and simplicity of the theory.

That logic does not therefore consist merely in a metatheory of some object language arises in the following way. It is found that ordinary theories, and perhaps any satisfactory theory, of deductive reasoning in the form of a metatheory will lead to analytic sentences in the object language, i.e., to sentences which, on the theory in question, are consequences of any arbitrary set of hypotheses, or it may be, of any arbitrary non-empty set of hypotheses.[1] These analytic sentences lead in turn to certain generalizations; e.g., the infinitely many analytic sentences A v ~ A, where A ranges over all sentences of the object language, lead to the generalization p v ~ p, or more explicitly $(p) . p$ v ~ p; and in similar fashion $(F) (y) . (x) F (x) \supset F (y)$ may arise by generalization from infinitely many analytic sentences of the appropriate form. These generalizations are common to many object languages on the basis of what is seen to be in some sense the same theory of deductive reasoning for the different languages. Hence they are considered to belong to logic, as not only is natural but has long been the standard terminology.

Against the suggestion, which is sometimes made from a nominalistic motivation, to avoid or omit these generalizations, it must be said that to have, e.g., all of the special cases A v ~ A and yet not allow the general law $(p) . p$ v ~ p seems to be contrary to the spirit of generality in mathematics, which I would extend to logic as the most fundamental branch of mathematics. Indeed such a situation would be much as if one had in arithmetic $2 + 3 = 3 + 2$, $4 + 5 = 5 + 4$, and all other particular cases of the commutative law of addition, yet refused to accept or formulate a general law, $(x) (y) . x + y = y + x$.

For our present purpose it is convenient to regard a language as being given when we have a set of primitive symbols and formation rules and, in some sense which it is not here necessary to make definite, meanings for the expressions (wffs) of the language. Thus let me speak of the rules of inference, not as constitutive of the language, but rather as belonging to a theory of deductive reasoning for the language – so that there may be different sets of rules of inference for the same language.[2]

There is then another consideration which leads us to count certain generalizations of analytic sentences as belonging to logic. This arises from the idea that logic cannot be taken as exhausted by what is special to particular languages.[3] Abstractly the laws of logic are not dependent on whether, for example, one uses C or [$\supset$] as sign of implication, or whether one writes P(x) or xP, the predicate before or after the subject. Thus the metatheoretic principle that from [B $\supset$ C] and [A $\supset$ B] may be inferred [A $\supset$ C] is to be regarded as special to a particular language; and the corresponding general principle of logic is rather something like $(p)(q)(r) . q \supset r \supset . p \supset q \supset . p \supset r$. In this connection the Fregean distinction of two kinds of meaning, the sense and the denotation, has the merit that the abstract general laws of logic may satisfactorily be formulated as extensional, since an intensional aspect of the meaning is still present in the sense. But from the point of view of a Russellian theory of meaning, which denies the sense in favor of the denotation, the variables p, q, r, F, etc., must be taken as intensional variables, having propositions, properties, etc., as their values. From this point of view, if one is inclined to minimize the domain allowed to logic, one might even take the extreme position that such assertions as $(p) . p \text{ v} \sim p$ and $(F)(y) . (x) F(x) \supset F(y)$, where p and F are extensional variables, having, respectively, truth-values and classes as their range, though they are analytic, do not belong to logic.[4]

Now from the point of view of such an account of what is meant by logic one may see the logicistic attempt to reduce mathematics to logic in its most favorable light. For it could be said that logic is at any rate one prerequisite for mathematics, since deductive reasoning plays so prominent a role in mathematics. This is the weak sense of the priority of logic, which was referred to above. And if we accept it, we may then well say that mathematics would be founded on a minimum basis if it could be reduced to nothing but pure logic.

Historically logicists have not been as explicit as this but have seemed just to assume that the laws of logic have so ultimate and fundamental a character that the reduction to logic is clearly desirable if possible, and that the true nature of mathematics would be revealed by such a reduction.

Now having the case for the logicistic thesis before us, let us proceed immediately to objections. There are three important ones to be cited, and possibly a fourth.

The first objection is simply that the attempted reduction of mathematics to logic has not been more than half successful. The history is well known. Frege – who held the logicistic thesis only for arithmetic as opposed to geometry – did indeed reduce arithmetic to his own formulation of pure logic. Frege's logic includes the extensional as well as the intensional. This is a feature which I do not regard as being a defect in itself. But it is precisely the extensional part of Frege's logic which, despite the immediate appeal of its principles as intuitively sound, leads to its inconsistency. And the historical fact is that Frege, confronted with the Russell paradox, gave up in despair.

To avoid the paradoxes, Russell, and later Whitehead and Russell in *Principia Mathematica*, introduced the theory of types, and this in turn compelled use of the axiom of infinity. The term "axiom of infinity" is due, not to Russell, but to C. J. Keyser. And in an early paper Russell had argued against Keyser that the axiom of infinity is not a special assumption which is required by mathematics above and beyond the laws of logic, because the axiom (or supposed axiom) can be proved on logical grounds alone. Thus when Russell later reversed himself and adopted an axiom of infinity, it is almost his own admission, it might be said, that he thus went beyond pure logic. Indeed the axiom of infinity might be described as half-logical in character, since it can be stated in the same vocabulary that is used to state the laws of pure logic, but is not analytic according to any known theory of deductive reasoning that I believe can be accepted as adequately and naturally representative of existing standard practice in mathematical reasoning. And though it is known that elementary arithmetic can be obtained without the axiom of infinity if based on a set-theoretic rather than a type-theoretic approach, it does not appear that mathematics as a whole can dispense with such an axiom if otherwise based only on a standard and naturally acceptable formulation of pure logic.

An incidental point is that Russell showed the derivability of mathematics from intensional logic, plus the axiom of infinity.[5] Or more correctly, Russell's logic is neither extensional nor intensional, but neutral. He assumes no principle of extensionality for his propositional and functional variables. Equally he assumes no different and stricter principle of individuation which would require an intensional range for any of these variables. He simply has no need of such an hypothesis, as he says. In accomplishing this, the role of Russell's elimination of classes by the device of contextual definition is perhaps not as widely appreciated as it should be. And though there may be objections to it which I would urge in a different context, they concern such matters as adequacy for the logic of indirect discourse, and certainly not the adequacy for mathematics.

To return, however, to objections against the logicistic thesis – the second one concerns the question of founding particular branches of mathematics on a minimum basis. If we wish to found the whole of mathematics – or to evade difficulties connected with the Gödel incompleteness theorem and related questions, let us say rather the whole of presently extant mathematics – it does indeed appear that pure logic in an appropriate formulation,[6] plus the axiom of infinity, affords at least an approximation to a minimum basis. But for most particular branches of mathematics, and especially for elementary arithmetic, this is not the case. For the Frege–Russell method requires predicate variables of higher order to obtain even elementary arithmetic. Such higher-order variables may well be regarded as belonging to the vocabulary of pure logic, since they arise naturally from even a first-order language if we first generalize from the analytic sentences in the way that has been described, then extend the language by adding the notations required for these generalizations, then formulate an extended theory of deductive reasoning to apply to the extended language, then generalize again from the analytic sentences, and so on. However, the higher-order predicate (or functional) variables, together with comprehension principles which are required for them, mean in the presence of an axiom of infinity that even the non-denumerably infinite has been admitted. A more satisfactorily economical basis for elementary arithmetic is provided either by one of the standard formulations of first-order arithmetic employing primitive notations special to arithmetic and special arithmetic postulates, or by a weak set theory which is adequate for the treatment of finite sets but omits all the standard set-theoretic axioms that are not needed for this purpose (including the axiom of infinity).

According to a third objection, it is not logic in the sense of a theory of deductive reasoning that is required for mathematics but only just various concrete instances of deductive reasoning. This third objection might be taken, like the second, as directed against the desirability of deriving mathematics from purely logical primitives, rather than against the success of the logicists in doing so. However, mathematical intuitionists in particular have urged such an objection in a stronger form, maintaining that mathematics is prior to logic in a sense which would make the derivation of mathematics from logic unsound on the ground of circularity. In fact intuitionists go far beyond denying that the strong logic required by Frege and Russell is an acceptable foundation for mathematics, and intend an objection as much against the weak sense of the priority of logic as against the strong sense.

Now it is true that any foundation of either mathematics or logic is in a certain fashion circular. That is, there always remain presuppositions which must be accepted on faith or intuition without being themselves founded. We may seek to minimize the presuppositions, but we cannot do away with them. Whether the minimum of presupposition that remains after reduction is to be called mathematics, or logic, or both, or neither, becomes a question of terminology. But I would remark, in criticism of the intuitionists, that it is at any rate much less that the total content of a mathematics library, or even of a few good mathematical books.

It is not clear to me just how far the intuitionistic denial of priority to logic applies against the use of the logistic method[7] in founding particular theories. For intuitionists, Heyting in particular, have used the logistic method and I think do not dispute its value. In fact it is by the logistic method that those who do not share the intuitionistic intuition are nevertheless able to see, at least in the case of particular mathematical and logical theories, what it is to which the intuitionistic intuition would lead. The crucial point in regard to the intuitionists' use of the logistic method is not whether they proceed by direct application of intuition before reaching the logistic formulation of a theory, but whether having once reached the logistic formulation they then regard it as definitive of the theory in the sense that a change in it or addition to it has to be regarded as a change to a different theory. Since it appears that they do not treat the logistic formulation as characterizing the theory in this way, or even as adequately representing it, we thus have the situation that no theory is ever fully intersubjectively determinate. If intuitionists are to be so understood, it would seem to me that this is the weakest point of their doctrine, and by no means essential to the rest of it. I believe that there is much more to be said in favor of their objections against particular classical theories, and against conventionalistic and "formalistic" aspects of the axiomatic method as classically understood.

From the point of view of the intuitionistic rejection of certain parts of the logic of classical mathematics, one might add as a fourth objection to the program of logicism that it is simply rendered impossible. And indeed this would seem to be the case, even if an axiom of infinity is conceded. Against the contention on behalf of logicism that logic in the broad sense is a natural extension and an essential completion of even the most rudimentary theory of deductive reasoning, there is the intuitionistic contention that the extension has gone too far and in the effort to achieve generality has passed beyond tenability. The objection will carry conviction only for intuitionists. But it agrees with the second objection in emphasizing the strength of the logic required by logicism.

Classically, even if we accept one or more of the first three objections and regard them as cogent, it does not follow that logicism is barren of fruit. Two important things remain. One of these is the reduction of mathematical vocabulary to a surprisingly brief list of primitives, all belonging to the vocabulary of pure logic. The other is the basing of all existing mathematics on one comparatively simple unified system of axioms and rules of inference. Such a reduction of the primitive basis of mathematics might indeed be made differently if one were less exclusively occupied with the logicistic doctrine, but it was nevertheless in the first instance an accomplishment of the logicists.

Notes

1 We may understand consequence either in the sense of provability or in any other, less effective, sense which the particular metatheory may provide, the distinction being not important for the immediate purpose.
2 The term "language" is of course often used by logicians in such a sense that a particular language is not determined until inference (or transformation) rules have been determined in addition to the other things named above. There is actually a need for two terms.
3 Else indeed, since Greek and Latin are different languages, the logic of Aristotle and the logic of Boethius could not be said to have even in part the same content or to treat the same topic.
4 I do not advocate this extreme position, and Russell did not do so. But it is worth noticing that it provides a very satisfactory motivation for Russell's avoidance of extensionality by means of his contextual definition of class abstracts which is mentioned below.
5 For a strictly historical account, the axiom of reducibility should also be added. But it is now usual to avoid this by the introduction of simple type theory, and it may therefore be ignored for our present purpose.
6 This does not hold if we include in the logic assumptions that require intensional values for the propositional and functional variables. However, as already

noticed, Russell, and Whitehead and Russell, do not do this, but regard the assumption of intensionality and of extensionality as alike superfluous.

7 That is, the method of metatheoretic statement of the formation and transformation rules of a language.